THE FLORENTINES

THE
FLORENTINES

FROM DANTE TO GALILEO:
THE TRANSFORMATION OF
WESTERN CIVILIZATION

PAUL STRATHERN

PEGASUS BOOKS
NEW YORK LONDON

THE FLORENTINES

Pegasus Books, Ltd.
148 West 37th Street, 13th Floor
New York, NY 10018

Copyright © 2021 by Paul Strathern

First Pegasus Books cloth edition July 2021

ISBN: 978-1-64313-732-2

10 9 8 7 6 5 4 3 2 1

Printed in the United States of America
Distributed by Simon & Schuster
www.pegasusbooks.com

To
Arabella

CONTENTS

SAVOY

Milan ○

DUCHY
OF
MILAN

REPUBLIC

MARQ. OF MANTUA

Padua ○   ○ Venice

OF VENICE

FERRARA   ● Ferrara

REPUBLIC OF GENOA

Genoa ○

Ligurian Sea

MODENA

○ Bologha

○ Imola

REP. OF
LUCCA

Pistoia ○

○ Forli

ROMAGNA

City of Florence ○

Pisa ○

R. Arno

REP. OF FLORENCE

Livorno ○

○ Arezzo

Volterra ○   ○ Siena

Urbino ○

Ancona ○

Elba

REPUBLIC
OF SIENA

PAPAL

○ Perugia

STATES

Adriatic Sea

CORSICA
(to Genoa)

Rome ○

Ragusa ○

KINGDOM

OF

SARDINIA

Tyrrhenian

Sea

○ Naples

NAPLES

Otranto ○

Mediterranean Sea

SICILY

0		100 miles
0	100 km	

Italy c. 1500

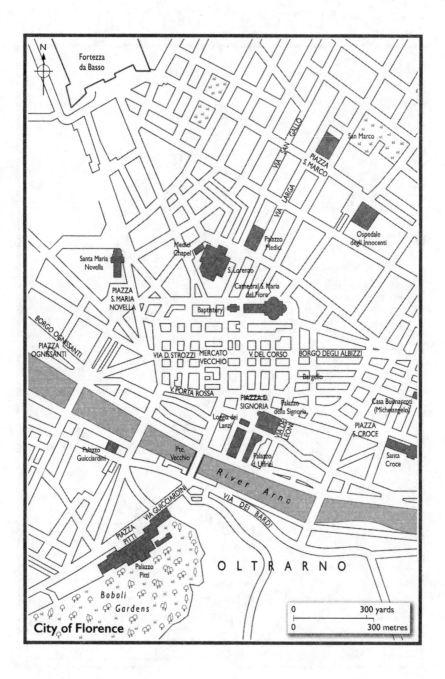

City of Florence

MEDICI FAMILY TREE

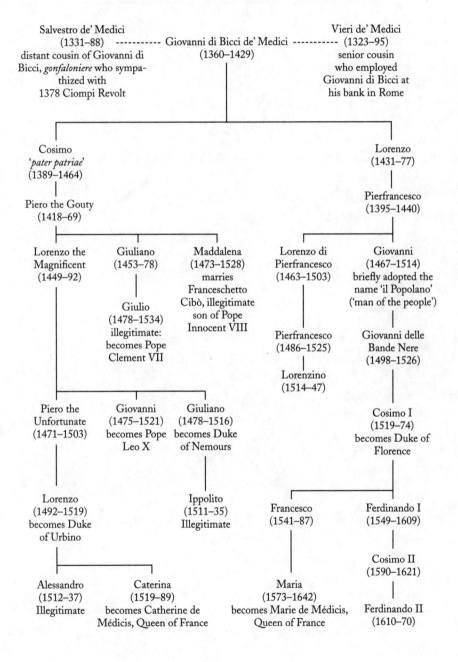

Salvestro de' Medici
(1331–88)
distant cousin of Giovanni di
Bicci, *gonfaloniere* who sympa-
thized with
1378 Ciompi Revolt
---------- Giovanni di Bicci de' Medici ----------
(1360–1429)
Vieri de' Medici
(1323–95)
senior cousin
who employed
Giovanni di Bicci at
his bank in Rome

Cosimo
'pater patriae'
(1389–1464)

Lorenzo
(1431–77)

Piero the Gouty
(1418–69)

Pierfrancesco
(1395–1440)

Lorenzo the
Magnificent
(1449–92)

Giuliano
(1453–78)

Maddalena
(1473–1528)
marries
Franceschetto
Cibò, illegitimate
son of Pope
Innocent VIII

Lorenzo di
Pierfrancesco
(1463–1503)

Giovanni
(1467–1514)
briefly adopted the
name 'il Popolano'
('man of the people')

Giulio
(1478–1534)
illegitimate:
becomes Pope
Clement VII

Pierfrancesco
(1486–1525)

Giovanni delle
Bande Nere
(1498–1526)

Lorenzino
(1514–47)

Piero the
Unfortunate
(1471–1503)

Giovanni
(1475–1521)
becomes Pope
Leo X

Giuliano
(1478–1516)
becomes Duke
of Nemours

Cosimo I
(1519–74)
becomes Duke of
Florence

Lorenzo
(1492–1519)
becomes Duke
of Urbino

Ippolito
(1511–35)
Illegitimate

Francesco
(1541–87)

Ferdinando I
(1549–1609)

Cosimo II
(1590–1621)

Alessandro
(1512–37)
Illegitimate

Caterina
(1519–89)
becomes Catherine de
Médicis, Queen of France

Maria
(1573–1642)
becomes Marie de Médicis,
Queen of France

Ferdinando II
(1610–70)

PROLOGUE

Bᴇᴛᴡᴇᴇɴ ᴛʜᴇ ʙɪʀᴛʜ ᴏꜰ Dante in 1265 and the death of Galileo in 1642, something happened which would transform the entire culture of western civilization. Painting, sculpture and architecture would all visibly change in such a striking fashion that there could be no going back on what had taken place. Likewise, the thought and self-conception of western European humanity would take on a completely new aspect. Sciences would be born, or emerge in an entirely new guise. Part of this cultural transformation would be influenced by the rediscovery of the pre-Christian literature of Ancient Greece and Rome, but much of it would result from how the novelty of this earlier – essentially pagan – outlook came into conflict with, and was assimilated by, the society in which it was rediscovered.

The collapse of the Roman Empire just under a millennium previously had left Europe largely in a state of historical and intellectual desolation often referred to as the Dark Ages, with the few persisting centres of learning mainly confined to isolated monasteries. Gradually, with the encouragement of Christianity, this dark age evolved into the medieval world. Consequently, the combination of intellect and faith

came to be regarded as such a precious commodity, preserving civilization itself, that a widespread orthodoxy prevailed in order to protect it.
However, over the centuries this orthodoxy permeated all aspects of life
to the point where it dominated intellectual debate, and a state of cultural
stasis began to prevail.

The ideas which broke this mould largely began, and continued to
flourish, in the city of Florence, in the region of Tuscany in northern
central Italy. Such novel concepts, which placed an increasing emphasis
on the development of our common humanity – rather than other-
worldly spirituality – would coalesce into what came to be known as
humanism. As its name suggests, this philosophical attitude emphasizes
our individual humanity and its central place in our lives, rather than
relying upon divine providence and concentrating on metaphysical
matters. Its founding insight can be seen in the assertion by the fifth-
century BC Greek philosopher Protagoras: 'Man is the measure of all
things.' As such, humanism led to an increased self-understanding, and
a radical extension of our psychological self-knowledge. We gained a
clearer picture of ourselves, and in doing so were inclined to seek more
rational solutions to our problems – rather than reverting to the power
of prayer.

This philosophical outlook would eventually spread across Italy, yet
wherever it took root it would retain an element essential to its origin.
And as it spread further across Europe, this element would remain.
Inevitably, other ingredients also entered this rich mix. Amongst the
trading cities of northern Europe humanism would flourish and develop,
absorbing local characteristics. In less cosmopolitan kingdoms it would
take on a more static element of empty show. At the same time, more
abstemious, narrow-minded populations could not, or would not, tolerate
such ostentation and luxury. Despite such apparent resistance, elements
of the new humanism would also subtly permeate even their repressive
mental outlook. This was in many ways the period in which the modern
era began. The way we think, the way in which we regard ourselves, our
modern notion of progress... these, and much more, originated from the
humanist era.

Transformations of human culture throughout western history have remained indelibly stamped by their origins, no matter how they have evolved beyond these local beginnings. The Reformation would always retain something of central and northern Germany in its many variations. The Industrial Revolution soon outgrew its British origins, yet also retained something of its original template. Closer to the present, the Digital Revolution which began in Silicon Valley remains indelibly coloured by its Californian roots. It is my aim to show how Florence, and the Florentines, played a similar role in the nurture and evolution of the Renaissance.

CHAPTER 1

DANTE AND FLORENCE

IN 1308, THE EXILED Florentine poet Dante Alighieri described how, midway through his life, he found himself lost amidst a dark wood, with no sign of a path. He had no idea how he had arrived where he was. His mind was fogged; it was as if he had woken from a deep slumber. After walking for a while, filled with trepidation, he came to the foot of a hill at the end of a valley. Raising his gaze, he saw the high upland bathed in the rays of the dawning sun. He began to climb the barren slope, finally pausing for a while to rest his weary limbs. Not long after restarting, he found his way blocked by a gambolling leopard, its dappled fur rippling as it skipped before his feet. By now the sun had begun to rise in the heavens, and the sight of this fine frisking beast in the morning sunlight inspired Dante with hope. But this suddenly vanished when he caught sight of a roaring lion charging towards him. No sooner had he escaped from this fearful beast than he encountered a lean and slavering, hungry she-wolf, which caused him to retreat in terror down the slope, back towards the dark silence of the sunless wood. As he stumbled headlong downwards, he saw before him a ghostly form.

'Help me!' cried Dante. 'Whatever you are – man or spirit.'

The shadowy figure replied, 'No, I am not a man. Though once I was. I lived in Rome, during the reign of the good Augustus Caesar, in a time of false and lying gods. I was a poet, who sang of Troy…'

'Canst thou be Virgil? The very one who has inspired me throughout my own life as a poet?'

'I am he.'

'Oh, save me from this ferocious wolf.'

'She lets no one pass, and devours all her prey. She will gorge on all who try to get by her, until one day the Greyhound will come. He will hunt her through every city on earth. In the end he will drive her back to Hell, whence she escaped after Envy set her free.'

Then Virgil continued: 'I think for your own good that you should follow me. Let me be your guide, and pass with me through an eternal place, where you will hear the hideous shrieks of those who cry out to be released, those who beg for a second death but are damned to torment for evermore. Next you will come to another place and gaze upon those who are happy amidst the fire, because they know that one day they will be purged and rise to take their place amongst the blessed. Then, if you wish, you too can see this blessed realm and its Emperor, to which I cannot lead you, because I was a rebel against his law. From that point on, only another spirit, far worthier than I, can lead you through Paradise.'

Dante replied: 'Poet, I implore you in the name of that God you never knew, lead me through that place you have described, as far as St Peter's Gate, which stands at the entrance to Paradise.'

So Virgil moved on, and Dante followed him.

Thus opens Dante's *La Divina Commedia* (The Divine Comedy), now widely regarded as the finest poem in the canon of western literature. Its full ambition and scope are realized by the imagination which Dante lavishes on his descriptions of the land of the dead and the souls he encounters there. In many ways, his poem is an outline of the past world and many of its leading historical figures. It is imbued with the spirit of the medieval era, yet Dante's psychological insight into the characters he encounters, and the vividness of their described after-life, prefigures the coming age of the Renaissance. Each soul he meets on his journey is rewarded according to the life he or she has lived during their time on earth. In this, Dante's thoughts are thoroughly medieval: this life is but a preparation for the life to come, when we will be rewarded, purged or damned, according to our just deserts. Yet although this 'divine comedy' is suffused with the theology of Catholic orthodoxy, as well as the Aristotelian philosophy which underpinned so much of its teaching, the poem is instantly recognizable as being of the modern era.

In a drastic break with tradition, the poem is written in the Tuscan dialect of Dante's native Florence. At that time, all serious communica-tion and learning was written in the Latin used by the Church, scholars and the educated classes. By writing in dialect, Dante was making his poem available to all. Even those who could not read were able to understand his words if they were read aloud. Indeed, Dante's poem would play a significant role in establishing Tuscan as the basis of the Italian language which is written and spoken today, causing him to be seen by many as the father of the Italian language.

Yet for all its virtues, *The Divine Comedy* undoubtedly has its dark and vicious side. In 1300, some eight years before Dante began writing his masterwork, he had been elected to the *signoria*, the council of nine who ruled Florence. Yet within two years of serving his two-month term of high office, he had fallen foul of the rackety 'democracy' which prevailed in the deeply divided city. Consequently, he was sentenced to perpetual exile from his native land, with the warning that if ever he returned he would be burned at the stake. Not surprisingly, several members of the opposing political faction which brought about Dante's downfall would feature in the *Inferno* (Hell), the first of the three major sections of *The Divine Comedy*. Typical of these was Filippo Argenti, who in life had been a tall, silver-haired aristocratic figure, notorious for his wrath. A contemporary commentator mentions that he had once slapped Dante's face in public, a major insult to which Dante would probably have had no recourse. Argenti's brother is said to have seized Dante's possessions after the poet's banishment, and Filippo's family were most vociferously opposed to those who sought Dante's pardon and recall from exile.

Argenti makes his appearance early in the *Inferno*, as Dante and Virgil are being rowed across the River Styx, in the fifth circle of Hell, which is reserved for those who succumbed to the sin of wrath. Even though Argenti is covered in filth, Dante recognizes him. Virgil explains that, in the world of the living, Argenti had been a man filled with pride, 'and there is no act of goodness to adorn his memory. He must live for ever like a pig in muck.' The sight of Argenti reminds Dante of the humiliation he suffered at his hand. Dante is filled with anger, and exclaims to Virgil: 'How I would love to see him submerged in this filth.' Virgil assures him that this will happen before they reach the other shore. Later, Dante sees Argenti being torn to pieces by his fellow wrathful damned. And such is Argenti's own wrath that he even turns on himself, biting at his own flesh.

Dante Alighieri was probably born sometime around May in 1265. This is deduced from the celebrated opening line of *The Divine Comedy* where he places himself '*Nel mezzo del cammin di nostra vita…*' (Midway through the journey of our life…). According to the Bible, 'The days of our years are threescore years and ten' – a 'score' being twenty. If Dante was halfway through his life during the events which he describes in his great poem, he would have been thirty-five. Although, as already noted, he in fact began writing the poem in 1308, he sets it in the year 1300, when as a serving *signori* he had achieved the pinnacle of his political career. This may well have been intended as a constant reminder to himself of how low he had fallen.

In a further indication of Dante's birth date, he at one point alludes to the fact that he was born under the astrological sign of Gemini, which was approximately 11 May to 11 June in the Julian calendar of the day. Gemini is the sign named for the twins Castor and Pollux of Greek mythology. The characteristics of someone born under this sign are said to include intelligence and a thirst for knowledge. However, their inclination to adaptability can lead to them appearing fickle or disloyal.

Although astrology is nowadays dismissed as a superstitious pseudo-science, during Dante's time many regarded it as inseparable from astronomy. The sign of the zodiac under which one was born played a significant role in determining one's character and fate. Around a millennium previously, the great Christian philosopher St Augustine had perceived that the determinism implied by astrology conflicted profoundly with the Christian doctrine of our individual free will. Nonetheless, the pre-eminent medieval theologian Thomas Aquinas, who was a contemporary of Dante, sought to reconcile astrology with Christian doctrine by appealing to the authority of the Ancient Greek philosopher Aristotle. According to Aristotle, the stars governed the course and fate of our 'sublunary' body, while it was God alone who had charge of our souls. An ingenious but fraudulent argument – as much so then as it is now. (Just over two centuries later, the notorious but immensely gifted Italian polymath Girolamo Cardano would push this anomaly to its logical conclusion by drawing up a horoscope of Jesus Christ, and would be cast into jail by the Inquisition for his temerity.) Even so, despite Dante's profound powers of intellectual discrimination, where astrology was concerned he was evidently willing to go along with the tide of contemporary superstition, which retained a deep-rooted belief in such matters.

However, such astrology should not be entirely dismissed. This practice did in its own way contribute to the advancement of genuine human knowledge. Although misguided and based upon false assumptions, astrology acted as an aid to the ancient philosophical injunction 'Know thyself'. As we have seen in the case of Gemini, the characterizations of astrology were no simple matter, being imbued with a distinct subtlety of their own. And here lay its legacy: in astrology's muddled attempts to categorize human personality, it was a forerunner of modern psychological practice.*

Dante's father was a small-time moneylender, who occasionally speculated in plots of land. His mother was from the distinguished, ancient Abati family, but died when Dante was still a child. This fact may explain a certain austerity and lack of emotion in his character. Dante's father would die when he was eighteen, leaving him to make his own way in the world.

By this time, Florence had risen to become one of the more prosperous city-states in the Italian peninsula, largely through its involvement in the trans-European wool trade and in banking, two trades which were intimately linked. In the days when almost every large European city issued its own currency, there was much confusion and room for chicanery in international trade, with more than a little debasement, forgery and 'clipping' of coins. The authorities themselves were liable to reduce the precious-metal content of their currency during hard times, and unscrupulous citizens would clip off the edges of the coins to gather sufficient metal with which to manufacture counterfeits. The introduction of coins with raised edges, often with milled or inscribed circumferences, was intended to overcome such practices.

When Florence coined its own *fiorino d'oro* in 1252, the authorities guaranteed each coin would contain fifty-four grains of pure gold, and instructed merchants to carry their coins in leather pouches to avoid the

---

* A similar phenomenon can be detected in the medieval practice of alchemy. This was certainly misguided in its endeavours to turn base metals into gold. On the other hand, it undoubtedly provided modern chemistry with much early expertise, by developing and passing on many of the sophisticated laboratory techniques and instruments which became central to the practice of this genuine science. It is no accident that Galileo's Irish contemporary Robert Boyle, the 'father of modern chemistry', also continued with alchemical experiments. Even Isaac Newton remained a secret devotee. If history is anything to go by, this uncovering of pseudosciences lurking amidst the genuine article will certainly continue to recur. Possible modern candidates include Marxism and even string theory, along with the forlorn hope that our ideas about climate change too might one day prove to be based on unscientific assumptions.

wear and damage which facilitated clipping and forgery. The coin, which became known as the florin, was soon a trusted item in trade throughout Europe and beyond, from the Baltic to the Levant. This reflected well on Florentine bankers and the city's burgeoning wool trade. The latter involved importing wool from England and Flanders (Holland and the northern part of modern Belgium), by trade routes down the Rhône valley and over the Alps. Later this would be supplemented by sea trade, with galleys being sailed and rowed from the Flanders port of Bruges around Spain to the Tuscan ports of Pisa or Livorno, and thence inland to Florence. Here, skilled wool combers and dyers turned the raw material into fine, tastefully coloured cloth garments and costumery, which could be exported as luxury goods.

Florence was a republic, its citizens proud of their democratic government. Its florins bore the head of no king or ruler – only the lily, the city's emblem, with an image of St John the Baptist (the city's patron saint) on the other side. At the time of Dante's birth, Florence had a population of approaching 80,000 – compared with 80,000 in London and 200,000 in Paris. But although Florence was nominally a democracy, in practice only a select number of its citizens had the right to vote. To qualify, one had to be male, over thirty years old, and a member of one of the city's guilds. Owing to continuing rivalry between the city's leading families and factions, the constitution of Florence underwent a number of short-term modifications during this period. These changes would eventually evolve into a more lasting form.

At elections, the names of all members of the town guilds who had not recently held office and were not in debt were placed in a number of leather pouches. The first eight names to be drawn from these pouches served on the *signoria*, the ruling council, with a ninth name being given the role of *gonfaloniere* (literally 'flag-bearer'), the ruling chairman of the council and titular head of the city. Like his fellow members of the *signoria*, he ruled for just two months. This cumbersome form of government met Aristotle's requirements for a democracy, in that it elected its rulers to limited terms of office, thus preventing a dictatorship. Yet the very frequency of the elections led to a lack of continuity, which in turn led to manipulation by the more powerful families in the city, who worked in their own vested interests despite being in almost permanent rivalry.

After Dante's father died, he was placed under the guardianship of the sixty-two-year-old Brunetto Latini, a renowned local scholar who also maintained a position in the public life of the city. Latini would be sent on a number of important missions for Florence, travelling as far afield as Spain and Paris. Dante is known to have formed a close bond with his guardian, who in turn proved to be a formative influence on the young man's reading and continued education. Latini translated works by Cicero and Aristotle; but most significantly he wrote in French a work called *Li Livres dou Trésor* (The Treasure Books). This is a compendium of medieval knowledge, regarded by some as one of the earliest encyclo-pedias. Despite Dante's deep fondness and admiration for his guardian, in *The Divine Comedy* he would place Latini in the seventh circle of the *Inferno*, which is reserved for those who have sinned against God and nature. Dante is filled with sorrow when he encounters Latini amongst his fellow damned, 'branded by flames, their flesh covered with old and new scars, all wailing at their torment'.

The usually reliable contemporary Florentine chronicler Giovanni Villani thought highly of Latini, writing: 'He was a worldly man, but we have made mention of him because it was he who was the beginner and master in refining Florentines and in teaching them how to speak well, and in how to guide and rule our republic according to policy.' This refinement of the Tuscan dialect is precisely what Dante set out to achieve in his poetry – so why is Latini damned?

The clue lies in Villani's opening words. The word 'wordly' covertly alludes to the fact that, for all his virtues, Latini was well known in the city for his sodomy. To modern sensibilities, Dante's conflicted emotions when he encounters Latini serving out his eternal punishment in Hell may appear somewhat convoluted, not to say suspect. If he loved and respected Latini so much, why did he place him amidst the excruciating and everlasting torments of Hell? The fact is, Dante profoundly believed in the immutable laws of God. Here, his temperament is utterly medieval.

For him there is no gainsaying the punishment meted out to those who commit a 'sin against nature' – a mortal sin – no matter how distinguished their life might otherwise have been.

It is telling to compare Villani's description of Latini with his characterization of Dante:

> This Dante, because of his knowledge, was somewhat haughty and reserved and disdainful, after the fashion of a philosopher, careless of graces and not easy in his converse with laymen; but because of the lofty virtues and knowledge of so great a citizen it seems fitting to confer lasting memory upon him...

Despite Dante's aloofness, the most significant and lasting event of his life was one of passion (though he certainly would have disavowed this vulgar description). The love of Dante's life was a woman called Beatrice Portinari. He fell in love with her early, and would remain so even after he married and had four children.

Dante wrote that he first set eyes on Beatrice when he was nine years old, and she was almost a year younger. This happened when Dante's father took him to a May Day party at the house of Beatrice's father, the prominent banker Falco Portinari. According to Dante's own later description of this event: 'She was dressed in a very noble colour, a decorous and delicate crimson, with a girdle and trimmings which suited her youth... She did not seem to be the daughter of a mortal, but of a god.'

Despite his age, Dante fell in love at first sight. But this was not to be a worldly passion. In fact, Dante's love of Beatrice would develop echoes of the courtly love as practised in previous centuries by the French troubadours. Characteristically, he would go on to describe his love in terms of Aristotle's theory of the soul. Aristotle saw the soul as the form which gave life to the inanimate matter of the body; but the soul also had a spiritual element, which was capable of a purely spiritual love, such as Dante felt for Beatrice.

Dante's second significant meeting with Beatrice would take place nine years later on the streets of Florence. In his autobiographical work

La Vita Nuova (The New Life), he describes how he encountered Beatrice 'dressed in pure white between two noble ladies who were older than she was'. As Beatrice passed Dante, she turned and greeted him – familiarly, yet without apparently stopping. This was the first time he had heard her voice, and her salutation confirmed his love. He was filled with such joy that he returned to his room to contemplate what had happened. As he thought of Beatrice, he fell into a shallow sleep, where he had a vivid dream of almost hallucinogenic intensity. For Dante, this was a purely symbolic event: indeed, he describes it as 'a marvellous vision'. To more modern eyes it might appear inhabited by all manner of Freudian imagery, open to interpretations far removed from those which Dante might have wished.

In Dante's vision, or dream, he became aware of his room being filled with 'a cloud of fire'. From the midst of this emerged 'a figure of fearful aspect, who yet seemed filled with joy'. This male figure began muttering various words, of which Dante understood only '*Ego dominus tuus*' (I am your lord). There was a woman asleep in the figure's arms, 'her naked body lightly wrapped in blood-red cloth'. Dante realized that this was Beatrice. The large figure was holding in one of his hands something that was on fire, and said to Dante: '*Vide cor tuum*' (Behold, your heart). After a while, he appeared to awaken the sleeping woman, inducing her to eat the burning object in his hand. According to Dante, 'she ate it fearfully'. At this, the figure holding her, previously so joyful, began shedding bitter tears. As he wept, he gathered up the diaphanous form in his arms, 'and it seemed to me that he bore her off to heaven'. This sight caused Dante such anguish that he awoke.

Dante then began pondering what this vision could mean, and decided that he would ask amongst his poetic friends. He turned especially to those older than himself who had already achieved a measure of fame and wisdom. Could anyone come up with an interpretation? As he would later write: 'No one at that time realized the significance of the dream, but now it is obvious to the meanest intellect.' Those less gifted amongst us might find this vision – so filled with emotion, yet redolent of sensuousness and violation – more than a little ambiguous. Indeed, Dante's poetic friends gave him 'various opinions'. But Dante was now certain of what his beloved Beatrice meant to him: 'She has ineffable courtesy, is my beatitude, the destroyer of all vices and the queen of virtue.' Beatrice would be the guide and protector of his spiritual life. Later, when he came to write *The Divine Comedy*, she would be the one who led him through Paradise. (However, it is also possible to see in Dante's description of his violent youthful dream a precursor of the images of savagery, terror and sorrow which he would encounter on his journey through Hell and Purgatory.)

Meanwhile, life in the real world continued. As was the custom, Dante's family betrothed him at an early age to a woman, Gemma Donati, whom he probably married in 1287, when he was twenty-two. Probably around three years later, Beatrice was to be married off to Simone dei Bardi, the scion of a powerful banking family. But this did not deflect Dante's feelings. Beatrice was fixed in his mind forever, the one still point in a changing world. His eternal beauty.

By now Dante had become a member of a circle of poets in Florence. Together they sought to create a novel way of writing, called *dolce stil novo* (sweet new style). This novel form of poetry was devoted to *amore* (love) and *gentilezza* (noble-mindedness), as well as establishing a new element of introspection in Italian literature. Along with such traits, it also introduced intelligence and style into the local Tuscan dialect, using literary devices such as symbolism, metaphor, alliteration and punning. What had previously been a distinctly provincial – almost rustic – vernacular began to develop into the most subtle and sophisticated version of the many Italian dialects which prevailed throughout the peninsula. With hindsight, it is possible to detect in this the beginnings of a renaissance in literature. The new style also enabled Dante to lend precision to his idea of Beatrice – not in any physical form, but as a guiding light to the spiritual aspects of his nature.

All this is far removed from the actual life in which Dante found himself involved. The Italian peninsula was plunged into political turmoil, its city-states divided against each other, and even internally. Florence was torn apart by increasingly bitter and violent events. These contained an explosive mix of religious and class conflict, involving a power struggle between the two most influential figures in Europe: namely, the pope and the Holy Roman Emperor.

The pope claimed spiritual leadership over the faithful throughout western Christendom, and as the inheritor of the throne of St Peter saw himself as God's representative on earth. The Holy Roman Emperor, on the other hand, claimed descent from Charlemagne, the powerful Frankish ruler who around 800 AD had established an empire spanning France, the German lands, much of Italy and northern Spain, and saw himself as the true successor to the emperors of the ancient Western Roman Empire.

The supporters of the pope called themselves the Guelf party, whereas the supporters of the Holy Roman Emperor rallied to the Ghibelline cause.* The Guelfs were determined to resist the increasing German influence of the Holy Roman Emperor in northern Italy. The Ghibellines, on the other hand, contested the temporal power of the pope. This division resulted in a period of violent conflict in northern Italy, particularly in Florence.

Here there had for centuries been intense and bloody rivalry between the different families. By around 1200, Florence was known as 'the city of a hundred towers'. Some of these were as much as 150 feet high and contained occasional apertures in the upper storeys. These might be boarded up in winter, but open or covered with waxed paper during the warmer months. In case of attack they could be used to pour slops onto the enemy below. The lower floors of such towers were usually storerooms of sorts, containing olive oil barrels, wine casks, tools, and comestibles like dried tomatoes or strings of garlic, as well as farming implements such as hoes and scythes. Living quarters for the different groups within the family

---

* Guelf and Ghibelline are Italianized versions of the original German adherents to the separate causes. 'Guelf' derives from the House of Welf, the family of the dukes of Bavaria. 'Ghibelline' derives from Wibellingen (modern Waiblingen), a town on the north-eastern outskirts of Stuttgart and formerly the realm of the German Hohenstaufen kings.

were on different floors, which were often connected by an open wooden stairway. The top floor would usually be a kitchen, so that the smoke and cooking smells dissipated rather than spreading through the tower. Living conditions could be comfortable, luxurious or sparse, depending upon the status of the family, or the group that occupied the floor.

It is difficult to conceive of Florence, whose walls then enclosed much less than a square mile, containing such a host of towering build-ings.* These tall square towers served as the ultimate protection for their owners, the family clan and their servants or dependants. Aristocratic, merchant and even artisanal families would lock themselves inside as dusk fell and the vesper bells tolled from the monasteries and churches. For a few hours, young hotheads might shout insults, threats and impre-cations across the chasms between the towers. Later, the silence of the night would descend, broken only by the occasional cries of the shrikes and nightjars in the nearby woods and fields, the echoes of the hooting owls calling from the hillsides, the squawk of a night heron (*squacco*) down by the river.

As the dawn light spread across the eastern sky, the heavy doors at the foot of each tower would be unbarred, and the inhabitants would emerge to go about their business. Groups of peasants would make their way out of the city to tend the fields, each heavily armed with farming imple-ments. Bands of workers in their wooden clogs clomped towards the wool-combing sheds and the dyeing houses. (These woolworkers were known as the *ciompi*, after the sound their clogs made on the cobbled streets.) Butchers, bakers and others set up their stalls; builders began setting up their ladders, sawing wood, hauling stones. Similarly, in later years the money lenders would set up their benches in front of their *palazzi*, which were attached to their towers. (They were the first bankers,

---

* All but a few of these towers have long since gone from Florence, for reasons which will be described. However, it is possible to gain an idea of how the city must have looked by visiting, or seeking images of, the small hilltop town of San Gimignano, some twenty miles to the south-west. San Gimignano still retains its clustered towers, some of which are 150 feet high. In medieval times, such towers were a feature of almost all northern Italian cities.

and took their name from the *banco*, or bench, at which they conducted their business.) Meanwhile the fishermen, nets slung over their shoulders, left through the river gate, their bare feet squelching through the mud and reeds along the banks of the mist-veiled Arno.

Amidst all this movement, if one group had the temerity to take a shortcut, trespassing on another's 'territory', they were liable to be confronted. Fights between rival gangs were frequent, scores settled and resettled. The Florentine chronicler Giovanni Villani evokes the scene, describing how the fighting 'was so fierce and unnatural that well-nigh every day, or every other day, the citizens fought against one another in divers parts of the city, from district to district, according as the factions were, and as they had fortified their towers, whereof there was a great number in the city.'

Even so, as Villani goes on to explain: 'This war among the citizens became so much of use and wont that one day they would be fighting, and the next day they would be eating and drinking together, and telling tales of one another's valour and prowess in these battles.'

Despite such behaviour, by 1200 Florence had a chilling rate of murder, followed by revenge, with feuds frequently persisting through generations. And in 1215, a number of circumstances – including two related incidents – would transform Florentine society for more than a century to come.

Besides having residences in the city, the aristocratic families also maintained fortified country residences in the *contado*, the swathe of countryside surrounding Florence which fell under its control. This was where the noble families were in the habit of retiring during the hot months of summer, ruling in feudal style over their estates. On a summer's afternoon in 1215, a noble family threw a banquet in the garden of their country house, which was some five miles outside the city walls. The custom when there were so many in attendance was for the guests to sit at long tables; those seated beside each other would share a plate, helping themselves to the piled food as they watched the entertainment. As often as not, this included musicians, jesters, jugglers, recitations of bawdy rhymes and the like.

However, at one table two young men sharing a plate happened to be from rival families – one being a Buondelmonti, and the other an Uberti. At one point, an overenthusiastic jester snatched the dish they were sharing. One of the young men blamed the other, and a fight broke out. Soon the entire party erupted into mayhem. Amidst the chaos, the young Uberti had a plate smashed over his head, while the Buondelmonti was stabbed. When eventually order was restored and the guests sent on their way, the leaders of the two families consulted about what should be done. Both wished to avoid a long vendetta of increasingly violent incidents. So it was decided that in order to patch things up, an eligible young man of the Buondelmonti family should marry a girl from the Amidei family, who were part of the Uberti clan.

On the day before the wedding, the betrothed young Buondelmonte de' Buondelmonti was riding his horse through the streets of Florence. A woman from the Donati family called to him from a window: 'Shame on you, Buondelmonte, for letting yourself become engaged to that Amidei girl. She is plain and not worthy of you.' The lady indicated her daughter, who happened to be particularly beautiful. 'I have kept her for you,' the lady told him. On seeing the girl, Buondelmonte was overcome and immediately changed his mind. Regardless of being betrothed, he swore he would marry the Donati girl.

The following day, with the Amidei family assembled at the church door in preparation for the wedding, Buondelmonte rode to the Donati house and pledged his troth to the beautiful daughter. When the Amidei family heard what had happened, they became enraged at this insult and swore vengeance upon the Buondelmonti family. According to an anonymous chronicler who recorded what took place some days later:

> when Messer Buondelmonte, in doublet of silk and mantle, came riding over the bridge, Messer Schiatta degli Uberti rushed upon him and striking him on the head with his mace brought him to the ground. At once [Uberti's Amidei friend] was on top of him and opened his veins with a knife, and having killed him they fled.

The bridge mentioned here is the famous Ponte Vecchio (Old Bridge) lined with shops, which spans the Arno from the city centre to the Oltrarno, the district across the river where the Buondelmonti family lived. The original Roman bridge had been swept away by the floods of 1117, and a new stone structure built. The incident described above was to prove of such import that an inscribed stone still marks the spot where Buondelmonte was murdered. Buondelmonte is even mentioned by Dante in the *Paradise* section of his great poem. Dante comments that his murder by the Amidei marked the end of a peaceful time in Florence, when there were 'no cursed woes to weep for, the city tranquil in her place and power'. A somewhat rosy view of the preceding era; yet understandable in the light of what was to come.

The warring families of Florence now set aside their divisive minor differences, coalescing into two large rival groups, which tore the city apart. One group proclaimed allegiance to the Ghibellines, while the other pledged their loyalty to the Guelfs. Thus Florence was to be plunged into the larger conflict which was raging throughout northern Italy and beyond. It was the aristocratic families such as the Alberti and the Amidei, intent upon preserving their feudal rights, who swore allegiance to the Ghibelline party and the Holy Roman Emperor. Meanwhile the city merchants and the *popolo* (literally 'the people'), mainly workers and shopkeepers, opted for the Guelfs and support for the pope.

In an attempt to stem the endless internecine conflict within the city, the *signori* had decided some years previously to appoint a *podestà*, whose duty it was to maintain public order and act as chief magistrate. To ensure neutrality, this post was given to a foreigner who had no links with any family within the city. By this stage, the Holy Roman Emperor had taken to appointing his own man as *podestà* in a number of northern Italian cities. In 1246, the Holy Roman Emperor Frederick II appointed his illegitimate son Frederick of Antioch as *podestà* of Florence. Despite the alleged neutrality of the *podestà*, Frederick of Antioch naturally sided with the Ghibellines, who then set about strengthening their hold on the city. After a vicious street battle between the Guelfs and the Ghibellines, the Guelfs were forced to flee the city for their houses in the *contado*, leaving their towers abandoned. The Ghibellines immediately broke into these properties and set about destroying them. In the end they smashed or pulled down thirty-six Guelf family towers.

In 1250, the Emperor Frederick II died. The Guelfs were determined to seize this opportunity, and mustered their forces. They confronted the Ghibellines in a battle at Figline, a village in the *contado* fifteen miles south-east of Florence. After the Guelfs were victorious, they marched into Florence and began imposing a new regime. All family towers were ordered to be reduced in height, to a maximum of seventy feet. At the same time, the Guelfs embarked upon an expansionist foreign policy, raising an army to attack the Ghibelline cities of Pisa and Siena.

In 1260, the Ghibellines wrested back power once more. They then set about eliminating the Guelf strongholds. It was reported that they ordered the destruction of no less than 103 *palazzi*, over 500 houses, and 85 Guelf towers. In 1266, the Florentine Guelfs joined an alliance of several Guelf cities, along with the troops of the French Pope Clement IV, and defeated the Ghibelline forces at the Battle of Benevento in southern Italy. This resulted in a decline in the power of the Holy Roman Emperor in Italy, and a period of abeyance for the Ghibellines.

The following year, the Guelfs marched on Florence, and the Ghibellines fled from the city. The Guelfs were determined that this time they would maintain permanent control of Florence, and immediately launched into a programme of transforming the city. The stronghold of the Uberti family, a large complex of towers and *palazzi* in the centre of the city, was razed to the ground. (This would become what is now the large open expanse of the Piazza della Signoria.) At the same time, the Guelfs set about paving the streets, as well as reforming the voting system. This took on the previously described form of an elected ruling council of nine *signori*, presided over by the *gonfaloniere* – a constitutional framework which would last for some centuries to come.

It was during this period that the wool trade began to flourish. Relations were restored between Florence and the Tuscan ports of Pisa and Livorno, allowing the city access to the sea. This meant more reliable commercial routes to international markets for importing wool and exporting fine dyed cloth garments. Now was the time when Florence entered an era of prosperity, and its banks began establishing branches in northern Europe to assist in financing the wool trade. At the same time, the city continued to mint the *fiorino d'oro*, which was beginning to establish itself as a reliable Europe-wide currency, further adding to Florence's commercial reputation. This was the city into which Dante was born in 1265.

The Alighieri family had long been supporters of the Guelf cause, and the intellectual young Dante would enter civic life. In order to do so, one first had to become a member of one of the city guilds, and Dante was duly enrolled in the prestigious *Arte dei Medici e Speziali* (Guild of Physicians and Apothecaries). The fact that many apothecary shops also served as booksellers at this time may well have influenced his choice. The Florentine archives contain reference to Dante speaking and voting on various councils. These were part of the civil administration that was subordinate to the ruling *signoria* and the *gonfaloniere*, and provided an advisory ministerial function. For instance, the Six of Commerce was the council which advised on trade; in times of war, a council known as the Ten of War took charge of the military.

Despite widespread Guelf victories, the rivalry with the Ghibellines continued in northern Italy, with several cities still adhering to the Ghibelline cause. One of these was the Tuscan city of Arezzo, some fifty miles south-east of Florence in the foothills of the Apennine mountains. Things came to a head in the summer of 1289, when the Guelfs of Florence fought the Ghibellines of Arezzo at the Battle of Campaldino. Here we learn of a different side to Dante, who as a twenty-four-year-old served in the front line of the cavalry at this battle.

According to the contemporary report by Villani, the Aretines (as the inhabitants of Arezzo were known) 'were 800 horse and 8,000 foot, very fine men; and many wise captains of war were among them'. Although the Aretine horsemen were outnumbered two to one, they had little regard for the Florentine cavalry: 'they despised them, saying that they adorned themselves like women, and combed their tresses; and they derided them'. In the battle, 'the two hosts stood over against one another, after more ordered fashion, both on one side and on the other, than any before in any battle in Italy'. (One can only assume that this description did not take into account the efficient military tactics of the Roman era.)

Yet there is no denying that this was a serious battle, involving experienced and well-ordered soldiers on both sides, even if some of Dante's fellow cavalrymen may have been somewhat over-coiffured. In all, the battle would involve some 20,000 combatants. As Villani recorded it: 'the Aretines were routed and discomfited, and between horse and foot more than 1,700 were slain, and more than 2,000 taken'.

Dante would not forget this battle, recalling in his *Divine Comedy*: 'I have seen knights riding forward, leading attacks and standing muster, and sometimes retreating to save themselves.' Heroes from this battle would find themselves placed by Dante in Paradise; enemies consigned to Purgatory or damned to eternal torment in Hell.

In the year following this battle, Dante would learn of Beatrice's death, at the age of just twenty-four. Dante was of course devastated, and wrote that he felt 'left like a widow, despoiled of all dignity'. He found himself 'weeping in the desolate city'. Despite his deep poetic grief, during these years Dante's wife, Gemma, is known to have given birth to four children. At the same time, he himself rose in civil life, eventually serving on the ruling *signoria* in 1300.

Yet once again the politics of Florence erupted in turmoil. The ruling Guelfs split into the Black party and the White party. The Blacks favoured a closer alliance with the papacy, while the Whites were opposed to papal interference in Florentine politics. Dante supported the Whites, who prevailed, expelling the Blacks from the city. When Florence learned that Pope Boniface VIII was backing a Black invasion of the city, Dante was sent as the head of a diplomatic mission to Rome to intercede with the pope. Dante himself seems to have been the driving force behind this delegation, a fact of which Boniface VIII was covertly informed. When the delegation met the pope he dismissed them, sending them back to Florence. However, Dante was ordered to remain in Rome. In a concerted move, the Black Guelfs seized power in Florence with the aid of outside militia, and Dante was then tried in his absence.

The Black Guelf Florentine authorities condemned Dante to exile for two years, and ordered him to pay an extortionate fine. Dante was unable to pay his fine, largely because all his possessions had been seized in Florence. He thus found himself condemned to several more years of exile, and was warned that if he tried to return during this period he would be burned at the stake.

Dante would retaliate against the pope for the deceitful role he had played in his downfall. In *The Divine Comedy* he would condemn Boniface VIII to the third ditch in the eighth circle of Hell. This was the destination of all popes guilty of the sin of simony: the awarding of benefices and ecclesiastical posts in return for money. The sinner is buried head first in a round hole, where his feet are constantly burned in an oily fire, whose heat varies according to the severity of his sin. Each sinner is eventually replaced by a worse sinner, before disappearing into the ground for evermore. Dante was aware that he could not meet Boniface VIII in Hell, as the pope was still alive at the time of the poet's journey through the land of the dead. In order to circumvent this technicality, Dante made Pope Nicholas III, the present incumbent of this fiery torture, predict that Boniface VIII would eventually take his place. This can also be seen as a metaphor for the increasing corruption of the Church.

Dante makes other references to Boniface VIII, at one point alluding to the fact that he had tricked the previous pope, Celestine V, into resigning so that he could himself ascend to St Peter's throne. Thus Boniface VIII also becomes a symbol of deceit, a further step down towards the worst sin of all: treachery. This moral descent reaches its nadir when Dante descends to the ninth circle, the lowest and darkest of the *Inferno*, the very pit of Hell itself. Through the dimness and the mist he fearfully makes out the monstrous figure of Lucifer (the Devil), frozen up to his chest in a lake of ice. From Lucifer's body extend three pairs of great flapping bat wings, and atop his giant torso his head has three faces, each dribbling with bloody slobber as he chews on his victims. In his central mouth is Judas Iscariot, the arch-traitor who sold out Christ for thirty pieces of silver. His other two mouths are devouring the bodies of Brutus and Cassius, the Ancient Romans who betrayed their benefactor Julius

Caesar, stabbing him to death in the Senate. It is important to understand that in Dante's eyes Caesar's murder was the turning point which led to the decline of the Roman Empire. The longing for a return of Italy's greatness was a constant and lasting preoccupation during these centuries – in Dante's case, second only to the pre-eminence of Christianity itself.

According to Dante's fellow Florentine, the writer Boccaccio, Dante's arranged marriage to Gemma was not a happy one, so it comes as little surprise that when he was exiled she chose to remain behind in Florence. It cannot have been easy being married to a man obsessed with his beloved Beatrice, a fact which had long since passed into the currency of local gossip. Also, Gemma was a member of the Donati family, who were known to favour the Black Guelfs.

Dante now began his wandering years of bitter exile, 'where another man's bread tastes like salt, and heavy it is to ascend another's stairs'. By this time, Dante had achieved some renown as an intellectual and a poet, and was well received at various courts and castles. It is also known that he lived for periods in Bologna and Padua, and that he lived in Lucca for some time with a woman called Gentucca. She would duly be rewarded with a place in Purgatory, on the sixth terrace reserved for gluttons – who are forced to starve while surrounded by trees bearing fruit forever beyond their reach, until their sins are purged and they are permitted to ascend to Paradise. While in exile Dante also played an active role in several plots to retake Florence for the Whites. Each time, the plotters were betrayed by spies, and in 1308 the city of Florence announced that Dante was sentenced to perpetual exile. The Black Guelfs were in complete control, and there was now no prospect of him ever returning to the city he so loved.

It can be no coincidence that 1308 was the year Dante started writing *The Divine Comedy*. Only then did he understand that his exile was to be permanent, and the spirit of the city he would never see again haunts this great work. In its three main sections (*Inferno, Purgatorio, Paradiso*), each containing thirty-three cantos consisting of forty-seven verses of *terza rima* (Dante's own three-line rhyme scheme), the people and events of Florence take their place amongst the saints and sinners, heroes, heroines and villains of all history. As we have seen in the case of Boniface VIII, these figures are not only real historical individuals, but also take on a mythic status, achieving archetypical significance. One of the delights of the poem is that it works on so many levels: realistic, symbolic, allegorical and theological threads weave their way throughout, each interpretation yielding its own meaning.

Particularly in the final section, where Dante is led through Paradise by Beatrice, the poem becomes a quest for divine understanding. Indeed, Beatrice herself symbolizes Theology. However, as eagle-eyed scholars over the ensuing centuries have been quick to point out, not all of Dante's theology is quite as orthodox as he would have us believe. For instance, Dante is on occasion guilty of the heresy of Averroism.

This requires an explanation – as well as an indication of context. With the fall of the Roman Empire, many works of classical literature, especially philosophy, were lost. However, copies of these works were carried to the Middle East, and in time would prove of great interest to the Arabic thinkers of the Caliphates, during the period when this progressive Islamic civilization extended from India to Spain. Arabic scholars studied translations of many classical works, and even wrote their own commentaries.

Averroes (the European corruption of Ibn Rushd) was a twelfth-century Arab scholar living in Al-Andalus (Islamic Spain, now Andalusia). Gradually, copies of Averroes's translations and commentaries on Aristotle began reaching Europe, where they were translated into Latin, the scholarly lingua franca of the entire continent. Since Aristotle formed the intellectual foundation of medieval Christian orthodoxy, these new works stirred up much interest. Indeed, they are now seen by many as presaging the great transformation of European thought which became known as the Renaissance. This term literally means 'rebirth', and it was the rebirth of these classical ideas which would prove such an early inspiration for Renaissance thought.

According to Averroes's interpretation of Aristotle, all humanity shared the same intellect, which accounted for the universalism of human knowledge. Averroes was condemned by the thirteenth-century Christian philosopher and theologian Thomas Aquinas, but his ideas persisted nonetheless. Hence his appeal to Dante, who favoured the interpretation of Averroism that saw each soul possessed of its own intellect, which was but a reflection of the universal intellect.

Dante was not willing to concede that the theology he was pursing in *The Divine Comedy* was in fact tainted with heresy. Indeed, Dante would reserve the sixth circle of Hell for heretics, who were condemned to burn in agony in flaming tombs throughout eternity. It comes as little surprise that, on his journey through Hell, Dante here encounters the Florentine leader of the Ghibellines, Farinata degla Uberti (head of the family whose *palazzi* were demolished to form the Piazza della Signoria). Also residing in the sixth circle is the Holy Roman Emperor Frederick II, who had presided over the Ghibelline cause in Italy. (Ironically, it was Frederick II's court in Sicily which played a leading role in promulgating the works of Arabic philosophers such as Averroes.) And, for good measure, Dante would include in this region of Hell his rival Florentine poet Cavalcanti, a fellow writer of *il dolce stil novo* whom Dante referred to as 'the first of my friends'. Apparently Cavalcanti had adopted the 'wrong' form of Averroism, which disavowed the immortality of the soul – the thesis upon which the entirety of *The Divine Comedy* depends.

Dante would finish writing the *Paradise* section of *The Divine Comedy*, thus completing his great work, in 1320. He had been living for the past two years at the court of Prince Guido Novello da Polenta in Ravenna. The following year, the prince sent Dante on a diplomatic mission to Venice. While Dante was returning across the marshy wastes of the Po delta he contracted malaria. Within days he died, aged fifty-six.

CHAPTER 2

WEALTH, FREEDOM
AND TALENT

B Y THE TIME DANTE died, the first stirrings of what we now call the
Renaissance* were already taking place in the city of Florence. Why
should this momentous sea change in European civilization have begun
in Florence? And why at this time? The first question has produced a
host of answers. Recurrent themes amongst these include money, a

---

* The first use of this word would not occur until over 200 years later, when Vasari
referred to a 'Rinascita' taking place. However, it would take more than six centuries before historians fully conceptualized this event by naming it the Renaissance.
It is important to bear in mind that most contemporaries did not fully understand
what was happening. All they perceived was widespread change taking place
around them. As we shall see, this could inspire wonder and imagination, but it
could also provoke consternation and profound existential uncertainty. As should
be particularly clear to us today, no age of profound change can be fully aware
of its own historical significance and implications. Ambivalence towards the
life-changing outcomes which may be produced by the development of artificial
intelligence is but one modern example. As in so many cases throughout history, at
the time we simply do not know what we are doing, but press ahead nonetheless.

certain civic liberty, and a lack of constraint on imagination: in other words, wealth, freedom and talent. Each of these elements encouraged the others, resulting in a sudden flourishing of individual talent in artistic, intellectual and commercial fields. Circumstances in the larger picture also seemed to have played their part.

The Italian peninsula was at the time occupied by a host of independent city-states, frequently at war with one another. The main powers were Milan, Venice, Genoa, Florence, Rome and Naples, with a number of lesser city-states forming tactical alliances with their powerful neighbours in order to preserve their existence. Most Italian city-states were presided over by more or less autocratic rulers: a king, dukes, the pope, aristocratic families, petty tyrants and so forth. Venice and Genoa were exceptions, in that they were ruled by elected oligarchies, and this comparative freedom, along with their coastal locations, enabled both of these city-states to develop into maritime commercial powers. The other major exception was Florence. This city alone had something approaching democracy. Ramshackle, often ineffective, and open to corruption this may have been, but it remained – in name at least – democracy. Its citizens were proud of this; the people felt they had a say in the city's affairs. As the twentieth-century American philosopher John Dewey understood (especially with regard to his own country), it is the *ethos* of democracy which appears to be vital in characterizing a society.

Freedom, agency and individualism are all encouraged by such an ethos. A frequent by-product of this is a belief in education. In the decade after Dante's death, Florence had no less than six primary schools and four high schools, educating 600 pupils (including girls). More and more children of guild members were encouraged to attend school; and, increasingly, upper-class women administered the household accounts, farms and estates of their husbands, tasks requiring both literacy and numeracy. Despite these advances, the city of Florence was frequently in a state of political ferment. This was of course encouraged by the powerful family divisions within the city, but it was also exacerbated by the constant political divisions between city-states throughout Italy. The resemblance to the fractious political situation which had prevailed 2,000 years previously in Ancient Greece is evident. This too had produced a profound transformation in western culture, centred on Athens. It is little stretch to see Florence as the next Athens.

Regardless of such generalized analogies, it was far from inevitable that the Renaissance should take place in Florence. The early-thirteenth-century court of the Holy Roman Emperor Frederick II in Sicily brought about something which many have come to regard as an embryo Renaissance. Not for nothing was Frederick II known as *stupor mundi* (the wonder of the world). A remarkable individual, he encouraged at his court all manner of learning – including science, literature, philosophy and languages (he himself spoke six fluently). According to the English twentieth-century historian J. H. Plumb, 'it was an Arab who taught geography and presented the Emperor with a silver sphere on which the map of the world was drawn'. The translation of Arabic versions of the Ancient Greek philosophers was a favoured project. Frederick II also maintained a menagerie of wondrous animals including African giraffes, leopards and an elephant, as well as some large and exotic white gyrfalcons from Greenland. His intellectual curiosity and sense of adventure appeared to know no bounds.

But Frederick II was also a wilful character, who took a particular delight in defying popes. (He would be excommunicated four times.) After being excommunicated by Pope Gregory IX, he set off in defiance of the pope on a Crusade which took Jerusalem, where he had himself crowned king. (This left the pope with little alternative but to dis-excommunicate him.) However, Frederick II's wilfulness eventually began extending into more questionable fields. In his court, he conducted his own original experiments in pursuit of scientific knowledge. A man was crammed into a cask, in order to observe whether his soul escaped when he expired. Two infants were isolated from all human contact, to discover if they would develop the original language imparted by God to Adam and Eve. Frederick II also ordered the eyes of a vulture to be sewn up, in order to discover whether it detected its food by sight or by smell.*

When Frederick II blinded his long-term chief adviser Pietro della Vigna and exhibited him in a cage, it became clear the Holy Roman Emperor's behaviour was extending beyond the field of science. Fortunately, the *stupor mundi* died the following year, in 1250; his court then dispersed, and this premature Renaissance fell into abeyance.

Coincidentally, 1250 was also the year in which another seminal figure of the pre-Renaissance died. This was the man we call Fibonacci (meaning 'son of Bonacci'), who was born in 1170 in Pisa and would be known during his lifetime as Leonardo of Pisa. At that time the port city of Pisa, by the mouth of the Arno some fifty miles downstream from Florence, was a major Mediterranean trading centre. Indeed, Pisa would briefly rival both Genoa and Venice as a major naval power throughout the Mediterranean. More pertinently, its trade links with Florence would facilitate the spread of ideas between the two cities.

The sea trading routes of Pisa, Genoa and Venice fanned out across the Mediterranean. These links stretched from Cádiz to the Levant (Near East), and from the Barbary Coast (North Africa) to the Crimean peninsula in the northern Black Sea. The main trade was in grain, salt

---

*The cruelty of such experiments should be placed in context. Some 400 years later, the French rationalist thinker and scientist René Descartes, generally regarded as the first modern philosopher, believed that the body was purely mechanical, only given feeling and consciousness by its soul. Animals did not possess souls, and were thus mere automatons. As such they only *appeared* to suffer and feel pain. This led Descartes to embark upon what can only be described as a campaign of vivisection. In the course of his scientific investigations he would cut open and examine the inner organs of innumerable living animals, from birds and rabbits to cats and horses. Most notoriously, he is known to have nailed his mistress's dog to a plank and sliced it open while it was still alive.

Yet it is worth bearing in mind that none of our contemporary lives are untainted by such wanton cruelty. Even contemporary vivisection makes use of unsedated living animals in the cause of furthering the development of medicine and pharmaceuticals for human use. Where would we be without antibiotics, innumerable vaccines, blood transfusions, organ transplants or even chemotherapy? Few vital medical breakthroughs achieve human efficacy without animal suffering.

and timber, while precious metals, slaves and oriental spices were the luxury items imported from the eastern Mediterranean.

However, trade with some Muslim regions proved problematic. This was the age of the Crusades, when Europeans were at war with the Saracens (the European term for Middle Eastern Muslims). As we have seen, Crusaders even took Jerusalem, and were beginning to establish their own 'kingdoms' on the Levantine coast. Despite this, trade with Muslims in other parts of the Mediterranean continued as before. Indeed, European traders would often be granted their own 'quarter' in a port, where they constructed warehouses to store their goods.

Around the time of Fibonacci's birth in 1170, Pisa is known to have had half a dozen trading colonies, ranging across the Mediterranean from North Africa to the Middle East. Fibonacci's father, Guglielmo, was a successful and respected trader, to such an extent that he was appointed as the Pisan consul and customs official at the North African port of Bugia (now Béjaïa, in eastern Algeria). We have no reliable evidence of the young Fibonacci's education. Indeed, he probably had no formal education, apart from learning commercial practice at his father's head office in Pisa. We do know that in 1185, when he was around fifteen years old, he set sail on the 500-mile voyage to join his father at Bugia. And it was here that he made the discovery which would transform European thought and practice.

At this time, Europe was still using the number system bequeathed by Ancient Rome over a millennium previously:

I II III IV V VI VII VIII IX X... XX... XL... L... LX... C

Which corresponds to our contemporary numbers:

1 2 3 4 5 6 7 8 9 10... 20... 40... 50... 60... 100

The Roman system is opaque, and becomes extremely cumbersome when one attempts numerical manipulation. Indeed, it is best suited to counting on fingers, or the use of a simple type of abacus, which was how most commercial calculations were carried out in medieval Europe. Addition is bad enough:

XII + IV = XVI

But when it comes to multiplication or division, the Roman numeral system becomes a thicket of complication, with the figures giving no indication whatsoever of the process at work:

XV x III = XLV

When Fibonaccci arrived in Bugia, he discovered that the Arab traders used their own number system:

٠	١	٢	٣	٤	٥	٦	٧	٨	٩
0	1	2	3	4	5	6	7	8	9

The lower line shows our modern equivalents, giving some indication of how one evolved into the other.

The Arabic numerals reveal two significant differences from Roman numerals. For a start, there was no Roman sign for nought – or 'no number'. The sign for 'no number' in the Arabic numeral system (much of which originated in India) was called *zephyrum*, which would initially be called *zefiro* in Italian before it was shortened in Venetian to *zero*. More important than this actual number was the fact that it could be used as a marker, thus introducing a decimal system. If we look at the table above, we can see how the figure after 9 can become 10, i.e. the numbers are now repeated, but preceded by a 1, to show that they are members of the next ten numbers. When this line reaches 19, it then passes on to 20, so that the sequence can begin again, and so on. All this may seem very simple to our modern ears, but it caused nothing less than a revolution in mathematics. Numbers could now be manipulated with ease. There was no need for the letter 'L' for 50, as this number was simply the beginning of the fifth repetition of the line of ten numbers. Similarly with the sign 'C' for 100, which was simply the beginning of the tenth repetition of the ten numbers. Accordingly, this became known as the decimal system, after the Latin word *decimus* (ten).*

The recording of transactions in account books now became inordinately easier. Addition sums were written down for sales, and subtraction sums for purchases. And these resulting figures could then be added up (and subtracted) with comparative ease to give a final reckoning. Such sums were simple to calculate using decimal methods; while at the same time mistakes (or fraudulence) became much easier to spot.

In the course of his work as a trader, Fibonacci travelled widely throughout the eastern Mediterranean. He would almost certainly have visited the Pisan colonies at Antioch, Acre, Jaffa, Tyre and Latakia, all the while gaining further insight into Arabic mathematics. It soon became clear to Fibonacci that Arabic mathematics was far in advance of its European counterpart.

In the first years of the thirteenth century, while Fibonacci was still in his early thirties, he seems to have returned to live in Pisa. Here he set about pouring all his newly acquired Arabic mathematical knowledge into a book that he called *Liber Abaci* (The Book of Calculation), which he completed in 1202. This was long before printing had been established in Europe, which meant that in order to circulate books it was necessary to have them copied by hand. Most copyists were monks in monasteries, whose work was mainly confined to copying religious texts. It thus took some time for Fibonacci's *Liber Abaci* to reach a broader audience. We know that one copy reached Frederick II, who was so impressed that he invited Fibonacci to visit his court.

Fibonacci is widely regarded as the finest European mathematician of the medieval era, and is best remembered today for the Fibonacci

---

* Unlike western languages, Arabic is written right to left, and its numbers follow this order, with the smaller decimal digits appearing on the left of a number. It is merely convention for westerners to read the numbers from left to right, or higher digits to lower ones, as this makes no difference to the actual number. E.g. 'two hundred and ninety-seven' or 'seven single digits, nine doubles, and two hundreds'.

sequence – 1, 1, 2, 3, 5, 8, 13 – where the next number in the series is generated by adding the two previous numbers. Over the years this sequence would be detected in an uncanny proliferation in nature – from the arrangement of seeds in a sunflower head to chromosome inheritance. It is also related to the golden ratio, making it somehow fundamental to both the physical and the abstract world.* Fibonacci would die in 1250 aged around eighty, a man much honoured in his home city. In time, his numerals would bring about a revolution in the account books of Florence, playing a crucial role in the way this city transformed Europe.

It was during the latter half of the twelfth century that an early form of banking became established in Florence. European banking appears to have originated in Venice in 1157, but it was soon being practised in most northern Italian cities. In order to expand, or undertake foreign enterprises, traders required financing, and this was only made possible through obtaining loans from banks. However, there was a major problem. Usury – the lending of money at interest – was strictly forbidden by the Bible. On the other hand, without the prospect of increasing their money, there was no incentive for the moneylender to lend the money in the first place – especially when there was a risk that the debtor might default. It was this fact which enabled the early

---

* The golden ratio holds an almost mystical fascination to mathematicians.

A ————————————————— B ——————— C

In the line above, suppose the ratio of length AB to length BC is the same as the ratio of the length AC to AB. This ratio appears in many disparate branches of pure and applied mathematics, ranging from geometry to nuclear physics. Amongst other applications, it has been used by artists and architects for its aesthetic appeal, musicians seeking new harmonies, and financiers looking for patterns in stock market fluctuations. Euclid knew of it in the fourth century BC; it is central to the Fibonacci sequence; and has been used by the contemporary scientific thinker Roger Penrose. The ratio is in fact an irrational number; in other words, this number cannot be expressed in any exact number or precise fraction. Attempts to calculate it on a ratio of 1 to a number reveal only an unending sequence of decimal places, as in 1:1.61803398... (i.e. it is incommensurable, as is π).

moneylenders, and then the larger bankers, to find a surreptitious way around the edict against usury.

When a sum was loaned, the debtor would be expected to repay an extra sum for 'insurance', to cover the banker's risk in lending the money in the first place. This method usually amounted to an insurance payment of around 10–12 per cent of the original loan. The fact that when the debtor repaid his debt any possibility of risk essentially vanished was deemed irrelevant. The profit motive easily overrode any question of logic.

Other methods of circumventing the ban on usury were also developed. With virtually every major trading city minting its own currency, there was always a question of exchange rates where intercity trade was concerned. The simple manipulation of such rates was commonplace, especially as so many currencies became debased or coins clipped, which undermined their original value. The incorruptible Florentine florin soon became a standard, and was followed a few years later by the Venetian ducat. Over the years, these two currencies would remain almost equivalent in monetary value. Yet that 'almost' left the way open for a certain degree of exchange rate manipulation.

The need to transfer money to distant cities was essential in such transactions as the wool trade between Florence and Bruges. It was also essential for the collection of papal dues, an operation which required the transfer of large sums of money collected throughout Christendom for dispatch to the pope in Rome. Mule trains of gold, silver or currency, even when transported under armed guard, were vulnerable to attack by robbers or gangs of armed bandits as they made their way across remote countryside or over the Alps. Likewise, galleys crossing the Mediterranean were vulnerable to piracy. However, if a bank had a branch at one of the main collection points, such as Bruges or Barcelona, as well as a branch in Rome – both holding sufficient assets – the transfer of money could be effected by promissory notes or bills of exchange. These pieces of signed and stamped paper could only be validated by the bankers themselves at either end, and were thus worthless to robbers or pirates.

Gradually, use of the new Arabic numerals spread to the account books of Florence, then Siena, then the whole of northern Italy and beyond. This enabled banking to flourish. However, Florence was by this time torn between the Guelfs and Ghibellines, while its independent rival Siena, some fifty miles to the south, remained staunchly Ghibelline. Consequently, Siena's banks fared better than those attempting to operate amidst the strife in Florence.

By 1255, the *Gran Tavola* (Great Table) had emerged as the largest bank in Siena. Its founder, the enterprising Orlando Bonsignori, won the friendship of Pope Innocent IV, who appointed the *Gran Tavola* as the papal bankers, securing papal dues from all over Europe and making a fortune in the process. Indeed, according to the twenty-first-century German historian Wolfgang Reinhard, the *Gran Tavola* soon became 'one of the largest commercial and banking enterprises in Europe'.

During the early twelfth century, Siena had been ruled by its bishop, but by the mid-century it had become a republic like its larger neighbour Florence. In this case, the democratic machine soon fell into the hands of the Noveschi, the mercantile banking oligarchy whose Council of XI ruled the city. Inevitably, the rivalry with Florence led to outright conflict during the Guelf–Ghibelline period; yet despite having a population of 50,000 (just over half that of Florence), Siena managed to retain its independence.

Here, once again, we see all the ingredients for a Renaissance: money, a measure of civic freedom, and talent. The banks proved generous patrons, and the city prided itself on the excellence of its artists, amongst whom Guido da Siena was the outstanding figure during this period. But Guido remained very much under the influence of the Byzantine style, which had prevailed in Siena and flourished during the Middle Ages. Such art lacked perspective, and its faces tended towards the stereotypical features which characterized Byzantine icons. Also, the city lacked a literary culture capable of producing the likes of Dante, or a philosophical tradition with interest in the new humanism that was beginning to develop. Despite this, Siena remained well placed to nurture its own Renaissance. But this was not to be.

Bonsignori died in 1273, and subsequent managers of the bank lacked both his vision and his expertise. Disputes arose over debts owed by the bank to important clients, such as King Philip IV of France. But the final blow came in 1298 when the *Gran Tavola* lost the papal account, which was transferred to Florentine bankers by Boniface VIII, Dante's nemesis.

The collapse of the *Gran Tavola*, followed by the bankruptcy of several other banks in Siena, may have benefitted the Florentine banks, but it also gave the Florentine authorities pause for thought. Why had this happened? How were they to prevent such a thing from happening to their own banks? Many amongst them were ignorant of banking practices, as were the local religious authorities. The influential Dominicans of the Santa Maria Novella monastery began preaching against bankers and moneylenders who were 'passing their time doing calculation instead of Christian practices'. As a result, in 1299 the relevant guild the *Arte del Cambio* (Guild of Exchange) was forced to issue an edict which forbade the use of Arabic numerals in banking and account books. Ironically, the reason given for this ban was that the Arabic numerals were too easy to manipulate, thus facilitating forgery – whereas in fact nothing was easier to forge than Roman numerals, which required little more than a single stroke of the pen to transform them.

Despite this setback, the Florentine banks continued to flourish. The three main banks were owned and run by the Bardi, Peruzzi and Acciaiuoli families. Of these, the Bardi bank was marginally the most successful, and would build up a network of branches stretching from Jerusalem to Barcelona, from Constantinople to London. These had to be managed by trusted men – mostly members of the family, or related by marriage. Such managers were often partners in the ownership of their branch, and sometimes held a small share in the larger bank or company. The manager's pay was closely related to the profits his branch was able to generate. Dependent upon the manager's experience or relationship with his employers, he would often be allowed a certain freedom to enter into business contracts for the bank on his own initiative. In this way, a manager could accumulate a considerable sum of money. But being a foreign branch manager, usually with a staff of less than half a dozen, was not easy. Witness the complaints of one Bernardo Davanzati, who ran a branch in Venice for over forty years: 'We can do nothing at present,' he wrote during a particularly difficult time between Florence and Venice.

'Foreigners have to endure ill treatment every day. I am one of those who have to suffer constantly at the hands of marshals, captains and anyone disposed to inflict such punishment. There is always someone ready to make trouble for us poor foreigners.'

During this period, the traffic of money between foreign branches and the bank's head office in Florence was for the most part effected by the previously mentioned bills of exchange, which worked much like modern cheques. These were transported between branches by trusted Bardi couriers, who were often expected to act as minor diplomats and even spies for the city. Such couriers played an important role in supplying Florence with intelligence or even local gossip, which could be used for defensive as well as aggressive purposes. (It was almost certainly a courier who informed the city of Dante's plots during his exile.) Throughout this period, small-scale wars were liable to break out between city-states at any time, and couriers who observed the presence of hired mercenaries camped outside a city could provide vital information.

As early as 1164, the head of the Bardi family had been granted a hereditary title (count) and an estate outside Florence by the Holy Roman Emperor. By the time the Bardi had become successful bankers, they owned the entire county of Vernio, which lay twenty miles north of Florence. This was so far out in the *contado* that it was all but independent of the city. Vernio contained its own fortified castle, as well as nine village communes. Such was the growing fortune and power of the Bardi family and its bank that the city authorities ordered them to sell their castle, as they considered it a threat to the Florentine Republic. The Bardi had no option but to obey if they wished to retain their presence in Florence, which included not only their bank but also a fine *palazzo* in Oltrarno. This had been built after the Bardi family bought a slice of land running along the left bank of the Arno, bordered by what is now the Via de' Bardi. Originally this had been inhabited by fishermen and some of the poorest families in the city, in a district of hovels known as the Borgo Pidigliosi (Den of Fleas).

The Bardi in fact had no designs on seizing the government of Florence, or of setting up their own independent state in Vernio. Their power base, in conjunction with other banking families in Florence, was sufficient to influence the elections for the *signoria*, as well as maintain an influence over most decisions concerning the freedom of banking within the city. However, the decision to ban Arabic numerals, and the order to sell the Bardi castle, indicates that the power of the bankers in Florence remained far from absolute.

Possibly to safeguard their banking interests, in the early 1300s the Bardi bank branched out into the wholesale commodities market. They specialized in the transport of grain, and soon gained a monopoly on the transfer of grain between France and central Italian cities. Such was the success of these industries that, by the early 1320s, the Bardi bank – along with their fellow Florentine bankers the Peruzzi – had become the most successful in Europe, in terms of capital, expertise and the number of branches they maintained throughout the continent, the Levant and beyond. Only north Germany and the Baltic remained beyond their reach, as this was the territory monopolized by the Hanseatic League, a confederation of northern ports and cities tied by a commercial and defensive alliance. The league maintained a trade monopoly in as many as eighty cities throughout the Baltic, north Germany and Flanders, and even had a link with England through the port of King's Lynn.

The port city which maintained a link between the Hanseatic League and the southern European (mainly Italian) banking operations was the Flanders city of Bruges. This became a hub of trade, which ranged from English wool to Greenland sealskins, Russian fur pelts to oriental spices. This last item arrived from southern Europe via the Spice Routes, which started in China, India and the Orient, crossed mid-Asia and terminated at ports in the Levant and the Black Sea. Spices were new luxuries in northern Europe and provided high profits for Italian traders.

Such European trade was initially carried out along well-established transalpine routes, but in 1277 the first Genoese galley arrived in Bruges, establishing a sea route around the Iberian peninsula, across the Bay of Biscay and through the English Channel to the North Sea. Venice soon followed. It comes as little surprise that the world's first bourse was established in Bruges in 1309. This is the earliest known stock exchange – handling bills of exchange, and more importantly 'shares' in various banks or commercial enterprises which their owners wished to exchange or sell for cash. This first bourse is said to have derived its name from the Bruges inn, run by the Van der Beurze family, where such transactions began taking place.

In fact, Bruges also seems to have fulfilled the requirements for a possible Renaissance. And Bruges was not hamstrung by the flaws which disqualified the other two previous candidates – namely the mental instability of Frederick II in Sicily, and the banking crash in Siena. However, there seems to have been one overriding reason why the Renaissance did not begin in Bruges: its geographical location.

The ideas which did so much to stimulate the Renaissance came from the East – the translation from Arabic of classical works which had been lost to the West for a millennium or more. On top of this was the fact that Arabic thinkers had done so much to expand these ideas, and had been able to develop and utilize a system of numerals first used even further east, in India. The transference of such ideas from East to West was facilitated by the Mediterranean, which provided easy passage between southern Europe and the Levant. Bruges remained isolated from such philosophical and scientific stimulation. Although these ideas and developments would eventually percolate north across the Alps to centres of learning such as Paris and thriving centres of international trade such as Bruges, this would take time. In many ways, Bruges, for all its inventive commercial expertise, still remained a world away from Italy.*

The Florentine bank owned by the Peruzzi family occasionally worked in cooperation with the Bardi bank. The chronicler Giovanni Villani is known to have been a shareholder in the Peruzzi bank, which employed him during 1300–08 to travel through Italy, France, Switzerland and Flanders

---

* Despite this, there is no denying that Bruges was the centre of its own quasi-independent northern renaissance, as epitomized by the painter Jan van Eyck, who died in the city in 1429. The realism and detail in his works – such as the *Arnolfini Portrait* – demonstrate superior skill and technique aided by the use of oil paint which enabled subtleties beyond the reach of Florentine artists working in fresco. This was assisted by the new invention and widespread use of spectacles, which facilitated meticulous attention to detail.

as a factor, buying and selling goods on commission. Unfortunately, little mention of this is made in his *Chronicles*, which are mainly concerned with the people and affairs of Florence. However, a batch of Peruzzi account books dating from the first half of the fourteenth century have survived. They give a unique insight into the workings of Florence's second-largest bank. During this period it would form strong links with the Knights Hospitaller, who ruled the strategically important island of Rhodes. The bank also began diversifying into the wholesale grain business, establishing with their Bardi partners a lucrative monopoly on the shipping of this commodity from southern France to the cities of central Italy.

The third of the great Florentine banking families, the Acciaiuoli (pronounced *achia-ioo-oli*), appear to have made the most constructive use of the fortune they accumulated. As we shall see, they became patrons of the arts, in particular supporting the writer Boccaccio and the painter Giotto. In the course of running the Naples branch of the bank, Niccolò Acciaiuoli became close to King Robert of Naples, and would eventually be appointed grand seneschal of the kingdom (a powerful position equivalent to a combination of chief courtier and chief administrator). Later, the Acciaiuoli family's former banking links with Greece would enable Nerio I Acciaiuoli to become Duke of Athens, ruling over the duchy that had initially been established in 1205 by the Burgundians on the Fourth Crusade. No less than five members of Nerio I's family would go on to succeed to this dukedom during the ensuing century.

It is also worth mentioning one important point concerning these three great Florentine international trading banks, as well as their contemporaries and Sienese predecessors. This is articulated by the leading medieval financial scholar Raymond de Roover, who wrote in 1963: 'The Italian merchants evolved a body of mercantile law, customary at first, but codified [much] later in ordinances... [These] rules, more or less universally adopted, still form the basis of commercial, or business, law today.'

The Renaissance would prove to be the beginning of our modern world in thought, science, art and literature. Often overlooked is the fact that it also laid the foundations for our contemporary society in what has come to be regarded by many as its fundamental aspect – finance and commerce.

CHAPTER 3

A CLEAR EYE AMIDST TROUBLED TIMES

B Y THE EARLY 1300S, Florence was beginning to emerge from its years of Guelf–Ghibelline strife to become one of the leading cities in Europe. The presence of wealth and a certain civic freedom have already been demonstrated. On the other hand, the exile of Dante in 1302 hardly augured well concerning the third requirement for the Renaissance – namely, original imaginative talent. However, Dante was not alone amongst Florentines in possessing this quality. Neither was it just his *dolce stil novo* circle of poets and writers who were manifesting such novel inspiration. If anything, the field which would be most transformed by the Renaissance would be that of art – and most notably painting. It is this which, for most of us, conjures up the essence of the Renaissance. The US-born contemporary Renaissance expert Lauro Martines suggests a profound reason for this:

> The critical point in the sociology of art centers on the way in which artists convert social experience into a figurative language.

It is what happens when a way of seeing, as a function of social structure and social change, finds its expression in style. Art is what we have always thought it was, but it is also a mysterious social language.

The origins of Renaissance painting are best illustrated by the works of Giotto di Bondone, usually known simply as Giotto. It was he who was to make the decisive break with the Byzantine tradition which at the time so dominated medieval art.

Giotto was born the son of a blacksmith in Florence, sometime around 1267. He was probably brought up by family or relations in the village of Vespignano, some twenty-five miles north-east of the city walls. He seems to have been an intelligent child with a playful, likeable character. At an early age he was put to work guarding sheep as they grazed on the hillside. For details of Giotto's life, we have to rely mainly upon the sixteenth-century painter Giorgio Vasari's *Lives of the Most Eminent Painters, Sculptors and Architects*. Vasari wrote of Giotto some 200 years after his death, long enough for tales of Giotto's life to have survived, but with little evidence to indicate whether these stories had become embellished over time. However, they remain illustrative, if nothing else.

According to Vasari, when the young Giotto was out looking after the sheep, he often spent his time drawing with stones in the ground or on nearby rocks. One day, the Florentine painter Cimabue was travelling from Florence to Vespignano and noticed Giotto drawing one of his sheep 'scratchily with a slightly pointed stone on a smooth clean piece of rock'. Cimabue was so impressed by the untutored child's realistic drawing that he offered him a job at his studio as an apprentice. Giotto's family agreed, and the young man travelled back with Cimabue to Florence. Cimabue was at the time the most renowned painter in the city. Although he painted in the Byzantine style, his work invested the stylized figures with an incipient lifelike quality, lending them an element of realism with properly proportioned limbs and certain effects of shadow.

Giotto seems to have absorbed his master's technique with alacrity, becoming especially intrigued with the realistic aspects of Cimabue's work, which enhanced the naturalistic aspects of his own earlier untutored drawings of sheep and such. According to one of Vasari's stories, when Giotto was left alone one day in his master's studio, he meticulously painted a realistic fly on the nose of a figure in one of Cimabue's paintings. His master noticed this, and Giotto was highly amused when Cimabue made several attempts to brush the fly away. This story (or legend) illustrates Giotto's attention to realistic detail.

Another of Vasari's stories indicates Giotto's precocious skill – as well as an element of independent self-confidence. Word soon spread beyond Florence of the talented young painter working in Cimabue's studio, eventually reaching Rome. The pope himself became intrigued, and dispatched a courier to Florence to fetch evidence of Giotto's talent. While the courier looked on, Giotto dipped his brush into a pot of red paint and drew a perfect circle, 'without moving his arm and without help of a compass'. When the courier asked for some drawings, Giotto insisted that this circle alone was sufficient to demonstrate his skill. The courier left, disappointed, convinced that Giotto had made a fool of him. In order not to disappoint the pope, he picked up some drawings by other artists, and took them back to Rome along with Giotto's circle. The pope is said to have been unimpressed with the drawings but fascinated by Giotto's red circle, especially when the courier told him how it had been drawn. The pope seems to have remarked to the courier: 'You are more simple than Giotto's O.' This witticism would become a proverbial term of abuse, largely because of the pun it contains. In Tuscan, the word *tondo* meant both a circle and an imbecile.

Giotto's teacher Cimabue was a formidable character, with very high standards. According to Vasari, when he detected a flaw in his own work, 'he would immediately destroy the work, no matter how precious it might be'. He was a hard taskmaster for Giotto. When Cimabue was commissioned by the town of Assisi to paint a number of large frescoes depicting the life of St Francis, Giotto accompanied him on the 120-mile journey south-east across the mountains and worked as his assistant. These frescoes can still be seen at Assisi, and to this day scholars continue to dispute which of them, or which parts of them, were painted by Cimabue and which by Giotto. This speaks volumes of Giotto's growing abilities, and what he had learned from his master.

Giotto was soon gaining commissions on his own behalf and developing his own individual style. This was referred to as *il vero* (the true), owing to its direct imitation of nature. His figures were realistically placed amidst realistic surroundings, adopting lifelike poses – as distinct from the stylized figures and settings of the Byzantine style.

This change in Giotto's painting has been likened to the other subtle pre-Renaissance transformations which were starting to emerge during this period. Owing to the nature of their business, the bankers had begun to adopt a more rationalistic approach to life. Where money and trade were concerned, there was little room for the mysticism and irrational elements of faith which the Church had encouraged during the medieval era. Precise account books – rather than ethereal visions – were the order of the day in commercial life. And this attitude was beginning to spread from the bankers and merchants through the *popolani* (the small traders and skilled artisan classes). As Martines puts it, Giotto's style 'caught the self-assurance and practicality of those who lived by trade'.

Yet this shift away from a mystical view of the world to the rational precision of account books should not be regarded as a diminution of religion. These accountants and merchants very much remained devout Christian worshippers. This can be seen from the contemporary merchants' habit of heading their accounts with the legend 'In the name of God and of profit'. In its own way, this heading indicates a deep accord with the medieval worldview. Profit could be gained in the account books of this world, but in the end it remained for us to be judged by God in the next world. After our death, our mortal life would have to be accounted for – as in a ledger. From the profit of our good deeds would be subtracted the loss of our sins. The day of judgement was the balancing of the account books of our lives.

Similarly, although Giotto's paintings took on a more measured and rational view of reality, this shift was in no way a departing from his faith. Giotto's paintings were almost exclusively religious – the nativity, madonnas, the crucifixion, and scenes from the life of St Francis and the like. Though amongst the depictions of onlookers he did include the occasional portrait of a living contemporary – or even a self-portrait. From these we have a good idea of what Giotto looked like. Despite the playful anecdotes about the painted fly and the perfect circle, Giotto appears in these portraits as a serious, self-contained character with a high regard for himself. At least, this is the picture of himself he wished to convey. Similarly, the most reliable portrait we have of Dante is by Giotto, who according to Vasari 'was a very good friend of Dante'. He is even known to have met the exiled poet in Ferrara, where Dante arranged at least one commission for him.

Giotto's portrait of Dante appears on a fresco in Florence. This is in the Chapel of the Podestà, in the Bargello, the large crenellated building which was being built to house the *podestà* (the foreigner who served as chief magistrate). The portrait is known to have been painted around fifteen years after Dante's death, but was generally agreed to have been a good likeness of Dante as a young man, at the time when he would have known Giotto. The Dante he conveys has a strong face, which nonetheless has more than a suggestion of femininity in its youthful sensitivity. This would chime precisely with the Dante we know from his twenties: the somewhat precious author of *La Vita Nuova* who was at the same time the man assigned to the front row of the cavalry at the Battle of Campaldino.

Giotto is known to have married a woman called Ciuta (short for Ricevuta) when he was in his early twenties. They would have eight children together, one of whom would become a painter. By 1301, Giotto even owned a house in Florence: no mean feat for a young shepherd who was the son of a humble blacksmith. By now, Giotto's innovative talent was such that his work completely outshone that of his ageing master, Cimabue. His new realistic style had caught the imagination of rich patrons, and he is known to have received commissions from both the Bardi and the Peruzzi banking families, as well as receiving support from the Acciaiuoli. He spent much of the rest of his life travelling through Italy fulfilling commissions, and even took on work as a sculptor and an architect.

Contrary to the rather austere picture Giotto painted of himself for posterity, Vasari portrays him as a somewhat humorous character. On his travels Giotto visited Naples, where King Robert asked him to decorate a chapel with some apocalyptic scenes. According to legend, Dante is said to have suggested the images which Giotto painted. Vasari describes the artist during this time: 'The king was always pleased to watch Giotto painting and listen to what he had to say. Giotto was never at a loss for a joke or a witty riposte, and the king was as intrigued by his painting as he was amused by his anecdotes.' Giotto even visited Pope Clement V in Avignon, where the papacy was at that time based. He is also known to have travelled further afield in France, possibly as far north as the Loire.

Back in Florence he became a friend of the writer Boccaccio, who also much admired Dante. And it is from Boccaccio that a rather different picture of Giotto begins to emerge. Vasari, drawing on Boccaccio, says of Giotto, 'there was no uglier man in the whole of Florence'. (Admittedly, one of Giotto's self-portraits does hint at this.) Another story seems to confirm Boccaccio's view. During the course of Giotto's many travels throughout central Italy, he was invariably accompanied by his wife Ciuta and their growing band of children. When Giotto was painting in the Scrovegni Chapel at Padua he was visited by Dante, who was somewhat taken aback to see the painter blithely immersed in his work while his scruffy young children ran amok around him. Dante asked him how a man who painted so beautifully could have produced such children. Ever the wit, Giotto replied: 'I made them in the dark.'

The series of frescoes which Giotto painted in the Scrovegni Chapel are deemed by many to be his masterwork. They include several scenes from the life of the Virgin Mary, as well as a large portrayal of the Last Judgement. These are not only original in style, but often also in the interpretation of the events they depict. Despite Giotto's lack of education, it seems that he was well versed in references to the scenes he painted. The Scrovegni Chapel frescoes also depict the seven virtues and their opposing seven vices. The allegorical figures in these scenes achieve a statuesque quality through the use of a monochrome grey palette, which subtly lends them the quality of marble. These murals date from around 1305, when Giotto was at the height of his powers.

While living in Florence, Giotto maintained a studio with several apprentices, who often helped with his paintings. By now the city had embarked upon a number of cultural projects – especially in the field of architecture – which were intended to reflect Florence's stature as the leading banking centre in Italy (a title which was hotly contested by Venice). Chief amongst these projected buildings was a new cathedral, to be named Santa Maria del Fiore (St Mary of the Flower).* Construction had started as early as 1296, under the charge of Arnolfo di Cambio, who had drawn up its essentially Gothic design. After Cambio's death a dozen or so years later, Giotto was appointed chief architect of this long-term project, and his main contribution would be the freestanding Campanile, an edifice of considerable grace. This is faced with white and polychrome marble, which matches the exterior of the cathedral and baptistery. Giotto may have been a proficient architect, but his ambitions and abilities in this field do not match the groundbreaking work of his painting. The Campanile, though indubitably a fine piece of architecture, remains strictly Gothic in style.

Giotto would die in his native city in 1337, aged around seventy. Vasari describes how 'Giotto was buried in Santa Maria del Fiore, on the left of the entrance to the church where there is a slab of white marble in his memory'. Not until excavations were undertaken in 1977 would this grave provide a surprising revelation, along with what purported to be Giotto's bones. When these were subjected to forensic examination in 2000, evidence confirmed that they had, during their owner's lifetime, absorbed a considerable amount of chemicals. Predominant amongst these were arsenic and lead, such as would be used in an artist's paint (which in those days he would have personally ground for himself). Furthermore, the teeth of the skull were worn down in such a fashion

---

* This is the building which to this day dominates the skyline of Florence, and is widely known as the Duomo. Contrary to popular misconception, the word *duomo* means 'cathedral' in Italian, and has nothing to do with the dome – which would not be incorporated into the design of this structure until well over a century later.

as to indicate that he frequently held brushes between them. The bones were undoubtedly those of a painter. But they would also disclose a secret. They had belonged to a very short man, with a very large head and a prominent hooked nose, as well as a protruding eye. He would have been around four feet tall, and probably afflicted with congenital dwarfism. This chimed with a centuries-old legend that a dwarf who appears in a fresco in the Florentine church of Santa Croce was in fact a self-portrait of Giotto. Other self-portraits go to some lengths to disguise this truth, especially the one which views his face from below, lending it a misleadingly haughty character that is utterly at odds with the personality we know from Vasari.

We now come to Giotto's friend, the writer Boccaccio, with whom the painter shared a similarly realistic (or unpretentious) view of life. Boccaccio was born in 1313, some twenty-four years before Giotto died, and just eight years before the death of Dante – whom he did not meet but certainly venerated, though not without reservations. As we shall see, Boccaccio was one of the trio of great Florentine writers responsible for the birth of Italian literature. (The third was Petrarch, who features in the next chapter.)

Giovanni Boccaccio seems to have been born out of wedlock. His birthplace was Certaldo, a small town some twenty miles south-west of Florence. Here was the home of his father, Boccaccino di Chellino, a Florentine merchant who worked for the Bardi bank. His mother remains unknown. The young Boccaccio was brought up and educated in Florence by a tutor who is said to have enthusiastically introduced him to the works of Dante.

By 1326, Boccaccio's father had married a Florentine woman of good family called Margherita dei Mardoli. Around this time, Boccaccio's father was appointed manager of a bank in Naples. The young Boccaccio accompanied him and was apprenticed as a clerk at his father's bank, where he learned arithmetic and accounting, to which he proved temperamentally unsuited. His father was persuaded to let him study law at the University of Naples – one of the oldest in Europe, founded by the Holy Roman Emperor Frederick II in 1224. The university was already renowned for the fact that Thomas Aquinas had studied there almost a century previously. However, Boccaccio quickly became as disenchanted with studying law as he had been with accounting.

Owing to the influence of his father, as a banker working with King Robert of Naples, the young Boccaccio, now in his twenties, began moving in court circles. Here he fell in love with a woman called Maria d'Aquino, who was a married illegitimate daughter of the king. At the same time he began writing prose romances, and his inamorata appears as 'Fiammetta' (meaning 'little flame') in a number of these pieces. Boccaccio also became a close friend of Niccolò Acciaiuoli, the member of the Florentine banking family who had such influence at court that he would eventually become grand seneschal of the Kingdom of Naples.

It was during this time that Boccaccio realized his true vocation as a poet, and began writing a number of long poems based on Ancient Greek myths. One of these was *Il Filostrato*, whose title is a blend of Greek and Latin meaning 'he who is prostrated with love'. It features the story of Troilus and Cressida, and although the story dates from the mythological siege of Troy, Boccaccio subtly suggests the atmosphere of the contemporary Neapolitan court, as well as his love for Fiammetta. (Boccaccio's version of this story would go on to inspire both Chaucer and Shakespeare.)

Boccaccio's feelings for Fiammetta soon became public knowledge. As with Dante's love for Beatrice, this almost certainly remained a chaste 'poetic' love – with one crucial difference. Boccaccio sometimes spoke to Fiammetta, and both were aware of their feelings for one another, which appear to have been mutual. Even so, Boccaccio is known to have left Naples in 1340, less than two years after their 'affair' had become a staple of gossip in court circles.

A nexus of events seems to have contributed to Boccaccio's departure. First, of course, there was the possible jealousy of Fiammetta's husband. We also know that in 1340 there was a minor outbreak of plague, which caused many who could to leave the city. At the same time, the political situation took a dangerous turn, with increasing tension between King Robert of Naples and Florence. A couple of years previously, this had led Boccaccio's father to return to Florence, and may well have been the cause of his bankruptcy the following year. Possibly making matters worse, it is thought that Boccaccio's birth mother died around this time.

Boccaccio was not happy to return to Florence, where it seems his father managed to find a minor post for him in the administration. Yet it was now that Boccaccio wrote his first great work, *Fiammetta*. Here Boccaccio's originality becomes strikingly apparent for the first time. This work is written in the form of an elegy, in the voice of Fiammetta herself, describing her feelings towards a certain Panfilo. Apart from the fact that this is a cover name for Boccaccio, it is also in itself highly ambiguous. Panfilo comes from the Greek *pan* and *philo*, meaning 'beloved by all', but also contains the suggestion 'lover of all'.

Fiammetta's feelings for Panfilo are similarly double-edged. She calls her elegy 'a warning sent by her to ladies in love'. In it, she graphically sets out the perils of her amorous relationship with Panfilo. As the nineteenth-century English critic John Addington Symonds noted: 'It is the first attempt in any literature to portray subjective emotion exterior to the writer; since the days of Virgil and Ovid, nothing had been essayed in this region of mental analysis. The author of this extraordinary work proved himself a profound anatomist of feeling by the subtlety with which he dissected a woman's heart.'

This indicates both the novelty and considerable insight expressed in *Fiammetta*. Its expertise is not only literary, but also psychological and emotional. Previously, Dante had described his dream of Beatrice literally eating his heart. But with Boccaccio, the precious – if in part psychologically suggestive – nature of Dante's feelings is abandoned for a more transparent suggestiveness. This is best illustrated by the following passage, in which Fiammetta describes how:

> Wearily I lay down amidst the soft deep grass. Then it seemed as if I was discovered by a hidden serpent. As I lay stretched on the

bed of grass, it pierced me under the left breast. The bite of the sharp fang, when it first entered, seemed to burn me. But afterward, feeling somewhat reassured, and yet afraid of something worse ensuing, I thought I clasped the cold serpent to my bosom, fancying that by communicating to it the warmth of that bosom, I should thereby render it more kindly disposed in my regard in return for such a service. But the viper, made bolder and more obdurate by that very favour, laid his hideous mouth on the wound he had given me, and after a long space, and after it had drunk much of my blood, methought that, despite my resistance, it drew forth my soul; and then, leaving my breast, departed with it.

Boccaccio is well aware of the feelings he is describing in this thinly veiled metaphor. Although he and Fiammetta had not consummated their love with an actual sexual relationship, here Boccaccio expresses (from Fiammetta's point of view) how she might have imagined this taking place – allusively, yet in vivid detail. This is almost as honest and heartfelt as a direct description of the love-making of which they both dreamt.

Yet, just as external events had contributed to Boccaccio's loss of Fiammetta and his departure from Naples, so would they contribute to his leaving of Florence and his conception of his best-known work. And to understand these circumstances fully, we must return once more to the turmoil of Florentine politics.

By the late 1330s, the vagaries of Italian intercity rivalry had caused Florence to enter a period of great economic uncertainty. The three great banks – those run by the Bardi, the Peruzzi and the Acciaiuoli families – were being surreptitiously undermined by their rivals on the European scene: the Venetian banks. This was made easier, and all the more serious, by the fact that all three of these Florentine banks were owed vast sums by King Edward III of England.

Once again, monarchs and rulers were exposing the fundamental flaw in the growth of such medieval banks: the banks possessed great fortunes, but no power. When a monarch approached a bank for a loan, this was an offer it could not refuse – as long as the bank depended for its livelihood on trade within that monarch's domain. The Florentine banks depended upon their offices in London to facilitate the wool trade upon which the Florentine cloth industry was based. Edward III was short of cash and embarking upon the war with France that would eventually become known as the Hundred Years' War, which would run almost continuously from 1337 until 1453. All three Florentine banks were obliged (if they wished to remain in business) to loan Edward III large sums of money to provide for his armies. Once one loan had been made, it was not possible to refuse another if there was to be any prospect of retrieving the original loan. Within a few years, these loans to the English king had multiplied to frightening sums. The Bardi bank, for instance, was owed well over 500,000 gold florins, with the Peruzzi bank being owed just under this sum.

So what part did the Venetians play in all this? Recent scholarship has unearthed that the Venetians were almost certainly a hidden factor which further undermined the Florentine banks. Florence, being a landlocked city-state, was dependent for its maritime trade upon the hire of sea-going galleys. The Pisan navy had been destroyed almost half a century previously by the Genoese, and it was Venice who stepped in to fill the gap for Florentine overseas trade. Thus Venice ensured that most of the Florentine wool trade between Tuscany and Bruges was transported on Venetian galleys, and the captains of these galleys were ideally placed to supply Venice with vital intelligence on the Florentine wool trade – its quantity, its value, its profits and losses, and so forth. And there was one further factor which lay in Venice's favour. The Venetian ducat was still but a rival to the Florentine florin. On the other hand, Venice had now taken control of the bullion market, and could thus manipulate the price of gold. The going exchange rate for the florin could be decided in Venice.

Meanwhile, Florence embarked upon a costly and foolhardy attempt to conquer the neighbouring small city-state of Lucca, which occupied the north-west corner of Tuscany and thus posed a potential, if unlikely, threat to Florence's trade route to the coast. The cost of this war, in the form of a steep rise in taxes, quickly led to widespread and serious discontent amongst the people. Fearing a revolt, the ruling families – both aristocratic old families and the bankers and merchants – took a drastic step. They began looking around for a powerful figure to take over as temporary ruler of Florence. In the end, they chose the French nobleman Walter de Brienne.*

In such times of crisis, the ruling families of Florence would call for a *parlamento*, in which all men over the age of fourteen would be summoned to the central Piazza della Signoria and asked to voice their assent (or dissent) to whatever question was put to them. In this case, they were asked to confirm Walter de Brienne as lord of Florence for one year. But by now the people were so against the ruling families that, instead of giving their consent, they began shouting '*A vita! A vita!*' (For life! For life!). They wished Walter de Brienne to become their permanent ruler.

Thus in 1342 Walter de Brienne was appointed, and as a reward for the people's loyalty he began promoting members of the *popolani* to the ruling *signoria*. This naturally outraged the ruling families. Yet it soon became clear that Walter de Brienne intended to rule as a dictator. When he refused to abolish the heavy war taxes, the people also took against him. Consequently, the entire population of the city rose up, and Walter de Brienne, along with his 400 troops, withdrew into the Palazzo della Signoria.†

This imposing stone building had been completed in the early years of the century by Arnolfo di Cambio, the architect responsible for the original design of the city's cathedral (Santa Maria del Fiore). He had

---

* As Count of Brienne, Walter owned a large estate in his home county, 100 miles east of Paris. Walter de Brienne was closely allied to King Robert of Naples, who had once again become an ally of Florence. Walter also happened to be Duke of Athens at the time, though this was largely titular, as Athens had been overrun by Catalans. It would be almost half a century before the Acciaiuoli family gained this title, when Nerio Acciaiuoli helped oust the Catalans.

† The building, now known as the Palazzo Vecchio, would be called several different names over the centuries, but for clarity I have referred to it as the Palazzo della Signoria throughout.

modelled it on the Bargello, which he had also designed, extending the proportions and giving its exterior the shape of a large cube with castellated battlements. The *palazzo* was intended to house the members of the ruling *signoria* during their term of office, and overlooked the expanse of the central Piazza della Signoria. The 300-foot-high bell tower which rose above the *palazzo* was based on one of the tall defensive towers that had dominated the city at the start of the previous century. It was the bell in this tower – known colloquially as *La Vacca* (The Cow), on account of its deep mooing tone – that was rung to summon the people for a *parlamento*. In this way, the Palazzo della Signoria became the focus of civic life in the city.

With Walter de Brienne and his men holed up in this imposing building, the citizens of Florence rose up as one. The chronicler Villani describes the scene he witnessed: 'Everyone was out on the streets, either on horseback or on foot. The citizens gathered in their respective neighbourhoods, brandishing their flags and bellowing, "Death to the Duke [of Athens] and his men! Long live the people! Long live Florence! Long live liberty!"'

Soon the mob had gathered beneath the high windows of the Palazzo della Signoria and began baying for Walter de Brienne's blood. In an attempt to defuse the situation, Walter commanded his soldiers to set free all the men he had condemned to the cells without trial. At the same time, he ordered the reviled man he had appointed chief of the police, and his son, to be ejected from the *palazzo* with the prisoners. Villani records how the mob responded to the appearance of these two hated figures:

> they set upon the son and tore him limb from limb in front of his father, chopping him into pieces. After that they did the same to his father. One of the mob even speared a chunk of flesh with his lance, and another stuck a piece on his sword. They then began making the rounds of the streets, chanting and holding aloft their trophies. Some were so overcome with bestial fury that they even began eating the raw flesh.

While the mob was distracted in its hysteria, Walter de Brienne and his men slipped out of the Palazzo della Signoria and fled for the city gates, making good their escape.

By the early 1340s, the three main Florentine banks – the Bardi, the Peruzzi and the Acciaiuoli – were in even more serious difficulties. In fact, they were only just managing to survive. On top of their debts, the secret currency machinations of the Venetians were beginning to have their effect on the Florentine currency. Villani records: 'In that year 1345, there was a great shortage of silver and no silver coinage in Florence... because all silver coins were being melted down and carried overseas.' This was a serious matter. The gold florin was used for international trade, whereas silver coins circulated within the city for local commerce. By now, owing to Venetian manipulation, the intrinsic value of the silver in these coins on the international market was worth more than their face value. Little wonder that profiteers were accumulating silver coins and melting them down so that they could sell the metal, usually abroad.

In response to this situation, the Florentine authorities began minting a new silver coin. According to Villani: 'They were very beautiful coins, decorated with the lily and with St John, and were called *nuovi guelfi*.' This, in fact, amounted to an underhand devaluation. The *nuovi guelfi* was given a higher face value than the previous coin, but its silver content was not increased accordingly.

After the expulsion of Walter de Brienne and his men, the mob had gone on the rampage against the leading families. The Bardi family in particular had suffered, with several of their houses looted and destroyed before order could be restored. Their situation hardly improved when it was learned that three members of the family had come to a secret agreement with some counterfeiters from Siena. Hidden coinage foundries had been set up in the mountains far to the south at Castro, on the border of the Papal States, where forgeries of the *nuovi guelfi* were minted. This was a serious matter, and the Florentine authorities soon raided Castro. According to Villani: 'Two of [the counterfeiters] were captured and burnt, and they confessed that the three Bardi had made them do it.' The three Bardi fled, and were condemned to be burned at the stake in their absence.

By this stage, the Bardi bank was in a desperate situation. Its debts owed by King Edward III of England had almost doubled, from 500,000 gold florins to 900,000. A further debt of 100,000 gold florins was owed by King Peter II of Sicily, a descendant of the Holy Roman Emperor Frederick II. At the same time, Edward III's debt to the Peruzzi bank had now risen to 600,000 gold florins, as well as 100,000 being owed by the King of Sicily. On top of this, the Peruzzi bank owed 300,000 florins to other account holders, whose deposits had been raided to facilitate these loans.

Then, in January 1345, 'an English Royal decree was promulgated, suspending the payment of monies due to creditors of the Crown'. King Edward III of England was reneging on his debts. The King of Sicily soon followed suit. The leading Florentine banks collapsed like a pack of cards, with the Bardi, the Peruzzi and the Acciaiuoli all going under. This was not all. As Villani records: 'Many other small companies and individuals, whose money was invested with the Bardi and the Peruzzi... lost everything.' Before the crash, there were known to be more than eighty banks operating in Florence, the banking capital of Europe. Many of these were small family concerns; all but a dozen or so went under.

Villani, who later in life worked for the Buonaccorsi bank, even found himself incarcerated in the Stinche prison. This fact is alluded to obliquely in his chronicle, in the form of a homily to all historians:

> One whose task it is to write a history of important events should not remain silent when it comes to the truth. He should be an example to future generations, and warn them to be prudent in their actions. For all that has passed we crave pardon, because what has happened has also befallen this author, weighing heavily upon him and his conscience.

Even so, there is no doubting his anger at his banker employers:

> Oh accursed and ravenous wolf, filled with greed which blinds us

and drives our citizens mad. Craving profit from rulers, they risk all their money, and that of other people. They gamble away their own power and position, losing everything, destroying the poor people of our republic.

According to Villani, the total amount the English king owed to the Bardi and Peruzzi banks alone was 'worth as much as the kingdom itself'. Unlike banking collapses in the twenty-first century, there was no question of any of these banks, large or small, being 'rescued' by the state. The big Florentine banks may have been, in modern parlance, 'too big to fail'; but, unlike modern governments, the city-state of Florence was in no position to step in. The Bardi bank and trading company had been 'the greatest merchants of Europe'. And all three of the big Florentine banks had been engaged in banking and trading on an intercontinental scale, with branches all over Europe, North Africa and the Levant. The Florentine government, on the other hand, was that of a politically turbulent city-state, forced to support itself with an annual *estimo* where officially everyone paid 'according to his capacity and possibilities'. The tax burden had multiplied during the long war against Lucca, which had dragged on over the previous years, and any further hike in taxes, especially to rescue the likes of the Bardi and the Peruzzi – to say nothing of the smaller banks – was simply unthinkable.

The *estimo*, as its name suggests, was in fact an estimate of a person's wealth, as indicated by his annual income. Such a system favoured the landowners at the expense of wage earners. As ever, those with high incomes did their best to conceal, or somehow minimize, their earnings. This meant that those with lower incomes invariably ended up paying a higher proportion of the tax.

The *estimo* could be, and often was, used by those in power to cripple enemy families, by saddling them with an inflated estimate of their income. However, one effect of the *estimo* system was that it discouraged ostentatious displays of wealth. This encouraged the democratic ethos of the citizens, maintaining the illusion that all were more or less equal.

In times of need, such as the ruinous war against Lucca, the government could impose a special tax known as the *prestanze*. This was a 'voluntary' loan in the form of a lump sum paid to the government. In return, the 'volunteer' received interest of 5 per cent on his loan. This became a contentious issue amongst the religious authorities, as the Bible explicitly condemned such usury. Unlike the banks, who charged 'insurance' or manipulated the exchange rates, the *prestanze* involved blatant usury, even if it was in a good cause. In the event, the Franciscans pronounced that the *prestanze* was not usury, whereas the Augustinian and the Dominican orders maintained that it was. On this occasion, the Franciscans won the day, but the controversy over usury – concerning the banks as well as the *prestanze* – would persist.

Despite the collapse of the Bardi, Peruzzi and the Acciaiuoli banks, these families do not appear to have lost everything. Small fry such as Villani may have gone bankrupt and been condemned to a spell in the Stinche – where sentences frequently included the odd spell of obligatory torture – yet many others seem to have salted away sufficient funds to avoid complete penury. Indeed, amongst the ruling families, few were totally ruined. Witness the subsequent success of the Acciaiuoli, who some forty or so years later would obtain the dukedom of Athens. Likewise, the Bardi still retained their family *palazzo*, built on the Bardi land of the Oltrarno. Meanwhile, the Peruzzi also remained a force to be reckoned with in Florentine affairs. But although the ruling families, and even the bankers, still held sway over the city, their hold was weakened. To retain loyalty, especially at the ballot box, one had to pay for it. And 'patronage' could be an expensive business. While the elite families competed, there was still an element of unpredictability concerning elections. It remained to be seen what would happen if any particular family emerged as dominant. Democracy in a republic where private banking had recently been much bigger than government was inevitably precarious.

At this point, it is worth briefly considering the full cost of the Florentine banking crisis. It is all but impossible to relate these medieval figures to modern values, owing to the changes in costs relative to their modern equivalents. The replacement of medieval craftsmanship by mass production, for instance, renders many costs and values incalculable.

However, it is possible to give an indication in terms of relative values. During the mid-1340s, an artisan could expect to earn the equivalent of up to forty florins a year. A senior government official might earn more than three times this amount, while a rich family could build a new medium-sized *palazzo* for around a thousand florins. Thus the Bardi bankruptcy alone, of more than a million florins, could theoretically have built 1,000 *palazzi*, paid the wages of around 25,000 artisans, or paid for the entire civic administration of the city – from the members of the *signoria* to the lowest copying clerks, collectors and menial labourers – for several years.

At the time, a majority of the city's population were so poor that they did not even have to pay the *estimo*. Though this is not to say that the poor paid nothing; they were still taxed indirectly. Each morning, as the smallholders drove their piglets, a sheep, a cow, carried their bales of hay or pushed their carts of fruit and vegetables in from the countryside for market, a tax inspector was waiting for them at the gate, extracting a regulated number of *scudi* (the lowest coins) for each item. Even wine, salt, and flour for bread could be made to carry an indirect tax in their prices. This was known as the *gabella*, and was effectively an import tax.

Then, in 1348, a far worse fate than a banking collapse was to befall the city. The bubonic plague is thought to have arrived in Italy on galleys from the Crimean port of Kaffa (now Feodosia), on the northern coast of the Black Sea. This city had come under siege by the Mongols, whose army of horsemen-warriors had carried the bacterium *Yersinia pestis* from central Asia. The Mongols catapulted the cadavers of those who had died of the disease over the city walls, where it spread amongst the besieged citizens.

After galleys containing infected men arrived at Venice and Naples in January 1348, the epidemic known as the Black Death began to spread through Italy. It is thought to have arrived in Tuscany after an infected galley put in at Pisa. By the spring it had spread to Florence. Later in the year, Villani recorded how 'it was more virulent here in Florence than it was in Pistoia and Prato [the two small towns a few miles up the road north from the city gates]. There were also less deaths in Bologna [fifty

miles to the north] and the Romagna [the Adriatic region beyond the
Apennine mountains to the east].'

Villani went on to describe the symptoms:

> The disease manifested itself with certain swellings in the groin
> and under the armpits. The victims began to spit blood, and
> within three days they would die… The plague would last until…

These are the poignant last words in Villani's chronicle. Before he
could write down the date, he too had succumbed to the Black Death,
which would quickly spread across Europe, killing between 30 per cent
and 60 per cent of the entire population – accounting for an estimated
25 million souls.

CHAPTER 4

BOCCACCIO AND PETRARCH

B OCCACCIO RETURNED FROM NAPLES to Florence around 1341. He
thus lived through the turbulent events which preceded the Black
Death. At the time of his arrival home, Florence was one of the leading
cities in Europe, with a population of just under 80,000. Yet even in such a
prosperous city, life was not easy. Of this population, 25,000 were gainfully
employed in the wool trade. During a slump, many would be laid off, with
a thousand or more being supported by public relief. Others were reduced
to joining the ranks of the city's beggars: figures in rags lined up outside
the churches or the monasteries; small groups gathered in the mornings
outside the *palazzi* of the rich, grateful for crusts, leftovers or pails of slop.

During the daytime these beggars would haunt the busy streets, the
piazzas and the marketplaces – haggard figures in rags pitifully imploring
passers-by for alms. Many of them would have been outcasts from families
who could no longer support them; others would have been servants who
had been dismissed by their masters; and others still were 'fallen' women
clutching a tiny bundle of human life, or disgraced daughters, ejected wives,
women too old or too disfigured to sell themselves as prostitutes. Evidence
suggests that some would have been maimed mercenaries returned from

the wars, feral children escaped from orphanages, or people of feeble mind or indeterminate age ravaged by starvation and illness, their bodies wrecked by spells in prison. Then there were the broken men returned from punishing years working on the galleys which sailed from Pisa, and the peasants forced to take refuge within the city walls, evicted from their smallholdings or driven out of the countryside by outlaw bands. All the frailty of human life was here, the victims of its scheming and its mishaps, brought low by weakness of mind or body or by simple misfortune.

Such was the background against which Boccaccio would compose his finest works. Unlike Dante, whose characters inhabited their allotted place in the afterlife, Boccaccio's characters would all be very much alive, roaming a familiar landscape, eagerly seeking opportunity to commit the very sins which Dante so condemned. Yet it was this very humanity, which the author shared with his creations, that informed his compassion.

Boccaccio was thirty-five when the plague struck Florence, and he would describe its effect on what had once been characterized as 'the most noble city in all Europe'. Now its plague-ridden streets were reduced to the hideous squalor of an open mortuary. With characteristic vividness, he recounts a scene 'which I witnessed with my own eyes':

> One day I came across the rags of a beggar who had died of the plague. They had been thrown out onto the street, where they had been discovered by two pigs. In typical fashion they poked their snouts into the clothes and began rooting about. Then they took them between their teeth and began shaking them vigorously, so that they flapped against their cheeks. Within no time they both keeled over as if they had been poisoned. Almost immediately they were dead, their bodies lying prostrate on the wretched rags.

Like all others who could, Boccaccio fled the city for the countryside of the *contado*. According to his own telling, he took refuge in a deserted villa amidst the seclusion of Fiesole, on the hillside overlooking Florence. Some years later he would recount his days here in the book which would make him famous (and notorious):

I propose to set down, in order to provide succour for ladies in love, a hundred stories or tales or parables, or whatever you wish to call them. These were related over the course of ten days by an honourable company of seven ladies and three young men during the time when they were taking refuge from the deadly pestilence. In these stories you will find opportunities for love, both joyful and tragic, along with accidents of fortune which take place today as much as they did in olden times.

These tales, ranging in length from novella to enlarged anecdote, are all told in the Florentine dialect which would become the Italian language, and provide the first great prose example of this form. Boccaccio called them the *Decameron* – deriving from the Greek *déka* (ten) and *hēméra* (days), reflecting the time frame of the story – though they are sometimes known as the *Umana Commedia* (Human Comedy), in contrast to Dante's *Divine Comedy*. And what a contrast they are. Instead of Dante's po-faced judgements and sublime reverence, we are treated to a series of vivid and explicit stories of the most secular nature. These range from parables of homely wisdom (often of a most unconventional kind) to scurrilous tales of trickery and bawdiness; from bold adventures to the most knockabout misadventures.

Rather than glorifying religion, as his hero Dante does, Boccaccio prefers to make a mockery of priests and the Church. This very much accords with the attitude of many who witnessed the effects of the plague – where no amount of piety was enough to save the pitiful victims in their hideous death throes. When faced with the horrors of the Black Death and the seeming inevitability of their own gruesome demise, many chose to abandon all decorum and simply surrendered themselves to a life of debauchery. Some ran naked through the streets or took part in impromptu orgies; others drank to excess, ransacked the homes of the rich or indulged in all manner of other profanities. Evidence of such behaviour crops up frequently in contemporary reports. And it would seem that there is an element of this in Boccaccio's impulse to tell his riotous and often bawdy tales.

The stories in the *Decameron* have all the rude health and trickery which many have come to associate with medieval life as it was actually lived. Yet, curious to relate, many of these are not original medieval tales at all. Most of them are stories that were adapted from a host of previous sources, from Herodotus to the tales recounted by Scheherazade in the *Arabian Nights*. Many are classical, others simply classic – and this is their strength. They have stood the test of time, even if their lofty pedigree may sometimes be difficult to detect. They remain funny, or instructive; they recount our foibles, our ignoble aspirations. They are simply human. And the more so for the way Boccaccio tells them. This is medieval literature advancing into the more knowing and sophisticated character of the coming Renaissance, which would embrace the new humanism. Yet what have all these pornographic tales, jolly japes and earthy yarns to do with philosophy? In this case, we might say that their humanism is manifest in their very humanity.

It is all very well pontificating on the morality of these tales, but what precisely are they about? Let's start with the one which caused such trouble that it was sometimes simply omitted altogether. (Foreign translators, aware that they were dealing with the classic prose work of early Italian literature, were wont to throw up their hands in despair, often leaving these pages in the original Italian.)

So what was this story which so many poetasters considered not fit for our ears? The 'heroine' of the tale is the 'simple-minded' Alibech, 'a fine and fully-developed girl around fourteen years old'. She lives in North Africa, and although not a Christian herself, she is so impressed by this religion that she asks a believer how she can best 'serve God'. The Christian replies that those who did this best distanced themselves from all earthly goods and went to live as hermits in the desert. So, 'prompted by nothing more logical than a strong adolescent impulse', she sets off into the Sahara to learn about the life lived by these hermits. The first holy man she finds, 'on seeing how young and exceptionally beautiful she was', sends her on her way, 'feeling that if he took her under his protection the devil might catch him off guard'. A second holy man is equally reluctant, but directs her to visit 'a young hermit called Rustico, who is both very kind and steadfast in his faith'. Eventually, Alibech arrives at Rustico's cell. 'Being keen to prove to himself that he had a will of iron', Rustico invites Alibech to spend the night in his cell, where he puts together a bed for her made of palm leaves.

During the course of the night, Rustico finds himself unable to think of anything else but the beautiful young girl asleep in his cell. He racks his brains 'as to how he could creep up to her in such a way that she did not think the plan he had in mind for her was in any way lascivious'. He then wakes her and launches into a sermon about how powerful the Devil is, and how God most appreciates those who put the Devil back in Hell, from which he escaped.

To cut a long story short, they end up naked, kneeling opposite one another to pray. Whereupon Rustico is so overcome with desire that he experiences 'a resurrection of the flesh'. The innocent Alibech asks Rustico, 'What's that thing I can see sticking out in front of you? I haven't got one.' Rustico informs her that this is 'the Devil I was talking about'.

Alibech thanks God that she does not have such a Devil to contend with. Rustico agrees with her, but then tells her that she has something which he does not possess. 'And what's that?' asks Alibech. 'You have Hell,' replies Rustico. He then tells her that God has sent him to her so that he can put the Devil back in Hell. 'Oh Father, I really do have a Hell. Let's try and put the Devil back in Hell, just as God wants.' This they proceed to do. Again and again.

Alibech then tells him: 'The way I see it, anyone who doesn't devote all his energies to putting the Devil back in Hell must be a complete idiot.' And so on, for several days, until eventually Rustico is so exhausted that he finds himself driven impotent by the constant demands of the 'enthusiastic Alibech'.

This may be a highly titillating, even unlikely tale, and although it continues beyond this, it ends with no discernible moral – other than 'if you need God's grace put the Devil in Hell, which will bring great pleasure for all concerned, even God and the Devil'. But despite Boccaccio's apparent frivolity, there is no mistaking his psychological insight in describing Alibech's adolescent impulses and Rustico's torments of desire. As for its originality, Boccaccio himself has the storyteller claim it is an old Genoese tale. Scholars have suggested that it was probably Venetian and inspired by tales of Kublai Khan by Marco Polo, who had returned from China at the end of the previous century. As for its final message, this would seem to be more appropriate to the 1960s than the 1360s, the date by which Boccaccio had probably finished his magnum opus (which runs to over 800 pages of similarly entertaining stories and cod morality).

During these years, Boccaccio had risen to an important position in the Florentine administration. Promotion had been rapid following the Black Death, which had reduced the city's population to less than 50,000. As early as 1350, Boccaccio became a diplomatic representative for Florence, leading delegations as far afield as Venice, Milan (Florence's main ally), Avignon (now the seat of the papacy) and Brandenburg. In the midst of this he found time to write a biography of Dante, who had died in Ravenna during Boccaccio's childhood. There would thus have been a few elderly people in Florence who had actually met Dante prior to his exile, and Boccaccio seems to have drawn on these sources – which in the event did not always prove reliable, according to modern scholarship. Boccaccio greatly admired Dante, despite the disparity in their characters. Thus he could not help remarking of Dante's chaste love for Beatrice that this was 'no small marvel in today's world'.

By now, Boccaccio had met the third in the Tuscan triumvirate of great literary figures, namely the poet Francesco Petrarch, who was ten years older than him and had spent most of his life in exile. Petrarch's philosophical humanism had proved a significant influence on Boccaccio since his younger years in Naples, though its influence on the *Decameron* was hardly philosophical. Boccaccio met Petrarch when the famous poet visited Florence and Boccaccio was appointed to lead the delegation to greet him. Boccaccio put Petrarch up in his house and they became close friends, continuing to correspond after Petrarch had departed. Petrarch appears to have had a calming influence on Boccaccio's more rumbustious literary character.

Sometime around 1360, Boccaccio began writing his other great work, *De Mulieribus Claris* (Concerning Famous Women), which consists of a collection of biographies of women, from the mythological and the historical to his own contemporaries. Despite the influence of Petrarch, and his own growing maturity, Boccaccio could not resist including a number of notorious women amongst the 106 biographies. Thus his subjects range from Eve to Cleopatra; from Flora, the Roman goddess of spring and patron saint of prostitutes, to the ninth-century Englishwoman Joan, who disguised herself as a man and eventually became pope, only to die in childbirth during a religious procession.

In 1361 there was a failed coup in Florence, after which the conspirators were rounded up and executed. Although Boccaccio played no part in this plot, some of his friends were involved and he decided it would be wise for him to retire to his family village, Certaldo. Here he would live out his days, a fat and grouchy old man, becoming increasingly embittered as woman after woman rejected his attentions. In the end he despaired of himself and the world. It was only Petrarch who managed to talk him out of burning his large library of books, which had been such a source and inspiration for his works. Boccaccio finally died in midwinter at the end of 1375, at the age of sixty-two.

Although Francesco Petrarch was born in the small independent Tuscan city of Arezzo, he was Florentine by descent on both sides of his family, his father having been exiled. Indeed, Petrarch would spend his early childhood in the village of Incisa, by the banks of the Arno, just upstream from Florence. During these years he was brought up by his mother, who received secret visits from her exiled husband. Petrarch's father had been a friend of Dante, who also remained in exile and would not die until 1321, some seventeen years after Petrarch's birth. By this time, Petrarch had been taken by his family to live in Avignon, in southern France, following Pope Clement V, who had controversially moved the papacy from Rome to

France.* Petrarch's father was an ecclesiastical notary (a lawyer who dealt in canon law), and he insisted that his son should enter the legal profession. Dutifully, but with increasing reluctance, the young Petrarch studied law for seven years, first at the University of Montpellier and then at Bologna, accompanied by his younger brother Gherardo. By now Petrarch had become inspired by his discovery of Latin literature. When his parents died, he returned to Avignon at the age of twenty-six and abandoned law.

Here Petrarch made friends with several high-ranking clerics at the papal court. His fluent wit and deep learning would attract many close friendships throughout his life, wherever he went, and in Avignon he developed firm friendships with two brothers of the aristocratic Colonna family – namely, the young Giacomo Colonna, Bishop of Lombez, and his older brother Cardinal Giovanni Colonna. Almost certainly it was through Giacomo's influence that Pope Benedict XII appointed Petrarch to a sinecure post as a canon in Lombez, a small town thirty miles or so south-west of Toulouse. This enabled Petrarch to live off the stipend.

During the ensuing years Petrarch would travel widely, including to Flanders, Bohemia (Czech Republic) and Paris, which was then the intellectual centre of medieval culture. And it was here that Petrarch discovered the works of St Augustine, who in the fourth century had been the last great philosopher of the Roman Empire. St Augustine had a profound and sometimes profoundly troubled relationship with Christianity. Interestingly, it was St Augustine who managed to marry the philosophy of Plato to Christian doctrine, giving it an intellectual appeal and depth which it had not previously possessed. As we shall see, the reawakening of interest in Plato would have a crucial effect on the Renaissance.

---

* According to Villani, Clement V had been bound to do this by a secret promise made to King Philip IV of France, who influenced his election as pope. (This had happened despite the fact that Clement V was neither a cardinal nor Italian, both of which had become customary qualifications for the occupant of St Peter's throne.) The move to Avignon would eventually precipitate the Great Schism, when there were two popes, one in Rome and one in Avignon. This was followed by a period when there were three popes, each of which excommunicated his two rivals.

Almost a millennium and a half before the seventeenth-century French philosopher Descartes cast doubt on everything, and famously came to the bedrock conclusion which survived all scepticism – '*Cogito, ergo sum*' (I think, therefore I am) – St Augustine would come to a remarkably similar realization, concluding '*Si fallor, sum*' (loosely, 'If I am deceived by the world, I still exist'). This great step into inwardness and self-realization would have a formative influence on Petrarch and his development of a humanist philosophy. In humanism, a new humanity was coming into being, no less. Wherever Petrarch went, he would always carry a work of St Augustine with him.

Petrarch has been called the 'first tourist', as he was constantly seeking out sights and places of interest. He also went out of his way to visit monasteries and ancient churches which were known to have large libraries. His searches amongst these would result in many exciting bibliographic discoveries, unearthing a host of forgotten or unrecognized manuscripts. During his sojourns in these spots, he would also make many close and lasting friendships. These would be maintained by a constant flow of letters.

Petrarch's first major work was an epic poem, written in Latin hexameters, called *Africa*. The poem describes the exploits of the Roman general Scipio Africanus, who decisively defeated the Carthaginians at the Battle of Zama in 202 BC. *Africa* won Petrarch widespread fame and led to him being crowned poet laureate in Rome, a recently revived honour, dating from antiquity, involving the recipient being crowned with a wreath of laurel leaves.

Both Petrarch's honour and his Latin epic can be seen as further indications of the revival of classical learning presaging the Renaissance and the falling away of the medieval era. Petrarch's definitive role in this can be seen in the fact that it was he who coined the term 'Dark Ages', though he used this to characterize the entire Middle Ages, whereas it is now usually taken to refer to the centuries following the fall of Rome in 476 AD and preceding the turn of the new millennium in 1000 – and even this usage is increasingly disputed.

Despite my earlier assertion that contemporaries invariably do not fully comprehend what is taking place around them, Petrarch seems to have been all too conscious that a great transformation was taking place in the Italian world of the fourteenth century. The guiding force for this sea change in European thought can be ascribed to the inspiration of humanism, of which Petrarch was an early advocate.

To understand the full import of the new outlook, it is necessary to grasp the intellectual world which preceded it. As we have already seen, during the medieval era the Christian religion was the dominant element in life. Our existence in this world was merely a preparation for the world to come; after we died, we would be judged according to how we had behaved in this life, and be sent to Hell, Purgatory or Heaven accordingly, just as Dante had portrayed in his *Divine Comedy*. Humanism, on the other hand, placed the stress on the expression of our humanity in *this* life. We should live our life as human beings to the full.

This essentially pagan spirit was what had informed the philosophers, writers and artists of the classical era. Hence the enthusiasm for classical authors whose rediscovered works were beginning to permeate western Europe – largely from the East, by way of the eastern Byzantine Empire and also the Arab world, viz. Avicenna's translations of Aristotle. And as we have seen, this new learning also involved other eastern ideas, such as the Indo-Arabic numerals introduced into Europe by Fibonacci. Latterly, scholars were also beginning to rediscover and collect old manuscripts of new-found classical works, ones which had previously been unknown or which many thought had been lost forever.* Here again, Petrarch himself would play a leading role.

---

* The Great Library at Alexandria contained the largest collection of scrolls and manuscripts in the ancient world, attracting scholars from all over the Mediterranean. In 48 BC the library was accidentally burned down by Julius Caesar, and many unique copies of classical works went up in flames. Sometime around 270 AD the greatly reduced library suffered another, similar catastrophe. The loss to human knowledge caused by the destruction of the Great Library of Alexandria is impossible to estimate. Likewise the inspiration and influence its works may have had on the advancement and course of human history.

Education, too, was beginning to change. Medieval education was based upon scholasticism, with its emphasis on grammar, rhetoric and logic: how to write (in Latin), how to speak, and how to think, i.e. clarity, sophisticated argument, and reason. But all of these were beginning to ossify in a rigid formalism. Latin may have been the universal language of scholars throughout Christian Europe, but it was not the language of everyday life, unlike the Italian used by Dante, Boccaccio and later Petrarch. Rhetoric referred to a form of persuasive discourse which also had little to do with everyday life, except in such areas as the law and the few regions where public political speeches were permitted. Lastly, logic still consisted of the rigid structure of syllogistic arguments set down by its founder Aristotle over one and a half millennia previously. The syllogism as a method of deductive reasoning relied upon drawing a new conclusion from two known premises. Thus:

All men are mortal.
Socrates is a man.
Therefore, Socrates is mortal.

As we shall see, new knowledge would increasingly be discovered by scientific method and by the investigation of experience, rather than by abstract thought such as syllogistic logic.

The range of these transformations can be seen in the broadening of education which would soon take place. Instead of scholasticism, the new humanism sought to emphasize what we now refer to as the human-ities (known at the time as *studia humanitatis*). The stock arguments of Aristotelian logic would be abandoned in favour of a mental and moral philosophy derived from the newly discovered classical works of Ancient Greece and Rome.

At this juncture, Latin may have been the universal language, but Ancient Greek was virtually unknown in western Europe. As Petrarch put it, 'Homer was dumb to him, while he was deaf to Homer.' The works of Ancient Greeks that were available were all Latin transla-tions from the original. However, the new translations arriving from the

Arab world provided new perspectives on works already known, as well as introducing totally unknown works. And with the coming of a new rationalist approach, reasoned argument began to prevail rather than the strictures of Aristotelian logic.

Petrarch's fame as poet laureate meant that he was welcome at courts throughout Italy. His intellect and learning caused several rulers to see him as an 'honest broker'. As such, they conscripted him as a diplomatic go-between, and he often helped to negotiate treaties between city-states. Petrarch's post as a canon may have given him a stipend, enabling him to travel, but it meant that he could not marry. Even so, during the course of his travels he had a number of relationships with women, and fathered a son and a daughter, both of whom he had legitimized by the Church.

In 1345, Petrarch made a major discovery. While searching through the cathedral library on a visit to Verona, he came across a previously unknown cache of Cicero's letters. In the first century BC, Cicero had achieved fame in Rome as an orator and a philosopher, even being elected as one of the two ruling consuls in 63 BC. Petrarch's discovery would have a transformative effect, with some even going so far as to see this discovery as marking the start of the early Renaissance. Indeed, an indication of Cicero's influence on European thought from here onwards can be seen in the mark he left on the Enlightenment (the age which was to follow the Renaissance). The eighteenth-century historian Edward Gibbon embodies Cicero's effect on both his own age and the preceding Renaissance when he writes: 'I tasted the beauties of language, I breathed the spirit of freedom, and I imbibed from his precepts and examples the public and private sense of a man.'

It is all but impossible to overestimate the importance of what Petrarch set in motion with his discovery of Cicero. From almost one and a half millennia previously, a voice spoke with ringing clarity of what it meant to be human. Humanity was beginning to develop a larger picture of itself – of what it could be, and what it could do, in the vivified new world around it. With this, and with his poetry, Petrarch would leave his indelible mark on the world. But the world would have a great and lasting effect upon Petrarch too.

When Petrarch was thirty-two years old, he climbed over 6,000 feet to the peak of Mont Ventoux in southern France, accompanied by his brother Gherardo and two servants. Petrarch claimed that he was inspired to this achievement by the feat of King Philip V of Macedon (a dashing descendant of Alexander the Great), who climbed the 5,000-foot Mount Haemo in 200 BC. Petrarch may have been characteristically inspired by his classical predecessor, but the transformation this climb would wreak upon Petrarch's mind would be wholly modern. It is often assumed that the early nineteenth-century English Romantic poets were the first whose imagination was transformed by the beauty of nature. Four centuries prior to this, Petrarch would also be transformed by his experience of nature, but in a subtly different way.

As Petrarch trudged up towards the peak of Mont Ventoux, despite his weariness he could not help but marvel at the view opening up before him. In one direction he could see as far as the blue Mediterranean off Marseille; in the other he looked down on the Rhône valley and the mountains beyond Lyon. When he finally reached the top of the mountain, he took out his copy of St Augustine's *Confessions* from his pocket. By chance it fell open at the following words:

> Men are struck with wonder at the peaks of mountains, by the mighty waves of the sea, the sweep of rivers and the tides of the oceans, as well as the passage of the night stars across the heavens, yet they consider not themselves.

Petrarch closed the book, angry with himself at being so distracted by the wonder of nature around him. He was struck by the realization that 'nothing is wonderful but the soul... I turned my inward eye upon myself, and from that time on not a syllable fell from my lips until we reached the bottom again...We look about us for what is to be found only within.' He chided himself: 'No mountain range can compare with the range of human contemplation.'

Petrarch's reactions on this occasion are open to interpretation. Some see evidence of modern man emerging in his entirety, achieving a new detachment and completeness. By contrast, others see Petrarch as torn between the profound inner world of the more spiritual medieval vision, and the will to adventure and the discovery of the new which characterizes the Renaissance mind – a conflict which would generate some of his finest work. Either way, it is evident that Petrarch was achieving a more profound self-realization, aware of himself inhabiting both an inner and an outer world.

Petrarch is best remembered for his sonnets to 'Laura', his 'poetic love'. Dante had his Beatrice and Boccaccio his Fiammetta, and Petrarch would be inspired in his own original way by his love for Laura. He would write well over 300 sonnets to Laura, who has been tentatively identified as Laura de Noves, a virtuous woman married to a local nobleman in Avignon. Little else is known of her life, apart from Petrarch's sonnets, which sketch an idealized figure. Even so, small details occasionally bring Laura tantalizingly alive. In one sonnet, Petrarch speaks of 'the breeze blowing through her curling blonde hair', and 'her bright eyes whose gaze stings him'. In this, she is more real than Dante's Beatrice, but devoid of the passion of Boccaccio's Fiammetta. Despite such paucity, some commentators have seen Laura as 'the ideal Renaissance woman'.

Often, as in Sonnet 33, she makes no appearance other than her effect upon the poet:

Alone, and pensive, near some desert shore,
Far from the haunts of men I love to stray,
And, cautiously, my distant path explore
Where never human footsteps mark'd the way.
Thus from the public gaze I strive to fly,
And to the winds alone my griefs impart;
While in my hollow cheek and haggard eye
Appears the fire that burns my inmost heart.
But ah, in vain to distant scenes I go;
No solitude my troubled thoughts allays.
Methinks e'en things inanimate must know
The flame that on my soul in secret preys;

Whilst Love, unconquer'd, with resistless sway
Still hovers round my path, still meets me on my way.

Here the poet seeks solitude, but can never escape from his love.

It appears that Petrarch spoke to Laura on several occasions, though she never encouraged his advances. On the contrary, when he once broached the subject of love, Laura informed him 'that she was not such a one as he seemed to think her'. This coldness on her behalf served only to purify Petrarch's passion even further.

When he finally heard of Laura's death, he was deeply moved, but remained honest with himself. He would later recall:

In my younger days I struggled constantly with an overwhelming but pure love affair – my only one, and I would have struggled with it longer had not premature death, bitter but salutary for me, extinguished the cooling flames. I certainly wish I could say that I have always been entirely free from desires of the flesh, but I would be lying if I did.

Meanwhile Petrarch's relationship with his native Florence was always ambiguous. Petrarch's father had been a man of exceptional talent, who had risen to a high rank in the administration of his native city (Chancellor of the Committee for Reform; also heading several diplomatic delegations). However, like his friend Dante, he had been a White Guelf and would be exiled on a trumped-up charge, losing everything but his family. Petrarch could never forget this. Yet at the same time he formed a deep friendship and conducted a lasting correspondence with Boccaccio, who would remain closely attached to Florence throughout his life. It was Boccaccio who persuaded the city to revoke the exile of Petrarch's family, as well as to return the property which had been seized from Petrarch's father some fifty years previously. Petrarch would visit his friend in Florence, but he would never settle there. Even so, throughout his travels Petrarch would always proudly refer to Florence as his *patria* (homeland).

After years of wandering, in 1369 Petrarch would finally settle in a modest house outside Padua, in the small town of Arquà (now renamed Arquà Petrarca in his honour). Five years after his arrival he would die here, at the age of sixty-nine. Some 500 years later, Florence would erect a full-length statue of Petrarch, which stands to this day in a niche of the Uffizi Palace, alongside those of other luminaries from the city's history.

Perhaps the last word on Florence's great triumvirate should be left to the eighteenth-century Renaissance scholar John Addington Symonds:

> Dante brought the universe into his *Divine Comedy*. 'But the soul of man, too, is a universe', and of this inner microcosm Petrarch was the poet and genius. It remained for Boccaccio to treat of daily life with an art as distinct and dazzling as theirs. From Dante's Beatrice, through Petrarch's Laura, to Boccaccio's La Fiammetta – from woman as an allegory of the noblest thoughts and purest stirrings of the soul, through woman as the symbol of all beauty worshipped at a distance, to woman as man's lover, kindling and reciprocating the most ardent passion... such was the rapid movement of Italian genius within the brief space of fifty years. So quickly did the Renaissance emerge from the Middle Ages...

CHAPTER 5

WAR AND PEACE

OUR NEXT FIGURE WOULD be born in a far-off land, but would pass his last years as an honoured man in his adopted home city of Florence. This was the legendary English *condottiere* Sir John Hawkwood, known in Italy as Giovanni Acuto (John the Acute, or the Sharp) or sometimes as Haukevvod, or just Acko in vernacular Italian.

During the fourteenth century many cities, such as Florence, maintained no standing army of their own. When they went to war, they were obliged to hire a *condottiere* (mercenary commander) and his army to fight for them. This could prove costly, as in the war with Lucca where the mercenaries hired by Florence proved somewhat reluctant to go into battle against those hired by Lucca. This reluctance was frequently the case, and battles often consisted of little more than military manoeuvres between two armies. The army finally manoeuvred into a tactical dead end would then signal its defeat. No one was hurt, and the two armies were free to return to their employers and collect their pay. Occasionally battles could turn nasty, but this was more a case of overenthusiasm, or employers stipulating that victory was one of the necessary conditions of payment. But while mercenary armies may frequently have proved battle-shy, the mercenaries themselves were usually a tough and unruly bunch who enjoyed nothing more than looting, rape and pillage to supplement their pay. Any towns which they conquered, or entered, were liable to receive such treatment.

During the latter half of the fourteenth century, Sir John Hawkwood achieved a reputation as one of the most successful *condottiere* on the peninsula. Unfortunately, his services were hired by powers such as Milan, Pisa or the pope, who were often involved in alliances antipathetic to Florence. Hawkwood's early dealings with Florence were hardly auspicious. In 1363, and again in 1369, his passing mercenary army had menaced the suburbs which had grown up outside the city gates, and on at least one occasion his archers had fired volleys over the city walls. But worse was to come.

In 1375, Hawkwood and his mercenary army marched into Florentine territory, looting and pillaging the countryside, their commander demanding large sums of money via menacing threats at every city he came across. It soon became evident to all that his ultimate destination was the city of Florence itself.

A small coloured drawing is the only contemporary picture we have of Hawkwood at this time. In the words of Hawkwood's biographer Frances Stonor Saunders: 'It shows him in the foreground, mounted on a caparisoned white charger, his fist clenched around his sword, his head and neck protected by a helmet and a gold cuirass. Behind the cavalry, prisoners are roped by the neck and dragged from an unidentified town in the territory of Florence.' The mercenary army in the image is led by a herald blowing his trumpet. From the long trumpet hangs a pennant with Hawkwood's personal coat of arms, containing three scallop shells. In the background it is possible to distinguish another coat of arms – namely, the mitre and crossed keys of the papal emblem. This is the significant clue. Hawkwood had recently been employed by Pope Gregory XI, but when he and his men turned up in Rome to collect their money the pope had been forced to confess that he lacked sufficient funds to pay the *condottiere* and his mercenaries. Instead, Gregory XI suggested to Hawkwood that he and his men could easily recoup their funds by invading Florence. It was the richest city in Italy, and at that time it had no mercenary army in its employ.

Hawkwood immediately marched his men north into Tuscany, laying waste to the countryside at will and receiving large sums of money for 'protecting' the cities in his path. When news of these events reached Florence, the *signoria* frantically debated how they could avert the sacking of the city. In the event, they decided to dispatch two envoys to meet up with Hawkwood. The envoys were ordered to 'Make agreement – at any price'. They immediately galloped from the city into the country-side, following local rumour concerning the whereabouts of Hawkwood and his men. Eventually they crossed the mountains, riding east, where they finally met up with Hawkwood at an old wooden bridge outside the small city of Imola. Negotiations proved predictably one-sided: Hawkwood demanded the outrageous sum of 130,000 florins, to be paid in four instalments, along with provisions, wine and 'gifts' for all his men. According to a contemporary chronicler, in less than six months 'all the gold in Tuscany was thrown at the feet of the Englishman'. Only thus was Florence saved.

John Hawkwood was probably born in 1323 in the village of Sible Hedingham in the Essex countryside, about forty miles north-east of London. This was a time of some hardship. During previous years, famine had swept through northern Europe. Harsh winters, accompan-ied by floods, had been followed by arid summers and crop failures. Hawkwood's father was squire of the local manor, but with seven children to support, life was by no means easy – even for minor gentry.

John Hawkwood was just seventeen when his father died, but such wealth as his father possessed was mainly passed on to his firstborn son (also called John). The younger John Hawkwood received little more than twenty pounds and a few fields. Some years later, Edward III began recruiting for the wars against France (which would eventually become the Hundred Years' War), and Hawkwood joined up. He appears to have begun as a longbowman, but his aptitude for military life ensured his promotion. He fought in the memorable English victory at Crécy in 1346, but seems to have returned home after this. Little is known of the following decade or so, except that after a number of thefts and brawls he was registered as a 'common malefactor and disturber of the peace'. During this period he is also known to have married and had a daughter.

No other mention of him appears until he turns up in 1356 at the Battle of Poitiers, another famous victory over the French. Here Hawkwood's bravery was such that he may well have saved the life of the Black Prince (Edward III's eldest son). It is possible that he was also knighted for his act, though there is no record of this. Following the truce a few years later, Hawkwood joined the White Company, a notorious army of mercenaries, which set off for southern France in 1361. This was no band of scruffy freebooters, but a well-drilled militia of up to 3,500 cavalry and 2,000 infantry. These were mainly English, but included a sizeable group of Germans, as well as other nationalities. The company was properly organized into lances, consisting of four mounted men and their attendants (often a shield-bearer and a page). In battle these would be accompanied by a spear wall of lancers; as well as crossbowmen, with their assistants to help them speedily reload. The White Company was renowned for its close camaraderie fostered by its military structure, which in turn fostered a democratic element.

Under its German commander, Albert Sterz, the White Company marched south and prepared to take advantage of the power vacuum which had arisen in southern France and northern Italy. This was largely due to the comparative weakness of the Avignon pope, Innocent VI, and the lack of involvement from the Holy Roman Emperor Charles IV. As the White Company approached Avignon it seized the Pont-Saint-Esprit, the strategic bridge across the Rhône, thus severing the route by which the papal dues were transferred to Avignon. Innocent VI retaliated by excommunicating the entire White Company, before deciding that perhaps it was better to employ them as his papal troops.

In 1363, two years after Hawkwood had joined the White Company, he was chosen as its leader, probably by a vote of acclaim from the assembled army. Sterz was now reduced to serving under Hawkwood, and seems to have resented this. Regardless, Hawkwood marched his men into northern Italy, where the company was soon hired by Pisa for six months for a fee of 150,000 florins, to fight against Florence.

In the midst of the hot summer of 1364, Hawkwood and his men arrived at Pisa. Here they heard that the Florentine forces, under the command of the *condottiere* Malatesta of Rimini, were camped at Cascina, a few miles to the east on the banks of the Arno. Malatesta was commanding a mercenary army of 11,000 infantry and 4,000 cavalry, mostly seasoned German mercenaries. Just prior to this, Sterz had deserted Hawkwood, taking a large number of the White Company with him. Hawkwood found himself left with just 800 English soldiers, and rapidly recruited 4,000 men from amongst the citizenry of Pisa. Most of these recruits had never fought before.

Undaunted, Hawkwood marched his men out of Pisa into the blazing sun. After a couple of miles he halted his columns, waiting for the midday breeze from the sea, which regularly blew up a dust storm on the plain. His idea was to attack under cover of the dust. In the distance, Malatesta's men could be seen stripped of their armour, bathing in the river. Unfortunately, Hawkwood's scouts had not noticed a detachment of 600 Genoese crossbowmen concealed amongst the nearby houses. Hawkwood's men charged towards the bathing soldiers, but the crossbows soon began slicing them down.

Hawkwood's mercenaries began a tactical retreat, while the Pisan recruits panicked and fled in all directions. Hawkwood could do nothing but watch the ensuing rout. Casualty figures vary wildly. One contemporary source claimed that Hawkwood lost some 30 dead and suffered 300 wounded, which seems a reasonable estimate for actual battles of the period (rather than the military manoeuvres often carried out by opposing *condottieri*). Other chroniclers claim up to ten times these figures. Whatever the truth, there was no denying that Hawkwood had suffered a crushing defeat.

As we shall see, the Florentines came to celebrate this as one of their greatest victories. Although few Florentines were actually involved, there was no doubt about what this victory meant to the city. Tales of the fates suffered by cities defeated by Hawkwood and his men were grisly indeed. But was there any truth in these tales? Was Hawkwood simply a callous mercenary interested only in extracting the highest sums from his employers, encouraging his men to rape and pillage? Was he a skilled military commander who did his best by his men, and responded gallantly towards those he defeated? Or was he simply used as a pawn by his callous ever-changing employers – popes Innocent VI and Gregory XI, the Visconti of Milan, the treacherous Cardinal Robert of Geneva, the rulers of Pisa, and so on? There seem to be as many variations on Hawkwood's character as there were variations of his employers, or variations of his name.

We know that Chaucer met Hawkwood several times during the course of his travels to Italy as an envoy of Richard II.* Hawkwood does not seem to have left a good impression on his fellow countryman, who saw him as a 'seasoned, cold-blooded professional soldier motivated by personal gain'. Others claim that Hawkwood inspired Chaucer with the idea for 'The Knight's Tale', the first of his *Canterbury Tales*. Chaucer's knight was a mercenary by any other name, who adhered but loosely to the medieval code of chivalry, which included such virtues as bravery, courtesy and gallantry (especially towards women). There is little evidence of chivalry in what we know of Sir John Hawkwood's behaviour; on the other hand, he did not always conform to the low expectations exhibited by the typical *condottiere*. Indeed, at times he even showed what might be described as glimpses of nobility. In her biography of Hawkwood, Saunders goes to the heart of the matter: 'the question of motivation'. She points out that he 'left no *apologia*, no personal account to provide a clear signpost to the inner forces that energised him, to the life lived in his brain'. She concludes that although there is all manner of documentary evidence concerning Hawkwood's

---

* It is plausibly suggested that Chaucer may indeed also have met Boccaccio and Petrarch, and it would appear that both of these figures influenced Chaucer in their own way, if only in their works. For instance, Boccaccio's *Decameron* is thought by many to have inspired Chaucer's *Canterbury Tales*.

life and career, in the end 'he appears as an enigma, through a glass darkly'.

Following Saunders's question of motivation, an insight into Hawkwood's character may be gained from his participation in a crucial event. We know for a fact that Hawkwood and his men took part in the notorious massacre at Cesena, which occurred over three days and nights in February 1377. Indeed, the events surrounding this carnage would seem to be emblematic of Hawkwood and the situation in which he found himself in Italy. According to Antonino Pierozzi, Archbishop of Florence (who would later become St Antoninus), what took place at Cesena – a small city in the Romagna, close to the central Adriatic coast – was 'an outburst of insuperable barbarity... the most iniquitous and serious of cruelties since Troy'.

This entire affair originated when the ageing Pope Gregory XI instructed Cardinal Robert of Geneva to put down a revolt in Cesena, which officially belonged to papal territory. Gregory XI ordered that the uprising was to be subdued 'no matter the cost'. Robert of Geneva and his mercenary army, which included Hawkwood and his men as well as a strong contingent of Bretons, quickly cowed Cesena into submission. Whereupon the cardinal took up residence in the Rocca Murata, the fortress which overlooked the city, while Hawkwood and his men, along with the Bretons, set up their winter quarters outside the city walls. It was freezing cold, and the mercenaries had so pillaged the surrounding countryside that they were reduced to starvation rations, of turnips and the like. On 1 February, some Breton soldiers ventured into town and tried to steal a haunch of meat hanging at a butcher's stall. The butcher retaliated by attacking them with a meat cleaver, whereupon the citizens set upon the Bretons, killing them.

Upon hearing what had happened, Cardinal Robert became mindful of the explicit orders given to him by his master, Gregory XI, that he should subdue Cesena no matter the cost. If he did not succeed in controlling the unruly citizens of Cesena, he would not only lose the favour of Gregory XI, but also risk losing his chance of becoming pope after the death of his ailing master (which would take place the following year). So Cardinal Robert hatched a plan. He issued a demand that the citizens of Cesena should immediately hand over all arms in their possession and surrender fifty of their men as hostages. These men would only be pardoned if the citizens behaved themselves. To encourage the citizens and reassure them that there would be no further reprisals, the cardinal let it be known that he had dispatched Hawkwood and his men twenty miles up the road to the city of Faenza.

That night, under cover of darkness, Cardinal Robert sent a fast messenger to intercept Hawkwood, with orders for him to return immediately but by stealth. As reported by the contemporary Sienese chronicler Donato di Neri, the cardinal told Hawkwood on his arrival back at Cesena: 'I order you and your men to go into the town and administer justice.'

Hawkwood replied, 'My lord, if it please you I will go and arrange that the people surrender their arms and submit to your authority.'

To which Robert said, 'No, I want blood and justice.'

'But just think of the consequences,' began Hawkwood.

Robert interrupted him forcibly. 'These are my orders.'

In the words of biographer Saunders: 'Two struggles were about to begin: one was for the life of every man, woman and child in Cesena; the other was for Hawkwood's reputation.'

The next night, a fully armed column consisting of thousands of Bretons and Hawkwood's men burst through the city gates, clattering down the dark streets yelling and brandishing their swords, knives and axes. Fires were started, and as the citizens fled from their houses they were hacked down. Hundreds fleeing in their nightshirts, with their wives and children, managed to run as far as the north-eastern gate of the city. Here they pulled open the gates only to find a line of fully armed Breton and English soldiers waiting for them. Horrific scenes ensued. As Marco Battagli, the chronicler of Rimini, wrote: 'As many men, women and infants as they found, they murdered, and all the squares were full of dead.'

Mayhem, murder and pillage were followed by the methodical sacking of every building in the city, including public offices. Of the estimated

15,000 living in the city, as many as half were slaughtered outright. Others were maimed, raped or fled – to be found wandering the freezing countryside, 'naked, bereaved and utterly destitute'.

Word of this outrage quickly spread throughout Italy, and then beyond. Within weeks, the news had even reached Hawkwood's homeland, where the English preacher and reformer John Wycliffe referred to it in one of his sermons.

Despite Hawkwood's attempt to deflect Cardinal Robert, there can be no doubt concerning his involvement. Yet, as many have pointed out, there remain curious omissions. None of the chroniclers, drawing on eyewitness reports, mention that Hawkwood personally took part in the massacre, or was even seen drawing his sword. Though as Saunders notes, he could have been up on the battlements of the castle overseeing the events. One of the chroniclers, the anonymous Ferrarese contemporary who wrote the *Chronicon Estense*, claimed that 'Sir John Hawkwood, not to be held entirely infamous, sent about a thousand of the Cesenese women to Rimini'. This hardly exonerates Hawkwood. And even Saunders is forced to concede: 'He may have questioned the strategic value of the slaughter, but as to the fact itself, he was desensitised: it was for him a mere incident of his profession.'

After this, the fifty-four-year-old Hawkwood turned down all future offers of work for him and his White Company in the service of Gregory XI. Later that same year he would contract a second marriage, this time to an illegitimate daughter of Bernabó Visconti, the ruler of Milan. Later still, he would command his troops in the service of Padua in a war against Verona. During the course of this, he won a famous victory at the Battle of Castagnaro. This was achieved by using his disciplined men to goad and lure the enemy to a site of his own choosing. Here he avoided head-on confrontation, harassing the enemy's flanks and wearing them down with cavalry charges (one of which he led himself). This battle has been described by Hawkwood's biographer William Caferro as his 'finest victory and one of the great feats of military prowess of the era'.

After a quarrel with his powerful Milanese father-in-law, Hawkwood signed up with Florence, which would remain his base during his last years. The city welcomed him as their defender and saviour. An anonymous eyewitness described how:

> Sir Hawkwood entered Florence with his Company... and dismounted at the Palace of the Archbishop of Florence, and great honour was paid to him by our *Signoria* and the other councils, and a great deal of wax and sweetmeats, and draperies of silk and wool were presented to him... and he was much honoured.

Not least amongst these honours was the granting of an immunity from taxes. By now Hawkwood had amassed a considerable fortune. This had been hard fought for, and he would not have been parted from it easily. Thus this rare exemption was probably as much expedient as it was honorific. The house where Hawkwood installed his second wife, and which he made his home, had formerly been a residence of the Bishop of Parma; it was a *palazzo* of sufficient grandeur to befit Hawkwood's exalted status. In this way the legendary Englishman came to end his days as a distinguished citizen of Florence. And here he would finally die in 1394, at the age of seventy-one.

Later, the *signoria* would decide to immortalize Hawkwood as a Florentine hero. They would commission Florence's finest artist of the time, Paolo Uccello, to paint a fresco of Hawkwood on a wall in the cathedral, which can still be seen today. It depicts an armoured warrior astride a sturdy white charger and bearing his baton of command. His gaunt features hint at the acuity after which he was so often named, though the veracity of this posthumous portrait remains as unknown as the man himself.

It is important to bear in mind that, throughout the era which produced the likes of Dante, Boccaccio and Petrarch, characters such as Hawkwood and his band of hard mercenaries roamed Italy leaving a trail of havoc and misery in their wake. The city that nurtured the Renaissance could so easily have been razed to the ground by Hawkwood, and Florence was fortunate indeed when he chose it as his home. In this negative aspect, Hawkwood can be seen, at a stretch, as a Florentine benefactor of the emerging Renaissance. It is a supreme irony that without this rough English warrior there might have been no locus in which this transformation of western culture could take place.

As was the case of Athens in Ancient Greece, civil strife was never far below the surface of Florence during this entire period, and it would erupt with the greatest force in 1378 with what came to be called the Ciompi Revolt.

For years the *ciompi* (woolworkers, including combers, dyers and so forth) had been forced to work in grim conditions for very little recompense. Their wages provided a subsistence-level existence, while the sheds and wash-houses where they worked were no more than sweatshops. Most worked a sixteen-hour day. The slightest insubordination brought harsh penalties from their employers, and malefactors could be flogged, imprisoned or even be sentenced to have a hand cut off. The *ciompi* were not permitted to form a guild, and this meant they had no vote or say in the government. Although the *ciompi* received too low a wage to pay taxes, the government could still extract money in the form of reduced wages in times of need, when other citizens were subjected to the forced loan of the *prestanze*.

The long war with Lucca had drained the exchequer, and the ending of this war brought widespread rejoicing in the city, with the wealthier citizens throwing celebratory parties and banquets. This rejoicing stirred deep resentment amongst those who could only listen from the doorways of their dark hovels as the choruses of cheers and music emanated from the candle-illuminated houses. Word spread amongst the *ciompi*, and on the morning of 18 July 1378, instead of their clogs clomping across the cobbles on the way to work, the *ciompi* marched in shouting procession to the Piazza della Signoria. Seeing what was happening, they were soon joined by the *popolo minuto*, 'the small people' – regarded as the lowest of the low – who took on menial work or were dependent upon charity for survival. At the time, a certain Salvestro de' Medici held the office of *gonfaloniere*. Although he came from an old family, it was common knowledge that Salvestro had sympathy for the downtrodden. He and his *signoria* had already used their time in office to take measures reducing the power of the wealthier families.

The mob gathered outside the Palazzo della Signoria, chanting '*Viva il popolo! Viva il popolo!*' By now anarchy had broken out on the streets, and gangs began trying to force their way into the barricaded *palazzi* of the rich. This soon focused on the Palazzo dell'Arte della Lana, the meeting place of the Wool Guild – whose members were those who bought and sold the commodity, rather than those whose work added value to it by turning it into cloth. The Wool Guild building was ransacked, along with the district meeting places of the ruling Guelf party. At the same time, the prisons were thrown open, and the *podestà* was dragged into the street and hanged.

In response to the situation, Salvestro de' Medici and the *signoria* issued a decree exiling the Guelf leaders and repealing many of the repressive laws the Guelfs had recently imposed. But it soon became clear that this was not enough; the mob was set on nothing less than revolution.

When Salvestro de' Medici came to the end of his two-month term of office and was replaced, the *ciompi* and the *popolo minuto* once again went on the rampage, led by a barefoot woolworker named Michele di Lando. This time they managed to overpower the guards and burst into the Palazzo della Signoria. Soon *La Vacca* was tolling out over the city, summoning the people to a *parlamento*. Michele di Lando was confirmed as *gonfaloniere* by public acclaim, and a new *signoria* was sworn in. Amongst their first acts was the creation of three new guilds. One was created for the *tintoretti* (the dyers), another for the *farsettai* (the doublet-makers) and a third for the *popolo minuto* (in which the rest of the *ciompi* registered, forming a majority).

Little is known of Michele di Lando other than that he was employed as a wool comber. His mother is said to have been a washerwoman and his wife to have worked in a butcher's shop. Although not amongst the poorest of the poor, he evidently had leadership qualities which appealed to the most downtrodden. However, these did not extend as far as the skills required of a ruler. Indeed, it has been claimed that he was secretly assisted in this capacity by Salvestro de' Medici.

The city would be ruled by a commune of *ciompi* supporters for the next three and a half years, until 1382. During the course of this period, the *ciompi* government would settle a number of old scores. Several members of the leading families were arrested on trumped-up charges and summarily executed. However, opinion amongst the citizenry as a whole eventually began to divide over such blatant violations.

The end was assured when the *gonfaloniere* allied his government with the *popolo di Firenze*, the broader-based shopkeepers and members of the lesser guilds, an act which antagonized the *popolo minuto*. The leadership split, and for a time there were two competing governments in the city. At this point, the leading families seized their opportunity. In a prearranged move of rare unity, they led their armed retainers and retook power amidst the increasing anarchy. The old order was quickly restored and the authorities soon felt sufficiently empowered to abolish the *ciompi* guild, which contained the most extremist elements. Michele di Lando fled from Tuscany, while several other leaders were executed. Salvestro de' Medici was extremely lucky to escape such a fate, but the entire Medici family was publicly disgraced.

Even so, a lesson had been learned. Tensions between the classes – loosely, the oligarchy of leading families, the *popolo* and the downtrodden *popolo minuto* – would remain. But the fear expressed by a contemporary chronicler that 'every good citizen would have been kicked out of his home and the cloth worker would have taken everything he had' was allayed, and things soon returned to business as usual in the wool trade.

Despite such political hiccups, during the latter half of the fourteenth century the city of Florence was laying the foundations for the period of unprecedented prosperity which would see the Renaissance come into full bloom. The range and continuity of this aspect of the century is perhaps best illustrated by the life and circumstances of Francesco Datini, better known as the Merchant of Prato. This is the title of the book written by the English-born twentieth-century biographer Iris Origo, who made exceptional use of a rich cache of letters and documents which had remained undiscovered in an ancient stairwell for over 350 years.

In the fourteenth century, Prato was a small town in the *contado* some ten miles north-west of Florence. It had previously consisted of two villages (the Town and the Castle), which merged in the eleventh century to become a free commune. By a quirk illustrative of the complexity of Italian politics during this era, Prato was now placed under the protection of the kings and queens of Naples, thus ensuring that it did not fall into the hands of its powerful neighbour Florence. This state of affairs persisted into the mid-fourteenth century. Indeed, Francesco Datini would have remembered this time, as he was born in 1335. Just over a decade later, Prato was sold by Queen Joanna I of Naples to Florence for 17,500 florins. The town nonetheless remained an independently minded place, and flourished from the cloth trade, taking its wool from the sheep in the surrounding hills.

When Datini was thirteen, his father, mother and two siblings succumbed to the Black Death, after which he and his younger brother Stefano were adopted by Monna Piera, who became their loving mother. A year or so after this Francesco moved to Florence, where he was apprenticed to a merchant. Francesco proved to be an ambitious character. At the age of fifteen he sold off part of his inheritance – a plot of land worth 150 florins – and joined some merchants travelling on business to Avignon, the seat of the papacy and a major European trading centre. Apart from all the other goods which travelled down the Rhône valley, this was also on the main overland trading route for wool from England and Flanders to Florence.

The pope and much of his Curia (the papal government) were housed in a magnificent fortress-palace, the Palais des Papes. The city also housed the cardinals and various ambassadors, officials and notaries (such as Petrarch's father had been). In Avignon, the riches of the papal court, and the medical, legal and rhetorical learning of the university, flourished alongside a burgeoning market for trade of all kinds, as well as a bustling, overcrowded under-city. Here, amidst the unpaved streets of the reeking slums, low taverns and bordellos, lived the humble craftsmen, servants, indigent students, washerwomen, sneak-thieves and the like.

The Hundred Years' War between England and France had ground to a brief hiatus with the Truce of Bordeaux in 1357, which meant that many mercenary commanders and their men had gravitated towards Avignon. (As we have seen, Hawkwood would menace the city in 1361.) Consequently, there was money to be made in the trade of arms, armour and military equipment. Datini seems to have entered into this trade before moving on to luxury goods and art.

In the latter, a profound transformation was taking place. Previously, works of art had been almost exclusively commissioned and purchased by the Church and wealthy religious orders; now paintings were being bought by private patrons. Instead of adorning places of worship, they were being hung in the family residences of the rich. This was a significant development which would presage the flourishing of Renaissance art. Once again, it would seem pertinent to question why the Renaissance did not arise in the melting pot of Avignon. And once again, it would seem evident that something was missing. Of the three ingredients – wealth, a measure of civic freedom, and talent – only the first was present. And even this would be considerably reduced when the papacy departed in 1377.

In 1376, Datini became engaged in Avignon to Margherita Bandini, the teenage daughter of a Florentine family living in political exile. (Her father had been executed for taking part in an anti-government plot.) Datini duly married Margherita and returned with his new wife to live in Prato in 1383. From now on his business would continue to flourish, which involved frequent long absences abroad – especially in Avignon, which remained the centre of his business interests. The exchange of letters over the coming decades between Datini and his wife provide a succession of vivid glimpses into fourteenth-century life.

From the outset, the Datini marriage was beset by difficulty. Although six years earlier Francesco had fathered an illegitimate child by a slave girl, he and Margherita could produce no children. This was a source of great anguish to all concerned. Monna Piera wrote from Prato, imploring her adopted son: 'Come home. God has gifted you riches in Avignon. Here he will give you a family.' Letters from friends and family proffered all manner of current fertility methods and advice. A male friend suggested to Margherita that 'she fed three beggars on three Fridays, and did not hearken to women's chatter'. A female friend recommended 'a poultice, which they put on their bellies' but warned that 'it stinks so much, that there have been husbands who have thrown it away'. All this prompted tetchiness and sadness on Margherita's behalf, as well as irritability and even more lengthy absences for business on Francesco's behalf. As Origo puts it: 'We see a girl married at sixteen to a man already tired and soured, and who required from her, most of all, what she could not give him: a houseful of children.' Francesco felt unfulfilled, and Margherita was temperamental. Yet as Origo points out, 'the marriage was not devoid of either affection or mutual respect'. When Francesco had returned to live in Prato with his wife, and was then called away to nearby Pisa to oversee a new branch he had set up, he wrote to Margherita: 'I eat nothing that pleases me…Were you here, I would be more at ease.' She replied: 'I have resolved to go not only to Pisa, but to the world's end, if it pleases you.'

Francesco established his head office in Florence. Margherita remained at home when he travelled to set up more or less permanent branches in Barcelona, Pisa, Genoa and Livorno. He joined a fine guild, the *Arte di Por Santa Maria*, which specialized amongst other things in the manufacture and export of cloth. He dealt in cloth, then wheat, then scissors, then soap, and even table knives and needles. According to Francesco's contemporary Domenico di Cambio, Francesco Datini had 'the finest *fondaco* [establishment] on the finest street in Florence'. He set up trade links as far afield as the Balkans and North Africa – though he did not personally travel to these places, despite stories to the contrary.

In one of these tales, which according to Origo was still circulating in Prato in the twentieth century, a merchant of Prato (usually taken to be Datini) once travelled to a distant land called the Canary Isle. Here, he was invited to dinner by the king. Datini arrived to find that each place at the table was all laid out with cutlery, napkins and 'a club as long as his arm', whose purpose mystified him. Only when the platters of meat and other food were brought in did he understand, as the odour of the food 'brought forth a great abundance of mice, who must perforce be chased away with these clubs'. Next day the merchant returned, having spent the night on board his ship. Concealed in the large medieval sleeve of his doublet was the ship's cat. When the meal was duly served, he produced the cat from his sleeve, 'and she speedily killed twenty-five or thirty mice, and the others ran away'. The king was delighted, and even more so when the merchant told him: 'Sire, your courtesy to me has been so great, that I can only return it by bestowing on you this cat.' The king rewarded the merchant 'with jewels worth 4,000 *scudi*'. The following year the merchant returned, this time bringing the king a tomcat for which he was rewarded 6,000 *scudi*.

This merchant is most unlikely to have been Datini, but such a story is illustrative of the travellers' tales being brought back to Tuscany by merchants who had been trading overseas; tales which quickly spread from house to house. News – from idle gossip to more reliable information – was mostly passed by word of mouth. More official sources of information, such as public decrees, were posted on walls or proclaimed in public places for the benefit of those who could not read. Other news was relayed in sermons preached in church. Even so, gossip, rumour and stories remained the living currency of conversation. Like it is today, popular news was retailed as much for its entertainment value as for its veracity.

The letters written by Francesco and Margherita Datini give sparse hints of this rich and ever-circulating currency. Likewise, they shed little light on the contemporary customs, manners and behaviour expected of a bourgeois family such as the Datinis. Contrary to our popular image of Italian family life, Origo claims: 'There was little room left for affection or tenderness; parental authority was too absolute, too severe.' Children were forbidden to sit down in the presence of their parents, unless given permission. Similarly, they were expected to incline their heads humbly when being told what to do. Or so instructed the contemporary Fra Giovanni Dominici in his *Regola del Governo di Cura Familiare* (Rules

Governing Family Behaviour): 'At least twice a day let them kneel down reverently at their father's and mother's knee, and ask their blessing.'

Such was the perceived, or expected, correct behaviour in the view of the friar (who would of course have had no family of his own). This advice, like the occasional stilted, excessively polite phrase which crops up in the Datini family letters, was in all likelihood a mere anomaly. The chasm between actual behaviour and formal expectations ran deep in the late medieval era. Evidence of this can be seen in aspects of social life, ranging from the contrast between the love poems of Dante and Petrarch and their actual love lives, to the behaviour of popes compared with the expectations of such exalted office. The popes of the late fourteenth century, on both sides of the Rome/Avignon schism, were notorious for their sacrilegious avarice – including nepotism, simony and peddling dispensations (which shortened the period to be spent in Purgatory by the purchaser). To say nothing of such matters as the Cesena massacre, which had involved both Gregory IX and (in Cardinal Robert) the future Pope Clement VII.*

By contrast, the Datini letters – both between husband and wife and from others to Francesco – contain mainly details of familial problems and actions which remain recognizable to this day. For instance, although Francesco may have been 'tired and soured', he remained generous. When one of his business partners died in Avignon, leaving four small children he had fathered with one of his slaves, Francesco took these children into his house, hiring a woman to look after them and providing dowries for the girls when they married.

At this point, it is necessary for a short digression on the question of slaves. In the decades following the Black Death there was a huge shortage of people available for manual work, menial tasks and domestic service. Farmworkers and servants of all kinds, as well as labourers, were all in very high demand. The Church forbade the use of Christians as slaves, so the only way around this was to import 'pagans'. This led to

---

* Now regarded as an antipope, owing to his seat being in Avignon. He should not be confused with the sixteenth-century Florentine Pope Clement VII, who ruled from Rome, and of whom we shall hear later.

a lucrative trade in young Muslims, 'heathen' Slavs and Tatars from the Caucasus and the Black Sea region – as well as Africans and Berbers, who were mainly imported to Italy via Venice.* They were taken in by families of almost all upper to middling ranks and became part of the household, which included sitting at the end of the same long table as the extended family during meals.

Inevitably, as young female slaves matured, they would attract the attentions of the master of the house. This was certainly the case with Francesco, who in 1392 fathered another illegitimate child, named Ginevra, with his twenty-year-old slave Lucia. It is not difficult to imagine the feelings of the childless Margherita, who would by now have been in her early thirties. It comes as no surprise that the infant Ginevra was almost immediately banished from the Datini household and discreetly farmed out to the nuns at the Hospital of Santa Maria Nuova in Florence. However, six years later Francesco's account books record that Ginevra returned to the family fold, where she was brought up as his daughter. At the same time, her mother Lucia was married off to one of Francesco's servants, Nanni di Prato, who was doubtless rewarded with a suitable dowry by Datini. From this point on it appears that Margherita's maternal instincts overcame her and she grew fond of little Ginevra, whom she frequently mentions in her letters to Francesco. Margherita refers to Ginevra's occasional illnesses, the purchase for her of a toy tambourine (costing twenty *soldi*), and how at the age of nine she was being taught to read by a local lady. As Ginevra grew up, Margherita supervised the purchase for her of 'a great many fine clothes'. If anything, it appeared that Ginevra was now being spoilt by her stepmother.

Over the years, Datini's various businesses prospered and he became increasingly wealthy. The correspondence between Francesco and Margherita Datini reveals that there were those who sought to prey upon their generous nature. Margherita's brother Bartolomeo seems

---

* The very word 'slave' dates from this period, deriving from the word 'Slav'. The long waterfront near the entrance to the Grand Canal in Venice is known to this day as the Riva degli Schiavoni – the Quayside of the Slavs (or slaves).

to have suffered from excessive bad luck. In January 1399, he wrote to his sister that while he had been away from his home in Fondi, some sixty miles south-east of Rome, the entire town and its surroundings had been sacked by mercenaries. 'The wheat and the vineyards have been cut down and burned; my family must be in grievous trouble… So I beseech you, Margherita, in charity, help me in some fashion to join my family.' Francesco was away on business, and Margherita seems to have helped Bartolomeo out on this occasion, but it is clear that she already had reservations about her brother.

A few months later, Bartolomeo turned up in Prato, once more in trouble. Margherita wrote to her husband: 'When I heard that he had come it was a greater grief for me than if I had seen him dead before my eyes… For he is after all my brother, and I cannot but love him… And I see him old and poor and not strong and burdened with children.' Once again she seems to have helped him out, but at the same time she sent him a letter containing some home truths, alluding to earlier dealings: 'You have behaved in such a fashion, you and my mother, as to seal up my mouth in Francesco's presence, and I dare not speak either of your needs or of those of my other kinsfolk.'

Undaunted, Bartolomeo wrote back: 'You say you bear a great burden, and dare not open your mouth with Francesco on behalf of your family. I would that I and your other relations were not in sore need – but since fate has willed it so, one cannot go against fate.' He then continued with an outline of his latest business plan, which would inevitably involve Francesco's financial backing to get started. By now it was the 'Holy Year' (1400), the centennial of Christ's birth. Thousands of extra pilgrims were expected to visit Rome, and 'the Roman court will be the most perfect place for profits in every field that man has ever known'.*

---

* This plan evidently fell through, for eight years later there are further complaints from Bartolomeo, who was working in Avignon as a customs official on an annual salary of 72 florins. (Francesco Datini paid his live-in maids – who had no family to look after and all household expenses included – 10 florins a year.) Sometime after this, Bartolomeo died, and Francesco was obliged to cover his brother-in-law's outstanding doctor's bills; he also provided 'mourning cloaks for the whole family'.

We learn that late in that year Francesco and Margherita, along with Ginevra, found it prudent to flee to Bologna, to avoid a further outbreak of plague which had spread into Tuscany. It is not certain quite how long the Datini family stayed in Bologna, but they appear to have met up with a number of local exiled Florentine Guelfs. Some of these relationships with Francesco seemed to have matured into close friendships, involving consequent business dealings. Then, even more than now – where the rule of law tends to be more extensive in such matters – trust was a major ingredient of commerce.

The Datini family eventually returned to live in their houses in Prato and Florence. A few years later, when Ginevra was fifteen, a friend from Bologna wrote to Francesco to congratulate him on the betrothal of his daughter. Francesco replied, describing how several men had already asked for Ginevra's hand, 'not for her own sake, but to get my money'. However, Francesco had sought out for her 'a companion who will not despise her, nor feel shame to have a child by her'. Ginevra was duly married to one Lionardo di Tommaso, a young Pratese who was a close relative of one of Francesco's business partners.

Francesco had by now turned seventy, an unusually great age during this era; and the proud father ensured that his daughter's wedding was a suitably lavish affair. Ginevra's dowry was 1,000 florins, larger than that provided by some of the great Florentine merchants for their daughters. Yet such was the expense of Ginevra's trousseau and the magnificent entertainment, which the canny Francesco saw fit to subtract from her dowry, that only 161 florins remained for Lionardo – while it was stipulated that even this sum should be returned if Ginevra should die of the plague within two years of her marriage. This, and several other examples, indicate that Francesco remained a hard businessman to the end.

Francesco Datini had by this time risen so high in stature that he was mixing socially with senior-ranking officials, and at the same time reprimanding Margherita for not being as agreeable as she could towards their wives. Francesco's social ascension reached its apogee in 1409. This was the year a political meeting was arranged between Pope Alexander V and Louis II of Anjou, to discuss the pope's support for Louis's claim to the throne of Naples. The venue chosen for this meeting was Prato, and it was decided that Louis should stay at Francesco's house. There is no doubt that this was a superlative honour, but in reality it meant that Francesco and his family had to find alternative accommodation. Meanwhile, Louis and his royal entourage took royal advantage of Francesco's provisions and wine cellar.

By now Francesco was aged and infirm, having long outlived all his contemporaries. But according to his closest friend and attorney, Ser Lapo Mazzei: 'He thinks that he has had a warrant of long life from God.' For a man who had so single-mindedly devoted himself to his business, 'it seemed to him very strange that he should have to die, and that his prayers should be of no avail'.

Francesco Datini would finally die on 16 August 1410, leaving a fortune of some 70,000 florins. Much of this was bequeathed, along with his grand house, to charity – to be administered by the municipality of Prato. Francesco's gift is remembered with gratitude to this day by the citizens of his home town.

His wife Margherita spent her last days living in Florence with her beloved Ginevra and Ginevra's husband, Lionardo di Tommaso. Despite the Black Death, the *ciompi* riots and the activities of Hawkwood and his ilk, it is from the letters and documents preserved by Francesco Datini and his family that we learn how everyday life persisted and maintained a semblance of normality throughout the tumultuous fourteenth century. Like the chronicler Villani during the century before him, Datini gives us an insight into the quotidian reality of life in and around Florence. Such was the unsung, unmemorable and largely unrecorded life lived by that vital stratum of society: the middle class.

This was how normal life (as most of us would recognize it) was actually lived. Despite the chasm wrought by material transformation and technological advances, it is still possible to see into such domestic lives, and recognize them as our neighbours.

CHAPTER 6

THE DOME

THE RENAISSANCE HARKED BACK to the culture of Ancient Greece and Rome. Both of these civilizations produced architecture of consummate skill and beauty. In Ancient Greece, this was epitomized by the Parthenon in Athens. Ensuing Roman architecture managed to overcome one problem whose solution had eluded the Greeks – namely, the arch. The stones which form this curved structure are held in place by a wedge-shaped keystone at its apex. This both locks the other stones into place and enables the entire structure to bear a weight.

The arch would feature in all manner of Roman architecture, from bridges to aqueducts to the Colosseum. This simple, counter-intuitive idea of genius works in two dimensions; it was but a step to translate it into three dimensions and create the dome. But, as we shall see, this was not quite so obvious, or so easy, as it sounds. For a start, it would involve the use of concrete. Variations of this substance had been known since Ancient Egyptian times; however, the full potential of concrete was only fully realized by the Ancient Romans, who adapted it for use in domes. The classic example of such a structure is to be found in the Pantheon in Rome, which dates from around 126 AD. Centuries would pass and the

Roman Empire would fall, leaving a city of crumbling ruins, but many of the arches of the Colosseum would remain standing. And so too would the magnificent dome of the Pantheon. However, the secret of how it had been built was lost. Posterity could only marvel at this wonder, gazing up at it in bemusement.

Then, sometime around 1403, two young Florentine intellectuals arrived in Rome. The slowly increasing, early Renaissance thirst for knowledge of the classical world had created an embryonic tourism industry. Pilgrims had for many years been in the habit of making the long and dangerous journey by means of the main highways, the rough and dangerous passes across the Alps, and the remnant Roman roads down to Rome. This was the centre of western Christianity, the Roman Catholic religion. Here was the centuries-old Basilica of St Peter's, reputedly built on the very spot where St Peter himself had been crucified (upside down, at his own request, as he did not consider himself worthy to be crucified in the same manner as Christ).*

Rome had been known as the Eternal City since early in Ancient Roman times, but this had taken on a new significance with the arrival of the Christian era. The city became the home of St Peter's representative on earth – the pope. People were prepared to travel far and wide to receive his blessing. Yet over the years a new type of traveller had been drawn to Rome. This early trickle of visitors travelled to see the ruins of the ancient city: the Colosseum, the Pantheon, and the Forum with its graceful pillars still standing amidst a vast rubble of classical relics. A few of these new visitors began removing whatever of these relics they could carry away. A number became collectors; others, of a less scrupulous nature, began selling them off to rich buyers, frequently concocting inventories for even the most innocuous stones to increase their pedigree (and price). Though

---

* As late as 1960, bones were excavated from beneath the altar of the 'new' St Peter's (which would replace the fourth-century structure during the sixteenth century). Forensic examination revealed that these were the bones of a sixty-one-year-old male, dating from the first century AD, i.e. precisely the same age as St Peter when he died and dating from the same period. In 1968, Pope Paul VI announced that these were almost certainly the bones of St Peter.

what we might regard as vandalism was in fact a public manifestation of the early Renaissance.

But the two young Florentines wandering amongst the ruins in 1403 had their own agenda. The twenty-six-year-old Filippo Brunelleschi and the teenage boy we now know as Donatello made an odd pair. Brunelleschi was a short, insignificant figure with a secretive personality; Donatello, on the other hand, was a good-looking young man whose flamboyant behaviour hinted at his homosexuality. Both were volatile characters who had a high estimation of their own worth. The older Brunelleschi had already exhibited extreme skill. He had entered the open competition to create the doors for the Baptistery (beside Florence Cathedral). The doors were to contain gilded bronze friezes of biblical scenes, a task which was ideally suited to Brunelleschi's early training as a goldsmith. His design was deemed equal to that of a hitherto-unknown illegitimate young painter called Lorenzo Ghiberti, who had perfected his art by meticulously copying the portraits depicted on ancient coins and medals. In the end, the thirty-four-man committee decided that the two winners should work together on this highly prestigious project. According to Brunelleschi's biographer Ross King, 'Filippo's arrogant self-confidence, irascibility, and stubborn unwillingness to work with others' led to him demanding complete control. When this was denied, he refused the prize and swore to himself that he would never again make another sculpture or even work in bronze.

Despite the difference in age between Brunelleschi and Donatello, and the fact that they were both possessed of somewhat prickly temperaments, they shared a deep enthusiasm for the new humanism which was becoming increasingly popular amongst the intellectuals of Florence. Another trait they had in common was their early apprenticeships: they had both been trained as goldsmiths. The young Donatello had exhibited such precocious skill in this sphere that he now harboured an ambition to excel as a sculptor. Indeed, it was in furtherance of this aim that he was visiting Rome: he wished to study first-hand the classical statues which adorned the ancient buildings, as well as the many fragments which still lay amongst the ruins. Donatello was under the misapprehension that, following Brunelleschi's bitter disappointment over the Baptistery doors, his somewhat-disgruntled travelling companion now shared a similar ambition to become a sculptor.

Unlike other visitors who came to view the ruins, both of these Florentine artists believed in scrutinizing their chosen relics close up, which often involved clambering over precarious ledges, balancing on balustrades, or even using ladders so that they could approach upper carvings. In this way, Donatello managed to perch in awkward spots as he drew painstakingly exact sketches of the classical figures which interested him. To Donatello, it appeared as if Brunelleschi was engaged in the same activity – yet in reality he was doing no such thing. True to his secretive nature, Brunelleschi was furtively making notes on buildings, jotting down their measurements, sizing up their proportions, their angles, their profiles, their elevations and such – not as they appeared from ground level, but close-up, precisely as they would have been viewed by their original builders.*

Having obstinately forsworn sculpture and bronze work, Brunelleschi was now determined to become an architect. According to King: 'He inscribed on strips of parchment a series of cryptic symbols and Arabic numbers: a secret code.' To be fair, this cannot be entirely ascribed to Brunelleschi's secretive nature. At the time there was no such thing as patent law. This meant that anyone was free to steal the new ideas and techniques which had been invented (or rediscovered) by others. Likewise, King's reference to Arabic numbers only appears to be anachronistic. The 1299 ban by the Florentine authorities on the use of Arabic numerals had long since fallen into abeyance, and many were now familiar with the numbers we know today. Yet as can be seen from the diagram on p. 34, use of the original Arabic numerals, rather than their evolved European

---

* Even the finest classical buildings frequently incorporated architectural tricks, which would not have been apparent to the lay viewer. For instance, the slender columns of the Parthenon do in fact bulge a little at mid-height. This eliminates the appearance of them having a slight waist when viewed from ground level. Such refinements provide a 'reverse optical illusion', thus enabling the building to retain its exquisite proportions for the spectator.

equivalents, would certainly have rendered Brunelleschi's figures incomprehensible to all but the expert prying eye.

Even Brunelleschi's actual measurements were unlikely to have been taken in contemporary units, which could vary considerably from place to place. For instance, the *braccio*, a commonly accepted measurement in the building trade, was traditionally taken as the length of a man's outstretched arm, a somewhat loose definition. This led to considerable variations between different Italian city-states. A *braccio* in Florence was almost 23 inches (just under 60 centimetres), a *braccio* in Milan was 23 1/2 inches (or almost exactly 60 centimetres), whereas in Rome the *braccio* was nearly 29 inches long (just over 73 centimetres). Brunelleschi would have used a measuring stick of his own, thus further encoding the precise proportions of the buildings he was assessing.*

But Brunelleschi's investigations were much more than skin-deep. We know for certain that he actually climbed up the Pantheon so that he could examine its dome in great detail. He was already well aware of the difficulties involved in erecting such a construction, whose problems had defeated architects for almost a millennium. When a dome was created, its sheer weight bore down heavily upon the circular walls which supported it. The trouble was, although such stone (or brick) walls could take great vertical pressure from above, the support of a dome involved extra horizontal pressures that forced the walls to bulge outward, in a manner which stone was less able to bear. This was the central flaw that had thwarted the building of any large dome for so many centuries.

Brunelleschi managed to see a way around this problem through a combination of painstaking investigation and architectural understanding. When he examined the concrete dome of the Pantheon, he discovered that this was far from being as uniform and weighty as it appeared. In order to construct it, 5,000 tons of concrete had been

---

* Before deriding such quaint medieval discrepancies, it is worth bearing in mind that until the nineteenth century – i.e. half a millennium later, and well into the Industrial Age – the clocks in Britain's major cities continued to run on their own different times. Only with the advent of the railways, and the need for meaningfully coordinated timetables, were these regional variations synchronized.

poured onto the dome-shaped wooden framework which was intended to support the dome as it was being built. This had been poured layer by ascending layer, and the framework shrank in circumference as it rose higher and higher. But these concrete layers were far from uniform.

Brunelleschi measured the wall supporting the base of the Pantheon dome, and found that it was an astonishing twenty-four feet thick. Yet, as the dome rose and curved inwards, the concrete forming it became thinner. Not only this, but the material itself had also ingeniously been reduced in weight. Brunelleschi noticed that, as it rose towards the peak, the concrete had been lightened by the addition of stones such as pumice. And near the top it had been lightened even further by the insertion of empty *amphorae* (light clay bottles for wine or oil), which had skilfully been pressed into the thinning layer of concrete.

The dome of the Pantheon was also both strengthened and lightened by the introduction of coffers, or sunken panels. These lined the interior of the dome in ascending rings of indented squares – the size of the squares decreasing with each ring. The borders of these panels served to form an ascending vertical and horizontal web of support. At the apex of the dome was an oculus, which let in the light.

After his first visit to Rome with Donatello, Brunelleschi returned for various periods over the next decade or so, each time absorbing further knowledge of classical architecture. In 1417 he would return to Florence permanently, taking up residence in the family home, which happened to have a fine view of the cathedral of Santa Maria del Fiore, which was still under construction.

During the following years Brunelleschi is thought to have supported himself by inventing a number of ingenious machines, including clocks, hoists, cranes and other devices for raising stones. This technical ingenuity was also allied to a penetrating mathematical mind. Brunelleschi had spent many years studying the works of Fibonacci – his *Practica Geometriae*, which Brunelleschi would have used as a school textbook, but also his *Liber Abaci* and more advanced works.

Brunelleschi's most important discovery in this field was the geometric effect of perspective.* Essentially, this enabled a two-di-mensional representation of a three-dimensional linear effect. The flat surface of the drawing renders this three-dimensional effect by making objects appear smaller as their distance from the viewer recedes, towards a vanishing point. This was a revolutionary development which would in time transform Renaissance art. Though not yet. As with so many insights of genius, it was unrecognized and ahead of its time.

It is also fair to say that Brunelleschi was not a painter, and thus had little opportunity to demonstrate or exhibit his new idea before the public. As a result, his activities during this period did not earn him much money. Meanwhile, his precocious friend Donatello had gone from strength to strength, attracting rich and influential patrons who had enabled him to develop to the full his skill as a sculptor. His works were becoming more and more admired throughout Florence. As if to add insult to injury, he had now begun working with Brunelleschi's rival Ghiberti, collaborating with him on the frieze for the north door of the Baptistery, the very work which Brunelleschi had spurned.

By now Brunelleschi was in his forties, and as a middle-aged man he hardly presented a prepossessing figure. His clothes were ragged and often dirty, while his aquiline nose and receding chin were set in a face which maintained a permanently pugnacious expression. Not surprisingly, he also remained unmarried – not a good prospect to any family of his class. He may have been impecunious and of a cantankerous disposition,

---

* This invention, or discovery, remains disputed. It is undeniable that the Ancient Greeks used a basic form of perspective in some of their paintings of figures. And there is no doubting the highly sophisticated use of three-dimensional effects in their sculptures and friezes. But the twentieth-century art critic E. H. Gombrich argues that if they could execute such realism with their sculptures, then surely their two-dimensional art (so much of which is lost to us) would have evolved alongside. Yet such Greek sculptures, friezes and paintings as have come down to us are arguably not a fully three-dimensional space conveyed on a two-dimensional plane. Did Brunelleschi gain his first inklings of perspective from his knowledge of Ancient Greek art? Even supposing he did, his profound realization and development of the possibilities of this method were certainly his own, creating as it did a new technique which would transform western art.

but he was a member of a guild, notably the prestigious one to which the goldsmiths belonged – the *Arte della Seta*.* This meant that he retained a certain social status. He could vote, and as such was not to be regarded as a member of the lower artisanal and working classes – the *ciompi* and the like. At the same time, his brilliant technical inventions and known mathematical abilities would seem to have set him apart from his peers as much as his appearance.

A year after Brunelleschi returned to live permanently in Florence, a competition was announced for the building of a dome to cap the cathedral of Santa Maria del Fiore. It is possible – indeed, more than likely – that for many years Brunelleschi had secretly been preparing himself for just this opportunity.

The city had begun building the cathedral as early as 1296, in the heyday of its early banking era, when the Bardi, Peruzzi and Acciaiuoli family banks held sway throughout Europe. Flush with money and the commercial confidence accruing from the wool industry, as well as trade links with three continents, the dreams of the Florentine authorities knew no limits. The architect commissioned to design and build this masterwork was none other than Florence's finest: the medieval sculptor and architect Arnolfo di Cambio, who had been born in the early thirteenth century, some thirty years or so before Dante. Di Cambio had already proved his worth by designing the Palazzo della Signoria – whose red-brick structure, with its soaring tower and fine, uncluttered Gothic lines, remains a city landmark to this day.

But the authorities were determined that their city's cathedral would be something more than this. It was to be a new wonder of Italy, and beyond. It would be finer than the great Gothic cathedral being built in Milan, superior to the centuries-old St Peter's in Rome, as well as being capable of housing a congregation of 30,000 worshippers. And, hubris upon hubris, it would be crowned by a dome similar to that of Aya Sofia, the cathedral of the Byzantine Empire, the capital of eastern Christendom

---

* The Silk-Workers' Guild, which also included the goldsmiths and bronze workers.

– an edifice which dated from 557 AD. Little matter that no dome had been completed during the eight centuries since that time: nothing could halt Florence and its civic pride. Such overweening ambition came to an abrupt halt in the 1340s with the collapse of almost the entire Florentine banking system, followed in a few years by the disastrous depredations of the Black Death.

For over half a century, the walls and foundations of the incomplete cathedral remained an abandoned building site, an eyesore dominating one of the main squares of the city. Weeds grew amongst its interior tiles; its walls cracked, inadequately protected against the destructive forces of hot summers and cold winters. No sooner had work restarted on the cathedral than all manner of further problems came to light. These included legacies of previous instructions by the *signoria*, as well as what looked suspiciously like intentionally vague prevarications amongst the plans drawn up by di Cambio, who had been dead for over a century now and was thus not available to explain himself.

Yet worse was to come. Scrutiny and measurement of the original model for the cathedral revealed that the dome which was planned to be the crowning glory of this building would require a span of no less than 138 feet. This was wider than that of Aya Sophia (104 feet), and only marginally smaller than the Pantheon in Rome (140 feet). Meanwhile, all that remained of the cathedral was the facade and walls of the nave, as well as the exposed foundations of the incomplete eastern end of the building, the location of the very walls which were intended to support the dome.

All knew that if this dome was not completed, the city of Florence would be reduced to a laughing stock throughout Italy, after its previous boasts. But how was such a structure to be supported by the narrow walls which di Cambio's blueprint proposed? And how would the dome be held up when it was being built?

A long list of ingenious proposals was submitted to the *signoria*. Only two of these survived serious consideration. The first of these asked whether wooden scaffolding could perhaps be erected to support the dome during its construction. But it was then discovered that there simply wasn't enough wood available. The other suggested that the entire cathedral beneath the planned dome be filled with a huge mound of earth, rising to a sufficient height so that the dome could be balanced on top of it while it was being constructed. But how would all this earth be removed afterwards? One member of the *signoria* came up with a potential solution: if the earth could be liberally mixed with *scudi* (the lowest-denomination coins), this would surely encourage young urchins to carry out buckets of earth. But such a scheme would require almost as many *scudi* as were in circulation... The problem of the dome remained unsolved.

So, in 1418, the *signoria* decided to announce a competition for its design. When Brunelleschi came before the competition committee, he took a typically aggressive approach. Contemptuously, he explained that not one of the committee had the first idea of what they were dealing with. They wanted a traditional hemispherical dome, yet under the present circumstances this was quite simply impossible. Brunelleschi then produced an egg, and asked if any of them knew how to make it stand on end. The committee remained silent, mystified. Brunelleschi then rapped the egg on the table, smashing the blunt end of its shell. The rest of the shell remained upright. This should be the shape of the dome, he said, and was how it would remain upright. Instead of a hemispherical dome, he would build an egg-shaped dome, with the thinner end at its apex. This would lessen the stress on the walls. And to further improve its strength the dome would be supported by stone ribs, reaching from the base up to the apex (much like the ribs of an umbrella). Yet how exactly did he propose to go about erecting such a construction, demanded the *signoria*? Characteristically, Brunelleschi refused to divulge his secret.*

Despite this somewhat challenging approach, the members of the *signoria* were eventually convinced; but as a precaution they decided to award the contract to two architects, just so that Brunelleschi could be

---

* There are a number of different versions of the egg story, none of which are totally convincing. I have chosen the simplest and in my view most plausible version.

kept in check. Once again, Brunelleschi's old adversary Ghiberti was chosen as his co-worker. This time Brunelleschi was so enraged that the *signoria* were forced to call the guards in order to have him forcibly ejected from the chamber where he was being interviewed.

Brunelleschi had been preparing a lifetime for this chance, and he was not going to pass it on easily. Or share it. Yet for once he appeared to swallow his pride. He began work, designing a number of ingenious hoists to raise the large heavy stones to the top of the cathedral walls. At last the supporting walls were all in place and the final construction of the dome could begin. Whereupon Brunelleschi fell ill (or so he claimed), and retired to bed in his house overlooking the cathedral site. Ghiberti was now left in sole charge, and Brunelleschi watched with amusement as Ghiberti attempted to solve the task of how to build the dome. In the end, Ghiberti was forced to ask the *signoria* if he could build flying buttresses to support the overstressed walls, but the *signoria* refused. This device had already been specifically ruled out. This was how the rival Milan cathedral was supported; the dome atop Florence's Santa Maria del Fiore was required to be entirely self-supporting.

From the outset, Santa Maria del Fiore was intended to break with the tradition of medieval Gothic architecture. In other words, this proto-Renaissance construction, which would one day come to symbolize Renaissance Florence, was in fact conceived before the Renaissance – at least in architecture – had even begun. This insistence upon novelty, or doing things the Florentine way, would in the years to come prove a vital element in the city's leading role in the Renaissance.

Meanwhile, Brunelleschi lazed in bed, before a summons arrived urgently requesting his presence on the cathedral building site. According to King, Brunelleschi arrived 'with his head bandaged and his chest poulticed'. Many were persuaded that he was at death's door; others were less convinced. Still others believed that he was suffering from a lack of nerve; they felt that he knew he could not complete the task. After providing no help to Ghiberti, Brunelleschi hobbled back to his bed. Ghiberti was now left to his own devices: 'This enormous obligation caused [him] no small amount of disquiet, for [Brunelleschi], true to his nature, had not made his colleagues privy to the structure… let alone the ultimate design of the dome.'

Such was Brunelleschi's obstinacy and arrogance that his 'illness', or sulking absence from the dome project, appears to have lasted for several years. Meanwhile, he was persuaded to take on another project: the building of the Ospedale degli Innocenti. This was to be the city's foundling home, the first of its kind in Italy. Although the financing of this building is usually ascribed to the *Arte della Seta*, Brunelleschi's guild, it is now suspected that several wealthy private citizens made a sizeable contribution to this prestigious project. The fine building would incorporate many of the lessons which Brunelleschi had learned during his time clambering amongst the ruins of Ancient Rome. Its most striking feature would be the row of elegant narrow pillars which support nine perfect hemispherical arches. It came to be regarded as a trailblazing revival of classical style, and remains to this day the finest early Renaissance building in Florence.

Even while building the Ospedale, Brunelleschi continued to make the occasional discreet visit to the cathedral site, just to see how things were progressing. Or rather, to gloat over how they were not progressing. Eventually Ghiberti gave up, defeated by the problem. Brunelleschi was entrusted with the building of the dome, and Ghiberti was delegated with overseeing work on the lower interior of the cathedral. As if by chance, Brunelleschi's old friend Donatello was assigned as one of Ghiberti's assistants during this work. Suspicious as ever, Brunelleschi wished to be informed personally concerning any schemes his nemesis had for the cathedral walls. The slightest weakness in these walls would have proved disastrous to the dome, and Brunelleschi had no wish to be blamed for this. Donatello would also assist the ageing Brunelleschi in his work on the dome.

Brunelleschi's ultimate scheme was both ingenious and utterly original. The supporting walls for the dome were not circular but octagonal, which enabled him to build up the quasi egg-shaped dome in eight distinct sections, each divided by a concrete rib (the umbrella effect). Even more daring was his plan to build *two* domes, one nestled inside the other, and to use no supporting inner structure while they were being built.

The inner dome was heavier and stronger, in order to support the outer dome. It was built of interlocking bricks, often forming a pattern of filled arches. As with all arches, these retained their strength as the weight of the next layer of arched brick was built above them. At the same time, a rising diagonal herringbone pattern of bricks was incorporated into the growing dome, enabling it to taper as it rose. This enabled the circumference of brickwork to shrink at each rising horizontal level, as well as transferring the weight and pressure of each brick to the nearest concrete rib as it ascended towards the apex.

As the horizontal rings of the inner dome rose in unison, Brunelleschi also incorporated a series of strong 'chains': rings of iron or sandstone, embedded at regular intervals in the dome in order to hold it in shape and prevent it from bulging outwards under pressure. The potential for such bulging was a very real problem, as the stronger – and heavier – inner dome was seven feet wide at its base, tapering to five feet at its apex.

Incorporated into the inner dome were a number of protruding struts, rising perpendicular from the surface of the outer horizontal bricks, in the manner of spines rising from the back of a hedgehog. These protruding struts were able to help support the much lighter dome above it, which was just two feet wide at its base, tapering to one foot at the top.

The basic facts of this structure are astonishing. For instance, its construction involved no less than 4 million bricks, weighing a massive 37,000 tons – well over three times the weight of the Eiffel Tower. And the peak of the outer dome itself reaches over 375 feet (about 115 metres) above ground level. At the time, it was the largest masonry construction in Europe: its diameter even exceeded that of the Pantheon. And to this day it remains the largest unreinforced brick-and-mortar dome ever created.

Brunelleschi was, amongst other things, a highly skilled mathematician – as seen by his discoveries concerning perspective. But the mathematical methods for calculating stress and compression of this order had yet to be invented – which meant that Brunelleschi had to rely heavily upon intuition. He may well have carried out a number of preliminary calculations, but true to character these were destroyed after he used them. Had he not done so, he may well have been credited with a number of fundamental mathematical discoveries concerning applied mechanics, which would later be attributed to others. But Brunelleschi preferred to keep such secrets to himself: he was interested in practical achievement rather than pioneering theory.

Brunelleschi would live to see Santa Maria del Fiore consecrated in 1436, some sixteen years after he had begun work on it. When he died ten years later at the age of sixty-nine, the grateful *signoria* would grant him the honour of being buried in the cathedral crypt. However, even at this stage there still remained a few finishing touches to be completed. The most important of these was the construction of the lantern and gilded ball atop the dome itself. These features would only be finished in 1469, by the artist Andrea del Verrocchio, who at the time had a precocious teenage apprentice in his studio named Leonardo da Vinci. The machines used to hoist the stonework of the lantern and the bronze ball to the top of the dome were some of the many which had been designed by Brunelleschi himself.

While such complex and powerful machines were being used to haul the stonework and gilded sphere to the very pinnacle of the dome, young Leonardo is known to have become fascinated by their mechanisms. So much so that he made a number of detailed sketches of these machines. Indeed, it was believed for many years that these intricate drawings were of machines invented by Leonardo himself – though this theory is now generally discounted. Another question arises from a sole cryptic entry made many years later in one of Leonardo's notebooks: 'Remember the way we soldered the ball of the Santa Maria del Fiori.' Does this mean that Leonardo may even have played a small role in the completion of Brunelleschi's dome?

Such questions lead to some interesting speculations. Brunelleschi was without doubt an early example of what has come to be known as a Renaissance man. That is, he had a wide range of disparate skills, especially ones derived from the classical learning that was coming to the fore in the early days of the Renaissance. These skills he built upon, and developed in highly original fashion – particularly in the construction of his double dome. He is also known to have busied himself with a number of more modern topics, such as optics – which almost certainly led to his development of the idea of perspective.

But despite all Brunelleschi's skills, experience and knowledge of classical techniques, we also know that his work on the dome of Santa Maria del Fiore involved more than a little luck. Brunelleschi was a pioneer: this meant that there were occasions when he was pushing beyond the limits of current knowledge, and he was not above guessing the mathematics as he went along. Put simply, there were times when he could not really be sure of what he was doing. But his well-tuned intuitions proved correct.

Brunelleschi's role as a proto-Renaissance man undoubtedly leads to comparisons between him and his illustrious successor, the greatest Renaissance man of them all – namely, Leonardo da Vinci. The fact is, early Renaissance artists such as Brunelleschi were expected to be well practised in a wide range of skills. Their 'art' could extend to everything from the cutting and setting of jewels, to painting and sculpture and architecture, as well as military and civil engineering. Specialization in such matters had not yet fully developed, and the rebirth of classical knowledge involved the heritage of an entire culture.

In an age when people invariably lived in the house of their family, or apprentices inhabited the studio maintained by their master, there was little room for solitude, privacy or peace. This meant that what one wrote down in a notebook, or drew in a sketchbook, no matter how well it was hidden, would invariably be discovered by others. Fellow apprentices, servants (if they could read), other members of the household – all were liable to discover any secret notebook, passing on its contents. Technical tricks intended for painting, or grinding and blending colours; descriptions of complex new machines; even one's most intimate thoughts – all could be circulated as gossip. Facts could be passed on to rivals, or used as blackmail, or posted in the little boxes provided on the streets by the authorities for gathering anonymous information. So it is little wonder that Brunelleschi wrote his notebooks in code.

The simple 'cryptic symbols and Arabic numbers' he used in the notebooks which have come down to us hardly constitute a sophisticated code. (Though it is possible that, amongst the many notebooks he destroyed, he employed more impenetrable ciphers.) This writing of secret notebooks is another factor Brunelleschi shared with Leonardo. And Leonardo's method of encryption – Latin, written in mirror image – was almost as simple as that employed by Brunelleschi. These codes appear to have been a by-product of similarly secretive temperaments. Yet they also seem to have served their purpose – protecting the contents from the prying eyes of ignorant apprentices or servants. The drawings included in both sets of notebooks were another matter: there was little way of encoding these. Yet, devoid of readable instructions, they would have proved of little value.

Brunelleschi certainly had great artistic skill – as demonstrated in his design for the Baptistery doors, not to mention his development of perspective – though he did not match Leonardo as an artist. His mathematical and architectural skills, however, would appear to have been superior. Leonardo made meticulous sketches for several buildings, but never involved himself in the practical business of constructing them. Where the designing of machines was concerned, Leonardo was far more imaginative and wide-ranging. On the other hand, Brunelleschi's machines worked (which was not always the case with Leonardo). Even though Brunelleschi destroyed many of his plans and designs, there can be no doubt that his imagination fell far, far short of that revealed in Leonardo's notebooks. The anatomical drawings, the flying machines, the investigation of everything from military machines and diving suits to the movement of clouds and water – such things were well beyond the scope of Brunelleschi's mind. Nonetheless, Brunelleschi may well have proved inspirational here. As the teenage Leonardo painstakingly committed to paper the precise details of the cogs, pulleys and winches of Brunelleschi's machines, trying to puzzle out how they worked, he was in many ways sketching his way into his own future.

CHAPTER 7

THE MATHEMATICAL ARTISTS

BRUNELLESCHI'S FIRST BIOGRAPHER WAS Antonio Manetti, a young
Florentine contemporary. Manetti was already twenty-three years
old when Brunelleschi died. As an adolescent, he would have witnessed
the completion of Brunelleschi's dome. He also encountered a number
of Brunelleschi's friends, as well as many from that much larger group
who constituted his enemies – thus acquiring a wide range of gossip
concerning his subject. Fortunately for posterity, Manetti admired
Brunelleschi and understood the magnitude of what he had achieved.
He also shared Brunelleschi's views on the newly circulating classical
learning, which along with humanism was becoming part of the education of young upper-class Florentines. This was beginning to influence
the entire outlook of a new generation of educated citizens, transforming
their understanding of both art and culture.

Despite Manetti's empathy with Brunelleschi, he was not above
revealing his subject's many faults of character. Most of all, Brunelleschi's
irascibility. On top of this, there was Brunelleschi's fanatical attention to
every detail of his work, which more than once caused his entire workforce

to down tools and abandon the site. Yet without such obsessive methods, the dome would not have been completed successfully.

During the course of Brunelleschi's work, he also embarked upon a series of side projects. Perhaps the most ingenious of these was the invention of a paddle boat, which was named *Il Badalone*. In Italian, *badile* means 'shovel', giving an indication of how the paddles worked. This boat was invented to transport heavy blocks of Carrara marble upstream from Pisa to Florence. In order to power it against the current, Brunelleschi set about devising a series of treadmills which would drive paddles on either side of the craft. Whereupon, one of Brunelleschi's many enemies, a certain Giovanni da Prato, composed a malicious sonnet mocking *Il Badalone*, prophesying that it would be nothing more than an *acqua vola* (water bird), a reference to how the paddles would do nothing more than make ugly splashes of water, like a fleeing waterfowl. In the exaggerated rhetoric of the period, which played a large part in the public enjoyment of such spats, da Prato referred to Brunelleschi's mind as 'a pit of ignorance', describing him as 'a miserable beast and imbecile'. He then made the rash promise that he would commit suicide if Brunelleschi's *Il Badalone* ever worked.

Brunelleschi gave as good as he got, replying with a sonnet describing Giovanni da Prato as 'a ridiculous-looking animal' devoid of sufficient intellect even to begin to understand his clever invention. When eventually *Il Badalone* was launched amidst general wonderment, Giovanni da Prato thought it wise to lie low for a while. By this time, such was the frequency and virulence of Brunelleschi's quarrels with his fellow citizens that, according to Manetti, the authorities obliged him to swear an oath to 'forgive injuries, lay down all hatred, entirely free [himself] of any faction or bias, and to attend only to the good and the honour and the greatness of the Republic, forgetting all offences received to this day through passions of party or faction or any other reason'.

Manetti himself was a man of eclectic intellect. He too was a mathematician and an architect, yet he chose to devote much of his considerable mental energies to an unusual project. Having studied the works of Dante in meticulous detail, he drew up a number of mathematically precise maps of Dante's *Inferno*. One included an overview of the descending rings of Hell; others included depictions of particular circles of Hell; while another pictured 'the Tomb of Lucifer' in its lowest pit. The dimension, shape and location of the subjects of these drawings were precisely calculated using references in Dante's poem.

Manetti was not misguided in his insistence upon the mathematical nature of Dante's universe. To mention just one aspect: Dante's obsession with the number three throughout the poem – which was even written in *terza rima*.* Dante saw the number three as fundamental to the way the universe was created, our place in it, and how it functions. This he believed to be eternal, for Aristotle had conceived of the natural world as operating according to a tripartite principle long before the birth of Christ. This would continue into Christianity in the form of the Holy Trinity (God the Father, Son and Holy Ghost), the afterlife (Heaven, Purgatory, Paradise) and many other aspects. In this way, Aristotle's science and Christian theology came together to describe otherwise apparently independent aspects of reality.

---

* A poem written in *terza rima*, literally 'third rhyme', consists of three-line stanzas with each stanza linked to the next by an interlocking triadic rhyme scheme. Thus the first and third line of each stanza rhyme. The middle line of this stanza then provides the rhymes for the first and third lines of the following stanza, and so on: a b a, b c b, c d c, etc. Thus the poem opens:

Nel mezzo del cammin di nostra vita
mi ritrovai per una selva oscura,
ché la diritta via era smarrita.

Ahi quanto a dir qual era è cosa dura
esta selva selvaggia e aspra e forte
che nel pensier rinova la paura!

Tant' è amara che poco è più morte;
ma per trattar del ben ch'i' vi trovai,
dirò de l'altre cose ch'i' v'ho scorte.

A loose prose paraphrasing of these lines appears at the beginning of Chapter 1.

Manetti's drawings of Dante's *Inferno* would not be published until 1506, some nine years after his death in 1497 at the age of seventy-three. Manetti's own architectural legacy stems directly from his closeness to Brunelleschi and his sympathy with his humanist ideas. He well understood the revolutionary nature of Brunelleschi's work and how it broke with the medieval tradition in which the soaring pinnacles of Gothic cathedrals aspired to mystic glory and metaphysical transcendence. Renaissance architecture, at least in its earlier flowering, confined itself to a more human scale, with fewer spires and embellishments. Likewise, exteriors eschewed such adornments as flying buttresses and gargoyles, instead harking back to a classical simplicity.

Manetti's finest work is the rebuilding of the Basilica di Santo Spirito in Oltrarno. There had been a church on this site for more than two centuries, and during the fourteenth century it had become particularly popular as a meeting place for Boccaccio and his humanist circle. So much so that, on his death in 1375, Boccaccio donated his entire library to the church. The rebuilding of this church had originally been assigned to Brunelleschi, but he only took sporadic interest in the work. After his death, Manetti took charge of the scheme. The long straight lines and plain white walls give this building an austere beauty, while its 320-foot interior aisle is lined by two rows of slender pillars echoing Brunelleschi's pillars at the Ospedale degli Innocenti. These pillars were in fact Brunelleschi's idea, and the first batch was delivered to the church during the last week of his life. However, Manetti decided against slavishly following his mentor's ideas. Brunelleschi had originally intended the front of the church to be adorned with a facade, but Manetti chose to ignore this aspect, thus lending the church a sparser, more modern character. While Brunelleschi's Ospedale is regarded as a pioneering precursor of Renaissance architecture, Manetti's Santo Spirito is now recognized as a fully realized achievement of this style.

Despite Brunelleschi's long and meticulous work on the dome of Santa Maria del Fiore, the actual interior of the building remained unfinished. For some years there had been ambitious plans. As early as 1393, the *signoria* had proposed erecting in the cathedral a large marble statue of the *condottiere* Sir John Hawkwood mounted on his charger. However, this grandiose gesture was not without hidden motives. The *signoria* intended to demonstrate to all Italy how Florence honoured the *condottieri* who entered their service and remained loyal to the republic. Such an honour for a living man was unprecedented, as would have been the cost in fine marble, to say nothing of the fee demanded by the sculptor. Further incentive to this project was added when the *signoria* learned of the ageing Hawkwood's future plans. He was at this very time discreetly liquidizing his assets – selling off his properties in the *contado*, as well as his valuables – with the intention of returning to his native England. The *signoria* hoped that bestowing upon him the unique honour of a statue in the cathedral would persuade him to remain.

When Sir John Hawkwood died the following year, the proposal to erect a marble statue was quietly shelved by the ever-pragmatic *signoria*. Instead, it was decided to commission the talented but inexpensive Paolo Uccello to paint on the cathedral wall a monochrome fresco, whose colours would be such that it at least resembled the promised marble statue. This effect was to be enhanced by Uccello's renowned expertise in perspective, so that the uneducated viewer standing beneath the twenty-four-foot by thirteen-foot fresco could easily believe that he was staring up at a statue, or at least a frieze, of the great *condottiere* astride his charger.

The artist we know as Paolo Uccello was born in the mountain village of Pratovecchio some twenty miles east of Florence. His date of birth is uncertain, but is estimated to have been around 1397. His father, Dono di Paolo, was a barber-surgeon, a respected lower-middle-class member of society. Besides shaving and cutting hair, he would also have pulled out teeth, supervised bloodletting (with leeches), and generally carried out practical medical procedures from which more superior physicians would have refrained without the inducement of a large fee. Uccello's mother Antonia came from the distinguished del Beccuto family of Florence. The less attractive or later-born daughters of such families were frequently dispatched to a convent when a suitable marriage could not be arranged. Antonia evidently preferred to be married off beneath her station to a suitor who would not expect a large dowry.

The doubt concerning Uccello's date of birth, and the fact that we know nothing of his childhood, is characteristic of his life. He may have grown up to become the finest Florentine artist since Giotto, but he was not a demonstrative character. The very opposite, in fact. He preferred, in his own quiet manner, to follow his own path. Giorgio Vasari, writing of Uccello a century or so later, castigates him from the outset:

> The most captivating and imaginative painter to have lived since Giotto would certainly have been Paolo Uccello, if only he had spent as much time on human figures and animals as he spent, and wasted, on the finer points of perspective. Such details may be attractive and ingenious, but anyone who studies them excessively is squandering time and energy, choking his mind with difficult problems...

As Vasari was intent upon pointing out, such artists usually ended their days 'solitary, eccentric, melancholy, and poor'. And this was certainly the case with Uccello, yet this does not seem to have bothered him. Uccello was genuinely and deeply interested in exploring the fascinating details and problems of perspective. Curiously, although perspective was very much a central feature of Renaissance art, Uccello chose to paint in a style more resembling the earlier Gothic tradition. He preferred to concentrate on the vivid hues and drama of a scene, rather than the more realistic method favoured by his Renaissance colleagues.

It is known that around the age of fifteen (or possibly several years earlier), Uccello travelled to Florence, where he was taken on as an apprentice in the studio of Brunelleschi's old enemy Lorenzo Ghiberti. And it was here amongst his fellow apprentices that he acquired the nickname by which we know him today – namely, Uccello, which is Italian for 'bird'. While Ghiberti's other apprentices spent their own time drawing from life models and figurines, Uccello became notorious for hiding himself away and indulging in his favourite habit – drawing animals, especially birds. At around this time he is known to have been taught geometry by the young Manetti, thus inspiring a lifelong obsession which overrode even his fixation with birds and animals.

In 1416 Uccello graduated from apprentice to fully fledged artistic status, when he was admitted to the prestigious guild of *Arte dei Medici e Speziali*, the very one which Dante had joined almost two centuries previously. Despite this, Uccello's early career proved to be something of a struggle.

As was often the case with young artists, Uccello was commissioned to paint frescoes of religious scenes in churches and monasteries. One of these commissions was from the abbot of San Miniato, who hired him to paint scenes from the lives of the Church Fathers, the Christian theologians of the first and second centuries. The monastery of San Miniato was on a hilltop overlooking the outskirts of Florence, and in order to devote himself fully to his work Uccello was obliged to take up residence amongst the monks. Here he received the same food as the monks, who subsisted on a meagre diet of cheese soup and cheese pies. Owing to his characteristic timidity, Uccello could not bring himself to complain to the abbot about the food – so he simply ran away. According to Vasari, he was only tempted back to complete his work when the abbot promised that he would be provided with a more mixed variety of meals.

From religious frescoes, Uccello graduated to larger commissions: one for three large scenes depicting the Battle of San Romano, where the Florentine forces had defeated the Sienese in 1432. Each of these paintings contains a striking rendition of the battle, showing mounted warriors charging with lances in the foreground, with the upright lances of the infantry in the background, which creates a superb effect. In formal terms, the long straight lines of these lances enclose the foreground, leading the eye of the beholder to focus on the main mounted protagonists, while at the same time conveying the dissonant clash of arms. Beyond the raised weapons and chaotic scenes of battle one can see distant vignettes amidst the countryside, where individual figures are hunting, picking grapes or fighting one another. The paintings in the trio each illustrate a stage of the battle, which continued for eight hours. Judging from the light, the first is of early morning, the second is noon, and the third illustrates the near darkness of dusk. Although the clatter of battle is evoked, with fallen men, dead horses and piercing lances, there is little or no blood. These paintings were not intended to be realistic, yet their almost ritualized antagonism and the gritted determination of the soldiers would seem to convey the very essence of battle – as envisioned by a man who had heard tell of its horrors but had never taken part in such mortal conflict.

Uccello would remain unmarried until he was fifty-six, very much an old man by the standards of the period. Whether this was due to his temperament, or his comparative poverty, remains unclear. He drew and painted continuously, year in year out, and Vasari claims: 'In many Florentine houses can be found a number of pictures by Uccello, all of them small, painted in perspective, to decorate the sides of couches, beds and so forth.' Uccello may well have given these away. At the same time, he continued drawing animals. But these are no sentimental sketches. Although he loved animals, he had no illusions about their nature. There are many drawings of animals fighting. One of especial ferocity depicts a cornered lion snarling up at a dragon, which is attempting to devour it.

When Uccello finally married, his bride was Tommasa Malifici, and within a year she gave birth to a son, whom Uccello chose to name Donato, after Donatello. This was an odd choice, in the light of Vasari's description of an incident involving the two painters. One day, Uccello was painting a fresco above the door at the church of San Tommaso in the Mercato Vecchio (Old Market). In characteristic fashion, Uccello erected a wooden screen in front of his work, so that no one could see it until it was finished. Even when his fellow artist Donatello turned up and asked if he could take a look, Uccello brusquely denied his request, telling him: 'You will just have to wait and see.'

Sometime later, when Donatello was in the Mercato Vecchio buying fruit, he noticed Uccello removing the screen from his finished work. Uccello was keen to discover Donatello's opinion of his work, and called him over. Donatello examined the fresco in some detail, and then remarked dryly: 'Well, now that it ought to be covered up, you're showing it to everyone.'

Three years after the birth of Uccello's son Donato, his wife Tommasa gave birth to a girl, who was named Antonia. When Antonia was ten, her father placed her in a Carmelite nunnery. Uccello claimed on his tax return that he was now too old and could not earn enough to support her, and that on top of this his wife was sick. Interestingly, Vasari describes Antonia as 'a daughter who knew how to draw'.

When Antonia died in 1491, just thirty-five years old, her name was recorded in the *Libro dei Morti* (Book of the Dead) of the *Arte dei Medici e Speziali* (her father's former guild, and by now recognized as the guild for the most prestigious artists). Such an action was unprecedented. And beside Antonia's name was written the word *pittoressa*, said to have been the first official use of the female form of the word for 'painter'. Over the centuries, several works have been attributed to Antonia, yet each identification has so far been disproved. The most likely explanation of this absence is that Antonia acted as assistant, and then collaborator, with her ailing father during his last years. There is a suggestion that she may also have continued with Uccello's animal drawings, providing a small income for her impoverished mother.

During the last decade of his life, Uccello was increasingly solitary and infirm. Yet it was in 1470, just five years before his death, that he painted his final masterpiece. This is usually known as *The Hunt*. It depicts men on horseback, accompanied by their spear-bearing attendants and baying hounds, chasing through a wood in pursuit of their prey, a number of leaping deer. Because the woods are so dark, the painting has often been called *The Hunt by Night*. Unsuccessful attempts have been made to explain away this darkness as a matter of deterioration of the pigment, for none of the participants in the hunt are bearing flares – which they would certainly have needed to illuminate their way.

Only a master of perspective could have constructed such a vista. There is in fact more than one perspective. The first has two elements: one created by the static positioning of the trees, and another by the melee of the charging hunters, their attendants and the chasing hounds. These figures (both human and animal) are informed with colourful life – prancing, running, leaping. In Gothic fashion, they achieve their vibrancy through colour and pageantry, rather than any classical realism. Yet they are at the same time unmistakably placed within the setting of a Renaissance perspective. This is a work of art between two worlds. As if to emphasize this point, there is a second perspective, daringly created by a stream, which runs straight from the right-hand side of the painting towards a vanishing point of its own, which is way to the right of the main perspective point.

All manner of subtle interpretations have been read in this painting. Is it perhaps a spiritual hunt, leading us further and further into the darkness of the unknown? Could this be an echo of the symbolic *bosco oscuro* (dark wood) in which the middle-aged Dante found himself lost at the beginning of his *Divine Comedy*?

Perhaps inevitably there appears to be no wholly satisfying explanation. Like the best art, it cannot be 'explained away'. It is an object to be contemplated – for its beauty, its skill, what it portrays, and whatever symbolic interpretations it inspires in the mind of the beholder. The hunt remains what it is, and at the same time is a metaphorical quest losing itself in the darkness. The initial, natural and human perspective suggests an objective – but it points only to darkness and night and impenetrable trees. On the other hand, this is not an entirely natural wood. It shows signs of cultivation: some of the trees in the foreground have stumps where their branches have been lopped off, while the stream is so straight that it may well be a canal. The picture is pervaded by a mystery that soon begins to take on a psychological resonance. Put simply, the darkness and rigidity of the medieval is placed in a setting of Renaissance clarity. This mysterious, almost secretive quality is what makes the whole scene so intriguing. Here the Renaissance is taking on a new, enigmatic depth – yet ironically that depth stems from a more spiritual past.

Given Uccello's personality, and his part-archaic manner of painting, it is little wonder that he had no followers – with the exception of Antonia, who may well have contributed her own female element to *The Hunt*, that epitome of male activities. Some have detected a female sensitivity in a number of the gestures, the running figures, the prancing animals. Yet there is no woman amongst the hunting riders or their attendants; and the deer too appear to be all male, possessing antlers.

If there is an allegorical content, this involves man as mankind, or humanity in its entirety. We are all riding headlong, on prancing horses, or reining in our steeds in fear; gesturing or pointing to our companions, accompanied by our attendants with their pikes, their knives tucked into their belts, all equally disparate in their attitudes – some running with enthusiasm, some calling out, some pointing, some hanging behind, as the leaping hounds bay after their prey, which scatter to left and to right, further and further into the darkness of the wood.

The third of our mathematical artists is Piero della Francesca, who was born around 1415, a decade or so later than Uccello. Piero hailed from Borgo San Sepolcro, a small town set amongst the hills at the very east of Tuscany, some forty miles from Florence. Unlike the two previous mathematical painters, during his life Piero would arguably be more renowned for his geometry at the expense of his painting, an injustice that has long since been overturned.

Vasari, writing in the following century, waxes indignant at the fate of Piero, viewing him as one whose life was cut short and whose work was plagiarized, with his glory often claimed by others: 'When Piero died he left in his studio many drawings and paintings that were only partly complete. Unscrupulous colleagues then stole these and passed them off as their own work. Thus donkeys attempt to aggrandize themselves by donning the skin of a lion.' He continues by extolling Piero's accomplishments as he had come to see them:

> He was widely regarded as a master for solving several difficult problems in both mathematics and geometry. However, his growing blindness prevented him from solving many further problems. This is one of the reasons why his original researches, as well as his finished works, remained unknown for so long.

Vasari holds one man responsible for many of the wrongs which befell Piero, identifying the culprit as a friar who is known to us as Luca Pacioli. Vasari claims:

> This was the man who was taught everything he knew by Piero, the master who passed on to him all the mathematical secrets he had discovered. Indeed, Fra Luca was the very man who should have done his utmost to publicise Piero's many mathematical achievements. Yet he wickedly chose instead to claim for himself all this wealth of original knowledge which had been passed on to him by his teacher.

Here Vasari unfortunately does a great disservice to both Piero della Francesca and his pupil Luca Pacioli, who was also born in Borgo San Sepolcro, probably around thirty years after Piero. Pacioli's great work, *Summa de Arithmetica, Geometria, Proportioni et Proportionalita* (The Sum of Arithmetic, Geometry, Extensive Proportions and Relative Size), was published in Venice in 1494, i.e. two years after Piero's death. There is no denying that it included the vast spectrum of mathematical knowledge which Piero had accumulated and passed on to his pupil. But Pacioli's work included much, much more.

The indicative word is in the title: *summa*. 'Summary' could perhaps be an alternative translation here. Pacioli's book was intended as an encyclopedic work of all mathematical knowledge known in Europe at that time. Besides including theorems first written down by Euclid, Pacioli also included work introduced to Europe by Leonardo of Pisa (including Arabic numerals), as well as a survey of algebra (whose name is derived from the Arabic *al-jabr*, meaning 'the reunion of broken parts').

Today, Pacioli's *Summa* is best remembered for its chapter containing the first complete exposition of double-entry bookkeeping, which was transforming the banking industry of Florence and had already begun to spread throughout Italy and northern Europe. Put simply, this involved entering each transaction in two separate columns in an account book. The left-hand column was for debit, and the right-hand column was for credit. Thus, for instance, when recording a loan of ten florins, this would be registered as ten florins in the debit column, and as ten florins in the credit column. Using this method enabled the banker to make a rapid calculation of his total assets: both his equity (readily available assets, cash, or monies owed to him) and his liabilities (debits or monies owed by him). This also facilitated the detection of fraud, and may be regarded as one of the first steps into the modern age of finance. For this reason, Pacioli is frequently dubbed the Father of Accounting.

Luca Pacioli wrote much of his work in the vernacular. Significantly, this was now the everyday language used in business – as opposed to the high Latin used by the educated classes and the Church. (Dante's use of the Tuscan dialect in *The Divine Comedy* had only been the beginning of a new pan-Italian language – as distinct from the various regional dialects, whose separate users were often incomprehensible to one another.) Pacioli intended his book to be a textbook for students at the universities of northern Italy. His aim was the dissemination of knowledge, rather than laying any claim to having invented the contents of the *Summa*.

The fact that Pacioli had his book printed in Venice indicates one of the few significant changes of the Renaissance era which did not have associations with Florence or Tuscany. Around 1440, the Rhineland German Johannes Gutenberg produced a moveable-type printing press. He was not the first to discover this method of printing, as it had already been known to the Tang Dynasty in China some six centuries previously. On the other hand, Gutenberg seems to have developed his idea without any knowledge of his East Asian predecessors.

Although Gutenberg was cheated out of the profits from his 'invention', the printing press itself quickly spread through Germany and then across the Alps to Venice, which soon became the printing centre of Italy. And it was through the publication of Pacioli's *Summa* that Piero della Francesca's mathematical ideas became widely disseminated throughout Italy, and then beyond.

As we have seen, Brunelleschi may have been the first to understand fully the secret of perspective, and he was certainly the first to develop this into a mature and highly effective artistic method. Later, his biographer, the artist and mathematician Antonio Manetti, would advance this work. Then Uccello became obsessed with perspective, to the point where he frequently valued it more than his painting. Uccello's introduction of such virtuoso touches as 'double perspectives' brought a further mathematical refinement into Renaissance art. However, this mathematization of painting would reach its peak with Piero della Francesca, who would take this element one step further than his predecessors.

At this point, it is worth asking what precisely was happening here. What were the intentions and aims of these early Renaissance artists? They and many of their contemporaries were also expected to work as architects, and the need for architectural drawing – with its reliance upon pattern, proportion and balance, and its aesthetic of numerical ratios – took a strong hold on these artists' imaginations. If buildings could be constructed according to such precise plans, why not paintings?

Here is another side effect of the shift from medieval thought to the new humanism. The mystical attitude of the Middle Ages was in many ways an inchoate attitude towards the world. Its paintings may have been stylized, but its essential vision of the world was holistic or cosmic. Like Dante's *Divine Comedy*, it included everything in the *cosmos* – the Greek word for 'world', 'universe' or 'order'. Humanism, on the other hand, would emphasize the human as the measure of things.

This had of course been the case for centuries, yet only in the most literal and practical sense: for instance, the *braccio* was the length of a man's arm. In other languages there were measurements such as a foot, a span (the width of a hand's span), a yard (the length of a man's belt) or a mile (based on the Roman *mille passus*, 'a thousand paces'). The Renaissance would add a psychological dimension to this idea of the human as the measure of all things. Humanity's position in the world shifted from being part of a vast mystical cosmos, instead centring on the individual consciousness and what it actually experienced.

The rediscovery of classical artistic techniques had led early Renaissance artists to depict increasingly lifelike figures, with techniques such as shading used to lend them a more fully rounded, three-dimensional presence. A predictable step on from this was the faithful rendering of realistic backgrounds in their paintings, by means of techniques like perspective, which included a vital element of mathematical measurement.

What had previously been a rule of thumb, so to speak ('foot', 'span' and so forth), now required a more mathematical exactitude. The world was becoming more subject to measure. It is no accident that the first clock towers and chiming clocks began appearing in cities throughout Europe. Time itself was being measured, with an exactitude approaching that which had previously only occurred in the account books of bankers.

From now on, numbers spilled from the precision of the account book into exact measurement of the world around us. Inevitably, this soon entered the artist's depiction of that same all-encompassing world. Pictures had an underlying pattern that could be measured. This could be drawn in arithmetic patterns, or in geometric terms (such as perspective). And it was Piero della Francesca who would take this mathematization one step further.

Just prior to Piero's birth in Borgo San Sepolcro, his father Benedetto de' Franceschi died. Benedetto had been a tradesman, but he and his wife were both descendants of the ancient Franceschi family of Florence. After his father's death, Piero took on his mother's (female) version of the ancient family name.

From an early age, he was apprenticed to a local 'artist-artisan' named Antonio d'Anghiari, who had been a friend of his father. D'Anghiari's art remained strictly Gothic, so that when some painters from Siena were hired for restoration work in San Sepolcro, their Renaissance style came as a revelation to Piero. However, his true originality as a painter did not become evident until he visited Florence in his early twenties.

It is known that Piero was present on 15 February 1439, when the Byzantine emperor John VIII Palaeologus, the patriarch (pope) of the Eastern Orthodox religion, entered Florence at the head of a Byzantine delegation. Florence had become the venue of a grand council aimed at reconciling eastern and western Christianity. The capital of the Eastern Church, Constantinople, now lay under serious threat from the Ottoman Muslims, who had already overrun western Anatolia (modern-day

Turkey) and much of the southern Balkans (most of the territory now occupied by Greece, Bulgaria and Romania).

The entry of the Eastern Orthodox delegation into Florence on that February day almost 600 years ago caused a sensation. This was particularly true of the emperor himself: an anonymous contemporary chronicler describes how he 'wore a white gown with over it a mantle of red stuff and a white hat coming to a point in front in which he had a ruby bigger than a pigeon's egg and many other precious stones'. This sight certainly made an indelible impression on the young Piero. Twenty years later, he was commissioned to paint a portrait of the fourth-century Emperor Constantine, the first Christian Roman emperor, after whom Constantinople was named. In this work, Piero would recall precisely what he had seen that day in Florence. The Emperor Constantine is not only painted wearing the hat worn by John VIII Palaeologus, but also bears his unmistakable features.

In Florence, Piero worked with Domenico Veneziano, who was born in 1410 in Venice but emigrated to Florence to pursue his childhood dream of becoming an artist. By 1439, Piero and Veneziano are known to have worked together on a fresco for the church of Sant'Egidio in central Florence, though this work has long since disappeared. By the early decades of the fifteenth century, Florence was home to several of Italy's leading artists. These included Donatello and Brunelleschi, whom Piero almost certainly met. Piero appears to have absorbed the primarily classical influence of these painters, and may well have been inspired by them to a deeper study of mathematics.

By 1450, Piero's style had matured, and would remain basically the same throughout the rest of his painting career. He soon began to attract work from a number of influential sponsors. The most important of these, as far as Piero was concerned, was the cultured *condottiere* Federico da Montefeltro, the ruler of Urbino, a small city seventy miles or so east of Florence, on the other side of the mountains. Montefeltro had pursued a successful career as a mercenary commander, often in the service of Florence. During the course of his career he had accumulated a large fortune, and became determined to transform the walled city of Urbino into a centre of Renaissance culture, inviting a number of leading artists and intellectuals to live and work in his city. The most important and influential amongst the artists was Piero, who became a member of Montefeltro's court.*

Piero is known to have worked in Urbino between 1455 and 1470, though it remains uncertain as to precisely how many of these years he actually lived in the city, for he also took on important commissions in many other cities, especially Florence, the Tuscan city of Arezzo, and commissions for Pope Nicholas V in Rome.

Perhaps the finest work which Piero painted in Urbino was *The Flagellation of Christ*. This enigmatic small masterpiece has provoked all manner of speculation concerning its complex and controversial perspective, as well as the identities of the highly individualized figures who occupy the right foreground and the left background. Astonishingly, contrary to all the rules of composition, the right and left sides of the painting are completely divided from one another. Yet Piero's skilful use of line and the guidance of the eye enable these two distinct halves to form a united picture. The painting is imbued with a classical calm, despite the violence of the subject matter – the whipping of Christ prior to his crucifixion. Interestingly, the main figure witnessing this torture wears the distinctive hat worn by the Byzantine emperor on his visit to Florence. This has led many to interpret Christ's suffering as symbolizing the suffering of Constantinople under siege by the Ottomans. (Constantinople had in fact been overrun by Sultan Mehmed II in 1453, almost twenty years prior to Piero's painting, but this remained a seminal

---

* Half a century or so later, a diplomat and member of this court named Baldassare Castiglione would begin writing *Il Cortegiano* (The Courtier), which would set down the morals and general demeanour expected of a contemporary courtier. This gives a fascinating insight into the manners and mores of cultured Renaissance life. *Il Cortegiano* would quickly become the handbook on etiquette throughout Europe. An indication of its influence and popularity can be seen from the fact that its first publication in Venice in 1528 would quickly be followed by translations into all major European languages. The first English edition was published in 1561 and would prove a vital influence in Elizabethan court life. This would most notably be reflected in many of the plays of Shakespeare.

event in the history of the era.) The many geometric, harmonic and aesthetic mathematical proportions incorporated in Piero's rendition of this scene would be 'rediscovered' by the cubists and abstract painters of the twentieth century.

No description of Piero's work would be complete without mention of his masterwork, *The Resurrection*, which depicts Christ risen from his tomb with the sleeping Apostles in the foreground, as well as a background of receding realistic barren hillsides. (Some critics have gone so far as to claim this as the inspiration for Leonardo da Vinci's use of a similar realistic motif in the background to the *Mona Lisa*.) Another memorable work is the portrait of Federico da Montefeltro, Duke of Urbino, which today hangs in London's National Gallery. This is unusual in that it is painted in profile, depicting only the left-hand side of Montefeltro's face. The pose was chosen to disguise the fact that Montefeltro had lost his eye and suffered shattering injuries to the right-hand side of his face during a jousting match in Perugia. The only hint at this disfigurement is the indentation at the top of Montefeltro's nose, which had in fact remained unharmed during the accident. Montefeltro himself had ordered surgeons to cut away the bridge of his nose, so that his remaining left eye could see to his right side as well as his left, thus enabling him to protect himself against any assassination attempt. (Assassination had been the cause of death of the previous ruler of Urbino, his half-brother Oddantonio da Montefeltro, a conspiracy in which Federico himself is thought to have played a hand.) Once again we see the characteristic Renaissance juxtaposition of great art and the murderous violence which seldom lay far below the surface of this glorious new era that heralded the modern world.

It was while Piero was living in Urbino that he probably first met his fellow citizen from Borgo San Sepolcro, Fra Luca Pacioli, who is known to have acted as a tutor to Montefeltro's son. Around this time Piero was also befriended by the Genoese humanist Leon Battista Alberti, whose polymathic interests included a deep understanding of mathematics. It was Alberti who encouraged Piero to write his work *De Prospectiva Pingendi* (On Perspective in Painting), which covers a large range of arithmetic, geometric and algebraic topics, as well as instructions on how to paint a face, the creation of perspective by means of colour, and other artistic subjects. Its influences range from Alberti's *De Pictura* to Euclid's *Elements*. According to Vasari, 'Piero studied Euclid so closely that he achieved an intimate knowledge of his work and methods. He understood better than any practised geometer the nature of perfect curves drawn on a basis of regular bodies.' *On Perspective* also includes aspects of perspective with relation to human anatomy, the beginning of a topic which would become of prime interest to the great Renaissance artists who followed Piero.

Piero did not finish *On Perspective* until around 1480, when he was in his mid-sixties. By now Piero's sight had begun to deteriorate drastically, and it was claimed that he finally 'went blind through an attack of catarrh at the age of sixty'. This claim is not borne out by the facts, as Piero continued to write mathematical works, some requiring precisely drawn geometric figures. Indeed, he completed *De Quinque Corporibus Regularibus* (On the Five Regular Solids) in 1485, sometime after he returned to live in the Tuscan family home at Borgo San Sepolcro. Here he is said to have lived out his remaining years alone, tended to only by family servants.

Piero would finally die at the age of seventy-seven on 12 October 1492, the very day that Christopher Columbus first set foot in the Americas. Europe was entering a new age, at the same time as it 'discovered' new worlds. Both of these developments would help expand the western mind beyond the previous limits of its imagination.

CHAPTER 8

THOSE WHO PAID THE BILLS

F EDERICO DA MONTEFELTRO'S TRANSFORMATION of the obscure walled city of Urbino into a centre of Renaissance art and learning was in direct imitation of Florence, which had relied upon his military services over many years. Florence, Milan, Naples, Rome – Montefeltro was hired on various occasions throughout his long and successful career to fight for each of these powerful city-states (and, on occasion, to fight against them).

Montefeltro himself may have aspired to be a man of culture, but those who made up the lower ranks of mercenary armies were tough soldiers of fortune hailing from poor rural areas of Italy, Germany, Switzerland, France and England. Even kilted Scots and ragged Irish warriors might make up the numbers. These men could be a murderous, uncouth lot – bent on rape and pillage, and often as willing to fight amongst themselves as they were against the enemy. Both courses of action which their commanders (and their commanders' loyal henchmen) did their best to suppress.

According to Italian medieval custom, campaigns were only conducted during clement weather – starting in late spring, and concluding before the first rains of autumn. In winter, the armies could be disbanded and paid off, allowing soldiers to return home. Or they could set up winter quarters, where their patron was expected to provide shelter such as rude felt tents or billeting, often in stables. At such times, hay and drinking water were required for the horses. On top of this, the soldiery expected adequate victualling and somewhat more plentiful supplies to quench their thirst. Other activities during this off season included the forging and sharpening of weaponry, gambling, roughhouse kickball with an inflated pig's bladder, and athletic competitions such as wrestling, weightlifting and high-jumping. Owing to cold weather, washing of bodies or clothes only took place inadvertently, during rainstorms. Little wonder that villagers throughout the land often first became aware of an approaching army by its smell on the wind, prompting them to flee for the woods or mountain caves.

Yet as ever in this age, the primitive coexisted with the cultural. Even a battle-hardened *condottiere* could make his contribution to the Renaissance. Montefeltro may have been the classic case, but he was far from unique – either in his pursuit of culture or in seeking social betterment. Montefeltro enjoyed accumulating titles. In 1437 he was knighted by the Holy Roman Emperor Sigismund, and would go on to be rewarded in similar fashion by no less than two popes. In 1462, Pope Pius II appointed Montefeltro to the official title of Gonfaloniere of the Papal Forces. Twelve years later, the subsequent pope, Sixtus IV, married his favourite nephew to Montefeltro's daughter Giovanna, rewarding him with the title of Duke of Urbino as a wedding gift.

In all, Florence would hire Montefeltro for more than six years, but there still remains the question of where the money came from. The source of the new duke's wealth, and his sponsorship of Urbino's renaissance, is clear enough. Yet how did those who rewarded him for his services gain their wealth?

Milan's large agricultural hinterland, its metal industry and the cultivation of silk around Lake Como provided a considerable income, which was increased by its strategic geographical position as a link between Italy and transalpine northern European trade. The extensive territory of Naples had made it a centre of power and wealth since before the era when the Holy Roman Emperor Frederick II chose to establish his court in Sicily. Rome's wealth derived from the vast papal dues which were collected throughout western Christendom, from Greenland to Vienna, from Sweden to Sicily. And the transfer of this money and other vital trading income was frequently facilitated by bankers whose strong contacts with northern Europe had been fostered by the wool trade. This naturally favoured powerful Florentine banks such as the Peruzzi or the Bardi, but they could not always rely upon papal preferment. With the city-states of Italy constantly squabbling, Florence often found itself at odds with a newly elected pope, whereupon a new papal banker was liable to be appointed. And as we have seen, banking would become an increasing source of wealth for the city.

The collapse of the Bardi, Peruzzi and Acciaiuoli banks in the mid-1340s left only a few small banks remaining in Florence. One of these was the Alberti bank, a minor family concern. However, the Alberti immediately took advantage of the gap in the market and successfully put in a bid to take over the papal business. Yet the Alberti proved a quarrelsome family, and the bank quickly split into several rival companies. According to the financial historian Raymond de Roover: 'Moreover, some of the leading members of the family fell into disgrace with the ruling Florentine oligarchs, with the result that from 1382 to 1434, the entire Alberti clan was sent into exile.'

This left four main family banks in Florence: the Pazzi, the Ruccellai, the Strozzi and the Medici. The last of these would eventually emerge as the leading concern. 'Although the Medici succeeded in overshadowing their competitors, they never attained the size of the Bardi or the Peruzzi, the giants of the fourteenth century.' Considering the immense power and influence which the Medici would later come to wield over the city of Florence, and indeed the Renaissance itself, this is a surprising claim. Yet its truth is indisputable, for as de Roover states: 'The business records of the Medici Bank have been preserved in sufficient quantity to give a fairly detailed picture... True, the extant material is uneven and full of gaps, but is more nearly complete than [almost] any other medieval firm.'

The Medici bank which rose to such prominence would be founded by the thirty-seven-year-old Giovanni di Bicci de' Medici in October 1397.* Previously he had worked for the smaller bank owned by his older cousin Vieri de' Medici, entering as a clerk and gradually working his way up to become a junior partner. By all accounts Giovanni was a rather dry character, meticulous, hard-working and immensely ambitious – though the latter quality he disguised well and kept to himself. The Medici family were still in some disgrace as a result of Salvestro de' Medici's involvement in the Ciompi Revolt, which Giovanni would have witnessed at the age of eighteen.

In 1385, Giovanni was promoted to a senior post requiring both skill and trust: he became the manager of the bank's Rome branch. In the same year, he was married to Piccarda Bueri, whose dowry amounted to a handsome 1,500 florins, at least ten times Giovanni's annual salary. For the time being, Giovanni seems to have invested this sum in two successful wool workshops in Florence.

By 1397 he was able to take over the Rome branch from his boss Vieri, who was retiring. According to custom, the new owner was liable for the bank's debts as well as its assets. The Rome branch of Vieri's bank had, like many others, competed to gain the accounts of the rich cardinals residing in the city. The extravagant living of these cardinals meant that many of them ran up debts they could not repay. In this instance, Giovanni was left holding debts of 860 florins when he took over. Yet he must have prospered in his commercial activities in the wool trade during this immediate period, for it was in the October of that same year that he opened his own bank in Florence with an initial capital of 10,000 florins. Despite his setback in Rome, he himself was able to put up a controlling share of 5,500 florins in the new Florence bank, with two smaller shares being taken by partners who seem to have been related to the Medici by marriage.

From the outset, Giovanni proved a cautious banker, anxious to consolidate rather than indulge in the risks he had been encouraged to

---

* For a family tree identifying the different members of the Medici family, see p. xi.

take on wholesale by his former employer Vieri, in the form of the extravagant cardinals' accounts.

Previous Florentine bankers had introduced considerable advances in the practice of finance. These included such innovations as double-entry bookkeeping, which was widely practised long before Luca Pacioli set down his 'explanation' of how this accounting method worked, in his *Summa* of 1494. Other financial instruments included bills of exchange, letters of credit and so forth.

Many bankers were innovative, introducing their own novel methods, or variations on the above practices. Giovanni di Bicci was very much the opposite. He insisted upon being cautious, and relying upon tried and trusted methods. The memory of previous bank crashes remained ever-present in his mind. However, besides its normal account books, the Medici bank did also keep its own *libro segreto* (a confidential ledger) – a widespread practice among banks of the period. De Roover describes how these *libri segreti* 'contained the partners' accounts concerning investments and withdrawals, the accounts for operating results, the accounts of capital allocated to branches, and sometimes the salary accounts of the factors and clerks'. In other words, they revealed the underlying structure of the bank, as well as the profits (or losses) accruing to its various foreign branches.

The Medici bank, like all others, also had its own rules. For instance, the manager of the new Venice branch of the bank, one Neri di Cipriani Tornaquinci, was instructed that under no circumstances was he to make any loans to Germans or Poles. When he disobeyed this instruction, loaning cash to a German merchant, he learned the reason for his boss's edict. The merchant immediately left Venice and crossed the Alps to Germany, from whence there was no hope of recovering the loan. Despite the efficient accounting methods of the Medici bank, Tornaquinci was able to conceal this hole in his accounts by quickly and quietly borrowing money at a heavy 8 per cent. As his working capital began to shrink, Tornaquinci began inserting into his books entries of non-existent profits. It took three years before the malfeasance was uncovered back in Florence, by which time the bad debts had risen to a staggering 13,403 florins, with unpaid salaries amounting to a further 683 florins. Tornaquinci was prosecuted in Florence, where the authorities ordered the confiscation of his family home in the city as well as a farm he owned in the *contado*.

Tornaquinci fled Florence and headed across the Alps to search for his debtor. Eventually, he managed to track the merchant down in Cracow, where he succeeded in recouping some of the money he was owed. But this he kept for himself. Sometime later, Giovanni di Bicci learned that Tornaquinci had tried to make enough to pay off all his debts, but in doing so had lost everything. On hearing of this, Giovanni took compassion on Tornaquinci and sent him thirty-six florins – enough for him to live on for a year. Despite all his financial caution, it seems that money was not everything for Giovanni di Bicci.

Such a story illustrates the day-to-day hazards of banking during this era. Yet despite such setbacks, Giovanni and the Medici bank soon began to make handsome profits – and the fortunes of Florence and those of Giovanni seem to have run hand in hand during these years. By now the *contado* had begun to expand far into the Tuscan hinterland, with Volterra and Pistoia both becoming Florentine cities. Florence could afford to buy Prato from the protection of the Queen of Naples as early as 1351; then in 1384, Arezzo came under Florentine rule. By 1406, Florence had finally taken control of its ancient rival, the city of Pisa, which gave Florentine trade unfettered access to the sea, with no possibility of Pisa peremptorily imposing import or export dues. Overseas trade was further enhanced when the city bought the port city of Livorno from the Genoese in 1421.

During this period the wealthy Albizzi family and their allies had effectively taken over the running of Florence. Gifts had bought friends; strategic marriages had extended influence; and their nominees now occupied senior posts in the committees which administered the city. At elections they ensured that their friends were rewarded with seats on the ruling *signoria*, and the *golfaloniere* was invariably an Albizzi supporter. With such power, they were also able to ensure that their enemies caused them as little trouble as possible. Dissidents or opponents were liable to be bankrupted by a heavy *estimo* of their taxable goods, or sent into exile. Most of the citizens were willing to tolerate such rule, as long as prosperity prevailed.

Meanwhile, the Medici bank began benefitting from the new overseas trade links, opening branches or establishing agents as far afield as Bruges and even London (for the wool trade), in Lyon and Avignon (for the big trade fairs), in Ancona (for enabling the shipment of fine Florentine cloth to the Levant), and in Naples and Gaeta for western Mediterranean trade – which soon prospered to such an extent that a further branch was opened in Barcelona.

Giovanni di Bicci was becoming a very rich man. Yet he knew better than to advertise the fact, and continued to live in an unostentatious fashion. Judging from the way he conducted himself in public, he had no aspirations whatsoever for political power. He wanted no quarrel with the Albizzi, nor with any of the other powerful families such as the Uzzano. Giovanni and his family lived in a modest house overlooking the cathedral square, and he would be seen every day emerging from his home for the three-hundred-yard walk down through the commercial heart of the city, past the bustling stalls and shops of the Mercato Vecchio (today the Piazza della Repubblica) to the Medici bank's main office on the Via Porta Rossa. The leaders of the important families never ventured out without a retinue to clear their way through the streets, as well as for protection; Giovanni, on the other hand, would make his way through the crowds accompanied only by his personal servant. The people respected him, and he knew he would come to no harm: the *popolo* had not forgotten the part Salvestro de' Medici had played in the Ciompi Revolt. The Medici family may have been publicly disgraced for this, but they still retained the covert respect of the common people. The Uzzano family in particular remained aware of this, and thwarted any attempt to vote a member of the Medici family into public office.

Yet, in the end, old suspicions were not enough to prevent a worthy citizen such as Giovanni di Bicci from being appointed to a position of authority. In 1401, Giovanni was chosen as one of the committee tasked with selecting an artist to create new bronze doors for the Baptistery. This was the occasion when Brunelleschi arrogantly refused to work alongside

Ghiberti, the joint winner. Later, Giovanni would be on the committee that chose Brunelleschi to build the Ospedale degli Innocenti. This time he also played a large role in financing the entire operation. During the course of this work, the canny old banker and the prickly artist struck up a surprising friendship. Both were meticulous in their work, and they appeared to develop a mutual admiration for each other's disparate expertise. As an orphanage, the Ospedale was also much admired by the *popolo*.

With a suitable show of reluctance, Giovanni allowed himself to be voted onto the *signoria* three times during these years. And in 1421 he received the final accolade of being voted *gonfaloniere,* serving two months as the city's nominal 'ruler'. This act could be said to have marked the final pardoning of the Medici family after their years of public disgrace following the Ciompi Revolt.

Giovanni gave no sign of trying to attain any lasting power in the city, even advising his son Cosimo that he should always be seen going to his place of business, and never to the Palazzo della Signoria, the seat of government. That is, he should at all costs avoid getting involved in local politics: those who hung around in front of the *palazzo* were gossips, political schemers, and people who wished to influence the meetings of the *signoria*.

However, it was during this very period that Giovanni revealed the full scope of his ambitions. He may have avoided taking any political power in Florence, but he would do so in the field of international politics and commerce. This required an act which appeared to be completely contrary to his public and professional character.

Giovanni's years of running an international bank had led him to a deep understanding of the larger world of Italian and European politics. He well understood that many senior churchmen had grown tired of the Great Schism that had resulted in two separate popes, one in Avignon and one in Rome. In 1414, an ecumenical council was summoned to resolve the issue between the two reigning popes: Gregory XII (Rome) and Benedict XIII (Avignon). This council was to be held in the German lakeside city of Constance under the auspices of King Sigismund of Hungary and Germany (who would later become Holy Roman Emperor).

However, by now a third claimant to the papacy had emerged. This was a maverick Neapolitan by the name of Baldassare Cossa. After an early life as a pirate, he had obtained a doctorate in law at the University of Bologna. He had then bought himself the position of papal legate, a senior diplomatic post carrying the rank of cardinal. By means of influence garnered from this post, he succeeded in persuading the religious authorities in France, England and Bohemia to let him be declared Pope John XXIII at Pisa. This newly declared pope remained a tough character, not without guile and charm, who refused to let high office in the Church interfere with his customary licentious behaviour.

Some years previously, Cardinal Cossa had managed to persuade the habitually cautious Giovanni di Bicci to become his banker. Giovanni may well have been privy to Cardinal Cossa's papal ambitions, and been persuaded that the prospect of gaining the lucrative papal account outweighed the risks involved. In which case, Giovanni was in for a shock. King Ladislas of Naples was outraged at the claim by the new pope, and launched a military campaign against him. John XXIII was soon forced to sign an expensive peace treaty, promising King Ladislas no less than 95,000 florins. He found himself bereft of funds and turned to his banker for a loan. After some thought, Giovanni di Bicci handed over the money. This was an enormous sum: the equivalent of 20 per cent of the profits accruing to the Medici bank's successful Rome branch over the previous twenty years. As security against this loan, John XXIII entrusted Giovanni with a jewel-encrusted mitre and a quantity of gold plate which he had somehow succeeded in removing from the papal treasury.

John XXIII was duly summoned to the Council of Constance, along with the two other claimants, Gregory XII and Benedict XIII. Such was the politicking and behind-the-scenes dealing at this ecumenical council that it would last no less than four years (1414–18). Pope John XXIII eventually found himself politically outmanoeuvred, and was put on trial. According to Edward Gibbon: 'The more scandalous charges were suppressed; the vicar of Christ was accused only of piracy, rape, sodomy, murder and incest.' Whereupon he was deposed and imprisoned by King Sigismund, who demanded 35,000 florins for his release. To widespread astonishment, the former pope managed to convince Giovanni di Bicci to pay this amount. There is no doubt that he was a persuasive rogue, but how had he induced the astute banker to part once again with such a large sum? It looked as if Giovanni's decision to enter international politics had been a colossal blunder.

Yet Giovanni had not built up one of the largest banks in Europe without also gaining insight into how the intertwined worlds of finance and power actually worked. By rescuing his candidate for the papacy, Giovanni was demonstrating the fact that when you were backed by the Medici bank it would never let you down, no matter the circumstances. This showed that not only was the Medici bank a trustworthy institution, but that it was also one with vast resources at its disposal. The bank's ability to raise such money, and at surprisingly short notice, was soon the talk of Europe.

The grateful former pope travelled from his prison cell directly to Florence, where he was put up by his only remaining friend, Giovanni di Bicci. John XXIII may have been a disgraced figure, but he had nonetheless once been a pope. The social standing of the Medici family rose considerably as word spread of their illustrious guest.

Back in Germany, the Council of Constance declared the other two claimants to the papacy similarly dismissed. In place of all three popes, an entirely new candidate emerged in the form of Cardinal Otto Colonna, scion of one of Rome's oldest and most distinguished families. Colonna was duly elected, and became Pope Martin V. He immediately set out to take up residence in Rome, but was forced to stop over in Florence, as the successor to King Ladislas of Naples, Queen Joanna II, could not be persuaded to vacate the Holy City, to which she now had no justifiable claim.

Giovanni di Bicci decided to take advantage of this stroke of fortune, and soon engineered a reconciliation between Martin V and the previous papal claimant, John XXIII, who was now ailing and on the point of death. Martin V expressed his extreme gratitude to Giovanni, whose services ensured that the new pope was now to all intents and purposes the first undisputed occupant of St Peter's throne since the Avignon papacy had begun in 1309.

It would take but a few years before Martin V expressed his gratitude in more concrete form. In 1424, after so many twists of fate, Giovanni di Bicci finally achieved his aim when the Medici were appointed as papal bankers. Not only was he running the most lucrative and extensive banking network in Christendom, but he could take on as many accounts of cardinals and senior members of the Church in Rome as he wished. And now that he was papal banker, he would no longer have to suffer the worry and risk which had so dogged his earliest years at the bank in Rome, working for his older cousin Vieri. Anyone who ran up debts and defaulted on their account with the pope's banker was automatically liable to be excommunicated.

By now, Giovanni was well into his sixties. In an era when life expectancy in Italy was around forty for the middle and upper classes, and just twenty-five for the lower classes, this made him an old man. He appears to have begun feeling his age around a decade or so previously, for it was then that the day-to-day running of the bank was passed on to Cosimo de' Medici, his oldest son. Cosimo had quickly proved his abilities, and by the time he was just twenty-five Giovanni had sufficient confidence in him to let him travel to the Council of Constance and do his best to sort out the difficulties posed by the ex-pope John XXIII and his antics. Giovanni would have given strict instructions, but the on-the-spot decisions were made by the able young Cosimo.

With Cosimo in charge of the bank, this gave Giovanni the opportunity to indulge in his new pastime. His service on the committees to select the candidates for the Baptistery doors and the Ospedale degli Innocenti had awoken in him a wish to become a benefactor of the city which had at last recognized the Medici once more as a worthy family. Giovanni's friendship with Brunelleschi flourished. It is surely no accident that in 1421, the year during which Giovanni served as *gonfaloniere*, Brunelleschi was granted by the authorities of Florence what is now considered to be one of the city's first patents. This was for the much-mocked paddle boat, *Il Badalone*, which Brunelleschi invented for transporting marble and stonework upstream along the Arno to Florence. This contraption was cited by a contemporary as being able to 'bring in any merchandise and load on the river Arno etc for less money than usual, and with several other benefits'. According to the modern technological historian Frank D. Prager: 'In cultural and political terms, the grant of the patent was part of Brunelleschi's attempt to operate as a creative and commercial individual outside the constraints of the guilds and their monopolies.'

The introduction of the idea of a patent would in time prove another significant step forward attributable to the Renaissance. The guilds of the medieval era may have provided a vital service in maintaining the standards and business practices of their various skills and professions, but they also operated as a closed shop. If you were not a member of a city guild, you could not practise that particular trade or expertise within the city. The granting of a patent to Brunelleschi for his paddle boat marked a crucial breach in this monopolistic state of affairs. As the guilds began to lose their grip, this paved the way for a new spirit of enterprise. From now on, there would be more opportunities for creative entrepreneurship.

The Renaissance extended far beyond a new self-realization in the fields of the arts and the sciences; its innovative spirit also extended into the commercial sector, including overseas commerce. Now that the coastal cities of Pisa and Livorno were operating as free ports for Florentine trade, with galleys travelling the Mediterranean and across the Bay of Biscay to Bruges, a new method was introduced to finance these expeditions – borrowed directly from the Venetian model, used to finance its eastern Mediterranean trade. Nonetheless, its introduction to Florence, Pisa and Genoa would revolutionize the European maritime trade between Italy and Flanders.

The financing of a galley travelling on such a trading expedition required not only the purchase (or hiring) of the galley itself, but also the purchase of goods for export, as well as monies for the goods (such as wool) to be carried on the return trip. Then there was the cost of victualling for the long journey, payment for the crew, and so forth. Such was the cost of these commercial expeditions that they often required financing by several different 'backers', each of whom would purchase a 'share' in the expedition. These are recognizable predecessors of the merchant venturers, who would come into their own in the ensuing centuries. A century later the English would be founding the Muscovy Company, then would come the Dutch East Indies Company, the East India Company of London and the like. All of these were chartered 'joint stock' companies, where shareholders purchased a portion of company stock. The value of the stock could go up or down, dependent upon the perception of the risk or profit involved in such an enterprise.

The East India companies are widely regarded as the first joint-stock companies. However, a century prior to their founding, such practices were already commonplace amongst the Italian traders and those of Flanders. Such stocks were initially bought and sold at the bourse which had been established in Bruges, with similar institutions soon operating in Venice and Genoa. As Genoese and Florentine galleys began arriving regularly in Bruges, so the market in stocks and shares on these exchanges began to emerge as a major financial activity.

Sophisticated financing, stocks and shares, exchanges, the transfer of capital across the continent – all the foundations of modern capitalism as we know it were now being laid down. The Renaissance is not usually seen in the light of such activities, yet they were undeniably a part of the transformation of humanity which had begun to take place – first in Florence, then all over Italy, and finally spreading to northern Europe and beyond. And the profits from these commercial activities were what provided the finances to pay for the Renaissance.

Although Giovanni di Bicci played no part in the invention of the new financial structures coming into play, there is no doubt that he was fully versed in their operation. Indeed, the Medici bank would refine much of this expertise to their own advantage. Giovanni maintained a tight control over the bank and its far-flung branches. However, he was aware that a sudden drain of money (or even bankruptcy) involving one branch could easily unbalance the finance of the entire bank. This could be due to incompetent, or even dishonest, management – even though Giovanni selected and trained up his managers with scrupulous care. But bankruptcy could also result from a change in Florentine political relations with another city-state or country. Consequently, Giovanni made each bank a separate company.

Although this action safeguarded the bank as a whole, it gave branch managers a degree of autonomy – strengthened by the fact that managers were given a personal share in their branch, though the majority holding invariably remained in Medici hands. Thus what had previously been a list of guidance was now written down as a formal set of rules: never loan more than 300 florins to a cardinal; no loans to local rulers who could renege on debt within their own realm; similarly with barons, who could be 'a law unto themselves'; no business whatsoever with Germans; and so forth.

Paradoxically, Giovanni became an increasingly generous patron in his old age. In 1419 he commissioned his friend Brunelleschi to rebuild the ancient church of San Lorenzo, which was a short walk from his house overlooking the Piazza del Duomo. This was a major operation, and would inspire some characteristic work by Brunelleschi that would be completed after his death by his friend and biographer Manetti. The rows of fine pillars supporting arches either side of the nave echo Brunelleschi's classical Renaissance pillars in the Ospedale degli Innocenti. In its crumbling, eleventh-century incarnation, the church of San Lorenzo had been the parish church of the Medici. In time, the newly rising Basilica di San Lorenzo would increasingly be recognized as the 'Medici Church'.

By the late 1420s, Giovanni was becoming increasingly infirm. He was now one of the richest men in Florence. His 1427 tax bill was 397 florins, a sum only exceeded by Palla di Strozzi – head of the distinguished ancient family that supplemented its income from the family bank with the wool trade and widespread agricultural holdings – who paid 507 florins.

By 20 February 1429, Giovanni di Bicci knew that he was dying and summoned his immediate family to his bedside. According to the contemporary local historian Giovanni Cavalcanti, he then proceeded to deliver a lengthy speech, which was especially aimed at his forty-year-old son Cosimo and Cosimo's younger brother, Lorenzo, who together ran the Medici bank and would succeed him as the senior members of the

Medici family. It is unlikely that this speech was quite as long as the two pages or so meticulously recorded by Cavalcanti. However, these would seem to catch the gist of what Giovanni passed on to his sons that day, along with the bulk of what he had impressed upon them since they had come of age and entered the family business. The following are the salient points he made:

> I leave you in possession of the great wealth which my good fortune has bestowed upon me, and which your good mother and my own hard work has enabled me to preserve. I leave you with a larger business than any other merchant in the Tuscan land, and in the enjoyment of the esteem of every good citizen and of the great mass of the populace, who have ever turned to our family as to their guiding star... be charitable to the poor, kindly and gracious to the miserable, lending yourself with all your might to assist them in their adversity. Never strive against the will of the people, unless they advocate a baneful project... Be chary of frequenting the [Palazzo della Signoria]; rather wait to be summoned, and then be obedient, and be not puffed up with pride at receiving so many votes.

In that latter sentence, he is indicating how a Medici should behave if voted to serve on the *signoria* itself.

Giovanni went on to advise them against becoming engaged in litigation, 'or any attempt to influence justice, for whoso impedes justice will perish by justice'. His last piece of advice was perhaps his most important, as well as being most in keeping with his character: 'Be careful not to attract public attention.'

It is difficult to overstress the importance of what Giovanni passed on to his sons. Even when Cosimo was eventually obliged to disobey this Medici credo, he would do his best to remain true to its guiding spirit.

Giovanni di Bicci de' Medici would die at the age of sixty-nine, shortly after delivering a version of this speech. (Immediately after finishing it, according to Cavalcanti, who writes: 'Saying this, he passed away from this life.') Despite Giovanni's paternal advice about the Medici keeping a low profile, his son Cosimo was unable to prevent his father's funeral from becoming a very public event. On the day of the funeral, all the city dignitaries turned up at the Medici residence. Consequently, his coffin was followed by a formidable procession – consisting of the foreign ambassadors to Florence, the *gonfaloniere* himself, and the heads of all the leading city guilds, as well as all who laid claim to the name Medici. The streets were lined with onlookers, whose unfeigned respect indicated the widespread regard felt for him amongst the *popolo*.

After Giovanni's death his estate was assessed at almost 180,000 florins. De Roover's opinion on this matter is of some interest: 'This figure is plausible, if not entirely accurate.' Giovanni had refused to make a testament and de Roover suggests: 'Perhaps this decision has something to do with the Church's usury doctrine. By ordering extensive restitution in a testament, he would have denounced himself as a usurer and might have caused considerable trouble for his heirs.'

Giovanni appears to have squared his conscience on the question of usury. He may have considered the funding of Church projects, such as the rebuilding of San Lorenzo, sufficient restitution to absolve his soul. As we shall see, his able son Cosimo would build on Giovanni's foundations, considerably increasing the power and wealth of the Medici. On the other hand, the more sophisticated Cosimo would not find it in himself to assuage his guilt over the sin of usury quite so easily. This would have immense consequences for both the Republic of Florence and the direction taken by the Renaissance.

CHAPTER 9

THE RENAISSANCE
SPREADS ITS WINGS

W E NOW COME TO three very disparate Florentines whose lives expanded the possibilities of the new Renaissance beyond its previous boundaries.

Leon Battista Alberti was born in Genoa in 1404. His father, Lorenzo, was a member of the well-known Florentine Alberti family, whose bank had attempted to take advantage of the collapse of the Bardi, Peruzzi and Acciaiuoli banks in the mid-1340s. However, the family soon fell from favour amongst the leading Florentine families, on account of their political meddling. As a result, Lorenzo ended up in exile in Genoa, home of one of the more prosperous branches of the family bank.

Leon Battista Alberti is best remembered for his polymathic learning, which would lead to him being regarded as the first 'Renaissance man'. In many ways he prefigures the most archetypal Renaissance man of them all, namely Leonardo da Vinci, who would be born almost half a century later. With hindsight it can be seen that these two giants of their time shared certain traits. Both were born illegitimate; and both appear to have been motivated by an insatiable need to learn. They shared a belief in science, a respect for mathematics, and were driven by an inner restlessness which they were never quite able to satisfy. For Alberti, like Leonardo, 'painting is science'. But beyond this point, their interests tended to diverge. To give a broad generalization: where Leonardo was drawn to the empirical and the practical, Alberti favoured a more theoretical approach.

Despite being exiled, Alberti's father was wealthy, and he is likely to have owned, or had access to, a well-stocked library. Either way, Alberti is known to have been a precocious child. As Vasari expresses it, in his short 'Life of Alberti': 'Artists who are strongly drawn to reading will gain the most benefit from their knowledge. This is especially the case with painters, sculptors and architects. Ideas derived from such studies will inspire their imagination.' Yet first and foremost there is a prerequisite for well-practised talent which must balance this intellect – as only then can the artist flourish. As Vasari continues:

When theory and practice are well-wedded they will produce fruitful art – for skill is thus enabled by learning, which draws it to perfection. Advice set down by practised and knowledgeable artists will always improve the skills of any, no matter their talent, who simply rely upon the practical side of their work.

This was certainly the case with Alberti. Vasari's words also reveal how closely the Renaissance concept of art was imbued with the idea of learning.

While Alberti was still a child, his father had fled Genoa to escape an outbreak of the plague, taking Alberti and his siblings with him. Together they travelled across northern Italy to Genoa's main rival as a seaport, Venice. Here Alberti's father took over the largest and most successful branch of the Alberti bank. Then disaster struck. According to the French historian Bertrand Gille, Alberti's 'father died suddenly, leaving his children in the care of their uncle, who disappeared soon thereafter'. Gille speculates: 'It is possible that unscrupulous relatives liquidated the

Venice branch in order to make themselves rich at the orphans' expense.' All this speaks of an unsettled later childhood spent amidst a fraught, unloving family atmosphere.

Whatever took place, the teenage Alberti was still able to pursue his studies at the nearby University of Padua. By 1421, at the age of seventeen, he had transferred to the University of Bologna to study law. At this point: 'Overwork caused him to fall ill and he had to interrupt his studies; nevertheless he received a doctorate in canon law.' Despite his illness, Alberti's insatiable thirst for knowledge led him to study mathematics and the sciences, especially physics. He was also the first to make a detailed study of *De Architectura* by Vitruvius, the finest Ancient Roman architect and engineer, who reached his peak during the first century BC. Vitruvius's work would make an indelible impression on the young Alberti, inspiring him to dreams of greatness in this field.

All this speaks of conflicted motives. The study of canon law was usually a prelude to entering the Church, or at least taking minor orders; while the study of science and architecture indicates that Alberti had other intentions. His illness may well have been caused by inner conflict as much as by overwork or family troubles. Alberti had a Renaissance mind, yet the science he was studying was 'still close to the expiring Middle Ages'. In other words, his scientific studies would have involved accepting the authority of Aristotle, whose teachings dated from well over one and a half millennia previously.

Notwithstanding the brilliance of Aristotle's investigative mind, it was becoming increasingly evident that many of his findings – and the subsequent interpretations of these findings – no longer matched with reality. For instance, Aristotle believed in the notion of spontaneous generation: sea creatures, such as scallops, formed spontaneously in sand; similarly maggots appeared spontaneously in rotting meat. Aristotle's teachings had over the years been adopted by the Church, thus becoming theological truth. In contrast with such learning, by reference to 'authority' (such as Aristotle or the Church) the Renaissance mind was becoming more inclined to question reality, trying to discover for itself how the world worked. Yet Aristotle's teachings were still seen as sacrosanct. To deny them was heresy, which risked excommunication, or worse. The prospect of conflict was inevitable, and such contradictions were already becoming apparent in Alberti's mind.

Despite Alberti's difficulties through 'overwork', he still presented a remarkable figure. His precociousness had not been limited to his mind; he also became known for his physical exploits. And as with the child, so with the man. The great nineteenth-century Swiss Renaissance scholar Jacob Burckhardt* describes how 'of various gymnastic feats and exercises we read with astonishment how, with his feet together, he could spring over a man's head; how, in the cathedral, he threw a coin in the air till it was heard to ring against the distant roof'. Likewise, Alberti was famed for his ability to ride 'the wildest horses'. Burckhardt asserts: 'In three things he desired to appear faultless to others, in walking, in riding and in speaking.' Burckhardt also notes that Alberti claimed to be a self-taught musician, whose compositions 'were admired by professional judges' – though doubt has been cast on this last assertion.

From such evidence, it would appear that Alberti was not only omniv-orous in his pursuit of learning, but also highly competitive. However, unlike most such driven figures, he was not devoid of humour or an interest in the ordinary things in life. He wrote a eulogy for his pet dog, was not above questioning cobblers 'about the secrets and peculiarities of their craft', and was renowned for his 'humorous dinner-speeches'. The person who wrote 'A man can do all things if he but wills them' and 'Nothing is at the same time both new and perfect' could also tell jokes which remind one of Boccaccio (e.g. A travelling merchant brags to his companion, 'I can screw around as much as I want, my wife never objects.' To which his companion replies: 'Same as me, because I know my wife is doing the same.').

A self-portrait in relief on a bronze medallion is generally considered to be the best likeness we have of Alberti. According to the National

---

* Burckhardt was one of the first historians to use the term 'Renaissance' in its modern sense, thus conceptualizing this period as a distinct age in European historical development.

Gallery of Art in Washington, where the medallion is now on display, it is 'one of the earliest, if not the earliest, of Renaissance portrait medals, and also the first independent self-portrait by a Renaissance artist and the first to show the artist dressed in the antique style'. Some have remarked on the shape of Alberti's head in this portrait, as well as his close-cropped curly hair, suggesting that his unknown mother may have been an African slave. Genoa is known to have had trading outposts in North Africa during this period, and also to have engaged in the slave trade, making Alberti's African heritage at least a possibility. Such recondite speculations are encouraged by the fact that Alberti's motto was '*Quid tum?*' (So what?), which was taken from the Ancient Roman poet Virgil's '*Quid tum, si fuscus Amyntas?*' ('So what, if Amyntas is dark?').*

Sometime during the late 1420s, the banishment of the Alberti family from Florence was revoked. A few years later, Alberti himself travelled to the city. Here he initially met with a mixed reception. Having been educated in the cities of northern Italy, he spoke and wrote in vernacular Latin, rather than the Tuscan dialect which had been promoted by Dante. The resident literati disapproved. Despite his broad learning, it would take Alberti some time before he felt fully at ease with Tuscan. On the other hand, he formed a close friendship with the middle-aged Brunelleschi, who shared his polymathic interests and eclectic enthusiasms. It was during these years that Brunelleschi was studying Fibonacci's mathematics, as well as inventing a number of the ingenious machines used to hoist and position the stones for his dome.

Brunelleschi proved in many ways an inspiration for Alberti, and may well have been instrumental in gaining the young man his first architectural commissions. But Alberti had already formed his own ideas, and proved adept at putting these into practice. By 1446 he had secured a commission from the ancient and distinguished Ruccellai family, which had made its fortune in both the wool trade and banking. Alberti was commissioned to design a suitably impressive *palazzo* for the family, and

---

* Fuscus can also mean 'black' or 'swarthy'.

this would prove to be his first masterpiece, with an imposing facade in revived classical style – the first of its kind in the city.

Alberti was consequently employed by the Ruccellai family to design the impressive marble facade which to this day adorns the Santa Maria Novella, one of the principal churches in Florence and the main place of worship for the Dominican Order. Alberti's restoration work on the facade of this church would transform Renaissance architecture. To paraphrase the authoritative *Gardner's Art Through the Ages*, Alberti attempted to bring the ideals of humanist architecture, proportion and classically inspired detailing to bear on the design, while also creating harmony with the already-existing medieval part of the facade. In the interior, this solution to the technical problem of visually linking the levels of the central nave and the lower aisles would become a standard feature for centuries to come.

Shortly after completing the Palazzo Ruccellai, Alberti travelled to Rome. Here, according to Vasari, the reigning pope Nicholas V 'had been turning the city upside down with all his building projects'. The pope had evidently been briefed on the achievements of Alberti, and was no less impressed by the charismatic Alberti in person. Nicholas V soon befriended him, taking his advice on architectural matters. Alberti was even induced to take up an official position in the Church, and entered minor holy orders in order to do so. This meant that he was given something of a free rein in restoring many of Rome's ancient ruins. The most prominent amongst these projects was the renovation of the old Aqua Virgo, which became known as the Acqua Vergine. This aqueduct once again, for the first time in well over a millennium, would transport fresh drinking water into the city, terminating at a central fountain where three roads (*tre vie*) met: the Trevi Fountain.

At the same time as he was renovating these ancient structures, Alberti also followed the advice and example of his Florentine friend Brunelleschi, spending much time walking amongst the ruins and learning from them the secrets of Ancient Roman architecture. Characteristically, this led Alberti to write a treatise on architecture, *De Re Aedificatoria* (On the Art of Building). This was the first of its kind during the Renaissance, and is generally regarded as the finest since Vitruvius, upon whose work it is in part based. Like Vitruvius, Alberti demonstrated an expert eye for aesthetic proportions, yet he combined this with a highly original gift for practical ingenuity.

As early as 1435, Alberti had written *De Pictura*, a highly informed treatise on the art of painting, which included analyses of classical optics, perspective, and elements of geometric proportion. However, in this case, Alberti's accomplished and original theoretical knowledge was not matched by practical expertise. According to Vasari: 'In painting Alberti achieved nothing of any great importance or beauty. The very few paintings of his that are extant are far from perfect, but this is not surprising since he devoted himself more to his studies than to draughtsmanship.'

This judgement would appear to be fair. Indeed, the lack of surviving evidence with regard to Alberti's painting – as well as the fact that he did not himself actually build many of the architectural works constructed according to his designs – has taken its toll on Alberti's reputation. Consequently, he has come to be regarded by many as the forgotten Renaissance man, overshadowed almost to the point of invisibility by his illustrious successor Leonardo. But this would appear surprising when one sees the list of Alberti's diverse technical achievements. According to Gille: 'He spoke of balances, clocks, sundials, pulleys, watermills and windmills, and canal locks. He developed topographical instruments and envisaged the odometer and the "sulcometer", which measured distances covered by ships. He studied the methods of sounding in deep waters.' To these can be added his pioneering work on maps and astronomy, both of which pointed a way to the future in these fields. And then there is his work on cryptography, which marked the first real advance in this sphere since the time of Julius Caesar.

Several sources also believe that it was Alberti who wrote the famous but mysterious work known as *Hypnerotomachia Poliphili*, an anonymous narrative which would eventually be read by scholars throughout Renaissance Europe. The title of this work derives from the Greek words *hypnos* (sleep), *eros* (love) and *mache* (strife), and may be translated as 'The Strife of Love in a Dream of Poliphilo'. *Hypnerotomachia Poliphili* was first published in Venice in 1499, and is one of the best-known exemplars of an incunable, the word given to printed works that appeared before 1501. It is a fantastical dreamlike novel written in a curiously imaginative version of vernacular Latin, which includes many ingenious neologisms – as well as turns of phrase in the Venetian and the Tuscan dialects. To make matters even more bizarre, this strange prose is also studded with Hebrew and Arabic words, as well as some fake Egyptian hieroglyphs lifted from medieval sources. Its pages are illustrated by a large number of stylistically unexceptional yet nonetheless inventive woodcuts depicting events described in the text.

As for the text itself, this contains a story in the tradition of the courtly romance, and is set in the year 1467. The hero, Poliphilo (meaning 'lover of many things'), wanders through a dream world in search of his love Polia (literally, 'many things'). The opening passage contains distinct echoes of the beginning of Dante's *Divine Comedy*:

> At length my ignorant sleepes, brought me into a thick wood, whereinto being a pritty way entred, I could not tell how to get out of it. Wherevpon, a soddaine feare inuaded my hart, and diffused it selfe into euery ioynt, so that my couler began to waxe pale, and the rather by reason that I was alone, and vnarmed, and could not finde any track or path, eyther to direct me forward, or lead me back againe. But a darke wood of thicke bushes, sharpe thornes, tall ashes…

As Poliphilo continues through an exaggerated landscape, filled with strange symbolism and hints of allegory, he sees all manner of curious buildings and encounters dragons, wolves and maidens. The narrative eventually concludes with Poliphilo being reunited with his Polia beside the 'Fountain of Venus'.

Over the centuries, *Hypnerotomachia Poliphili* has been subjected to a wide variety of interpretations, ranging from the spiritual to the symbolic, depicting the moral and psychological advancement of its hero as he resolves the problem of his initially rejected love for Polia. A more recent interpretation by the twentieth-century Swiss psychologist Carl Jung sees its dreamlike images as prefiguring Jung's own concept of 'archetypes' deriving from the 'collective unconscious'. One of the opening passages of the book itself claims that it contains 'not only knowledge, but as you will see, more secrets of nature than you will find in all the books of the ancients'.

This, and many other aspects of the work, suggests that it was written by a leading polymath during the early years of the Renaissance. Alberti would certainly fit this description. However, others who have scrutinized the original text have discovered that the first letters of the chapters of the book form an acrostic which reads (translated into English): 'Brother Francesco Colonna dearly loved Polia'. Like the book itself, this leads to further mysteries. Does this confirm that the text was written by one Francesco Colonna, or is it a secret joke suggesting that the work is a description of Brother Francesco's love for Polia? And who is this Polia?

Alberti, of course, was close to Nicholas V, who was a member of the aristocratic Colonna family. At this time there were several Francesco Colonnas, most notably a Dominican monk of that name who lived in Venice and even preached at St Mark's. He is known to have written an unpublished work called the 'Dream of Delfilo', whose title bears more than a passing resemblance to the 'Dream of Poliphilo'.

Whether or not Alberti wrote *Hypnerotomachia Poliphili*, this work certainly illustrates how the Renaissance imagination was beginning to extend itself. Here, possibly for the first time in human history, was a phantasmagorical epic which expressed a unique range of imagery, happenings, metaphors and so forth, rising as if directly from the unconscious mind. Alberti, or Colonna, would lead Renaissance intellectuals throughout Europe into a polymathic realm which both informed and gave greater depth to the everyday world around them.

But what of Alberti's lasting reputation? Why is it that he remains so frequently overlooked? It is Gille who seems to pinpoint the more profound reason for our oversight concerning this early Renaissance man: 'He contributed no new principles, but seems to have had a very profound knowledge. In short, he seems to have regarded science as a means for action rather than a system of organised knowledge.'

This is all the more surprising when one considers that Alberti's finest and most influential works are mainly his theoretical ideas: his treatises, his outlines of the possibilities of his subjects and how they could be achieved. The Renaissance may have been spreading its wings, but it had not yet achieved full flight. By the time Alberti died in Rome in 1472, at the age of sixty-eight, his conclusive successor to the title of Renaissance man, Leonardo da Vinci, was just twenty years old.

Another example of how the Renaissance mind was beginning to extend itself can be seen in the life of Paolo Toscanelli. He was born in Florence in 1397, seven years before Alberti, but his lasting effect would be felt long after his death, which came ten years after that of Alberti.

Toscanelli is thought to have studied medicine, mathematics and astronomy at the University of Padua, in the Venetian Republic. By this time the university was nearly 200 years old, making it the second-oldest in Italy after Bologna, which was founded in 1088. After Bologna and Padua, universities would be founded in Naples (1224), Siena (1240), Rome (1303), Perugia (1308) and then Florence (1321). The existence of such universities throughout Italy certainly played its part in the advent of the Renaissance, despite the limited nature of the learning imparted at these establishments. Even during Toscanelli's day, the curriculum in universities throughout Europe was limited to Aristotelian thought and scholasticism (largely a blend of medieval theology and the 'theologically correct' interpretation of Aristotle's ideas).

While Toscanelli lived in Padua, he gained a reputation as the finest mathematician of his generation. At the same time, his astronomical studies led him to dabble in the current craze for the 'science' of astrology. When he returned to Florence, sometime prior to 1430, his reputation preceded him. Consequently, the *signoria* offered him the post of adviser on 'judicial astronomy' – the forecasting of coming events and their likely outcome, according to the movement of the stars in the heavens. This seems to have been a part-time post, earning him only a small stipend, for Toscanelli soon found himself a better-paid post in the Florence branch of the Medici bank.

During this period, he also became friends with Alberti and Brunelleschi. The latter friendship would result in Toscanelli putting together a scientific instrument, known as a gnomon, which can still be seen in Florence to this day.

While Brunelleschi was completing his work, Toscanelli persuaded him to incorporate a bronze plate, with a one-inch-diameter hole, beneath one of the windows of the lantern which tops the dome. When a ray of the sun passes through the small hole it falls onto a marble slab set in the cathedral floor some 300 feet below. The slab is inscribed with a meridian clock, over which passes the disc of light formed by the sun's ray. On 21 June, the summer solstice – the longest day of the year, when the sun is at its highest – the falling disc of light aligns perfectly with the disc inscribed in the marble slab, enabling the measurement of time with a precision of less than a second. This intriguing instrument remains the largest and most accurate of its kind.

Indeed, during the following century this simple but highly accurate device would be fundamental in changing a vital component of our world. Measurements taken by Toscanelli's gnomon would assist in the replacement of the Julian calendar, which had been implemented as early as 46 BC. A slight inaccuracy in this calendar resulted in the addition of three-quarters of an hour every four years. By the 1500s, the spring equinox (when the hours of day and night are equal) appeared on the Julian calendar ten days earlier than it actually took place. In 1582, Pope Gregory XIII would introduce the Gregorian calendar, which is still in use to this day. This more accurately synchronizes the calendar year with the time it actually takes the earth to orbit around the sun. Yet even the Gregorian calendar is not absolutely accurate: it accelerates by twenty-six seconds per year, meaning that by 4909 it will be a full day ahead of the solar year.

Although this calendar reformation took place at a time when the Renaissance was all but over, there is no doubt that it was a legacy of the rebirth of European culture. And measurements taken by Toscanelli's gnomon in Florence Cathedral would play their part in the change of mind required to bring about this reform.

Amongst Toscanelli's other scientific achievements was his measurement of the passage of comets through the night sky above Florence. He made precise observations of the comets that appeared in 1433, 1439, 1456, 1457 and 1472. His observations of the 1456 comet would later enable the English astronomer Edmund Halley to predict its return in 1759, whereupon it would be named Halley's Comet. Yet the achievements mentioned so far are dwarfed by Toscanelli's major contribution, which ironically would come about as a result of a giant mistake on his behalf.

As well as studying the heavens above, Toscanelli developed a deep interest in measuring the earth below. This led him into the field of cartography, which was undergoing a new surge of interest inspired by the Renaissance thirst for knowledge of all kinds. Foreign travellers passing through Florence would seek out Toscanelli, informing him of the geography of the regions through which they had passed. In this way, he built up a wide range of correspondents; and although he is known to have travelled no further afield than Padua and Rome, he soon became recognized as a leading geographer.

It is thought that Toscanelli was in attendance when a Chinese delegation arrived in Rome during 1432. As a result of information passed on by members of this visiting delegation, a number of new maps were drawn and soon began circulating. These outlined Cathay (China) and Cipangu (Japan), as well as the fabled Spice Islands which were thought to lie east of Cathay.

In 1439, the Council of Florence was held, with the aim of unifying the Catholic Western Church with the Byzantine Eastern Church, which was under threat from the Ottoman Empire. Amongst the Byzantine delegation was the Greek Orthodox philosopher Gemistos Plethon, who would do much to introduce forgotten Ancient Greek works to the West. It was he who introduced Toscanelli to the works of Strabo, the Ancient Greek geographer who had lived in Asia Minor (modern Turkey) during the first century AD, when this territory became part of the Roman

Empire. Strabo had travelled far and wide – journeying as far west as the coast of Tuscany, south through Egypt and into Ethiopia. During the last years of the first century BC he wrote *Geographica*, which gathered in encyclopedic form all the knowledge he had gained during his travels, as well as information relating to many places he had only learned about second-hand. In this way he described most of Europe, ranging from Britain through Gaul and Germania, and beyond to the northern Black Sea coast and North Africa.

Toscanelli had been persuaded by his reading of Strabo and the Ancient Greeks that the world was round. This, together with the information he had gathered from the visiting Chinese delegation, led him to realize the possibility of sailing west across the Atlantic to reach Cathay and the Spice Islands. With this in mind, he drew up a map, which he sent to one of his correspondents in Portugal. This map is now lost, but it is known to have eventually fallen into the hands of the Genoese sailor Christopher Columbus. Sometime in the 1470s Toscanelli wrote to Columbus. In this letter, he described how he had spoken with a member of the Chinese delegation to Rome:

> I had a long conversation with him on many subjects, about the magnitude of their rivers in length and breadth, and on the multitude of cities on the banks of rivers. He said that on one river there were near 200 cities with marble bridges great in length and breadth, and everywhere adorned with columns. This country is worth seeking by the Latins [i.e. Europeans], not only because great wealth may be obtained from it, gold and silver, all sorts of gems, and spices, which never reach us; but also on account of its learned men, philosophers, and expert astrologers…

Toscanelli went on to suggest that this land could be reached by sailing west across the Atlantic:

> The said voyage is not only possible, but it is true, and certain… But you cannot know this perfectly save through experience and

practice, as I have had in the form of the most copious and good and true information from distinguished men of great learning who have come from the said parts, here in the court of Rome, and from others being merchants who have had business for a long time in those parts, men of high authority.

In the light of the information he had garnered, Toscanelli drew up a map. Unfortunately, travellers' reports, as well as exaggerations arising from Marco Polo's tales of his travels, led Toscanelli to miscalculate the extent of China – assuming that it stretched 5,000 miles further east than was in fact the case.

When Toscanelli's map eventually reached Columbus, he was much encouraged by what it showed. Further encouragement came from Columbus's mistaken belief that the circumference of the globe was 25 per cent less than the true figure. Armed with this combination of erroneous 'facts', Columbus confidently approached his backers – Queen Isabella of Castile and King Ferdinand II of Aragon. The royal couple eventually agreed to finance Columbus's voyage to 'Cathay and the Spice Islands', and on 3 August 1492 Columbus set sail westwards across the Atlantic.

Some ten weeks later he made landfall on an island in the Bahamas. Reliant on the copy of Toscanelli's map that he had brought with him, as well as his own underestimation of the world's circumference, Columbus was convinced that he had reached Asia. The twentieth-century writer Isaac Asimov echoes many commentators in referring to this as 'one of the more fortunate coincidences of history'. Sadly, Toscanelli would not learn of this momentous event which he had been so instrumental in encouraging, as he had died in Florence ten years earlier.

Two of the most significant developments which took place as a result of Columbus's discovery would also be directly attributed to a Florentine. This was Amerigo Vespucci, who was born in Florence in March 1454, the third son of a local notary from an ancient noble family. Not much information is available on Amerigo's early life, but he is known to have been born in a house close to the Arno river, east of the city centre. For reasons which will become evident, he is thought to have been baptized in the local church of Ognissanti (All Saints), often known locally as San Salvatore.

Amerigo's two older brothers were sent to study at the nearby University of Pisa. Presumably because of insufficient family funds, Amerigo completed his education in Florence, where he was tutored by his uncle Giorgio Vespucci, a Dominican friar who was also a respected humanist. Another of the friar's pupils happened to be Lorenzo di Pierfrancesco de' Medici, a member of the junior branch of the Medici family and a distant cousin of Cosimo de' Medici. Amerigo joined the Medici bank as a clerk, but soon demonstrated his abilities and his loyalty. His friend Lorenzo di Pierfrancesco succeeded as head of the Medici bank in 1492, and immediately dispatched the thirty-eight-year-old Amerigo on a mission to Cádiz in Spain to investigate the local branch of the bank, whose manager appeared to have been entering into unauthorized business on his own behalf, using the bank's money.

While in Spain, Vespucci travelled from Cádiz to nearby Seville, where he made contact with the local Medici agent Giannotto Berardi. Besides handling bank matters, Berardi also acted as a shipping agent, outfitting and supplying ships sailing from southern Spanish ports. In this capacity, he had outfitted the three vessels which Columbus had taken with him on his first voyage of discovery in 1492. Vespucci almost certainly witnessed the return of Columbus in 1493.

Working with Berardi, Vespucci assisted in the outfitting of Columbus's second and third voyages, during which he further explored the islands of the Caribbean – erroneously known to this day as the West Indies, owing to Columbus's mistaken belief that he had reached islands off the coast of India. During these ensuing voyages, Columbus remained convinced that he had found a way to Asia, but the royal court in Spain was becoming increasingly disillusioned with him, owing to his failure to return laden with the treasures he had vowed to bring them from the East. During this period Vespucci certainly met and conversed with Columbus.

When Berardi died in 1495, Lorenzo di Pierfrancesco appointed Vespucci to take over the Seville agency of the Medici bank. Contact with naval life and meeting Columbus appear to have stirred some deep romantic impulse in Vespucci. He realized that he was unfulfilled: there was more to life than working as a banker and a mercantile agent, no matter how successful he might be. Despite being middle-aged, Vespucci fell in love with the sea and the idea of travel to unknown lands. From then on, he set himself to learning as much as he could about nautical life. More than knowing the details required for a ship's chandler and outfitter, he studied navigation and sought out news of distant discoveries, tales recounted by sailors returning from voyages across the ocean.

By now, Vespucci's mercantile work meant that he had established close links with the Spanish royal court. His enthusiastic knowledge of nautical life, and the latest discoveries, must have impressed the authorities. Soon he was being financed to undertake a number of voyages to the land which Columbus had discovered, in the hope that he would prove more successful in locating treasure.

It is at this point that Vespucci's life becomes somewhat blurred. We know of his voyages through letters which he wrote back to Lorenzo di Pierfrancesco de' Medici, who probably in part financed these expeditions. Vespucci also wrote to Piero Soderini, the *gonfaloniere* of Florence, a long-term friend who in youth had studied alongside him under his uncle Giorgio. However, many reputable historians claim that a number of these letters are outright forgeries. Others accept them, or suggest that they may have been 'put together' by contemporaries from original sources now lost.

The gist of the matter is that Vespucci may well have made four voyages west across the Atlantic between 1497 and 1504, but evidence for the first and last of these voyages remains disputed. However, the second and third voyages are certain. The second voyage took place between May 1499 and June 1500, under the command of the experienced Spanish sailor Alonso de Ojeda. Vespucci was appointed 'navigator' of the expedition, a responsible post which meant that he was not only the royal representative, but also in charge of mapping and of undertaking trade with any newly discovered territories. Some see this as implying that he already had experience from a previous voyage. But we will stick with what is known for certain: this alone is sensational enough.

After several weeks, the expedition reached the coast of what is now Guyana, where Vespucci became the first European to set foot on the mainland of what is now known as South America. (Columbus had only made landfall on the islands of the Caribbean at this point; meanwhile the explorer John Cabot had sailed from England and made landfall on the island of Newfoundland as early as 1497.) While sailing along the coast, Vespucci's expedition rounded a cape and entered an extensive gulf. Here in the shallows they encountered a large tribe, 'which dwelt in houses whose foundations had been built in the water like Venice'. This was duly named Venezuela (Little Venice).

Around this time, the expedition appears to have split, with Vespucci leaving Ojeda and heading south-east along the coast, in the hope of finding a route around this into the Indian Ocean. In the course of his voyage, Vespucci discovered the mouth of the Amazon at the Equator and sailed on as far as Cape St Augustine (eight degrees South), before returning home to Spain.

By now Vespucci was convinced that if he could sail further south he would be able to round a cape into the Magnus Sinus (Great Gulf) and cross this to reach the port of Cattigara, which was marked on a map by the second-century AD Alexandrian geographer Ptolemy and believed to be on or near the coast of Cathay. From here he could sail to the island of Taprobane. This was the Ancient Greek name given to Sri Lanka, tales of which had been heard as early as the fourth century BC by Alexander the Great when he reached the approaches to India.

But the Spanish authorities proved disappointed by Vespucci's findings, and were unconvinced by his reasons for a return voyage. So Vespucci turned to the Portuguese, who proved more amenable. In May 1501, Vespucci set sail west once more. This time he sailed further down the coast of South America, south of Cape St Augustine. He continued past Guanabara Bay (site of modern Rio de Janeiro) and beyond. Some claim that he continued as far south as Patagonia, but doubt has been cast on this by the fact that he makes no mention of the broad estuary now known as the Río de la Plata (location of modern Buenos Aires).

Either way, voyaging down this coast convinced Vespucci that he was not sailing along the coast of Asia towards an entrance into the Indian Ocean, but was in fact charting the coast of an entirely different land mass. In a letter which Vespucci later wrote to Lorenzo di Pierfrancesco after his return in 1502, he would assert that the land he encountered was entirely different from the world described by Ptolemy and Marco Polo, and for this reason 'we observed [it] to be a continent'. Vespucci referred to this 'continent' as Mundus Novus, the New World, making him the first to use the term. This is the major realization for which Vespucci is best remembered. However, another discovery of his would advance seafaring itself into a new era.

While making his voyages, Vespucci developed a new method of celestial navigation. This involved observing and measuring the hour of the moon's conjunction with a planet while he was in Spain, and then comparing this with the hour of its conjunction when observed in the western New World which he was exploring. This eventually enabled him to estimate the earth's circumference, coming up with a figure that was accurate to within fifty miles.

Vespucci's method would later be improved upon, with the advent of more precise chronometers and more accurate instruments for measuring the heavens. According to Vespucci's biographer Frederick J. Pohl, an 'extension of Amerigo's method then became the accepted one and continued so for more than three hundred years'. No less than the eighteenth-century British explorer Captain James Cook would declare: 'The method of lunar distance from the sun or stars is the most priceless discovery which the navigator ever could have made, and must render the memory of the first discoverer of this method immortal.'

Vespucci would return to Portugal with evidence of his sensational new findings in 1502. Five years later, in 1507, the geographer Martin Waldseemüller of Lorraine produced a world map showing the new continent (South America), suggesting that it should be named 'after its discoverer, Americus*... or let it be named America, since both Europa and Asia bear names of feminine form'. This explanation of the name 'America' has been disputed, but would seem the most plausible.

Curiously, although a Florentine and a Genoese played such a pivotal role in the discovery of South America, it is Venice whose name is lastingly commemorated in Venezuela. There is also a land named Colombia, for Christopher Columbus. Yet there is no country named Fiorenzetto or Nueva Florentina (Little Florence or New Florence). Even so, Vespucci ensured that Florence did leave its mark on the continent. The large bay which he discovered in northern Brazil he named the Bay of All Saints, in part because it was discovered on All Saints' Day, but also with the added personal reference to the Ognissanti church in Florence where he had been baptized. This is confirmed by the fact that the Florentine church was also known as San Salvatore, accounting for why the first early settlement on the edge of this bay became known as Salvador – the name of the city which now stands on this spot.

In Toscanelli and Vespucci, we can see how Florentine influence stretched to the furthest reaches of the known world. Had it not been for Toscanelli's (mistaken) map, Columbus might not have set sail on his momentous journey in 1492. And, as Pohl points out, 'Vespucci gave meaning to 1492 – the foremost meaning which 1492 has acquired.'

It was the Florentine Amerigo Vespucci who had realized that the New World was in fact a separate continent, and his was the name which would be bestowed upon it.

---

* The Latin form of Amerigo.

CHAPTER 10

MEDICI RISING

D URING THE PERIOD COVERED by the previous chapter, Florentine
politics underwent some of the most turbulent moments in its long
history. Yet in the midst of this, the Medici bank continued to flourish.

In 1429, Cosimo de' Medici had inherited the bank from his father,
Giovanni. He was now forty years old and running the richest bank in
Europe, with branches in locations ranging from Lübeck on the Baltic to
Ancona in eastern Italy. It also had agents operating in places stretching
from Portugal to the Levant. An idea of the financial might of the Medici
bank – and the size of the Medici income derived from it – can be seen in
the fact that, between 1397 and 1420, the bank made a profit of 151,820
florins, of which 113,865 florins went to the Medici. This, at a time
when the annual papal dues from churches all over western Christendom
amounted to around 300,000 florins.* Indeed, much of the profit for the
Medici bank came from facilitating the transfer of these dues to Rome
from places as far afield as Greenland and Sicily. Such transfers often

---

* At this time, a small merchant could expect to earn around fifty florins a year.

involved convoluted barter, as well as exchange between currencies. For instance, the (literally) impecunious Greenland diocese was liable to pay its dues in the form of whalebones or sealskins, which would be shipped to Bruges. Here the Medici manager would sell such goods on the open market, and then dispatch a note of credit to Rome. These transactions enabled the bank to circumvent any mention of 'interest' in its ledgers, and thus avoid committing the sin of usury.

Despite the deathbed warning given by his father, Cosimo was soon deeply involved in the machinations of Florentine politics. He realized that if he did not control the ballots for the election of the *gonfaloniere* and the ruling *signoria*, his enemies amongst the leading families were liable to seize his wealth. The prudent Giovanni di Bicci had ensured that his son married Contessina di' Bardi, thus cementing an important alliance with the Bardi clan. This, and other interlinked alliances, enabled Cosimo to use his wealth in order to influence the elections and protect the family fortune.

But a rival faction, headed by the powerful and headstrong landowner Rinaldo degli Albizzi, was now beginning to outmanoeuvre Cosimo. As a consequence of yet another unsuccessful and ruinously expensive war against neighbouring Lucca, the Florentine exchequer was all but bankrupt and in dire need of cash. Previously, such funds had mostly been raised by the *estimo*, where the wealth of a taxpayer was measured by his estimated income; or in emergencies by a one-off *prestanze* – government bonds 'voluntarily' purchased by citizens. But through Albizzi influence, the city instituted a new form of taxation called the *catasto*, which took into account the entire wealth and possessions of a citizen, rather than just his income. Each citizen was required to list all his worldly goods in a register, the accuracy of which was enforced by government inspectors, who had the power to enter a citizen's home; at the same time, informers were encouraged to assist these inspectors. Ironically, the *catasto* affected the landowning Albizzi more than the Medici, whose genuine income remained hidden within their *libri segreti*. But it soon became evident to Cosimo that the Albizzi intended to use the *catasto* to ruin him.

In order to forestall such a move, Cosimo instructed the manager of the Florence branch of the Medici bank to loan the Florentine authorities sufficient funds to service their debts and continue the orderly running of the city. Cosimo was well aware that this 'loan' would never be repaid, but it immediately turned public opinion in his favour. Yet public opinion in Florence was fickle, as Cosimo well knew. So he covertly began transferring much of the bank's funds to its Venice and Rome branches. Other assets, such as gold, were quietly hidden away in sympathetic monasteries within the city. The new Venetian pope Eugenius IV had demonstrated his friendship by continuing to employ the Medici as the official papal bankers. Cosimo knew that the Albizzi would never risk incurring the pope's wrath by having the city authorities raid any of the Church's monasteries.

By now, the Albizzi had begun to wage a war of nerves against the Medici. One morning in May 1433, Cosimo woke to discover that the doors to his residence had been daubed with blood. Although he had a reputation as a bold and skilful schemer, he was not possessed of a similar physical courage. Immediately he gathered up the family and fled the city for the safety of the Medici ancestral home in the Mugello, way out in the *contado* some twenty miles north of Florence. Here he sat out the long hot summer, biding his time.

Following the September elections, a new *golfaloniere* and *signoria* were installed in the Palazzo della Signoria. Immediately, an official messenger was dispatched to the Mugello ordering Cosimo to return to Florence and present himself before the *signoria* so that 'some important decisions can be made'.

There are two main sources for what took place next: Cosimo's not-always-reliable diary, and the similarly informed but not entirely dependable history of Florence written early in the following century by Niccolò Machiavelli. However, these important sources do concur on several salient points. Although Cosimo's friends attempted to dissuade him, on 4 September he rode back into Florence. After presenting himself at the Palazzo della Signoria, he immediately mentioned the rumours which had been relayed to him in the Mugello. According to these, the *signoria* was planning a revolution in the city, during the course of which all Medici property would be seized. According to Cosimo himself: 'When I told them what I had heard, they denied it, and told me to be of good cheer, as they hoped to leave the city in the same condition as they found it when their time was up.' Should he have any concerns, Cosimo was told to present himself at the meeting of the *signoria* in three days' time.

As soon as Cosimo left, he went straight to the Medici bank on Via Porta Rossa. Here he instructed the manager, Lippaccio de' Bardi, his wife's cousin, to take charge of the bank and all its branches, and guide them as best he could through any coming events. On 7 September 1433, Cosimo duly presented himself at the Palazzo della Signoria as instructed. He was surprised to hear that the *signoria* was already in session. The captain of the guard and his men-at-arms escorted Cosimo up the main stairs, but instead of leading him into the council chamber he was hustled up the long, dark, stone stairway which led to the top of the 300-foot tower. Here he was unceremoniously bundled into the tiny cell, known locally as the *alberghetto* (little inn).

As word spread of what had happened, the city descended into chaos. Medici followers and Albizzi groups roamed the streets, engaging in skirmishes – while the market stalls vanished, shops closed, and the rest of the population locked themselves in their houses, barring doors and windows. Cosimo might have managed to spirit away his fortune, but the Albizzi were more prepared in every other way. Rinaldo degli Albizzi summoned his son and ordered him to take control of the Piazza della Signoria, guarding against any concerted protest by Medici supporters. Looking down through the little window at the top of the tower, Cosimo watched as events unfolded far below. Unless he acted quickly, he knew that he was liable to be put to death.

When Albizzi's men finally restored order, the *gonfaloniere* and the *signoria* were prevailed upon to prosecute Cosimo for 'attempting to raise himself above the rank of an ordinary citizen'. This was considered an extremely serious charge in republican Florence. And the evidence was plain for all to see: through the Medici bank, Cosimo was amassing a vast fortune, which he intended to use in order to subvert the elections on an increasingly drastic basis. In the view put forward by the Albizzi, it was evident that Cosimo was planning to install himself as a tyrant. Rinaldo degli Albizzi did his best to browbeat the *gonfaloniere* and the *signoria* into signing Cosimo's death warrant; yet despite such pressures the *signoria* dithered, fearful of such an action, which would doubtless have had serious repercussions for all concerned.

A stalemate ensued, during which Cosimo's life hung in the balance. In fact, Cosimo had already begun taking some counter-measures, through his bribed gaoler. Several members of the *signoria* were informed that if no harm came to their prisoner, they too would be well rewarded, and the *golfaloniere* understood that Cosimo was willing to pay off the considerable debts owed by his family. Consequently, despite all the pressure and the bullying, the *signoria* would not agree to any sentence of death for the captive in the tower. Instead, Cosimo de' Medici was sentenced to exile. Skilfully avoiding any secret assassination attempt, Cosimo and his family were whisked out of Florence by a side gate in the city walls. Having eluded any pursuers, they followed the road into the mountains and across the Apennine pass. Cosimo would eventually take up residence in Venice.

The Albizzi may have gained nominal control of Florence, but they still had many enemies within the city. The *popolo minuto* remained loyal to the Medici; and although the leading families were mainly for the Albizzi, there were many powerful figures who remained sympathetic towards the Medici. This was particularly the case amongst the educated class of humanists and the flourishing artists within the city, many of them beneficiaries of Medici patronage. Indeed, it could be said that around this time the humanists and artists were beginning to attain an awareness of their common cause: a growing consciousness that a profound cultural transformation was taking place. Some sources, such as Medici historian Christopher Hibbert, even go so far as to suggest that this was when the word *Rinascimento* (Italian for 'Renaissance') was first used – though it would be many centuries before the full conceptualization and understanding of this historical process came about. Even so, such ideas were anathema to the reactionary Rinaldo degli Albizzi and his followers, who regarded humanism as an anti-Christian development bordering on heresy.

However, the Albizzi and their followers had underestimated Cosimo de' Medici, who had powerful friends, not least the Venetian pope Eugenius IV. On arrival in Venice, Cosimo took up residence in the monastery of San Giorgio Maggiore, which stood on the island at the entrance to the Grand Canal. This was where Eugenius IV had once been a monk. Cosimo quickly endeared himself to the city and its pope by using part of his fortune to commission a new library for the monastery.

As the months passed, it was becoming increasingly evident that the Albizzi were incapable of ruling over the divided city of Florence. In desperation, Rinaldo degli Albizzi hatched a scheme to overthrow the *signoria* and put an end to Florence's democratic system. Florentine democracy may have been somewhat ramshackle, and was certainly open to manipulative corruption, but the citizens themselves were inordinately proud of being part of the only democracy in Italy. Tensions further heightened amongst the populace, and the city was soon faced with the prospect of outright civil war. Albizzi fled, and word was sent inviting Cosimo to return to Florence. It was just eleven months since he had been imprisoned in the tower of the Palazzo della Signoria, in fear of his life.

As Cosimo and his entourage travelled back through Florentine territory, crowds lined the roadside to welcome him. In a spontaneous gesture, Cosimo was being greeted as the city's saviour. Within days of his arrival he had established himself as the de facto ruler of the city. But Cosimo remained mindful of his father's advice. He maintained a low profile, and paid lip service to the city's long-standing traditions. Democratic procedures continued as before, with the regular elections for the *gonfaloniere* and the *signoria*. Yet more than ever these were covertly under the control of the Medici faction and their friends. Cosimo had the pulse of the people; he knew that most citizens would tolerate firm government as long as it guaranteed peace and stability. So he acted decisively in order to achieve this.

The Albizzi and many of their leading supporters were exiled. Other powerful members of the leading families had their wings clipped by the infliction of a drastic *catasto* – not enough to ruin them, but a suffi-cient warning. Meanwhile, Cosimo himself went to great pains to show that he was not above the law; he was merely a citizen like any other. In exemplary fashion he made sure that his declared tax returns were always far and away the highest in the city. Despite this, as Raymond de Roover demonstrates in his classic *The Rise and Decline of the Medici Bank*, the public declarations of the Medici bank profits were always considerably less than the actual profits recorded in the bank's *libro segreto*. There was a limit to how far Cosimo was willing to go to become an 'ordinary citizen'.

A profound but subtle change had taken place in Florentine politics. During the following years, visiting delegations from foreign powers understood that they should first pay their respects at the Medici residence. Similarly, citizens hoping for official assurances would seek an audience with Cosimo. There was even a special hour of the day set aside for such visits and petitions. At the same time, Cosimo began receiving – and accepting – invitations from leading families to become god-father of their firstborn child and heir. This practice suited Cosimo's needs perfectly. It was unostentatious, yet ensured loyalty. Even if it was not as binding as a marriage into the family, it served a similar purpose, and could be extended over a wider range. Cosimo de' Medici was effec-tively becoming the godfather of the city, in the accepted Italian manner. As we shall see, this role would soon broaden to make the Medici godfa-thers of the Renaissance itself, both within the city and beyond.

Cosimo had always been more than just an astute banker. Under his father, Giovanni di Bicci, he had represented the Medici bank, along with his father's interests, on the international stage. It had been the young Cosimo who had been entrusted to look after the difficult antipope John XXIII at the Council of Constance, and it was his success in this role which had led to the final coup for the Medici, when Martin V appointed them as papal bankers.

Now, some fifteen years later, in 1439, Cosimo would achieve another great diplomatic coup, this time for Florence rather than just the Medici bank. The previous year, a delegation had set out from Constantinople to attend the ecumenical council being held in Ferrara. By this time,

Constantinople stood under increasing threat from the Ottoman Turks, who had begun extending their territory through Anatolia and the Balkans. The Byzantine emperor John VIII Palaeologus had appealed to Pope Eugenius IV for aid 'in the name of Christ'. The pope had responded by suggesting a reconciliation between the Eastern Orthodox and the Western Catholic Churches, and the ecumenical council in Ferrara was intended to iron out any doctrinal difficulties which might arise with this union.

The arrival of the Orthodox delegation in early April 1438 had caused consternation. The Byzantine emperor had brought with him an entourage consisting of more than 700 delegates. The difficulty of housing so many foreign visitors in the small city of Ferrara was matched by the fact that Eugenius IV was already short of funds, and financing the ecumenical council was forcing him further and further into debt. Nonetheless the council went ahead, debating differences over matters ranging from who should be the supreme leader of any newly unified church, to the composition of the Holy Trinity and disputed doctrine concerning the existence of Purgatory. To all this was added the question of what to do about the Coptic Church (of Egypt) and the Abyssinian Church, neither of whom recognized the authority of either Rome or Constantinople. Then, as the negotiations continued into the hot summer months, the city of Ferrara found itself under threat from an outbreak of plague.

At this point, Cosimo de' Medici saw his opportunity, and stepped in with an offer to host the council in Florence. He even assured the pope that he would cover the expenses of the council, which were already running up to 1,500 florins a month. Mindful of the immense prestige this would bring to the city, the citizens voted Cosimo into the post of *gonfaloniere* to welcome the delegations to the city in early 1439.

The papal delegation was housed in the monastery of Santa Maria Novella, while the Byzantine emperor John VIII Palaeologus and his extensive entourage were moved into the *palazzi* and houses recently vacated by the Peruzzi family, who had been banished into exile for supporting the Albizzi. The citizens of Florence lining the streets (amongst them the young Uccello) were spellbound by the sheer spectacle of the Byzantine delegation, with its bearded priests in their curious ancient headdresses, and their dark-skinned servants, many of whom were of Mongol, Moorish or Black African descent. Yet all this was as nothing compared with the extraordinary pets which accompanied the delegation – said to have included monkeys, birds of exotic plumage, and even a pair of chained cheetahs. (Several of these would consequently appear in paintings by Florentine artists.)

The council sessions were held at various locations throughout the city, but the differences between the two delegations remained as irreconcilable as ever. The main sticking point was still 'the origin and nature of the third Person of the Holy Trinity' – namely the Holy Ghost. At one stage during the lengthy deliberations, an Orthodox priest attempted to scratch out a passage in an ancient manuscript which appeared to undermine the arguments being put forward by the Byzantine delegation. Uproar ensued when this was discovered. However, in his nervous haste, the priest had in fact scratched out the wrong passage. In an attempt to defuse the situation, and overcome the problem of the desecrated and partially obscured sacred text, the Byzantine emperor proposed that a replacement manuscript be fetched from Constantinople. To which a Roman cardinal replied: 'Sire, where you go to war you should take your arms with you, not send for them in the middle of battle.'

Despite such fractious disputes, an agreement was eventually effected by the skilful diplomacy of the Orthodox Archbishop of Nicaea, Johannes Bessarion,* who was one of the few senior delegates who spoke both Greek and Latin fluently. On 6 July 1439, a solemn ceremony was held amidst the echoing splendour of Florence Cathedral, with Archbishop Bessarion and a senior Roman cardinal symbolically embracing each other beneath Brunelleschi's magnificent dome. Church bells rang out over the city. Christendom was finally united, and the main Byzantine delegation set off back to Constantinople, assured of spiritual and military support against the advancing Ottoman army.

However, this agreement would prove short-lived. When the

---

* More correctly known as Basilios Bessarion.

Orthodox delegation arrived back in Constantinople, and the compromising contents of the agreement became known, the populace rose up in
anger, rioting in the streets until the agreement was publicly disavowed by
the Orthodox authorities. Constantinople's fate was sealed: there would
be no help from western Christendom against the advancing Ottomans.
Just over a decade later, in 1453, the city fell to Sultan Mehmed the
Conqueror, and his Ottoman troops ransacked the last capital of the
Roman Empire.

Despite the apparent failure of the Council of Florence, its presence in the
city would have a decisive and lasting effect. As a result, the Renaissance
would enter a new philosophical phase, and humanism would be transformed by the rebirth of Plato's works. It is possible to trace precisely how
this came about.

Following the days of disagreement at the public sessions of the
Council of Florence, private meetings would take place in a more informal
and friendly atmosphere. After dinner at the Medici residence, the vener-
able Greek Orthodox philosopher Gemistos Plethon, now in his eighties,
would expound on Plato's theory of ideas. Human beings were no more
than chained prisoners sitting in a dark cave facing its inner wall; the
world they perceived was no more than shadows cast by the sun playing
over the cave wall. In order to understand the truth, we must turn away
from the world of shadows and face the true reality of ideas which exists
in the bright sunlight outside the cave.

Cosimo de' Medici and the humanists of Florence listened in awe
to Plethon. Compared with the shadowy world of Neoplatonism inherited from Roman interpretations and the commentaries of the medieval
philosophers, Plethon's exposition, which drew directly from Plato's
work, was a revelation. The absorption of such ideas would prove a
turning point in Cosimo's thinking. Previously preoccupied with banking
and political matters, his outlook now took a more spiritual turn. One of
the effects of this would be to instruct his protégé, the young humanist
scholar Marsilio Ficino, to learn Greek, and to embark upon a translation

of the entire works of Plato from the original Ancient Greek into Latin, still the lingua franca of contemporary European learning. The undertaking would occupy Ficino for most of his coming life, but Cosimo and his circle would not have to wait that long to become further acquainted with Plato's ideas. In an echo of the Academy, originally set up in Athens by Plato to teach his philosophy, Cosimo instigated a series of regular meetings, during which Ficino would expound and discuss the ideas he was discovering during his translations of Plato. The Florentine Academy, as it became known, would prove a formative influence on the literary and artistic culture of the Renaissance in the city. Later, these Platonic ideas would begin to permeate mathematical, scientific and political thought, both in Florence and beyond. They would also provide a much-needed intellectual underpinning for the new humanism.

A further aid to the promulgation of these new ideas would be provided by Cosimo de' Medici's library. In his earlier years, Cosimo had developed an interest in collecting ancient manuscripts. The managers of foreign branches of the Medici bank, as well as Medici agents in other cities, had been instructed to keep an eye open for rare ancient manuscripts. These Cosimo assembled in a library which was open for the use of local scholars. He even employed skilled scribes, so that copies of the works could be loaned out for serious study, or for the purpose of translation. Perhaps the most significant feature of Cosimo's library was that it provided knowledge from a source other than the Church. These freely available classical manuscripts were the initial public manifestation of a new secular learning.

Cosimo would over the years also finance a number of building projects throughout the city. These would mostly be designed by the architect Michelozzo, who would become a close personal friend.

Michelozzo Michelozzi had been born in Florence in 1396, the son of a tailor of French origin. As a young man, he was apprenticed to Lorenzo Ghiberti, the sculptor whose joint victory in the competition to build the Baptistery doors had so upset Brunelleschi. Michelozzo then went on to study under Brunelleschi's friend Donatello. During the course of these apprenticeships Michelozzo developed an architectural style which was a blend of late Gothic (medieval) influences and ancient classical form (Renaissance). From an early age, Michelozzo had been drawn towards Cosimo de' Medici and his intellectual circle. In the words of the eighteenth-century Italian historian Angelo Fabroni: 'Michelozzo was more agreeable and accessible to the advice and desires of Cosimo than the turbulent Brunelleschi, and was willing to follow the strong personal tastes of his patron.' Such was Michelozzo's closeness to Cosimo de' Medici that he chose to follow him into exile in 1433, returning to Florence for his triumphal welcome a year later.

Around this time, Pope Eugenius IV banished the Sylvestrine monks from the monastery complex of San Marco in the north of the city. The pope may well have acted on Cosimo's behalf, as it was common knowledge throughout Florence that the Sylvestrine monks were guilty of 'laziness and laxity'. This appalled Cosimo, and not only because it reflected badly on the city's name. During these years Cosimo found himself increasingly drawn to religious observance. This was at least in part fuelled by his guilty conscience concerning the sin of usury, the foundation on which his entire banking empire was based. Although measures had been taken to circumvent this sin, as Cosimo grew older he became more and more troubled, going to increasing lengths to allay his conscience by making ever-larger contributions to the Church. Yet despite Cosimo's conflicted soul, he nonetheless remained a meticulous and highly successful banker. All this largesse had to be paid for; and even Christian doctrine proclaimed that God gave us our talent, and that by using that talent we gave it back to God.

When the Sylvestrines were expelled from San Marco, the monastery was taken over by the more orderly and pious Dominicans. By now the buildings of San Marco were in an advanced state of dilapidation, so much so that the friars were reduced to living in cramped dormitories with water running down the walls, while others were forced to take shelter in decrepit wooden huts in the monastery grounds. Cosimo saw his opportunity, and offered to pay for a complete refurbishment of San Marco. This offer was gratefully accepted, and Cosimo commissioned Michelozzo to undertake the task.

The result was a transformation. The gloomy, all-but-windowless buildings were converted into a light and airy monastery, complete with inner courtyards surrounded by covered walkways with graceful slender columns. In recognition of Cosimo's charity, the Dominicans allowed him to have his own private chapel built within the complex, to which he could unobtrusively retire for periods of sober silent contemplation. This chapel and the newly designed individual cells for the resident friars were to be decorated with religious frescoes by chosen artists under Cosimo's patronage. In all, Cosimo would spend over 40,000 florins on the project. This gesture may have gone some way towards assuaging Cosimo's conscience, but it was also in its way his own memorial. He had few illusions about the Medici de facto rule of Florence. His friend, the librarian Vespasiano da Bisticci, recorded him declaring: 'I know the ways of Florence, within fifty years we Medici will have been exiled, but my buildings will remain.'

Such a stoic attitude utterly befits Cosimo's temperament. All his life he suffered from the 'Medici curse', namely gout. This highly painful disease is the result of an excess of uric acid in the blood. It causes tiny sharp crystals to form around the joints, inflicting excruciating pain, particularly in the lower leg and toes. Gout was prevalent amongst the Florentine upper classes, largely owing to a lack of vitamins in their winter diet, which eschewed seasonal fare like turnips and parsnips. Such coarse root vegetables were regarded as fit only for peasants and animals, and were consequently shunned by the upper classes. Instead, it was their habit to dine on various meats, invariably smothered in rich, sweet and spicy sauces. These condiments were intended to mask the taste of the meat, which could be tainted, owing to faulty preservation, or over-salted from being pickled in brine.

One of the symptoms of gout was inflammation of the joints, which often caused the entire body to appear twisted. This is certainly indicated in one of the few portraits of Cosimo de' Medici which have come down to us. It depicts a sallow-skinned, hollow-cheeked figure, his body posed awkwardly in a chair, the disfigurement of his limbs masked by a full-length crimson robe. This was painted by the young Florentine artist

Jacopo da Pontormo, whose mannerist style aptly reflects the disguised distortions of Cosimo's frame. Although the painting dates from over half a century after Cosimo's death, it is almost certainly taken from a sketch made during his lifetime. Indeed, the Medici were so impressed by the candid verisimilitude of Pontormo's work that he was taken on by the family, who ensured him a regular succession of commissions.

After Cosimo de' Medici had embarked upon his restoration of San Marco, his next major project was the building of a family *palazzo*. With this in mind, he had purchased a central plot of land on the corner of the Via Larga, just around the corner from the cathedral. At the time, Brunelleschi was generally recognized as the finest architect in Florence, and despite Cosimo's antipathy towards Brunelleschi's 'turbulent' temperament he decided to commission him for this highly prestigious project. After some delay, Brunelleschi duly produced a design for a magnificent *palazzo*, which would far outshine all others in the city. But it seems that Cosimo now became mindful of his father Giovanni di Bicci's deathbed advice, warning against drawing attention to oneself with displays of opulence. Consequently, Cosimo rejected Brunelleschi's painstakingly meticulous model, and instead turned to his friend Michelozzo. According to Vasari, this rebuff so upset the fiery Brunelleschi that he flew into a rage 'and smashed his model into smithereens'.

The building that Michelozzo designed would be redoubtable, yet not overpowering. Its plain stone facade expresses the Renaissance spirit of rationality, order and classicism on a human scale. Although larger than other *palazzi*, its unadorned exterior ensured that it did not stand out in any ostentatious fashion.* The building would always remain approachable, with stone benches set against its walls, where the petitioners for justice, or alms, or favours could sit waiting their turn before being summoned inside to explain their case. Although similar charitable practice was commonplace amongst the leading

---

* A testament to the lasting influence of the Palazzo Medici can be seen in the lower stories of the Federal Reserve Bank building in New York, which directly imitate the exterior style of Cosimo's palace.

families – ensuring, as it did, loyalty to their cause – the scale of such Medici activities has inevitably led to comparison with the behaviour of a modern Mafia godfather.

The interior of the Palazzo Medici was another matter. Here was a residence fit for housing, exhibiting and protecting the increasing number of artistic treasures which the Medici family were accumulating. Beyond the formidable arched entrance gates were two secluded courtyards, one containing a peaceful garden. The other was lined with a covered walkway supported by slender columns – an echo (and acknowledgement) of Brunelleschi's pioneering Renaissance building, the Ospedale degli Innocenti. This courtyard would be the setting for Donatello's sculpture of David, the biblical figure who would come to be regarded as an emblem of the city of Florence. Donatello's life-sized figure represents one of the great advances of Renaissance sculpture, being the first freestanding bronze male nude created since the classical era. Donatello chose to represent this heroic figure in a manner which reflected his own homosexuality. Donatello's *David* is a frankly erotic nude, heightened by its skin of polished bronze; the subject is clad only in a laurel-bedecked hat and a pair of knee-high boots, holding a large sword as he poses provocatively above the severed head of the slain Goliath.

The city's relaxed attitude towards homosexuality during this period was widely recognized. Indeed, it was notorious: so much so that the contemporary German slang term for a 'sodomite' was *Florenzer*. And as a local proverb blatantly put it: 'If you crave joys fumble some boys.' The predilection for homosexual encounters amongst the young men of Florence at this time was hardly surprising. The young women of the city were jealously guarded by their families and seldom allowed out – and never unchaperoned. Virginity was essential for young females, who were mostly married off in their teens to older partners selected by the head of the family. Meanwhile boys usually had to wait until they were a decade or so older before their father would arrange a propitious marriage. Little wonder that the passionate and deprived young men of Florence turned to each other. (Though this could also be seen as the renaissance of a practice that was widespread in Ancient Greece.)

The authorities frequently issued edicts forbidding homosexuality. For instance, edicts were issued in 1415, 1418 and 1432, all to little avail. When Florence lost the war against Lucca in 1432, the city's senior military officers blamed their defeat on the homosexuality of the recruits, claiming that they all ran away at the first sign of danger. In fact, the defeat was largely due to inept leadership, but the authorities chose to recognize that they had a 'problem'. Consequently, a number of registered bordellos were opened up in the back streets near the Mercato Vecchio. The licensed prostitutes who worked from these bordellos were made to bedeck themselves with little tinkling bells in their hair and wear distinctive gloves – as a sign of their profession. These women became known as *meretrici*, meaning 'to merit payment', the source of our word 'meretricious'.

Over the decades following Cosimo de' Medici's return from exile, he would consolidate his position in Florence to the point where Pope Pius II would write of him: 'Political questions are settled at his house. The man he chooses holds office… He it is who decides peace and war, and controls the laws… His mind is keen and alert [although] he frequently passes entire nights without sleep. Nothing goes on in Italy that he does not know about… He is king in all but name.' Cosimo's sleepless nights would probably have been due to the increasing pain of his gout, as much as they were to problems at the bank or worries over the governance of the city.

As head of the Medici bank, Cosimo received intelligence from all its branches, and it was this which enabled him to guide Florence's foreign policy with such skill. The politics of the Italian peninsula remained as volatile as ever – still relying upon a precarious balance between the five major powers: Milan, Venice, Rome, Naples and Florence. As the weakest of these powers, Florence had long relied upon its alliance with powerful Venice for protection. However, Milan posed a constant threat, and the enemies of Cosimo de' Medici were beginning to make use of this. Within four years of being sent into exile, Rinaldo degli Albizzi had the ear of the mentally unstable Duke Filippo Maria, the Visconti ruler of Milan, who harboured fantasies that he would one day rule the whole of Italy. In 1437, and again the following year, Albizzi would lead a Milanese army into Florentine territory.

Fortunately, Cosimo had foreseen this threat, and since returning from exile he had cultivated a friendship with Francesco Sforza, the most powerful *condottiere* in the peninsula at the time. Francesco had been born in 1401 in San Miniato, in the *contado*. His father had been a farmer from the Romagna, the remote hilly territory of city-states across the mountains east of Florence. Nominally these city-states owed allegiance to the pope, but they were in fact mostly ruled by petty tyrants. Owing to its poverty and general lawlessness, the Romagna was a well-known recruiting ground for tough mercenaries.

Around the time of Francesco's birth, his father returned from Tuscany to the Romagna and set up as a *condottiere*. Here he recruited a legion of peasants whom he trained into a formidable fighting force, offering his military services for hire. Indeed, to reinforce his reputation, he even changed his name to Sforza, meaning 'force'. In his early twenties, when his father died, Francesco took over his father's army. He immediately gained popularity amongst his men, owing to his physical prowess (he could bend an iron bar with his bare hands) as well as his tactical abilities (most notably his outmanoeuvring of his mercenary enemies into a position where they were forced to surrender, thus relinquishing their booty without a fight).

Such was Francesco Sforza's military prowess that he was soon hired on a quasi-permanent basis by Filippo Maria, the Duke of Milan, who came to regard Sforza as his trusted right-hand man. Filippo Maria had no legitimate heirs, and despite Sforza's coarse appearance and humble origins, he soon began harbouring dreams of marrying the duke's illegitimate daughter, Bianca Maria, and inheriting his title.

In 1436, just two years after Cosimo de' Medici's return from exile, he had invited the thirty-five-year-old Francesco Sforza to Florence. This was a calculated risk. Sforza had already carved out a small territory for himself in the papal territory of the Romagna, and in asking him to visit Florence, Cosimo risked incurring the displeasure of the pope. The invitation was also liable to rouse the suspicions of the volatile Filippo Maria of Milan. But the shrewd Cosimo saw all this as an opportunity similar to the occasion when his father, Giovanni di Bicci, had gambled on befriending the unreliable Baldassare Cossa, who later became Antipope John XXIII. Cosimo, like his father before him, was playing the long game.

The Francesco Sforza who arrived in Florence was an uncouth character, yet not without a certain rough charisma. Despite his fearsome appearance and coarse manners, he remained touchy concerning his lack of social graces. The sophisticated, middle-aged Cosimo de' Medici quickly gauged Sforza's character, and proceeded to charm him with a display of paternal affection. Sforza was treated with the same courtesy and easy friendship as Cosimo showed to his circle of intellectual humanist protégés and the brilliant artists who graced his table. Sforza had never before been treated as an equal in such company, and quickly warmed to his host. After Sforza returned to his home in the Romagna, he began writing regular letters to Cosimo, addressing him in his mixed Italian dialect as '*Magnifico tanquam Pater carissime*' (Magnificent and dearest almost father).

When Rinaldo degli Albizzi led a Milanese army into Florentine territory in 1437, Cosimo de' Medici immediately contacted Francesco Sforza, sending a large sum of money. Sforza responded by bringing his mercenary army to Cosimo's aid. Cosimo ordered Sforza to drive Albizzi and his Milanese force out of Florentine territory, and then continue on to take Lucca, a move he knew would be popular with the people of Florence. Sforza drove out Albizzi, but was reluctant to press his victory by taking Lucca, which he realized would upset Filippo Maria of Milan. Sforza still had hopes of marrying his daughter. At the same time, Florence's main ally, Venice, refused to support the city in any attack on Lucca, not wishing to see Florence increase its territory.

When Albizzi marched into Florentine territory once again in 1438, Cosimo travelled to Venice, in the hope of persuading his ally to come to Florence's aid. But Venice turned down Cosimo's plea, insisting that it wished to remain neutral. Cosimo now knew what he had suspected for some time: Florence could no longer rely upon Venice as an ally in the ever-shifting politics of the Italian peninsula. Meanwhile, Sforza had been rewarded for his covert loyalty to Milan in not attacking Lucca, and Duke Filippo Maria sanctioned his engagement to his daughter Bianca. He even hinted that he might make Sforza his heir. Albizzi found that he could no longer rely upon Milan in his attempt to overthrow Cosimo de' Medici, and his invasion came to nothing.

In 1447 Duke Filippo Maria of Milan died, leaving no legitimate heir to his dukedom. Sforza immediately launched his claim to the duchy, but was rebuffed by two other claimants to the title – King Alfonso of Naples and the French Duke of Orléans, who both regarded Sforza as a mere upstart. In the end, the citizens of Milan took matters into their own hands, and declared the city and its territory a republic, along the same lines as Florence. But after three years of troubled republican government, Sforza seized his opportunity and installed himself as ruler of Milan, proclaiming himself a duke in the process. Florence's old enemy had now become its closest ally.

Venice sought to retaliate by seizing the assets of the Medici bank at their branches in Naples and the port of Gaeta, but Cosimo had already anticipated such action and quietly withdrawn all money and merchandise. However, Florentine commerce with Venice suffered a severe blow, as all Florentine merchants, bankers and agents were expelled from the city. This signified a serious loss for Florence, which had a growing trade with the eastern Mediterranean, much of it using hired Venetian galleys. It also meant the closure of one of the most profitable branches of the Medici bank after those in Rome and Florence. An indication of this can be seen in the fact that, during the previous decade, the Venice branch had on one occasion made an annual profit of more than 8,000 ducats, equal in fact to its entire capital – 'a truly spectacular result', according to Raymond de Roover.

Yet consolation was at hand. Francesco Sforza invited his friend Cosimo to open a branch of the Medici bank in Milan, granting him the use of a group of somewhat rundown buildings in the city centre.

Cosimo immediately brought in Michelozzo, who refurbished these on the grand scale, turning them into a splendid *palazzo*. As manager of the new bank Cosimo installed the thirty-one-year-old Pigello Portinari, who as well as being a close friend of Cosimo was also one of his most trusted and accomplished employees.* Pigello's father had died when he was ten, whereupon Cosimo had taken the young orphan into his household, where he received his elementary education – at the same time mingling with Cosimo's intellectual circle of humanists and artists, one of whom would almost certainly have acted as his tutor. At the age of thirteen, Pigello had been sent to Venice, which Cosimo used as a training ground for his young up-and-coming managers. According to de Roover, when Pigello Portinari took charge of the Milan branch of the Medici bank, 'he was a very successful manager, who kept the favor of the Sforza court without compromising the solvency of the bank by granting credit indiscriminately'.

Cosimo's switch of allegiance from Venice to Milan had deeper reasons than the exposed unreliability of Florence's alliance with Venice. He had read the situation on the Italian peninsula with the eye of a skilled diplomat. Milan's weakness after the death of Filippo Maria and the installation of a weak republic had left it at the mercy of its rival Venice. Should Venice have taken Milan, it would have ruled most of northern Italy, leaving Florence exposed to any further Venetian expansion. Cosimo's deft diplomatic moves had not only neutralized any threat to Florence, but also restored the balance of power in Italy. For the first time in years, the peninsula faced the prospect of peace.

In 1455, this peace would be placed on a formal basis by Pope Nicholas V, when he announced a Holy League. This initiated a twenty-five-year mutual defence pact between Milan, Venice, Rome, Naples and Florence. Separate alliances between an Italian state and any foreign power were expressly forbidden, and the borders of the signatory states were to be recognized by one and all. It was during these years of comparative peace that the Renaissance would reach its greatest heights. Little wonder that

---

* One of Pigello's ancestors was Beatrice Portinari, Dante's muse.

the near-contemporary Florentine historian Francesco Guicciardini would write of Cosimo that he 'had a reputation such as probably no private citizen has ever enjoyed from the fall of Rome to our own day'.

During Cosimo de' Medici's final years he became increasingly bedridden with gout. His two sons, Piero and Giovanni, also suffered from the family ailment. On one occasion, when the Milanese ambassador called at the Palazzo Medici for an audience with Cosimo, he was surprised to find himself ushered into the bedroom. Here he found himself witnessing a tragicomic scene. The elderly Cosimo was lying in the master bed, his middle-aged sons lying either side of him, all three stricken with gout.

Cosimo de' Medici eventually died in 1464, while lying in his bed listening to Ficino read one of his translations of Plato. Cosimo was by then seventy-four – an exceptional age for the period.* His funeral would be a modest affair, in keeping with that of his father. Yet the entire population of the city is said to have silently crammed the streets around the Medici church of San Lorenzo as his coffin was laid to rest. Afterwards, the *signoria* decreed that on his tombstone should be carved the words *pater patriae* (father of the country).

The 'succession' passed to his ailing elder son Piero di Cosimo de' Medici, who would become known as Piero the Gouty. Prior to this, Florence had remained a republic, if only in name; the Medici ascendancy had not been officially acknowledged. From now on, this illusion could no longer be maintained. The ascendancy of Piero to the leadership was a purely Medici matter, with no democratic process involved. For the time being, Florence was a Medici city, in name as well as in fact.

---

* Precise and reliable figures for life expectancy in Italy during this time are hard to come by. However, discounting the high rate of death in early infancy (estimated to have been around 30 per cent), the labouring classes could now expect to live into their thirties. More privileged members of society usually lived into their forties. As we have seen, Cosimo's father, Giovanni di Bicci, died aged sixty-nine, so there was probably a genetic aspect to Cosimo's longevity. On the other hand, in the ensuing four generations of this branch of the Medici family, almost all died in their forties.

CHAPTER 11

A MEDICI ARTIST

ALESSANDRO DI MARIANO DI Vanni Filipepi, now known to us as Sandro Botticelli, was born in Florence sometime between 1444 and 1446, according to information gleaned from his father Mariano Filipepi's tax records. The house where he was born, now number 28 Borgo Ognissanti, still stands, with some alterations, a few doors along from the Ognissanti church. Botticelli would be baptized in this church some nine years before Amerigo Vespucci; but unlike his adventurous contemporary, Botticelli would live all his life in and around this street, apart from a brief visit to Pisa and some ten months he spent in Rome. Botticelli's travels would take place in his restless mind, and his imagination would conjure up scenes of such vivid colour and clarity that they seem to come from the dawn of an earlier, timeless era.

Typical of these are his *Primavera* (Spring) and his *Birth of Venus*, which have now become central images of the early Renaissance. Despite this, his reputation would lapse after his death. Some attribute this to Vasari's unwillingness to grant him a place in the evolutionary line of Renaissance art – an astonishing omission. Others attribute this eclipse to the vicissitudes of his life: his fall from the brightest star in the Medici firmament to the tragic figure described by Vasari as 'grown old and useless, unable to stand upright and moving about with the help of crutches… ill and decrepit'. Almost four centuries would pass before Botticelli gained his rightful place in the pantheon of Renaissance art.

At the time of Botticelli's birth, the Ognissanti district down near the right bank of the Arno was a working-class location inhabited by cloth-workers, with the flowing water of a nearby canal driving their mills. The ground in front of the Ognissanti church was an open stretch of rough grassland, beside a larger meadow reaching west to the city walls and the Porta al Prato (Prato Gate). This meadow was where the local lads came to let off steam playing the rough-and-tumble medieval *giuoco del calcio fiorentino* (Florentine kick game). An early forerunner of modern football, this involved gangs of local young artisans known as *potenze* (powers). Each *potenze* consisted of two dozen or so youths, chosen to represent one of the six districts of the city. There were few rules, and the two teams fought and punched and struggled to get the ball, which usually consisted of an inflated pig's bladder encased in pieces of leather sewn together. The aim was to kick or carry this ball through the opponents' goal. When the ball became bogged down under a pile of players, a bull was sometimes driven onto the pitch to scatter them and free it. This game may have originated from a similar Ancient Roman game called *harpastum*. As early as 1490, a game of *calcio fiorentino* is known to have been played on the frozen surface of the Arno.

Some sources speak of Botticelli being a sickly child, though his self-portrait as a young man suggests a burly figure who could well have taken part in games of *calcio fiorentino*. His father was a poor tanner, and had ambitions for young Sandro, but according to Vasari he became irked when Botticelli 'refused to settle down or be satisfied with reading, writing, and arithmetic'. Botticelli's older brother ran a successful wine shop, and around this time young Sandro appears to have worked for him, thus gaining the nickname Botticelli, which means 'little barrel'. Other sources claim that the brother ran a successful pawnbroker's shop with a sign marked 'Il Botticelli'. Vasari suggests a third explanation: how, 'exasperated by his son's restless mind, his father apprenticed him as a goldsmith to a close companion of his own called Botticelli'.

Some decades earlier, the profession of goldsmith had been held in high regard in Florence; at the same time serving as an apprenticeship or initiation for many artists and architects. Witness the case of Ghiberti, whose bronze Baptistery doors remain one of the formative wonders of the 'new art' in Florence, which we now recognize as the beginning of the Renaissance. But those days were past, in part due to a recent downturn in economic life and a lack of gold. It soon became clear that young Sandro was more interested in drawing and painting than the humdrum and exhausting task of burnishing his master's works. When Sandro was sixteen, Mariano arranged for him to be taken on as a *garzone* (meaning 'boy', i.e. an assistant) by Fra Filippo Lippi, who had long been under the patronage of the Medici family.

Fra Filippo Lippi would appear to be a curious choice as a master for an impressionable young artist like Botticelli. There was no doubting Lippi's talents, and Cosimo de' Medici had been quick to spot these. Likewise, Vasari refers to Lippi as 'a great painter of that time'. On the other hand, Lippi's life also qualifies him as one of the great rogues of the era. It was picaresque, to say the least.

Lippi had been orphaned at an early age, and poverty had induced him to become a Carmelite friar at the age of sixteen. He is said to have learned how to paint by studying the early Renaissance artist Tommaso Masaccio, who had been commissioned to paint a series of frescoes in the chapel of the Carmelite friary. In his twenties, Lippi left the monastery (without being released from his vows) and travelled to southern Italy. Here he was captured by Barbary pirates and held as a slave in North Africa; but according to his own story he managed to secure his release by painting a portrait of his Berber master.

It was sometime after Lippi returned to Florence that he attracted the attention of Cosimo de' Medici, who took him into the Medici house-hold and secured for Lippi some important Church commissions. But in the midst of painting these exquisite and uplifting religious scenes, Lippi was in the habit of disappearing for days on end into the bordellos and wine shops around the Mercato Vecchio. In the end, Cosimo took to having Lippi locked in his studio until he fulfilled his work, but Lippi would pick the lock or escape by knotting the sheets of his bed to form a rope. Then there was the occasion when he was commissioned to paint an altarpiece at a nunnery in Prato, and ran off with one of the nuns. On this occasion Cosimo de' Medici used his influence with Pope Pius II, who happened to be visiting Florence, and Lippi was given dispensation to marry his pregnant nun.

Such was the man who took on Botticelli as his apprentice. Yet, according to Vasari, 'Botticelli threw all his energies into his work, following and imitating his master so well that Fra Filippo grew very fond of him and taught him to such good effect that very soon his skill was greater than anyone would have anticipated.' Vasari was a man of superlatives, and it is interesting to see how he damns Botticelli with faint praise. Despite this assessment, which would dog Botticelli's reputation for centuries to come, he would soon follow Lippi into service with the Medici, where his talent was recognized by Cosimo's son, Piero the Gouty, now de facto ruler of the city following the death of his father in 1464.

One of Botticelli's most important early commissions was to come from the Vespucci, the leading family of the Ognissanti district, who were in fact close allies of the Medici family. They appointed Botticelli to paint a fresco of St Augustine in the church of Ognissanti, which was run by the *Umiliati* order of priests, who were often married men who had forsworn the secular life.

In accepting this commission, Botticelli found himself in direct competition with the much-admired Florentine artist Domenico Ghirlandaio, who had painted on the opposite wall a portrait of the fifth-century theologian St Jerome, who had exchanged letters with St Augustine. This was a highly skilled portrait, filled with illustrative detail. It depicted the bald, white-bearded St Jerome resting his head on his hand as he sat writing in his study, surrounded by objects indicating his devotion as well as his everyday life – including open books in Hebrew and Greek, as well as a vase, some fruit and an hourglass.

According to Botticelli's biographer Ronald Lightbown, such competition 'was always an inducement to Botticelli to put out all his powers'. Spurred to emulate Ghirlandaio, Botticelli chose to depict St Augustine in a similar room, also writing and surrounded by familiar objects. But where Ghirlandaio's St Jerome is meditative, Botticelli's St Augustine is a troubled soul, just as he was in life. Botticelli's painting dramatically trumps Ghirlandaio's in its vividness and virtuosity, with a cunning *trompe-l'œil* open drawer and the text of an opened book above the saint's head. This text is for the most part meaningless, yet cunningly incorporates the words '*Dov'è Frate Martino? È scappato. E dov'è andato? È fuor dalla Porta al Prato*' (Where is Brother Martino? He went out. And where did he go? He is outside Porta al Prato). This is a characteristic practical joke by Botticelli, yet it is open to a variety of interpretations. Was this just a scrap of everyday conversation which Botticelli had overheard while painting the fresco in Ognissanti? If so, Lightbown claims this shows that Botticelli thought 'the example of Jerome and Augustine likely to be thrown away on the Umiliati as he knew them'. Others have gone so far as to suggest that this scrap of dialogue might allude to a contemporary scandal involving one of the *Umiliati* named Brother Martino.

Botticelli's painting contains all this and more, even before one understands the central secret inherent in its composition. As Lightbown points out: 'In fact the link between the two frescoes [of St Jerome and St Augustine] is even closer than has been suspected.' St Augustine's frowning features are overwhelmed with awe as he looks up from writing a letter, witnessing a vision. Although we do not see this vision, Botticelli manages to suggest not only what it is, but also what St Augustine is doing and what is happening.

The clock behind St Augustine's head on the wall indicates that it is the end of the twenty-fourth hour. In medieval times, the first hour began at sunset, so although Botticelli shows no windows, we know that the scene depicted is taking place around sunset. This subtly links Botticelli's painting with that of Ghirlandaio – for, according to legend, in 420 AD St Augustine had a vision at sunset while writing a letter to St Jerome.

The vision was accompanied by a sweet smell (the odour of sanctity) and a voice which told St Augustine that 'he might as soon enclose the ocean in a small vessel, as soon clasp the whole earth in his fist, as soon halt the movement of the heavens as describe the beatitude of the saints without having experienced it, as he who spoke was now experiencing it.'

In a tremulous voice, St Augustine asked who was speaking, and the voice answered that it was St Jerome. Later, St Augustine would learn that St Jerome had died in Jerusalem on precisely that day at precisely that hour.

This story is told in an apocryphal epistle written by St Augustine which had recently begun circulating in Italy. It is evident that Botticelli had studied this letter closely, ingeniously devising indicative visual parallels which could be incorporated into his painting. As Lightbown perceptively observes:

> This power of keeping his imagination chained to a text, yet of transfiguring what the written word imposed on him into a powerful pictorial equivalent, was to remain with him until the end of his working life and is one of the essential keys to a true understanding of his art.

Yet Botticelli was painting far more than a visual parallel to a written text, no matter how ingeniously he did it. In this work he renders St Augustine's face and posture with a psychological depth. Botticelli 'had come to note the signs and actions by which our faces and limbs reveal what passes within our minds'. And by doing so, Botticelli also revealed that he had read Alberti's *De Pictura*, which recommends that artists should aim to do just this.

The most accomplished evidence of him fulfilling this aim can be seen in St Augustine's right hand, which is loosely placed over his heart. This registers his surprise at witnessing the vision and hearing its voice, as well as indicating his reverence in its presence. Here Botticelli succeeds in going one better than Alberti's recommendation. Instead of St Augustine's gesture revealing one state of mind, it involves two – surprise and reverence. Indeed, it succeeds in expressing St Augustine's passage from one state of mind to the other.

The fact that Botticelli had seen a copy of St Augustine's apocryphal letter,* as well as the evidence that he had read Alberti's treatise on painting, indicates how deeply involved he was with the circle of humanists, poets and artists who gathered at the Palazzo Medici. Botticelli was closely associated with the Medici family during its 'golden era' – the period of its ascendancy over Florence and its greatest influence on the Renaissance. He would have been around twenty years old when Cosimo de' Medici died and was granted the title *pater patriae*.

Botticelli would remain closely involved with the family during Cosimo's son Piero the Gouty's brief reign from 1464 to 1469; and he would be at the height of his artistic powers during the ascendancy of Piero's son Lorenzo the Magnificent. When Lorenzo survived the violent assassination attempt known as the Pazzi conspiracy, it was Botticelli who was commissioned to paint a public fresco of the eight leading conspirators, on a wall between the Palazzo della Signoria and the Palazzo del Podestà. Seven of these figures were shown hanged, each with a noose around his neck and a mocking inscription in Latin verse composed by Lorenzo himself. The eighth, who had managed to escape, was depicted hanging by his foot, above Lorenzo's description of him as 'an outlaw awaiting a crueller death'.

Botticelli would outlast the death of Lorenzo the Magnificent in 1492, and would be deeply conflicted during the fall of the Medici and the rise of the fundamentalist priest Savonarola, which would cast a shadow not only over his radiant art but also over the pathetic figure which he became in old age.

Although the history of the ruling Medici would provide the dramatic backdrop to Botticelli's life, it was in fact a member of the less prominent, junior branch of the Medici family who would be Botticelli's main

---

* Now thought to have been a thirteenth-century forgery.

benefactor. This was Lorenzo di Pierfrancesco de' Medici, the man we have already encountered as manager of the Medici bank, and the recipient of letters from Amerigo Vespucci which revealed the sensational nature of his discoveries.

Lorenzo di Pierfrancesco was descended from Cosimo de' Medici's younger brother, Lorenzo, and would thus be a cousin to Cosimo *pater patriae* and his son Piero the Gouty, as well as his grandson, Lorenzo the Magnificent. Relations between the senior and junior branches of the Medici family were complex. Lorenzo di Pierfrancesco's father had died when he was just twelve years old, whereupon the twenty-eight-year-old Lorenzo de' Medici, now ruler of Florence, decided to take him and his younger brother into his care. Lorenzo the Magnificent moved his two young cousins into the Palazzo Medici, and ensured that they were given the best available education, being tutored by members of his humanist circle. These tutors included Marsilio Ficino, who was still involved in translating the works of Plato, and the humanist friar Giorgio Vespucci, who was at the time tutoring the young Amerigo Vespucci. (This would be the beginning of the lifelong friendship between Lorenzo di Pierfrancesco de' Medici and Amerigo Vespucci.)

However, along with this charitable gesture, Lorenzo the Magnificent also took possession of the young brothers' considerable inheritance. Both sides of the family held large partnerships in the branches of the Medici bank, sharing its overall profits. But the capital of the senior branch of the family had been considerably reduced, owing to the extravagance of Cosimo de' Medici's patronage of the arts and his large building projects such as the refurbishment of San Marco and the construction of the Palazzo Medici. Similar patronage had continued under Piero the Gouty and Lorenzo the Magnificent. As a result, Lorenzo the Magnificent's costly lifestyle would begin to drain the coffers of the Medici bank, which was itself beginning to experience difficulties.

The inheritance of Lorenzo di Pierfrancesco and his younger brother thus proved a timely windfall, and Lorenzo the Magnificent was soon extracting 'loans' from this large sum under his protection. Such was the extent of these 'loans' that by the time Lorenzo di Pierfrancesco came of age in 1485, Lorenzo the Magnificent had diverted from his cousins' inheritance the sum of 53,643 florins, according to the surviving records. Some sources suspect that he took even more.

However, it should be noted that not all of this money was for Lorenzo the Magnificent's personal use. The maintenance of the Medici party machine, the ensuring of election results, and the necessary 'presents' involved in the servicing of this apparatus were a costly business. Then there was the cost of putting on traditional entertainments for the people, to ensure popular support. These included everything from the public staging of bawdy farces to colourful pageants and even jousting tourna-ments.* Although such events encouraged the popularity of Lorenzo the Magnificent, and bolstered his position as a ruler amongst the people, it should be remembered that they also ensured the privileged position (and safety) of the Medici family as a whole.

In rising to their present position of eminence, the Medici had inevit-ably made enemies, and there remained a number of powerful families in the city who were biding their time, just waiting for an opportunity to strike against them. Some of these enemies even maintained contact with the exiled Albizzi, who had suffered the public insult of having their leaders painted as traitors on the wall of the Palazzo del Podestà, in a precursor to Botticelli's paintings of the Pazzi conspirators. Such insults were not forgotten, and the maintenance of Medici supremacy was an expensive business. Furthermore, the Medici cause had hardly been helped by Piero the Gouty's inept running of the family bank. In his attempt to bring some order to the books after his father Cosimo's spending spree, Piero had begun calling in the bank's overdrafts. Many of these accounts were held by family friends, whose debts had been kindly overlooked by Cosimo for many years. Piero's unexpected move resulted in several bankruptcies, and in the end only increased the cost of maintaining Medici supremacy and popularity.

---

* It was during just such a contest that the *condottiere* Federico da Montefeltro, ruler of Urbino, had lost his right eye.

According to Raymond de Roover, when Lorenzo di Pierfrancesco de' Medici and his brother discovered the hole in their inheritance, 'Lorenzo [the Magnificent] was forced to transfer to his cousins the ancestral villa of Cafaggiolo and other properties in the Mugello'. There is also mention of him paying back 50,000 florins, which suggests that the sum he 'borrowed' from their inheritance was a lot more than the 53,643 florins of which there is a record. And where did Lorenzo the Magnificent obtain that extra 50,000 florins, when he appeared to be so strapped for cash that he had raided his cousins' inheritance? There are suggestions in fifteenth-century sources that he may have appropriated this sum from the public funds.

The separation between the financial dealings of the city of Florence and those of the Medici had started to become blurred as early as Cosimo de' Medici's time. However, Cosimo appears to have paid back with interest any 'loans' he took from the public exchequer; indeed he may even have done more than that on occasion, rescuing the city itself from bankruptcy. This may have been what happened after the disastrous war against Lucca, for instance, when the bank's funds appeared all but limitless.

Piero the Gouty's attempt to put the Medici bank back on a firm footing had backfired badly. And it appears that Lorenzo the Magnificent had increasingly begun to identify his personal and family finances with those of the city exchequer. His particular penchant was for siphoning off money from the *Monte delle doti*, the state fund which provided dowries for daughters of the poor to enable them to get married. Unfortunately, all but a few of the relevant records from this period would be destroyed by a later generation of the Medici, thus obliterating any evidence of malfeasance. With regard to the Medici finances during this 'lost' period, no less an authority than de Roover would opine: 'It is likely, therefore, that bankruptcy after [1478] was averted only by dipping into the public treasury.'

So although the junior branch of the Medici family had no power, by this stage they had considerably more in the way of assets and cash. But while Lorenzo the Magnificent may not have had sufficient funds to support the artists in his circle, he ensured that they gained lucrative commissions. This was particularly the case with Sandro Botticelli, who had become deeply influenced by the ideas which circulated amongst the humanists attached to the Palazzo Medici, especially those of the Platonist Ficino.

Lorenzo the Magnificent persuaded his cousin Lorenzo di Pierfrancesco to commission several works by Botticelli, most notably the two masterpieces which would hang in Lorenzo di Pierfrancesco's family residence, the Villa di Castello, in the *contado* a few miles north-west of the city walls. These two large paintings are today the best known of all Botticelli's works.

The Birth of Venus depicts the goddess of love, originally known as Aphrodite by the Ancient Greeks. According to the myth, Venus emerged from the sea fully grown and possessed of all her beauty. In Botticelli's painting, Venus rides naked on a scallop shell, blown across the sea towards the wooded shore by Zephyr, the god of wind. The painting is suffused with a timeless quality, embodying the Platonic ideal. This is not the shadowy world which humanity sees flickering on the wall of the dark cave. Instead, it is the radiant world of ideas: the true reality in the light beyond the cave.

Botticelli was not known for his anatomical verisimilitude. In his St Augustine, for instance, the saint's body is merely suggested, covered beneath his tunic and his flowing cape. Yet in this painting Botticelli turns his very weaknesses into strengths. The nude body of Venus has her modesty masked by her flowing red hair, and her right hand is placed above her left breast in a gesture reminiscent of St Augustine's. But her entire pose is anatomically impossible. Her neck is elongated; the curve of her head and body unbalanced. Nor is her body given sufficient solidity or perspective. As a result of such 'faults', Venus appears to float, her left foot only lightly resting on the scallop shell which is bearing her across the waves. All this only adds to the idealistic aspect of the painting.

The Birth of Venus has been subjected to all manner of deep analysis. And, like Botticelli's St Augustine, it almost certainly contains many hidden indications and secrets. But here, amidst the freshness of the seascape and the wooded land beyond, such interpretations seem super-fluous. Like Plato's ultimate reality of ideas, this scene is what it is: perpetual, elemental. It is real, yet ethereal, and this has endeared it to so many art lovers. This is the image which conjures up the full glory of the early Renaissance.

The other painting that Botticelli created for Lorenzo di Pierfrancesco's Villa di Castello was the similarly delightful *Primavera* (also known as the *Allegory of Spring*). *The Birth of Venus* and *Primavera* are frequently seen as a pair, though this was not intended by Botticelli. Their original shared location and the matching brilliance of an artist at the height of his powers perhaps adds to this association. *Primavera* too is a large painting (more than two metres by three metres), but it is altogether different with its elusive, shadowy nature and the power of its enigmatic symbolism. Here is a scene which begs interpretation: eight expressive figures from classical mythology in a dark orange grove, above whom flies a cherub. These figures can be read from right to left. Emerging from the darkness of the trees to the right is the shadowy figure of Zephyrus, the cold wind of March, who is in the process of carrying off the figure of Chloris, who will marry him, becoming goddess of spring. The next figure appears to grow out of the fading Chloris. This is Flora, the full embodiment of the goddess of spring, whom Chloris is destined to become. Flora, the eternal bringer of life, is resplendent, clad in a flower-bedecked robe, scattering roses from her lap. In the centre of the painting, set slightly back from the others, is a pregnant Venus, symbol of the fecundity of spring. Beside her to the left are the Three Graces – Pleasure, Chastity and Beauty – clad in diaphanous robes and dancing together. These robes cleverly serve the dual purpose of clothing the nudity of the Graces and obscuring Botticelli's weakness in portraying precise anatomy. The central figure of the Three Graces is casting a lingering gaze left towards the last figure in the painting. This is the youthful Mercury, his torso exposed, who is reaching up with a staff towards the oranges in the trees above his head.

Hovering above the entire scene is the chubby, childish form of a blindfolded cherub: a cupid drawing back the string of his bow, on the point of firing an arrow of love towards the figure of the gazing Grace.

This alludes to the actual occasion which the painting was intended to commemorate – that is, the marriage of Lorenzo di Pierfrancesco de' Medici to Semiramide Appiano, daughter of the Lord of Piombino, who was related to the Aragonese royal family of Naples. In keeping with the custom of the time this was an arranged marriage, organized by Lorenzo the Magnificent for strategic political reasons: a strengthening of ties with Naples for the protection of Florence.

Such large pagan scenes as *Primavera* were virtually unknown in the centuries since classical times. Many attempts have been made to pin down the precise allegory which *Primavera* depicts. There is no doubt that Botticelli intended this painting to be as richly allusive as his depiction of St Augustine, and the intellectuals and poets of the Palazzo Medici evidently encouraged him to embody elements of classical myth and Platonic idealism. However, although he may well have intended a precise meaning, such as in the painting of St Augustine, it has continued to elude all manner of penetrative analysis. Consequently, apart from the surface interpretation, no deeper symbolic and personal reading has emerged which satisfies all the complex visual elements which Botticelli incorporated into the painting. Indeed, its very mystery has only contributed to its popularity. Perhaps the last word on this should be left to Botticelli's biographer Lightbown, who claims that the Renaissance echoed antiquity in developing two attitudes towards classical myths:

> On the one hand philosophers and the learned sought to rationalise and deepen their meaning by treating them as allegories concealing philosophical, moral or historical truths. Far more generally influential was the exoteric tradition that took them simply as lively and beautiful images of the forces and impulses that govern man's nature and the world.

In 1483, a year after the occasion of the marriage of Lorenzo di Pierfrancesco de' Medici for which Botticelli had painted *Primavera*, Lorenzo the Magnificent sent the twenty-year-old bridegroom to France as the Florentine ambassador at the formal betrothal of King Charles

VIII and Anne of Austria, intended to seal an alliance between France and the Habsburgs. Botticelli's *Portrait of Lorenzo di Pierfrancesco de' Medici*, painted around this time, depicts a callow young man whose formal expression appears to mask a somewhat pugnacious character: the man who dared to take on his powerful older cousin over his purloined inheritance. Botticelli's portraits sometimes tend towards caricature, emphasizing a predominant aspect of his sitter's personality; and this would seem to be no exception.

The Medici presence at the wedding of Charles VIII would strengthen a vital alliance for Florence, as France was at the time the most powerful nation in Europe, and there is no doubting the importance of the mission Lorenzo the Magnificent entrusted to his young cousin. It was following this visit to France that serious disagreement broke out between the junior and the senior branches of the Medici family. As we have seen, when Lorenzo di Pierfrancesco discovered the vast amount which Lorenzo the Magnificent had looted from his inheritance,* Lorenzo the Magnificent felt obliged to hand over several ancestral properties. These were no mean concessions. The Cafaggiolo villa was a fortified residence which had been in the family since the time of Giovanni di Bicci's father in the fourteenth century. In the following century, Cosimo de' Medici had commissioned his friend Michelozzo, architect of the Palazzo Medici, to transform this modest villa into an expansive 'hunting lodge'. As such, it had later become a favourite location for his grandson Lorenzo the Magnificent to spend the hot summers with his family or to meet up with his intellectual friends such as Ficino and the poet Angelo Poliziano. Following 'protracted negotiations', this treasured residence eventually passed into the hands of Lorenzo di Pierfrancesco de' Medici. Seven years later, on the death of Lorenzo the Magnificent, Lorenzo di Pierfrancesco would take over the ailing Medici bank. It was during these years that he would once more become involved with Amerigo Vespucci, and probably had a role in financing at least one of the voyages which resulted in the transformation of our knowledge of the world.

---

* Some sources go so far as to suggest that he drained the entire inheritance.

As for Botticelli, according to Vasari, 'he earned a great deal of money but wasted it all through carelessness and lack of management'. As we shall see, this was only a contributory factor towards the pitiful figure he eventually became. Even so, when he fell on hard times towards the end of his life, it was Lorenzo the Magnificent, as much as his great benefactor Lorenzo di Pierfrancesco de' Medici, who came to Botticelli's rescue: 'So finally, as an old man, he found himself so poor that if Lorenzo [the Magnificent]... and then his friends and other worthy men who loved him for his talent had not come to his assistance, he would have almost died of hunger.'

Portrait of Dante (centre); detail of *Paradise* by the School of Giotto.

An early Florentine gold florin (*fiorino doro*) showing the fleurs-de-lis on one side and St John the Baptist on the other.

Above: Portrait of Boccaccio.

Right: Paolo Uccello's fresco of Sir John Hawkwood in Florence Cathedral.

A detail from Ghiberti's Baptistery doors, showing Jacob about to sacrifice his son Esau.

The inside of the dome of the Pantheon in Rome.

Santa Maria del Fiore (Florence Cathedral), showing Brunelleschi's dome to the right, and Giotto's Campanile to the left.

Above: Paolo Uccello, *The Hunt*.

Below: Uccello's painting of the
Battle of San Romano.

Opposite: Piero della Francesca,
The Flagellation of Christ.

Above: Leon Battista Alberti, self-portrait.

Left: Portrait of Federico da Montefeltro by Piero della Francesca.

Facade of Santa Maria Novella by Alberti.

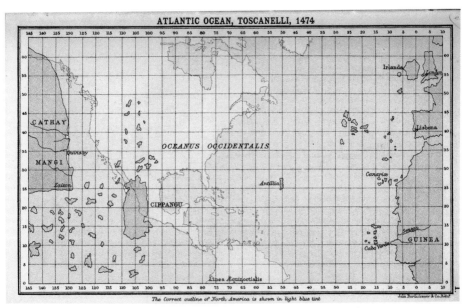

Above: A modern reconstruction of Toscanelli's map, with the actual position of the Americas imposed in light blue.

Right: Jacopo da Pontormo's portrait Cosimo de' Medici.

David by Donatello.

CHAPTER 12

IL MAGNIFICO

L ORENZO THE MAGNIFICENT, OR more correctly Lorenzo de' Medici *il Magnifico*, certainly lived up to his nickname.* But there was much more to him than mere magnificence, although his personal belief that he possessed this quality cannot be denied. Lorenzo's personality, his legacy, and indeed much about him, remain deeply contradictory.

It was certainly not Lorenzo the Magnificent's appearance which earned him his nickname. He was far from good-looking, yet it seems the very ugliness of his striking dark features only contributed to his

---

* *Il Magnifico*, 'the Magnificent', was initially a term of respect, used to address a person of superior rank or wealth. For instance, when the managers of the Medici bank wrote home to the head of the bank, they appended to the name of the person to whom the letter was addressed the epithet *magnifico*. De Roover makes the significant point: 'As the Medici, after Cosimo's death, reach princely status, the tone becomes even more obsequious and Lorenzo [de' Medici] is commonly addressed in the third person as *la Magnificenza Vostra* (Your Magnificence). This is how he came to be known as Lorenzo the Magnificent.'

charisma. They were undeniably attractive to women, and he appears to have used these charms to seduce young men as well.

Similarly, his deep flaws were equally at odds with his flamboyant skills. As ruler of Florence, he may have identified himself with the city and its welfare, to the immense benefit of the city; but as we have seen he also identified his own financial interests with those of the city, using the exchequer for his personal benefit as well as for the maintenance of Medici rule. This would involve chicanery and dark deeds, as well as grandiloquent gestures and reckless bravery.

Lorenzo the Magnificent was the first of the Medici to be openly invited to rule the city. After the premature death of his father, Piero the Gouty, in 1469, the twenty-year-old Lorenzo received, as he later wrote, a delegation of 'leaders, knights and citizens' the next morning. These had called at the Palazzo Medici 'to offer me condolences for my loss and to urge me to take over control of the city and the state'. Despite his youth, Lorenzo had for many years been groomed for this role. And in many ways he would become the epitome of Renaissance Florence during its period of greatest achievement.

Lorenzo had been born in 1449. He was old enough to have known, and learned from, his illustrious grandfather Cosimo de' Medici, who would die when he was fifteen years old. Despite being brought up amidst the splendours of the Palazzo Medici and its dazzling intellectual circle of poets, painters and philosophers, Lorenzo would prove a boisterous child. In early adulthood he took part in the roughhouse *calcio fiorentino* games. Though, unlike Botticelli, he participated in the games held in the Piazza Santa Croce, where the young bloods of the better families played their football – presumably in a rather less brutal fashion.

Lorenzo's father, Piero, was confined to bed with gout for much of Lorenzo's early years. Indeed, if anything, this was the somewhat incongruous throne from which he conducted the day-to-day business of his court: spending his time dealing with government matters, diplomacy, receiving important visitors, looking after the affairs of the family bank, dispensing patronage and so forth. Lorenzo's mother, Lucrezia, on the other hand, played a leading role in his upbringing. Lucrezia was a

Tornabuoni, one of Florence's oldest noble families, who had close links with the Medici.* Although Lucrezia had poor health herself, she took on a guiding role in her husband's political activities. She also read Latin, and more unusually Greek. In this way she had become well versed in the classics, to the point where she even composed her own poetry. As a protective mother she would be a guiding force in her son Lorenzo's upbringing, ensuring that his education was conducted by her chosen tutors from amongst the Medici intellectual circle. Young Lorenzo and his younger brother Giuliano learned Platonic philosophy and humanism from Ficino, as well as being tutored by the polymath Gentile de' Becchi, who wrote poetry, often composed hymns and would later be rewarded by the Medici family with the bishopric of Arezzo, an indication of how closely this once independent city had become integrated into the Florentine Republic.

From an early age, Lorenzo demonstrated the literary facility which would ensure that his mature poems would one day enter the canon of Italian literature. As part of his education, Lorenzo also become a talented player of the viola and the flute, an accomplishment which enabled him to set some of his poems to music. At the same time, Lorenzo enjoyed such open-air pursuits as hunting, falconry and horse riding. In 1469, he won first prize in a spectacular jousting tournament held in the Piazza Santa Croce. As Machiavelli would write in the following century in his *History of Florence*, Lorenzo achieved this victory 'not by way of favour, but by his own valour and skill in arms'. As so often with Machiavelli, it is difficult to separate the truth from the irony. The tournament had of course been sponsored by Piero, who arranged that his son should sport a banner specially painted for the occasion by no less than the distinguished artist-architect Verrocchio, the man who had put the finishing touches to

---

* The Tornabuoni had changed their name from Tornaquinci. Neri di Cipriani Tornaquinci had been the manager of the Venice branch of the Medici bank during Giovanni di Bicci's time, when he got into such a scrape that he fled across the Alps to Cracow. However, it was not this disgrace which caused the family to change its name. The Tornaquinci came from an aristocratic lineage, and were thus liable to the longstanding ban on aristocratic participation in the public life of republican Florence. Revoking their time-honoured name enabled the family to elude this ban.

Brunelleschi's dome. It would have taken a reckless (and skilled) competitor to have dislodged Lorenzo from his jousting horse.

By this time, Lorenzo's charismatic ugliness was already beginning to charm the ladies. He is said to have had a penchant for more mature women – often widowed, but not invariably so. This amorous success was all the more astonishing given the fact that he had a beetle-browed protruding forehead, jutting chin and pronounced lower lip. His prominent nose was squashed so flat that he had no sense of smell, and according to Guicciardini 'his voice and pronunciation [were] harsh and unpleasing, because he spoke through his nose'.

Not surprisingly, Lorenzo soon gathered about him a gang of like-minded young men from good families – most of whom, like himself, were as interested in earnest discussions of Plato as they were in jolly japes and drinking too much wine. Machiavelli, in particular, seems to have been intrigued by this double-sided aspect of Lorenzo's character: 'to see him at one time in his grave moments and at another in his gay, was to see in him two personalities joined as it were with invisible bonds'. Others were less intrigued, in particular his high-minded tutor Becchi, who reprimanded him exasperatedly for 'going out late at night wenching and engaging in buffoonery that shames those who must have dealings with you the following day'.

Lorenzo's equally exasperated father decided to get him out of Florence, away from his roistering companions. In order to do this, yet at the same time retain a modicum of control over his behaviour, Piero dispatched Lorenzo on a number of minor diplomatic missions. Initially these were a mere formality, but Lorenzo seemed to enjoy exercising his charm and was surprisingly successful on missions to Bologna and Ferrara. Consequently, when Piero the Gouty realized that he was now too ill to travel, he decided to send Lorenzo on an important mission to Milan. He was to represent his father at the wedding of the daughter of the ageing Duke Francesco Sforza to the son of King Ferrante (Ferdinand I) of Naples. This was a vital diplomatic occasion: the strengthening of the alliance between Naples and Milan, and thus Florence too. Such an alliance guaranteed the balance of power in Italy. Piero the Gouty wrote to his son with solemn advice: 'Act as a man, not as a boy. Show sense, industry, and manly endeavour, so that you may be employed in more important things.' Here, too, Lorenzo acquitted himself impressively.

Piero the Gouty decided that it was now time for his son and heir to learn the workings of the family banking business. In February 1466,* Lorenzo was dispatched to Rome, where he was to be instructed by the manager of the most important branch of the Medici bank, namely his uncle Giovanni Tornabuoni. This proved to be a fiasco. All Lorenzo's instincts were contrary to those required of a banker. His poetic temperament, his flamboyant personality and his love of humanistic debate were utterly unsuited to perusing dry ledgers, financial prudence, and calculating the minutiae of profit and loss. Lorenzo learned practically nothing, and the gap in his knowledge would later prove a serious flaw. This would be exposed when he came to rely upon the advice of Medici bank managers who would not all prove to have the Medici interests at heart as much as his uncle did.

It was while Lorenzo was in Rome that his father received news of the death of Francesco Sforza, Duke of Milan, who had been Florence's most protective ally. At a stroke, Lorenzo's visit to Rome was transformed into a vital diplomatic mission. In March, Piero the Gouty wrote to Lorenzo that he must meet with Pope Paul II. His task was to impress upon the pope the importance of allowing Francesco Sforza's son, Galeazzo Maria Sforza, to succeed as Duke of Milan. This was no simple task. Francesco Sforza had usurped the dukedom from the previously ruling Visconti family, and recognizing the Sforzas as rulers of the dukedom would set a decisive precedent which would not be well received by the hereditary rulers of states throughout Italy. To make matters more difficult, Paul II was a Venetian, and his city now viewed Florence as an enemy following Cosimo de' Medici's switch of alliance to Milan. This had already resulted in the Medici bank losing the lucrative papal account, as well as Florence forfeiting all its commercial activities in Venice.

---

* The records show this was February 1465. In accord with medieval practice, the New Year began in March. I have translated this into the modern usage.

Inevitably, Lorenzo's time in Rome was not without its social side. He cut a dashing figure on his visits to the *palazzi* of the local nobility, such as the Orsini and the Colonna families. Yet in a letter Piero the Gouty sent to Lorenzo, he demonstrated that he knew his son all too well. He instructed him to 'put an end to all playing on instruments, or singing and dancing'. Now was the time for him to demonstrate his qualities as a future ruler of Florence.

It appears that Lorenzo was granted a number of audiences with the pope, after which he travelled south in April to Nola, in Neapolitan territory. Here, King Ferrante of Naples went so far as to break off his hunting trip in order to meet his young Florentine visitor. Piero the Gouty obviously intended Lorenzo's visit to bolster the Florentine alliance with Naples, but Ferrante was a difficult character at the best of times. According to Jacob Burckhardt, 'Besides hunting, which he practiced regardless of all rights of property, his pleasures were of two kinds: he liked to have his opponents near him, either alive in well-guarded prisons, or dead and embalmed, dressed in the costume which they wore in their lifetime.'

Indeed, King Ferrante delighted in treating his guests to a guided tour of his beloved 'museum of mummies'. An eyewitness to Lorenzo's meeting describes how 'the king took Lorenzo by the arm and, alone with the Secretary, escorted him into the ante-chamber'. But once again, Lorenzo's celebrated charm appears to have won the day. He would later write to his father of his meeting with Ferrante: 'I spoke with him, and he replied with many kind words, which I want to tell you in person.' In early May, Lorenzo arrived back in Florence to find the city split, on the verge of civil war.

An anti-Medici faction had coalesced around Luca Pitti, who had formerly been a close ally of the Medici. Pitti was a successful banker, and the wealth of his bank now well exceeded that of the ailing Medici institution. In order to demonstrate the superiority of his fortune, Pitti had decided to build himself a vast *palazzo* on the Oltrarno, close to the Ponte Vecchio. This *palazzo*, on its prominent hill, overlooked the city; and, according to a contemporary account, it was purposely intended to outshine the Palazzo Medici, with 'windows as big as the doors of the

Medici residence and… an internal courtyard that was large enough to contain the whole of the Medici's palace on the Via Larga'.

Pitti was not satisfied with just being the richest man in Florence. He wanted power, and to this end he had covertly gathered about him a group of supporters calling themselves the Party of the Hill – a reference to the hill on which Pitti was building his grandiose palace. By contrast, they referred to the Medici faction as the Party of the Plain, as their *palazzo* was across the river in the low-lying city centre.

This challenge to Medici rule had been some years in the making. It had gained its appeal, and its strength, with the promise of reform of the city government. The reformists' declared intention was to reduce the Medici stranglehold on power and open up effective governance to a larger section of the political class. However, the Medici had realized that, despite such promises of reform, Pitti's motives were in fact more about replacing their power with his own.

The leaders of the Party on the Hill were a mixed bunch. Pitti may have been their figurehead, but he was now approaching seventy and looked an unlikely candidate to take over the city. Other leaders such as Salvestro Nardi and Diotisalvi Neroni had their own agenda, wishing to seize power for themselves and their own families. Though another leader, Niccolò Soderini, seems to have harboured genuine reformist ideas, seeking to establish a truly democratic government in the republic.

Initially, Cosimo de' Medici, and then his son Piero the Gouty, had tried to placate Pitti, by ensuring that he was elected to important government posts. When this failed to assuage Pitti's ambitions, Piero the Gouty hinted to Pitti that he was willing to arrange for one of the Medici family to marry Pitti's eldest daughter, Francesca, the implication being that her bridegroom would be Lorenzo. This would have united both factions – at the same time consolidating the Medici hold on Florence.

However, Piero the Gouty had a habit of making seemingly beneficial decisions which eventually led to disastrous consequences. Typical of these was his attempt to settle the books of the Medici bank at the beginning of his reign by calling in its debts, a move which had alienated many of his father Cosimo's oldest friends. Accompanying this flaw was his penchant for indecision and subterfuge. Piero the Gouty now realized that he could never fully trust Luca Pitti, so instead of letting Pitti's daughter marry Lorenzo, he would have her betrothed to his younger son, the eleven-year-old Giuliano.

It had long been customary for the scions of Florence's leading families to be married off to members of the other leading families, thus consolidating the bonds between them. But in an unprecedented move to strengthen the Medici position, Piero the Gouty decided that it would be best if his son and heir was married outside the leading families of Florence, in order to ally the Medici with a powerful external power. He began putting out feelers to the leading aristocratic Orsini family of Rome, suggesting that Lorenzo should become betrothed to one of their eligible daughters, a young girl called Clarice.

The Orsini were the most powerful of all the ancient Roman families. Amongst their ranks were the rulers of a number of petty states in central Italy, some of whom were *condottieri* with their own private armies. They also boasted many highly placed members of the Church, including a cardinal. Linking the Medici to the Orsini seemed like a prudent move, as Piero suspected that the Venetians were at last making plans to march on Florence, in retaliation for the switching of their alliance to Milan. The Medici needed external allies, rather than inward-looking bonds to strengthen their position at home. Without such powerful allies, Florence could not hope to survive as an independent state.

Florence's reliance upon Milan was beginning to look increasingly unwise. The new Duke of Milan, Francesco Sforza's son Galeazzo Maria Sforza, was already proving to be an unpopular ruler. Unlike his *condottiere* father, Galeazzo was a man of some culture, with a deep love of music; but he was also possessed of a sadistic tyrannical streak. The latter caused him to inflict bizarre punishments on those who crossed him. A friar who predicted that Galeazzo would have a short reign was bricked up in a room and left to starve to death. A poacher who was caught on his estate was suffocated by having an entire rabbit stuffed down his throat. Tales of such deeds hardly endeared Galeazzo to the common people. And his habit of raping the daughters and wives of his nobles was quickly alienating him from the upper classes too. It was Piero the Gouty's realization that he could hardly rely upon such an ally that had finally persuaded him to disappoint Luca Pitti's daughter and seek to join the Medici with the Orsini of Rome instead.

However, when Luca Pitti got wind of this move, he took it as an insult to the honour of his daughter as well as his entire family. He quickly rallied the leaders of the Party of the Hill to a secret candlelit meeting in one of the halls of his vast unfinished *palazzo*. It was time to make plans for a decisive strike against the Medici.

Through the long summer of 1466, the streets of Florence sweltered in an ominous peace. As usual, most of the leading citizens had retired to their villas in the comparative cool of the nearby hilly countryside. Piero the Gouty was no exception, having moved with his family to the Medici villa at Careggi, a few miles north of the city walls. Here news reached him that, across the Apennines, the Venetians – along with their ally the Marquis of Ferrara – were assembling their forces under the command of the *condottiere* Bartolomeo Colleoni, who had taken over Sforza's mantle as the finest mercenary commander in Italy. This move could only be a preparation for the long-expected Venetian attack on Florence. As if this was not threatening enough, Piero also learned that Luca Pitti and the Party of the Hill were plotting a move of their own.

In desperation, Piero the Gouty dispatched a messenger to Galeazzo Maria in Milan, pleading with him to send Milanese troops to his aid as soon as possible. He knew this was but a forlorn hope. At the same time, he decided that it was imperative he return to the city. If he was to rally the Party of the Plain and unite Florence against her enemies, both internal and external, he would need to direct operations from the Palazzo Medici.

For some time now, Piero had been so stricken with gout that he was unable to walk. He was carried out of the Careggi villa on a litter, accompanied by a detachment of armed men. Meanwhile, the seventeen-year-old Lorenzo rode on ahead with a group of retainers, to make sure the way was clear. As Lorenzo was riding in the direction of the city gate, some labourers in the nearby fields warned him that they had noticed a large group of armed men preparing an ambush further up the road. Lorenzo immediately galloped back, warning his father. Whereupon Piero the Gouty ordered his entourage to carry him through the back lanes, skirting the ambush, so that he could enter the city by another gate. Lorenzo's dashing action had saved the day, at least for the time being.

No sooner had Piero the Gouty reached the Palazzo Medici than he learned that the Marquis of Ferrara was marching his troops towards the city. Piero conferred with his advisers. They drew up a list of citizens they thought they could rely upon for support, and another of those who were known to support the Party of the Hill. To their consternation, they found that many names appeared on both lists. So who could they rely upon? Around this time, the Milanese ambassador, Nicodemo Tranchedini, arrived at the Palazzo Medici. Tranchedini was a former soldier, and according to the contemporary Florentine chronicler Marco Parenti he at once took charge of the proceedings, 'erecting scaffolding above the windows to serve as battlements, with many stones and other arms of war, and occupying the streets around the house with armed troops'. Tranchedini also brought some unexpected good news: Galeazzo, Duke of Milan, had in fact responded to Piero the Gouty's plea for help, and had ordered 2,000 of his soldiers to march for Florence. The men acting under Tranchedini's command 'seized as well the gate of San Gallo in order to allow the entrance of his own men, who were expected to arrive, while the others were closed to ensure that their enemies would not be able to enter the city'.

At the same time, Piero the Gouty sent out men to buy up all the bread in the bakeries, as well as all the wine in the wine shops. These were to be laid out on tables in front of the Palazzo Medici, with the aim of attracting support from the people.

Back in the unfinished Palazzo Pitti, the leaders of the Party of the Hill learned that their ambush had failed and were thrown into disarray by the news that Piero the Gouty was safely ensconced in the Palazzo Medici, surrounded by armed supporters. They then learned that the Medici supporters had seized the keys to the city gates and were locking them against the arrival of the Marquis of Ferrara and his troops. This seizure of the keys to the gates of the city has been seen by many as the pivotal moment. It swung things in favour of the Medici, but more importantly it marked a point of no return. Previously, the Medici may have corrupted the ballot boxes, but they had never before directly taken the law into their own hands. According to the city statutes: 'The keys to the gates of the city of Florence must be kept under the power and custody [of the *gonafaloniere*]'. This marked more than a symbolic tipping point. According to Parenti and others, 'this act alone made Piero a tyrant of the city'.

Nonetheless, events continued to unfold. On hearing that the gates of the city were barred to the Marquis of Ferrara and his men, the Party of the Hill decided to act of their own accord. Their leaders rode out through the city streets, attempting to rouse the populace with cries of '*Popolo e Libertà*' ('the People and Liberty', the traditional rallying call of the Florentine citizens against their rulers).

Despite such stirring calls to arms, the fearful population remained for the most part locked in their homes. Others, finding themselves without bread, now heard about the tables laid out in front of the Palazzo Medici. Many soon began making their way to the Medici palace, where they began eating bread and drinking wine, at the same time being encouraged into chanting the Medici slogan: '*Palle! Palle! Palle!*'*

Through the next few days there was a tense standoff outside the city walls between the troops from Milan and those under the command of the Marquis of Ferrara, before the latter decided to withdraw. The attempted coup by the Party of the Hill was over, and the Medici were consolidated

---

* *Palle* literally means 'balls', and referred to the six red balls that appeared on a yellow background in the Medici coat of arms. The precise meaning of these balls is disputed. Some claim they are pills: the word *medici* means 'medical doctors', and the family may originally have had connections with this profession – or at least been apothecaries. Others insist that the six balls are copied from the arms of the Guild of Exchange (*Arte del Cambio*), of which the Medici were members. Variations in the number of balls and their colour would appear as the Medici coat of arms evolved over the ensuing years.

in power.* Pitti was reduced to a pitiful old man, and begged forgiveness from his erstwhile friend, grovelling at his feet. Piero the Gouty forgave him. Other leaders, such as Nardi, Neroni and Soderini, were sentenced to death by the authorities, but Piero the Gouty decided that leniency would be the less divisive option, and their sentences were commuted to lifelong exile.

In the year following Pitti's attempted coup, Lucrezia de' Medici (née Tornabuoni) was dispatched to Rome to assess Clarice Orsini as a future bride for her son. Lorenzo had in fact met the then sixteen-year-old Clarice at a social occasion at the Orsini residence during his earlier visit to Rome. Lorenzo's mother wrote approvingly of the tall, red-headed Clarice: 'I don't think Rome at present has a more beautiful girl to offer in marriage.' In reality, beauty had little to do with the matter. This was to be a dynastic union.

Two years later, in June 1469, the twenty-year-old Lorenzo de' Medici and the nineteen-year-old Clarice Orsini were formally married in Florence. Clarice brought with her an impressive dowry of money and gifts, equivalent in overall value to 10,000 florins. But more importantly she forged a link between the Medici bankers of Florence and the aristocratic and powerful Orsini of Rome. The event was marked by three days of public celebration throughout the city.

---

* Piero the Gouty later claimed that his would-be ambushers on the way to Florence were a detachment of the Marquis of Ferrara's soldiers, and that it was this attempt on his life which made him take up arms – thus precipitating the events which led to the defeat of Pitti and the Party of the Hill. Some sources have suggested that the attempt on Piero the Gouty's life was either fictional or staged, a view to some extent reinforced by such events as the opportune arrival of the Milanese ambassador at the Palazzo Medici. As is so often the case, there are several differing versions of this story. My views have been changed by wider research since I originally wrote about these events in *The Medici: Godfathers of the Renaissance* (2003). The differing 'facts' make any interpretation of the principal actors' motivations slippery. Was Piero the Gouty forced to act as he did? Or did he purposely precipitate the events in order to consolidate Medici power?

These began on the morning of Sunday, 4 June 1469, when Clarice Orsini rode down the Via Larga on the white horse gifted to her by her bridegroom. The crowd, filled with curiosity and awe, watched as she led a long procession of thirty maids of honour (one for each leading family in Florence). Clarice was wearing a white hooded gown sparkling with gold thread, and her passage was accompanied by heralds playing trumpets and flutes. On either side, the buildings were bedecked with flags, flowers and bunting. When the procession arrived at the Palazzo Medici, Clarice was assisted from her mount and entered through an archway of olive branches (symbolizing fertility). The *palazzo* itself was decorated with hanging tapestries and awnings displaying the Medici and Orsini coats of arms.

An anonymous contemporary chronicler who witnessed the event recorded: 'In the house here, where the marriage feast was, every respectable person who came in was at once taken to the ground-floor hall... The common folk were not invited.' During the ensuing days, several banquets would be held in the courtyard, garden and loggia of the Palazzo Medici. At these, wild boar and suckling pig, together with quantities of poultry, were served, along with some 300 barrels of the finest Tuscan wine, cakes, jellies, marzipan and sugared almonds. As the guests dined, minstrels serenaded them from the balconies.

The festivities continued until the Tuesday, when a ceremonial High Mass was celebrated in the nearby San Lorenzo – the Medici church bearing the name of the family's patron saint. Here the bride was presented with a book of hours, bound with crystal-studded silver and costing some 200 florins. Those who bore witness to these events seem to have been aware of the exact price attached to each item.

In the Roman fashion, Clarice had received no more than the traditional female education: dancing, singing and the social graces. Lorenzo, on the other hand, possessed as fine an intellect as any young man in Florence, being cognizant with the latest humanist ideas, appreciative of the superlative art produced by the Medici 'family artists', and already capable of writing verse whose skill and sentiments would be appreciated long after his death. This difference between the bride and groom does not seem to have bothered the opinionated Lorenzo, who wrote: 'The defect which is so common in women and makes them insupportable is their affectation of understanding everything.'

Lorenzo would prove a difficult husband to live with. Clarice, for her part, remained convinced of her aristocratic superiority, regarding Florence as little more than a colourful backwater compared with her native Rome, the Eternal City. However, in time they would each become reconciled to the habits and opinions of their partner. And both would go to considerable efforts to maintain the appearance of a normal Italian marriage of the period. In doing so, the appearance would eventually become reality. Clarice and Lorenzo would go on to have no less than ten children (with three dying in childbirth). They would frequently be apart, and the letters between them reveal a gossipy cosiness, tinged with playful irony. As Clarice wrote on one occasion: 'If you have any news which is not a state secret, do write and tell me.'

However, little courtesy was extended to Clarice by Lorenzo's charmed circle of intellectuals and artists. Amongst these, she was regarded as frumpy and ignorant, and was frequently slighted. But when such slights descended into rudeness, Lorenzo would be the first to take his wife's side, admonishing his friends, and even on occasion expelling them from the Palazzo Medici for a period to cool their heels. Meanwhile, the ties between the Medici and the Orsini would later be further strengthened when Lorenzo used his influence to ensure that Clarice's older brother Rinaldo was appointed Archbishop of Florence.

Just six months after Lorenzo's marriage to Clarice Orsini, his father Piero the Gouty finally succumbed to the affliction which had crippled him during his final years. The twenty-year-old Lorenzo was invited by the *signoria* to become leader of the city, and duly accepted. The republic was now little but a sham, the Medici machine ensuring that their men were appointed to all the major administrative offices. Lorenzo would justify this state of affairs, explaining the real reason he was willing to 'take care' of the city: 'I did so in order to protect our friends and property, since it fares ill in Florence with anyone who is rich but does not have any control over the government.' Despite such self-serving pragmatism, Lorenzo would prove to be a lot more than a wholly selfish ruler. When necessary, he would identify himself with Florence. In the good sense, he saw its survival as his own. In a less magnanimous sense, he regarded its assets as his own. And, as we shall see, on one vital occasion these two motivations would prove identical.

Despite the Medici hold on power, the politics of Florence never lost their turbulence. As before, it was the ethos of democracy that counted. The citizens of Florence always remained republican at heart, no matter how 'fixed' their democratic process became. The political volatility which had been a constant factor during the years of the early Renaissance would continue during the reign of Lorenzo the Magnificent, when the High Renaissance blossomed into its greatest flowering: once again, the parallels with Athens in Ancient Greece would prove uncanny. One of the greatest transformations of western culture would continue to take place against a background of internal political turmoil and external squabbling city-states.

As early as the spring of 1470, there was an uprising in Prato, north of the city. This was led by Diotisalvi Neroni, along with several other exiled members of the Party of the Hill. Together with a column of armed men, they took over Prato, and were rumoured to be making plans to march on the city itself. On hearing this news, the *signoria* at once summoned the city militia and ordered them to march on Prato. By the time the militia arrived, they discovered that the local mayor, Cesare Petrucci, had acted swiftly and decisively, rousing the people to seize the leaders of the uprising. Neroni had managed to escape but the others had been summarily hanged in the main piazza, along with a number of their fellow conspirators.

This was heartening news for Lorenzo the Magnificent. Petrucci's action had not only saved Florence, but had also demonstrated how firmly the people of the *contado* backed Medici rule. Lorenzo took note of Petrucci, who was not a known Medici man, earmarking him for future promotion. The Medici had often found that such 'outsiders' proved more loyal to the cause than long-term members of the Medici faction. (This would certainly prove to be the case with Petrucci, who would rise to hold the post of *gonfaloniere* at a particularly auspicious time. It would be his brave actions which played a crucial role in overcoming the Pazzi conspiracy, the most serious threat to Lorenzo the Magnificent's rule.)

One of the first things that Lorenzo had done on coming into power was to sit down with Francesco Sassetti, the long-term general manager of the Medici bank, and go through the bank's ledgers – as well as the *libri segreti* which invariably reflected a more realistic picture. Lorenzo was no expert in accounting, but with the help of Sassetti he grasped the basics: when everything was totted up he 'found that we possessed 237,988 scudi' (at the time, probably around 230,000 florins). Under Piero the Gouty's cautious management, the bank had to a certain extent recovered from the extravagant patronage which marked the last years of Cosimo's reign. Even so, the bank remained in a parlous state where profits were concerned. And without profits there was simply not enough money to finance the Medici political machine, to say nothing of maintaining the precarious balance of power in Italy which ensured Florence's survival as an independent state.

This was brought home to Lorenzo the Magnificent when he invited Galeazzo Maria Sforza, Duke of Milan, on a state visit to Florence to thank him for his help in overcoming the Party of the Hill. Galeazzo duly arrived in Florence with an entourage of more than 2,000 nobles, courtiers, servants and the like. The citizens of Florence were dazzled by the seemingly endless procession of Milan's brocaded knights, liveried soldiers, falcon-bearers, and even 500 hunting dogs. Playing host to such a huge delegation proved a costly business. On the other hand, the Milan branch of the Medici bank, under its skilled manager Acerrito Portinari (who had succeeded his brother Pigello), was now to all intents and purposes the Milanese state exchequer – and as such, one of the few branches guaranteed to bring in a profit.

Galeazzo's stay in the Palazzo Medici proved a resounding success. The Duke of Milan was more than impressed by the wealth of cultural artefacts which adorned the walls, stairways and courtyards of Lorenzo's *palazzo*. Milan, for all its glory as a commercial centre and the wealth it had obtained from the silk trade, remained very much a medieval city, barely touched by the cultural transformation of the Renaissance. This was exemplified by its huge cathedral, a classic of Gothic architecture with its flying buttresses and host of intricate spires. By comparison, the clear-cut lines and marble facade of Florence's cathedral were very much those of a contemporary masterpiece; its towering dome an unsurpassed feat of engineering. Furthermore, Galeazzo's visit was marked by lavish banquets and public pageants, with arches and tableaux created by Lorenzo the Magnificent's finest artists, such as Botticelli and the up-and-coming Leonardo da Vinci.

Despite the vast cost of this ducal visit, relations between Florence and Milan did not noticeably improve. Italian politics remained as difficult and divisive as ever, and Florence's dazzling display for Galeazzo of Milan hardly improved relations with her other ally, Naples. Why was Lorenzo being so lavish to a mere duke like Galeazzo? The ever-suspicious King Ferrante of Naples was jealous.

As if this was not enough, Lorenzo the Magnificent also found himself obliged to lay on regular expensive and spectacular pageants to keep his own citizens happy. Meanwhile, as his reign continued, the finances of the Medici bank began to take a turn for the worse. Lorenzo became desperate to find another source of income to fill his coffers.

The Medici family and its bank had long been involved in the lucrative alum trade. Alum was the mineral salt which was primarily used to fix vivid dyes to cloth. Crimson robes, doublets and hose, as well as delicate dresses, all required alum. As such, this substance was essential to the Florentine textile trade, as well as to markets as far afield as the Low Countries and England.

Alum was a rare commodity, and the main European source was discovered in 1460 at the small town of Tolfa, some thirty miles north-west of Rome, near the port of Civitavecchia. This was in papal territory, and Pope Pius II immediately took control of these mines, creating a virtual monopoly of the alum market. At the time, the Medici were the papal bankers, with the Rome branch under the experienced management of Giovanni Tornabuoni. Within two years Tornabuoni had negotiated exclusive distribution rights for this alum with the pope. The Tolfa mines transported the alum to warehouses at Civitavecchia, and from there the Medici shipped the alum by galleys to their agents in northern Europe. Few but the Medici bank had sufficient expertise and capital to run the alum business properly. They alone could afford to equip the galleys necessary for the long voyage from Italy, around Spain, to the Low Countries. They alone could afford to cover any losses which might be incurred by shipwreck or piracy.

Surprisingly, this agreement survived when the Venetian Paul II became pope in 1464 and Florence became involved in a warlike situation with Venice. The Medici commercial organization was seemingly indispensable.

The only reliable details of this commercial enterprise were entered in the Medici bank *libri segreti*, which are now lost. The public accounts produced by Tornabuoni were purely for inspection by the requisite tax authorities. It seems that initially the alum trade may have brought in an annual sum of over 70,000 florins. (A vast amount, when one remembers that the entire profits of the Medici bank during the twenty-three years up to 1420 were 151,820 florins.)

However, it soon becomes evident that things in the alum trade did not continue in this vein. Although Tornabuoni did his best from the Rome end to ensure that the price and supplies of alum remained stable, the Medici bank's manager in Bruges, Tommaso Portinari, complained that there was a glut in the market, which meant that he was having to sell the alum at reduced prices just to get rid of it. Tornabuoni suspected that Portinari was siphoning off money for himself, and passed this on to general manager Sassetti in Florence. Portinari was well established in Bruges, where he had firm relationships with several important noblemen. The sheer distance, the time it took for mail to reach Bruges, and the subsequent inability to control Portinari meant that the Medici bank was soon sinking back into its old unprofitable ways, dragged down by the ailing alum trade and a contract which obliged it to pay large sums to the pope.

But luck was at hand. In 1471, a rare deposit of alum was discovered in a cave by the small town of Volterra, in Florentine territory some thirty miles south-west of the city. The Volterra authorities initially assigned the mining concession to a company with three Medici supporters as the main shareholders, but it soon became clear that the deposits were much larger than had previously been estimated. Whereupon it was decided to revoke the concession and sign it over to a consortium of local citizens. This move was vetoed by the *signoria* in Florence, but when news of the decision reached Volterra a riot broke out, during which several Florentines resident in the town were killed. One of the Medici shareholders was thrown out of a window, and the local mayor, a Florentine appointee, was hacked to death by a mob as he attempted to barricade himself in his *palazzo*.

The twenty-three-year-old Lorenzo the Magnificent had already demonstrated his considerable diplomatic skills, but wisely decided to refrain from acting at once. He sought the advice of the *signoria*, who replied with an old Florentine proverb: 'Better a lean peace than a fat victory.' Lorenzo was inclined to agree. But he then learned that Neroni and other exiled members of the Party of the Hill had made contact with the Volterra rebels. Neroni and his supporters wished to sign a secret pact with Volterra which would lead to 'the destruction of the house of Medici'. Lorenzo at once decided that a show of force was essential. If Volterra broke with Florentine rule, other cities were liable to follow suit. Tuscany could well splinter into various independent city-states, followed by the downfall of the Medici in Florence.

Lorenzo the Magnificent now hired Federico da Montefeltro, Lord of Urbino, and his mercenary army, who were ordered to march on Volterra, which was soon placed under siege. After four weeks, the citizens surrendered, opening the city gate to allow Montefeltro's troops to enter. But at this point Montefeltro lost control of his troops, who went on the rampage, murdering, raping and looting their way through the city.*

When news of this outrage reached Lorenzo in Florence, he was horrified and set out at once for Volterra. Here he found the city devastated, its ruins smoking, the streets littered with mangled corpses. The remaining survivors had fled naked and were hiding out in the woods. After riding through the ruins, Lorenzo pledged 2,000 florins towards the rebuilding of the city. However, according to Machiavelli in his *History of Florence*: 'The news of this victory was received with very great joy by the Florentines, and because it had been altogether Lorenzo's campaign, he rose to very great reputation for it.'

Paradoxically, this represented both a low point and a high point in Lorenzo the Magnificent's career as ruler of Florence. This would not be the last such occasion during his twenty-three-year reign.

---

* Technically speaking, according to the widely accepted contemporary 'rules of war', when a city was placed under siege the commander of the besieging forces would offer the citizens the opportunity to surrender. If this was accepted, no harm would come to the citizens. If, on the other hand, the citizens refused to surrender, hoping that they could outlast the besiegers until allied forces came to their rescue, the besiegers had the right to everything they could take when they overran the city. In practice, the city was usually forced to hand over spoils to the invaders. Massacres were a rarity.

CHAPTER 13

LEONARDO

A SIMILAR AMBIGUITY CHARACTERIZES THE most widely talented of all those who began their careers amongst Lorenzo the Magnificent's charmed intellectual circle.

Leonardo da Vinci, who would be befriended by dukes and even royalty, was born illegitimate and spoke with a common rural accent. If he was educated at all, it was at a medieval abacus school for clerks; in his early years he did not even learn Latin, let alone come into contact with the new humanist ideas. As a precocious young artist he quickly gained a reputation for leaving his commissions unfinished.

Further ambiguities abounded throughout his life. At the height of his artistic abilities, he would choose to give up painting altogether, in order to pursue a career as a military engineer. In an era when the dissection of human bodies was forbidden, he would explore human anatomy at a level of detail unknown to his predecessors. Yet none of his findings would have the slightest influence on medical science, as they remained hidden in his private notebooks and then scattered when these were taken apart and sold piecemeal – all this, over half a century before the

Flemish physician Andreas Vesalius completed his *De Humanus Corporis Fabrica* (On the Fabric of the Human Body), the work which founded modern anatomy.

Similar 'firsts' by Leonardo which would provide no benefit to humanity, for much the same reason, include flying machines, an underwater breathing apparatus, tanks, sluice gates, time and motion studies, a machine gun… the list goes on and on. According to the art historian Helen Gardner: 'Leonardo was well known in his time as both a sculptor and an architect, though none of his sculpture has survived and no actual buildings can be attributed to him.' She even goes so far as to suggest that the architect Donato Bramante 'may well have remembered a drawing by Leonardo when he prepared his original designs for the great church of St Peter's in Rome'. In her view, Leonardo's 'mind and personality seem to us superhuman, while the man himself [remains] mysterious and remote'.

These last aspects of Leonardo's personality come to the fore in his best-known work, the *Mona Lisa*, where the mysterious ghost of a smile on the sitter's face seems to express some profound inner emotion which we can never quite grasp. This may now be regarded as his masterpiece, yet it too remained (in his eyes at least) unfinished. He returned to it obsessively; had he not died, he would certainly have continued this restless quest for perfection, with the result that we might today be seeing a subtly different face. What has come down to us is the forever unfinished portrait in which he sought to express the mystery of self – of his self, of the human self. It remains forever unsatisfactory, in that its artist himself remained unsatisfied by what he had achieved. Wherever Leonardo travelled during his last wandering years, he took this painting with him. He even transported it, carefully bundled up amongst his cartload of worldly possessions, when he set out in 1516 as an old man on his final journey north across the Alps to France, where he would die at the age of sixty-seven, his head cradled in the arms of his friend King Francis I.

Leonardo da Vinci was born in 1452 in the countryside near the small Tuscan town of Vinci, some fifteen miles west of Florence. His father was a respected Florentine notary, Ser Piero da Vinci, and his mother was a local woman called Caterina – probably the daughter of a woodcutter, or possibly a slave of Middle Eastern origin.* Leonardo appears to have been close to his mother, but otherwise spent a largely solitary childhood roaming the countryside. As he would write many years later in his notebooks: 'While you are alone you are completely yourself; and if you are accompanied by even one other person you are but half yourself.'

Not until he was fourteen did he go to Florence, where he was employed by, and later apprenticed to, the artist and sculptor Andrea del Verrocchio, whose previous apprentices included Botticelli and Ghirlandaio. Verrocchio passed on much of his work to be finished by his apprentices; stirred by such challenges and high expectations, Leonardo's talent flourished, as did his technical skills. He also acquired the new technique of painting in oils.

This novel method of painting, which would play such a vital role in Renaissance art, was invented far away in northern Europe some years before the influence of the Renaissance reached that region. According to Vasari, the technique of mixing powdered pigments with linseed and other oils was invented by the Flemish brothers Jan and Hubert van Eyck around 1420. Modern evidence points to an earlier discovery of this method, involving multi-layered painting and the extensive use of glazes, but it is safe to say that it was developed considerably by the van Eyck brothers.†

Previously painters had favoured tempera or fresco, where the pigment is bound by water mixed with a glutinous material such as egg yolk. In tempera, the paint is applied to dry plaster or a wooden panel. In fresco, the paint is applied to wet plaster. In both cases the paint dries quickly, and is extremely difficult to paint over without blurring. Oil painting does not suffer from these drawbacks; it can also be applied in thick

---

* The Italian anthropologist Luigi Capasso has studied a clear left index fingerprint in one of Leonardo's notebooks and claims: 'The one we found in this fingertip applies to sixty per cent of the Arabic population, which suggests the probability that his mother was of Middle Eastern origin.'

† The multi-panelled Ghent altarpiece, painted between the 1420s and 1432 by Jan and Hubert van Eyck, is regarded by many as the first complete oil painting.

layers, allowing it to render subtleties of depth, colour and light, as well as innovative precision or suggestiveness.

At the same time, artists began using canvas, which amongst its other advantages made paintings more portable. They could be commissioned by the increasing class of wealthy merchants, who could hang them on the walls of their homes. Prior to this, such works of art had largely been commissioned by the Church. This meant they were painted on walls, altarpieces and chapels, and portrayed religious scenes. The advent of oil painting encouraged secular art, especially portraiture.

In these early years, Leonardo became known for his obsession with drawing, together with a similarly compulsive interest in experimenting with pigments and oil, as if trying to discover some perfect recipe for the application of paint. This habit of experimenting with materials would prove ruinous for a number of commissions during his later years.

Leonardo is known to have assisted Verrocchio in his large work *The Baptism of Christ*. This is the earliest example we have of Leonardo's painting. He is thought to be responsible for the angel holding Christ's robe on the far left of the scene, as well as for the background, which appears to be reminiscent of his solitary wanderings through the Arno valley near his home in Vinci. Several other points are immediately apparent in Leonardo's contribution to this work. For instance, while Botticelli was weak on anatomy, it is clear that the young Leonardo was already well versed in this skill. Where Botticelli frequently used robes to mask the bodies of his subjects, Leonardo goes so far as to subtly suggest the anatomy of the kneeling angel beneath the fabric of his clothing. Yet this is but a passing comparison with his illustrious predecessor. More pertinent is the view of Leonardo's biographer Serge Bramly, who noted that the face of Leonardo's angel 'shines with a luminous light quite unknown in Florence before this'. (Leonardo's contribution to this work is painted in oils, while Verrocchio's painting is in tempera. At this stage, Leonardo's 'experiments' were wholly successful, contributing to his originality.)

According to Vasari, when Verrocchio saw Leonardo's depiction of the angel carrying Christ's garment he was so overcome by his apprentice's superior technique that he swore never to paint again. This is certainly a myth, though the occasion may well have marked Leonardo's early promotion to Verrocchio's chief assistant. Most sources agree that Verrocchio's *Baptism of Christ* was begun around 1472, when Verrocchio put Leonardo's name forward for membership of the painters' guild, the Guild of St Luke.

It was around this time that we learn of Leonardo's early involvement with Lorenzo the Magnificent. When preparations were made for Duke Galeazzo of Milan's visit to Florence, Lorenzo ensured that no expense was spared. Verrocchio's studio was commissioned to redecorate the guest apartments at the Palazzo Medici, and much of this task was delegated to Leonardo. He was also responsible for designing some of the pageants and displays which took place during the visit itself. Such entertainments involved all manner of special effects. According to Vasari, there were *trompe-l'œil* temples, with pillars topped by gold and silver figures, as well as skies 'crowded with living creatures with lights that flashed on and off as swiftly as lightning'. These displays would also have involved fireworks, which had been introduced from China during the previous century. It comes as little surprise that the final pageant descended into chaos, catching fire and destroying the church in which it was being staged.

Although the citizens of Florence were initially dazzled by the arrival of Duke Galeazzo and his large exotic entourage, they soon became wary of the huge influx of soldiers. Florence had no standing army, and the citizens were unused to heavily armed warriors swaggering through the streets, to say nothing of their unruly behaviour. Likewise, the novelty of the finely hosed Milanese courtiers and other exotic hangers-on, not to mention their assumed superiority, soon began to pall. Why had Lorenzo the Magnificent laid on such exaggerated hospitality for these people? What had these Milanese strangers done to deserve such a welcome? Superstitious as ever, the Florentine populace were quick to blame the Milanese for the fire which burned down one of their churches. These foreigners had indulged in too much feasting, especially when it was now Lent and they should have been fasting.

Even so, such displays could not help but influence the locals' own conduct. Machiavelli's description of the transformation of current behaviour was typical of the general reaction:

> There now appeared disorders commonly witnessed in times of peace: the city's youth, being more independent, spent excessive sums on clothing, feasting, and debauchery. Living in idleness, it consumed its time and money on gaming and women; its only care was to seek to outshine others by luxury in costume, fine speaking, and wit... These unfortunate habits became even worse with the arrival of the courts of the Duke of Milan... If the Duke already found the city corrupted by effeminate manners worthy of courts and quite contrary to those of a republic, he left it in an even more deplorable state of corruption.

Although Florence had detailed sumptuary laws governing the costume and appropriate adornments to be worn by different classes and by women, these were falling into increasing abeyance during the period. Lorenzo the Magnificent and his charmed circle were certainly guilty of such transgressive behaviour. And it seems that Leonardo was no exception. He may not have been an intimate amongst Lorenzo's friends, but there is no doubt that he entered the fringes of this group. His limited education, as well as his complete lack of Latin, would have excluded him from the philosophical and humanist debates conducted by the likes of the Platonist Ficino and the humanist poet Poliziano. Though Leonardo would certainly have been heartened by the pronouncements of the great Alberti, such as: 'A man can do all things if he but wills them.'

Even so, Leonardo felt excluded. His lack of formal education, society mores and external self-confidence would have ensured that he never shone amongst such company. Yet he *did* believe that he could do anything, and his inner ambition and self-regard would have ensured that he saw himself as the equal of any of these dazzling figures. But he was shy, only able to be fully himself in his own company.

Leonardo's response to such contradictions seems to have taken on a characteristic psychological guise. In order to mask his shyness, he adopted a peacock style in his everyday wear. He would not directly participate, but he would shine from afar. This would become a typical response for the gauche young Leonardo, who became known both for his reticence and for his flamboyant red-headed appearance. His low, soft-spoken voice was initially to disguise his 'yokel' accent; his courteous manners to mask his lack of a 'good' education. In later years, when his country vowels had long been smoothed over, while his polymathic knowledge and skills had become a thing of legend, his manner would still retain this apparent diffidence. Yet he still could not help asserting himself in display. Leonardo may not have lived 'in idleness' like the foppish young men criticized by Machiavelli, but he certainly exhibited the 'effeminate manners worthy of courts and quite contrary to those of a republic'.

Leonardo would eventually pay for this. Quite how overt the homosexual element in his behaviour actually was, is difficult to tell. He made only the rarest oblique references to sexuality in his voluminous but secretive notebooks: 'The act of procreation and anything that has any relation to it is so disgusting that human beings would soon die out if there were no pretty faces and sensuous dispositions.'

Homosexuality was against the law in Florence, even if the law – like the sumptuary laws – was more honoured in the breach than in the observance. Despite this, it left Leonardo exposed. In Florence at this time, and indeed throughout the period of the Renaissance, there was a letterbox at the Palazzo della Signoria where those with a grievance, or who had witnessed wrongdoing, could post secret denunciations. In 1476, while Leonardo was still at Verrocchio's studio, an anonymous accusation was posted accusing a certain Jacopo Saltarelli, an artist's model, of 'being party to many wretched offences and consents to please those who request such wickedness of him'. Named amongst those who 'requested' such things of Saltarelli was Leonardo – along with a member of the Tornabuoni family. Theoretically, at least, those found guilty of 'homosexuality' in any form (this even included men who sodomized their wives to avoid having more children) could be sentenced to death. Such punishment was very rarely enforced, but it must nonetheless have remained a nagging fear in such cases.

In this instance, the accusations were not pursued. This was almost certainly at the instigation of Lorenzo the Magnificent. Not only was he himself prone to such practice on occasion, but the important Tornabuoni family had long been closely linked with the Medici (and Lorenzo's mother was a Tornabuoni). Although this accusation would certainly have frightened Leonardo, his subsequent behaviour would seem to justify his biographer Michael White's opinion that 'there is little doubt that he remained a practising homosexual'.

Despite Leonardo's youthful reserve, there is evidence that at least one Florentine intellectual proved a close and formative influence. In his notebooks, Leonardo mentions a certain '*maestro Pagholo medico*'. This is generally understood to be a reference to Paolo Toscanelli – the renowned map collector who did so much to encourage exploration of the New World – who would by now have been in his seventies. Toscanelli's great learning and age would certainly have merited him the title *maestro*, and we know that he had studied medicine, hence the description of him as *medico*. Toscanelli was a close friend of Verrocchio, and would thus have had ample opportunity to meet Leonardo, as well as to encourage the scientific interests which now began to appear in his secretive notebooks.*

---

* 'Secretive' may well be too strong a word. It is not clear how much Leonardo kept his constant jottings to himself. His habit of sketching and writing in his notebooks would hardly have escaped notice. The meaning of some of the drawings would certainly have been evident, but his coded writing would have been less easy to decipher at first sight. Less easy, but far from impossible – after all, Leonardo's code consisted simply of mirror writing. This entailed writing from right to left (easy for a left-hander such as Leonardo), with the individual letters written back to front, so that their meaning only became transparent when a mirror was held to the text, transposing it laterally to the eye of the reader. Some scholars have suggested that such writing was intended to keep it opaque only to the gaze of the casual inquisitive eye. Anyone of persistence and intelligence would soon have worked out the code. So why did Leonardo use mirror writing? The usual answer is that he wanted to prevent anyone from stealing his ideas. As we have seen, there was no fully effective notion of copyright during this period. Inventions and ideas could gain their creator employment or a simple one-off payment. All this seems plausible enough. On the other hand, such writing would also seem to mirror an aspect of Leonardo's complex psychological make-up.

But it was Toscanelli's maps and his talk of exotic far-off lands which seem to have had an inspirational effect on Leonardo.

In Leonardo's notebooks, he writes several long descriptions of voyages abroad. These initially led some to believe that he had actually undertaken these journeys, despite the fact that some of his descriptions have plainly fantastical elements. Travellers at the time often inserted such stories into their genuine descriptions, much as map-makers sometimes inserted drawings of mythical sea monsters and the like in their maps.

One of Leonardo's voyages is in the form of a letter to a Florentine merchant called Benedetto Dei, who certainly existed and is known to have travelled widely. Leonardo writes to him recounting 'news from the East', telling of a black giant with bloodshot eyes and a 'face most horrible' who terrorized the people of North Africa. 'He lived in the sea and fed on whales, leviathans, and ships.' When the locals tried to kill him, swarming all over his body like ants, 'he shook his head and sent the men flying through the air like hail'. This tale involves what would become a recurrent preoccupation of Leonardo: cataclysmic scenes of devastation, floods, monsters and the like.

He himself often becomes involved in these events, and at one point is swallowed by a giant: 'I do not know what to say or what to do, for everywhere I seem to find myself swimming head downwards through that mighty throat and remaining buried in that huge belly, in the confusion of death.' Beneath Leonardo's serene exterior – a serenity which he frequently achieved in his paintings – he appears to have been beset by dark thoughts welling up from his subconscious mind. Over the years these have been subjected to all manner of analysis and psychological interpretation, but they remain nonetheless elusive. Suffice it to say that the impulse which drove him to create also plagued him with negative feelings. Perhaps it was these, as much as his perfectionism and his constant need to experiment with his materials, that prevented him from finishing those works which he could not bring himself to regard as complete.

The frequent crossings out and insertions in the storytelling sections of Leonardo's writings would seem to indicate that he was trying to maintain an entertaining fictional narrative, with the prerequisite elements of suspense and excitement. One 'letter' addressed to the 'Devatdar of Syria, lieutenant of the sacred Sultan of Babylon' describes Mount Taurus in southern Anatolia, as well as the Euphrates river, and is even decorated with maps. Other mentions are made of travels to the Red Sea, the Nile, Gibraltar and even England. However, at one point he makes a penetrating scientific observation: 'When I was at sea, at an equal distance from a flat shore and a mountain, the coast of the flat shore seemed much farther away than the mountain.'

Of similar apparent veracity (alongside similar whoppers) is his tale of climbing to the peak of a 14,000-foot mountain in the Alps. This must have taken place during his time in Milan, which began in the early 1480s. He depicts his feeling of awe at the view from the peak – the sparkle of the glaciers below, the silver thread of the streams – and how he was looking down at 'the four rivers that water Europe', i.e. the Rhine, the Rhône, the Danube and the Po. Here he would have been at well over twice the height of Mont Ventoux, which had been climbed by Petrarch a century and a half previously.

This story may have elements of truth in it, exaggerated from the tales told by travellers visiting Toscanelli. On the other hand, imagining such a feat may well have inspired Leonardo's very real ideas for constructing a flying machine.

It was this sense of adventure, of exceeding the known, which was to make Leonardo's mind unique. And although few of his more fantastical 'engines' would ever be created in solid form, in his lifetime or after it, they are crucial to our understanding of the Renaissance – what it was, what was taking place in the human mind, and what effect it had. Here is an imaginative blueprint of what the beginning of modern science looked like – from inside the mind of one of the first modern scientists. In Leonardo's *Mona Lisa* we see the glimpse of an inner mind given expression. In Leonardo's notebooks we can actually see – as never before – the inner thought processes of one of the most inventive minds history has known, at a crucial moment in human mental evolution.

Toscanelli's inspirational presence in Florence can thus be said to have played a part in two of the most significant developments of his age.

Firstly, Amerigo Vespucci's exploration and his realization that America was in fact a New World. And secondly, Leonardo's inward impulse to discover and interrogate what he saw of the world around him.

According to the unknown contemporary Florentine chronicler usually referred to as Anonimo Gaddiano, by 1480 Leonardo was living in the Palazzo Medici, having been taken in by Lorenzo the Magnificent. Apparently, Leonardo was often seen working in the garden adjacent to the Piazza San Marco, just around the corner from the *palazzo*. This 'garden' was an open stretch of ground where the Medici family had begun storing their collection of Ancient Roman statues and fragments, initially chosen for Cosimo de' Medici by his friend Donatello. From all accounts, the garden had a pavilion, which was used as a sculpture school by the ageing former pupil of Donatello, Bertoldo di Giovanni. During the hot summers, the students would emerge from the pavilion and sit in the shade making drawings of the sculptures and fragments which were scattered throughout the garden. This also served as a general meeting place for Lorenzo the Magnificent and his intellectual friends, where they would listen to readings from classical works and have debates on humanism. (These meetings, and others held at Medici villas in the countryside, are often referred to as the Platonic or Florentine Academy.)

It may well have been at one of these gatherings that Leonardo first encountered Botticelli. Nearing the height of his powers, Botticelli was seven years older than Leonardo. Despite their differing temperaments, they became close friends. By now Leonardo had left the studio of Verrocchio and set up a studio of his own, almost certainly aided by his father, Ser Piero da Vinci; and he had begun receiving independent commissions. These may have come through his membership of the Guild of St Luke, but more likely resulted from his connection with Lorenzo the Magnificent.

Unlike his father and his grandfather, Lorenzo the Magnificent seldom commissioned works of art for himself, largely because of the parlous state of the Medici bank. On the other hand, he certainly went out of his way to encourage others to commission 'his' artists. This was how his cousin Lorenzo di Pierfrancesco de' Medici came to commission

Botticelli, and may well have been why in 1478 Leonardo da Vinci was commissioned to paint an altarpiece for the chapel in the Palazzo della Signoria. Three years later, Leonardo would be commissioned to paint *The Adoration of the Magi* by the Dominican monks of San Donato in Scopeto, which was then just outside the western walls of the city.

It is known that, in preparation for this work, Leonardo studied Botticelli's painting of the same subject which hung in the church of Santa Maria Novella. Botticelli's work is thought to have had an influence on Leonardo's overall composition, but little else. He and Botticelli may have been friends, but Leonardo was highly critical of his painting: in particular Botticelli's failure to use perspective and his lack of attention to background detail.

Leonardo made several preliminary sketches for his *Adoration of the Magi*, introducing realistic elements which are lacking in Botticelli's work. Leonardo was keen to stress the sheer awe and emotion of the Three Wise Men as they encountered the infant Christ. Botticelli had been more intent on depicting the various members of the Medici family and their circle amongst the crowd gathered before Christ, and we can identify these by their characteristic poses. The young Lorenzo, for instance, strikes a haughty figure, his hands resting on his sword: the hero who had saved his father Piero the Gouty's life. Botticelli even paints a portrait of himself, standing at the edge of the crowd, gazing out at the spectator.

Botticelli, as we know, had difficulties with depicting the human form, preferring to mask this in robes, or a thick braid of hair in the case of Venus. Leonardo, on the other hand, was determined to play to his strengths. His initial drawings for his *Adoration* depicted his figures nude. According to his biographer Walter Isaacson, this was because he 'had come to believe in Alberti's advice that an artist should build a picture of a human body from the inside out, first conceiving of the skeleton, then the skin, then the clothing'.

This preliminary work laid the foundation for a complex and extensive scene. The central focus is on the Virgin, holding the infant Christ on her lap, seated beneath a palm tree. This tree hints at the final stage of Christ's life, which began with his triumphant ride into Jerusalem along a way bestrewn with palm leaves. The palm tree also symbolizes his ensuing death and resurrection.

This central focus is enclosed within a vortex of worshipping figures. Amongst these many figures there is a self-portrait; it is placed at the far right of the picture, in imitation of Botticelli's self-portrait in his *Adoration*. It depicts a young man dressed in a cloak, but his face does not gaze out at the spectator like Botticelli's self-portrait. Instead, this shadowy and elusive figure gazes away from the Virgin, obliquely beyond the picture, as if looking at something we cannot see. It is difficult to know what to make of this seemingly disinterested gaze. The face has strong features, and would seem to confirm the general opinion that Leonardo was possessed of a striking beauty in his youth.*

The left background of Leonardo's *Adoration* is dominated by an ornate ruin, which imposes a strong line of perspective. This building is said to be the Basilica of Maxentius, which according to medieval legend was destined to remain standing until a virgin gave birth, and is said to have collapsed on the night of Christ's birth.†

This highly ambitious work had all the makings of a masterpiece. However, it remained unfinished. According to Vasari, who is not always reliable, Leonardo had a 'capricious and unstable' temperament which led to him frequently leaving work incomplete: 'His intelligence of art made him take on many projects but never finish any of them, since it seemed to him that the hand would never achieve the required perfection.'

He was forever seeing problems in his work that were 'so subtle, so astonishing' that, despite his immense skills, he could never quite solve them. Others have suggested that the Dominican monks of San Donato

---

* The bearded sage of the best-known portraits dates from the end of Leonardo's life. It is thought that he did not grow a beard until his late fifties.

† In fact, this building was not erected until well over two centuries after Christ's death. It would be the largest building in the forum of Ancient Rome, and its impressive ruins can be seen to this day. These bear no resemblance to the ruins depicted in Leonardo's painting, but served as an inspiration for the old Penn Station in New York City.

fell behind with their payments, and this accounts for why in the painting
the disaffected Leonardo is looking away from the scene.

The Dominican monks were not the only ones who suffered from a lack
of cash during this period. These were stirring times for Florence. In
1478, Lorenzo the Magnificent had survived the assassination attempt
known as the Pazzi conspiracy. This had been organized by the powerful
Pazzi family, with the covert backing of the powerful Pope Sixtus IV.
When the coup failed, the Pazzi and their supporters were run out
of town, but their backers were a more difficult matter. Sixtus IV was
outraged when he learned that, during the course of the disturbances
in Florence, the Archbishop of Pisa had been publicly hanged from a
window of the Palazzo della Signoria, still clad in his ecclesiastical robes.
Forthwith he excommunicated the entire city of Florence and seized the
assets of the Medici bank in Rome, amounting to some 10,000 florins.
He then summoned his ally King Ferrante of Naples to assemble an army
and march on Florence.

Meanwhile, Florence's most trusted ally, Milan, was in the midst of
its own political turmoil. Duke Galeazzo Maria Sforza had been assas-
sinated two years previously, and now the backers of his eleven-year-old
son, Gian Galeazzo Sforza, were locked in a power struggle with his
uncle, Ludovico Sforza. Consequently, Milan was only able to raise a
token force to support its ally. Florence was alone, bereft of defenders.
Even its favoured *condottiere*, Duke Federico da Montefeltro of Urbino,
had been in on the plot and refused to be tempted from his long-held
papal sympathies.

What was to be done? What could possibly rescue friendless
Florence? Lorenzo the Magnificent now made the boldest move of his
life. He decided to ride to Naples in a desperate attempt to dissuade King
Ferrante from launching an attack. Bearing in mind Ferrante's penchant
for embalming his enemies for display in his museum of mummies,
Lorenzo's move showed considerable daring. But he was convinced that
nothing less could save Florence. Even so, this mission was not without

its questionable side. Lorenzo knew that in order to make a success of this dash to Naples, he would need money – and a lot of it. But owing to his need to grease the wheels of the Medici political machine simply to keep himself in power, Lorenzo remained as short of cash as ever. The financial records for this period were all later destroyed by the Medici family; however, one document did survive. It is undated, but would appear to be related to this moment in Lorenzo's rule. It simply states that Lorenzo diverted 74,948 florins from the city funds to his own account, 'without the sanction of any law and without authority'. This may have been embezzlement, but it would save the city.

Lorenzo the Magnificent rode post-haste for Pisa, accompanied only by his secretary and two manservants. His sole pause was halfway down the road, at San Miniato, where he dispatched a letter to the *signoria*, informing them of what he was doing. Lorenzo intended to present the *signoria* with a fait accompli:

> I believe that by placing myself in their hands I can be the means necessary to restore peace to our city… If His Majesty the King [of Naples] intends to take from us our liberties, it seems to me better to know it as soon as possible, and that only one should suffer and not the rest… My greatest wish is that by my life or by my death… I should make a contribution to the good of the city.

It would seem churlish to point out that no mention was made of money: the very means by which Lorenzo hoped to secure 'the good of the city'. Did the *signoria* know what he had done? They surely must at least have guessed.

Lorenzo the Magnificent had chosen his moment well. It was midwinter, and the forces assembled by the pope, as well as those of Naples, were confined to winter quarters. Wars in Italy were still only fought in clement weather. Lorenzo's biographer Miles J. Unger makes a salient point about this heroic dash to Naples, writing that 'for Lorenzo it shifted the contest away from areas where he had little experience or aptitude – such as in financial administration or military strategy – and onto ground where he felt more comfortable. Face-to-face with his rival...'

Upon arrival in Naples, Lorenzo installed himself at the premises of the Medici bank and launched his charm offensive with a series of noble gestures which he knew would reflect well on him. The hundred Neapolitan galley slaves who had rowed him from Pisa had their freedom purchased by Lorenzo, who also gave them ten florins each to set up their new lives. He then established a fund to dispense money amongst the poor, providing them with dowries so that their daughters could make good marriages. King Ferrante granted him an audience at his *palazzo*, but remained equivocal. Lorenzo was welcomed, but at the same time informed that he would not be permitted to leave Naples.

There is no doubt that King Ferrante was deeply touched by Lorenzo the Magnificent's bravery, and by the fact that he had come to see him personally – throwing himself at His Majesty's mercy. On the other hand, Sixtus IV had recently made one of Ferrante's sons a cardinal, a rare honour for both the king and his kingdom.

Months passed as King Ferrante prevaricated, and Lorenzo continued with his lavish spending on the people of Naples. But the longer he remained in Naples, the more it became clear to Lorenzo that the king had deep difficulties of his own. The Ottoman fleet now sailed the waters around much of southern Italy, and were becoming more and more daring in their raids upon Neapolitan territory. At the same time, the King of France, the most powerful ruler in Europe, had claimed that by right of birth the Kingdom of Naples belonged to him. Despite such pressing distractions, King Ferrante was eventually persuaded to sign a peace treaty with Lorenzo the Magnificent. Pope Sixtus IV was furious, yet soon realized that he had little choice but to join this treaty, if he did not wish to alienate his most powerful ally.

King Ferrante released Lorenzo the Magnificent, who was welcomed back in Florence as a conquering hero. Lorenzo soon took advantage of this to strengthen his hold on the government. A new committee of seventy citizens was set up: its members were to hold office for five years, and could even overrule any decision made by the *signoria*. At the same time, Lorenzo took wise counsel from his advisers, and began acting in a less flamboyant fashion. Mindful of the deathbed advice issued by his grandfather Cosimo de' Medici, still fondly remembered as the *pater patriae*, Lorenzo became more modest in his behaviour. He also began involving himself more in the city's external relations, using his new-found renown for the good of the city. Recent events had brought home to him Florence's vulnerability. From now on, he would strive to ensure Florence had a place amongst the leading powers of the peninsula, using his diplomatic skills to achieve a balance of powers and maintain peace – for the good of defenceless Florence, as well as for the good of Italy as a whole.

Lorenzo the Magnificent's first move was to patch up relations with Sixtus IV. Compared with the other leading states in Italy, Florence had little to offer. It was rich, certainly, but it had no real power. Lorenzo decided to play to Florence's strengths – the one thing above all that it possessed was its culture, which was the envy of all Italy. Lorenzo would use this as a weapon of diplomacy.

Sixtus IV had recently completed the new chapel in Rome which would take on his name (Sistine). In 1481, Lorenzo the Magnificent dispatched two of his leading artists – Botticelli and Ghirlandaio – to Rome to paint the interior. A year later, he would extricate Leonardo da Vinci from his sorry mess of unfulfilled commissions, and send him to work for Ludovico Sforza, who had emerged as the de facto ruler of Milan.

In this way, Lorenzo the Magnificent would, over the years, become known as 'the needle of the Italian compass': guiding the Italian people through the rocky seas of political turmoil, and bringing an era of peace to the peninsula, which would remain free of war – but for a few minor lapses. At the same time, Lorenzo's diplomatic policy had the effect of encouraging the spread of the Renaissance beyond its founding city and throughout the whole of Italy.

CHAPTER 14

SHIFTING GROUND

LEONARDO DA VINCI SET off for Milan with high hopes. His *amour propre* had been deeply offended when Lorenzo the Magnificent had chosen Botticelli and Ghirlandaio to work for the pope in Rome. He well knew in his own heart that his painting was far superior to that of either of these artists, even if they were his friends. The insult stung. So when he was chosen by Lorenzo a year later to go to Milan, he decided to hatch his own plan. Instead of pursuing his career as an artist, he would present himself to the court of Ludovico Sforza as an engineer.

Milan owed its prosperity to its geographical location, commanding the trade routes across the Alps into Italy. It also had its own thriving trade in silk manufacture and millinery (the latter even takes its name from the city). To facilitate all this trade, a network of navigable canals linked Milan to the Po river in the south, and to Lake Maggiore and Switzerland in the north. These canals were known to be much in need of a skilled hydraulic engineer to maintain and extend them, and Leonardo saw this as his opportunity. Yet over and above this, Leonardo viewed his trip to Milan as an opportunity to establish himself as a *military* engineer. This was a curious ambition for one whose gentle nature had already gained him a reputation as a pacifist – a man who abhorred the infliction of suffering of any kind. Indeed, according to Vasari: 'Often when he was walking past the places where birds were sold he would pay the price asked, take them from their cages, and let them fly off into the air, giving them back their lost freedom.'

Perhaps it was simply overweening ambition – an ambition that he felt had been thwarted – which prompted Leonardo to write in his introductory letter to his new employer, Ludovico Sforza, ruler of Milan:

> My most illustrious Lord,
>
> I have seen and examined the inventions of many creators of instruments of war, and have found that none of these is in any way different from those that already exist. I would therefore like to place before you, my Lord, and demonstrate, all the more advanced and secret weapons which I myself have created…

He then goes on to list the 'instruments' whose secrets he would reveal to Ludovico Sforza: mobile bridges, siege engines, cannons capable of raining a hail of stones on the enemy, tunnelling devices, armoured vehicles, catapults… the list goes on and on.

All this was, of course, a colossal exaggeration. At the time, Leonardo had little more than a few speculative drawings in his notebooks. Nothing had actually been constructed, despite his offer to 'place before' Sforza 'and demonstrate' these secret weapons. Leonardo's biographer Charles Nicholl says of Leonardo's letter: 'The document has a sci-fi air about it, as if his imagination is running ahead of him. It is the pitch of a multi-talented dreamer who will fill in the details later.'

Here we see the dark underside of the Renaissance, that innovative era which came into being amidst a time of strife. It is as if its jewels, all its crystalline wonders, could only be created in the crucible of a blast furnace: the warring city-states of Italy.

At the very end of Leonardo's letter to Ludovico, almost as an afterthought, he refers to his artistic skills: 'in painting I can do everything that it is possible to do'. He had heard that Ludovico wanted to erect a large equestrian statue in honour of his illustrious father, the *condottiere* Francesco Sforza, who had been the first Sforza to take over as ruler of Milan. With this in mind, Leonardo presumed to add: 'I would be able to begin work on the bronze horse...'

This was another excessive boast, spurred on by hubris. During the many centuries since Ancient Roman times, the difficult process of casting and erecting large bronze equestrian statues had fallen into abeyance, its art all but lost. Then, in 1453, Donatello had succeeded in creating a life-sized equestrian statue in Padua of the *condottiere* known as Gattamelata. This had caused a sensation. By now, Leonardo knew that Verrocchio, his friend and former master, had recently received another commission, this time from Venice: the ruling *signoria* wished Verrocchio to cast a larger-than-life equestrian statue of the city's great *condottiere* Bartolomeo Colleoni. Despite Leonardo's lack of experience in this field, he wished to go one better. He would create an even larger, fourteen-foot bronze of Francesco Sforza; furthermore, while previous statues had projected their image of power and forward movement by depicting the horse with its left foreleg raised, Leonardo promised a far more striking pose. His statue would depict Sforza seated on a rearing horse, with only its hind legs on the ground – the ultimate image of power.

Such a feat had never previously been attempted, let alone achieved. Balancing the three legs of a horse had proved difficult enough: Donatello had been forced to resort to the Ancient Roman trick of placing a sphere beneath the horse's raised hoof, to prop up its weight. Now Leonardo found himself faced with the problem of balancing the weight of his massive bronze statue on just the slender hind legs. By following Leonardo's drawings in his notebooks, we can see how he strove to overcome this difficulty. First he tried to insert a fallen enemy beneath the horse's raised front hoofs; then the wide stump of a tree was incorporated... but neither of these appears practicable.

It would be several years before Ludovico Sforza finally gave Leonardo the go-ahead for this project. By this time, Leonardo had managed to visit Padua and had seen for himself Donatello's statue of the *condottiere* Gattamelata. This had proved a challenging, yet nonetheless inspiring, experience. Leonardo had been struck with wonder and admiration at Donatello's feat. Realizing at once that his plans for a rearing horse were impossible, Leonardo had in his own words 'begun again'. He would follow Donatello's pose, but he would strive to surpass this by rendering the sheer animation of the horse's presence. In his notebooks, he writes, 'The one in [Padua] is to be praised most of all for its movement', after which he adds: 'Where natural vivacity is missing we must supply it artificially.' His notebooks also contain a number of studies of horses taken from life. These achieve a striking muscular vitality: his statue may have been reduced to a standard pose, but its superiority would be achieved by the visceral realization of its animality.

Leonardo embarked upon a full-scale clay model in preparation for the casting of his statue. This was created in a central courtyard of the dilapidated and semi-deserted Corte Vecchia, the former ducal *palazzo* which Ludovico Sforza had assigned to Leonardo as a residence and studio space. Word soon spread of this marvel Leonardo had created: the ensuing bronze statue would surely become one of the wonders of Milan.

But disaster struck. In 1499, Milan found itself at war with France. The large quantity of bronze set aside for the casting of Leonardo's statue was commandeered by the army for casting cannons. Worse was to come. After the war was lost and Sforza had fled, the victorious French soldiery burst into the courtyard where Leonardo had set up his model. Fifty years later, the contemporary Milanese humanist and chronicler Saba da Castiglione would write: 'I remember, and with sadness and anger I say it now, this noble and ingenious work being used as a target by Gascon crossbowmen.' Leonardo's model was shattered beyond recognition or repair, reduced to a heap of rubble.

Leonardo's period in Milan working for Ludovico Sforza would last seventeen years, from 1482 until 1499. He would arrive a somewhat disillusioned and headstrong thirty-year-old, who had yet to reach his potential. He would leave a wiser and more fulfilled middle-aged artist and polymath (who nonetheless retained his dream of becoming a military engineer). By now he had completed many of the masterpieces upon which his supreme reputation rests. Apart from these works, he had also been commissioned by Ludovico Sforza to waste his talent creating ephemera to entertain the court and its guests at various celebrations, banquets and other entertainments. These are known to have included elaborate ice sculptures, wondrous firework displays and ingenious theatrical devices. Leonardo appears to have undertaken these duties with little cavil – accepting them as the price he had to pay for his comparative freedom. For between fulfilling his few serious commissions and the occasional trivial party piece, he had largely been left to follow his own pursuits.

In his notebooks we see his creativity expanding as never before. His mind remained a cornucopia of ideas, from manned flight to monsters, from depicting deluges to anatomical investigations. And in the midst of all this, he even found time to befriend the mathematical monk Luca Pacioli, who moved in with him and began teaching him arithmetic and geometry, of which he became an avid student. But Leonardo would suffer one further catastrophe to match the destruction of his clay horse, though in this case the disaster was largely self-inflicted.

In 1495, Ludovico Sforza had embarked upon a widespread renovation of many of Milan's older buildings, amongst which was the Dominican monastery of Santa Maria delle Grazie. To celebrate this renovation of their monastery, the monks commissioned Leonardo to paint a fresco of the Last Supper. Leonardo's realization of this scene was to be one of his finest works, with each of the Apostles skilfully characterized at the very moment when Christ reveals that one amongst them will betray him. However, instead of adhering to the tried-and-tested methods of fresco, Leonardo chose to incorporate a more experimental technique of his own. This involved painting on a dry surface (as distinct from the usual damp for fresco), as well as adding an undercoat of white lead paint to increase the luminosity of the figures. This proved disastrous. As a result, by the time the French conquered Milan four years later, and the French king Louis XII asked to see this great work, it was already showing signs of deterioration. And when Vasari saw it in 1556, just over half a century after its completion, he described it as nothing more than 'a muddle of blots'.* The painting we know today consists almost entirely of various restorations based upon contemporary copies.

After the French invasion, Leonardo set off with his friend Luca Pacioli for Venice, where he produced a number of complex geometrical drawings to illustrate Pacioli's *Divina Proportione*. And in 1503, Leonardo finally returned to Florence. But the city Leonardo had left just over twenty years previously had undergone a series of the most traumatic upheavals in its history, and was now utterly transformed.

The seeds of this transformation were already germinating beneath the surface when Leonardo set off for Milan. Lorenzo the Magnificent may have consolidated Medici rule over Florence following his heroic dash to intercede with King Ferrante of Naples, but his theft of almost 75,000 florins from the city's exchequer was indicative of a deep malaise in Medici affairs. The Medici bank, for so long the source of funds which had facilitated the family's control of the city, was on the brink of collapse.

These troubles had been a long time in the making. As we have seen, in order to secure the bank against any wholesale collapse, such as had befallen the Bardi, Peruzzi and Acciaiuoli banks in the mid-fourteenth century, Giovanni di Bicci had from the outset established each branch of the Medici bank as a separate company. The Medici family had retained a majority share in each branch, and the chosen manager was invariably a trusted member of the family or inner circle. Thus, when Cosimo de' Medici had switched Florence's alliance from Venice to the *condottiere* Francesco Sforza's Milan, the man chosen to manage this all-important branch was Pigello Portinari, who had been brought up in the Medici household.

Over the years, the managers of the Medici bank's foreign branches

---

* Admittedly, this was not entirely Leonardo's fault. Part of the deterioration was due to the excessive dampness of the wall, consequent to inept restoration work on the monastery.

had grown accustomed to an increasing degree of autonomy. This was inevitable, owing to the distances from Florence and the lack of speed in communications. (A letter from Florence to Bruges was liable to take six weeks at best.) Consequently, Cosimo de' Medici had frequently encouraged a limited degree of initiative, especially when the bank's managers had become part of a network of agents and representatives which stretched throughout Europe and even as far as the Middle East.

However, he expected to receive regular reports on their activities, including any commercial enterprises undertaken on their own private initiative or which extended far beyond their banking duties. Managers of foreign branches often became involved in the import and export of a wide range of goods, such as spices, furs and dyestuffs. And the bank's influential customers frequently required them to supply items ranging from sacred relics to exotic fruits. (The late fifteenth century saw the arrival of easily transported goods such as pineapples on the European market.) On top of this, Cosimo expected his managers to act as spies, supplying him with information which might prove of benefit to the interests of the Florentine Republic. Often such intelligence might consist of little more than the latest local news or commercial developments, yet even such snippets could be useful in unexpected ways. A rumour that the King of England was recruiting an army, or that the Duke of Burgundy* was increasing import taxes into Bruges, could well – in conjunction with other information – indicate crucial changes in the European market.

Likewise, managers and agents were often expected to mix bank business with their master's pleasure, especially with regard to Cosimo's avid collecting of ancient manuscripts. Witness Edward Gibbon's description of Cosimo de' Medici: 'His riches were dedicated to the services of mankind; he corresponded at once with Cairo and London; and a cargo of Indian spices and Greek books was often imported in the same vessel.' Yet such enterprise on behalf of Medici bank managers had not always been beneficial: for instance when Lorenzo di Pierfrancesco de'

---

* During this period, the Duchy of Burgundy extended along the North Sea coast from eastern France, through Belgium, into Holland, and as far south as Alsace and the border of Switzerland.

Medici dispatched Amerigo Vespucci to Cádiz to investigate unauthorized business by the local manager, who was using the bank's funds to
finance his own enterprises.

Cosimo de' Medici was a skilled judge of character, and had kept
a wary eye on his managers, scrutinizing their ledgers when they were
sent to Florence for his regular inspection. Little escaped his eagle eye.
His son Piero, on the other hand, would prove somewhat less skilled,
and would find it difficult to devote sufficient attention to the bank's
affairs while simultaneously devoting his energies to running the city. As
ever, the prescient Cosimo had been prepared for this. In order to assist
Piero, he called back to Florence the experienced manager of the Geneva
branch, Francesco Sassetti, appointing him general manager of the bank.
By now Cosimo was growing old and tired, and in this case his judgement failed him. Far from being a skilled manager, Sassetti was in fact
incompetent and lazy, faults which he had managed to disguise by means
of his consummate skill in flattery.

In the opening days of Piero de' Medici's rule, he had made the
ill-advised attempt to call in the bank's debts. Later, his lack of judgement
allowed the Albizzi and the Party of the Hill to threaten his political
power. Despite this, Piero's five-year reign inspired sufficient confidence
among the leading citizens of Florence for them to decide, on his death,
to retain Medici rule. This was the deciding factor which prompted the
delegation of 'leaders, knights and citizens' to present themselves at the
Palazzo Medici and beseech the dashing twenty-year-old Lorenzo to
take on the role of 'looking after the city and the government as [his]
father and grandfather had done'.

Yet for all Lorenzo's obvious charisma and skills, he proved even less
capable of running the family bank than his father. This was a task for
which he had neither the expertise nor the inclination. Though there
was one aspect which he did not neglect: reading the regular reports
sent by the bank's managers from other Italian cities, as these would
aid him in his assessment of the Italian political scene, a field in which
he became increasingly involved and influential. Meanwhile, the financial aspect of the business was left almost entirely in the hands of the

obsequious Sassetti, and it soon became clear that his neglect and inept-
itude were already leading to dire consequences.

The man who had taken over from Sassetti at the important Geneva
branch of the Medici bank was Lionetto de' Rossi, who had recently
married Piero the Gouty's illegitimate daughter Maria de' Medici. As
such, he was to all intents and purposes Lorenzo the Magnificent's
brother-in-law. The so-called Geneva branch, a big earner for the Medici
bank, had recently been moved to Lyon in central France, which had now
become the financial centre of the country and played host to important
European trade fairs. Once prosperous, this branch had already begun
to languish during Sassetti's time. Under Rossi, business slumped even
further. According to one of Rossi's reports to Lorenzo the Magnificent,
this was because the account books 'were too full of slow debtors and
stocks of merchandise'. This was evidently of sufficient concern to warrant
Lorenzo sending him a letter reprimanding him, and telling him to stick
to the bank's policy of getting rid of such encumbrances. Lorenzo even
ordered Lorenzo Spinelli, the Medici agent in Montpellier, to travel to
Lyon and see that Rossi followed his instructions. Rossi was upset by this
move, and wrote back to Sassetti in Florence that he resented Spinelli
'spying' on him.

Rossi's behaviour now became increasingly 'eccentric'. In 1482, he
even went so far as to send two different balance sheets back to Florence.
According to the meticulous analyst Raymond de Roover, one of these
balance sheets was sent to Sassetti 'in the usual form, [but] full of puzzling
details', while a second sheet was sent to Lorenzo the Magnificent 'with
everything explained in the most plausible way'. As de Roover puts it:
'What Lionetto [de' Rossi] expected to achieve is in itself a riddle, since
at headquarters the two would certainly be compared.'

Things now began spiralling out of control. Rossi boasted that he had
succeeded in clearing debts of 22,000 écus,* at the same time building
up reserves of 12,000 écus. He also stated that he had 'nearly as much

---

* At this time, the French écu was worth a little more than the Florentine florin,
with an exchange rate of around nine écus to ten florins.

in jewels and commodities' stored on the premises. What he omitted to mention was that such jewels 'could only be sold to great lords who were not the best payers'. Worse was to come. Soon the Rome branch of the Medici bank was complaining that the Lyon branch was falling seriously behindhand in forwarding several cardinals' benefices to Rome. Then the Lyon branch began issuing promissory notes against the Rome branch to cover debts it had accrued at the trade fairs. It soon became obvious that Rossi's behaviour was threatening the assets (and the good name) of two of the most important branches of the Medici bank. For once, Lorenzo dithered. What would be the effect on his family if he dismissed his brother-in-law? Most of the branch managers throughout Europe had similar family connections.

As de Roover points out, Rossi's next balance sheet 'was a fraud and figures had been juggled around to cover huge losses'. Lorenzo's exasperation finally gave way to rage, and he contemplated the drastic step of 'sending to Lyons someone in authority to have Lionetto [de' Rossi] arrested and, perhaps, brought back to Florence as a prisoner'. But in March 1485, Sassetti advised against such a move. In the words of de Roover: 'Instead, Lorenzo, by friendly letters, coaxed Lionetto to come to Florence for a conference.' Initially it looked as if Rossi had decided to ignore Lorenzo's letter. But finally, in June 1485, Rossi arrived back in Florence, whereupon 'he was arrested and incarcerated in the Stinche, the debtors' jail'. Some partners of the bank now claimed that he owed 30,000 florins – a colossal sum, which he certainly had no means of recovering.

Rossi's arrest set tongues wagging in Florence. In banking circles at Lyon, 'the news caused great consternation'. Likewise in Rome. It soon became evident that 'something was amiss and that the Medici Bank was in serious trouble'. Fortunately, skilful handling of the Medici bank's transactions at the next trade fairs managed to avoid a run on the bank, and confidence was somewhat restored. The worst had been averted, for the time being at least.

Meanwhile, in 1484 the Greek-Genoese Cardinal Giovanni Cibò was elected pope, taking on the name Innocent VIII. By now Lorenzo the

Magnificent's 'cultural' diplomacy of lending out his artists had secured Florence's alliances with Milan and Rome. Venice may have persisted in its antipathy towards Florence, and King Ferrante of Naples may have remained as unpredictable as ever, but Florence's alliances were sufficient to secure the balance of power in the Italian peninsula. Innocent VIII proved a weak pope, more interested in nepotism and his own pleasures than matters of state. Lorenzo the Magnificent took full advantage of this, using his influence to further the cause of peace in Italy. Indeed, it was the grateful Innocent VIII who would publicly confirm Lorenzo's standing as 'the needle of the Italian compass'.

But Lorenzo the Magnificent also had further ambitions. In 1487, he agreed to marry his daughter Maddalena to the pope's illegitimate son Franceschetto Cibò. It was very much to Innocent VIII's advantage to see his son married into such a renowned family, thus ensuring him a link to a powerful patron when he no longer had papal protection. Yet Lorenzo the Magnificent extracted a high price for this favour. He persuaded Innocent VIII to promise that he would make Lorenzo's second son, the thirteen-year-old Giovanni de' Medici, a cardinal. Even in this lax era, such an appointment was unprecedented. Innocent VIII only agreed as long as this appointment was not made public until Giovanni came of age three years later.

By now, the middle-aged Lorenzo had grown old beyond his years. The dashing youth who had excelled at jousting and *calcio fiorentino*, the golden young man who had gathered about him a circle of artists and humanist philosophers, the talented poet capable of penning high art to impress his intellectual friends and bawdy verse to entertain the people at public festivals, was now a thing of the past. Lorenzo the Magnificent's body had succumbed to the family curse of gout, his limbs so twisted and swollen that he could no longer walk. He had begun to suffer constant fevers, which according to his close friend the poet Angelo Poliziano increasingly consumed his body, 'attacking not only the arteries and veins, but the limbs, intestines, nerves, bones and marrow'. Like his father before him, Lorenzo was no longer capable of moving under his own power and had to be carried on a litter.

By the time Lorenzo's son Giovanni had reached the age of sixteen, it was clear that his forty-three-year-old father's days were numbered. Lorenzo was carried on his litter to the balcony above the inner courtyard of the Palazzo Medici, where he could gaze down, unobserved, as his chubby beaming son, wearing his mantle, scarlet hat and sapphire ring, presided over the banqueting table of dignitaries celebrating his elevation to the College of Cardinals. This was the last Lorenzo would see of his son. The next day, Cardinal Giovanni de' Medici set off for Rome, bearing with him a letter from his dying father. Though racked with pain, Lorenzo was still capable of long periods of mental lucidity. In the family tradition, Lorenzo's letter advised his son to adopt a modest lifestyle and to celebrate feast days with moderation, stressing that he should maintain 'a well-ordered and cleanly household [rather than] magnificence and pomp. Let your life be regular and reduce your expenses...'

Just as the traditional Medici deathbed advice of Lorenzo the Magnificent's father Piero the Gouty had fallen on deaf ears, so in turn would Lorenzo's advice to his precocious son. Cardinal Giovanni de' Medici would take to Rome, the city his father referred to as 'the sink of all iniquities', with the enthusiasm of a born sybarite. Yet he, like his father, would outgrow his hedonistic youth. By securing a cardinalate for Giovanni at such an exceptionally young age, Lorenzo had ensured that when the older cardinals died off, Cardinal de' Medici would gradually rise through the College of Cardinals, gaining further influence as the years passed. And in conformity with his father's secret wishes, Cardinal Giovanni's seniority, intelligence and diplomatic skills would ensure that in twenty-one years' time he would ascend to the papal throne, becoming Leo X.

The day after the sixteen-year-old Cardinal Giovanni de' Medici set off for Rome to take up his post, Lorenzo had himself carried out of Florence on his litter to his villa at Careggi, amidst the countryside north of the city walls. This was the villa which his grandfather Cosimo de' Medici had commissioned the architect Michelozzo to build some seventy years previously. It was here that Cosimo de' Medici had died.

It was here that Cosimo's son Piero the Gouty, Lorenzo's father, had died. And now Lorenzo himself was returning to the meadows and wooded hills of his childhood, where he too had come to die. But if Lorenzo hoped that his last days would be free from the turbulence of Florentine politics, he was to be disappointed.

CHAPTER 15

UNDERCURRENTS

WITH HINDSIGHT IT BECOMES clear that, by the late fifteenth century, western humanity had entered a new era. For a start, its world had suddenly become much larger than had previously been supposed. In 1488 the Portuguese explorer Bartolomeu Dias had sailed deep into the South Atlantic, becoming the first European to round the Cape of Good Hope and enter the Indian Ocean. Four years later, Columbus would sail west from Spain across the Atlantic and arrive at a hitherto unknown continent. Meanwhile, a gradual renaissance of ancient learning had begun to transform the entire outlook of western culture. Mathematics and banking, art and architecture, literature and philosophy had all taken on a new perspective. It was as if a lens had focused, bringing into sharp relief an entire landscape which had previously been no more than a blurred, incomplete sketch.

The focus of this Renaissance was the city of Florence. Just as the mind, the eye and the stature of western humanity was beginning to take on a new dimension, so Florence had grown into a city filled with novel wonders. Brunelleschi's dome atop the cathedral, paintings by the likes of Uccello and Botticelli adorning the city's churches, young intellectuals discussing Plato on the street corners, the colourful pageants laid on by Lorenzo the Magnificent... things would never be the same again.

Yet something else was happening too. Beneath the flow of new entertainments, new wonders and new ideas there was an undercurrent of increasing bewilderment, as well as a growing resentment, especially amongst the *popolo minuto*. As they trudged back to their homes in the narrow fetid streets of the slums after the festivals in the *piazze* were over, it was as if nothing had changed. If anything, their lives had got worse. By now England and the Low Countries had begun manufacturing their own fine cloth; consequently, they were selling less wool and the Florentine cloth industry had undergone a slump. As usual, the *ciompi* had been the first to suffer. Many woolworkers were laid off, and they and their families had fallen into destitution, dependent upon public charity. There was a mounting bitterness towards the new ways, the new buildings, the new luxurious lifestyle of the leading families.

In the midst of this growing bewilderment, which in its own fashion had begun to permeate all levels of society, only one man appeared to offer hope and certainty – a Dominican friar called Savonarola. His passionate sermons proclaimed a new fundamentalist Christianity, a return to the old ways – with a vengeance. His fiery prophecies of doom and destruction had begun to turn the people against the extravagant and flamboyant ways of the ruling elite, which were epitomized by the Medici. More and more citizens were becoming inclined to reject the rule of Lorenzo the Magnificent, in favour of the new simplicity preached by the ugly little friar with a thick provincial accent.

Try as he might, Lorenzo the Magnificent found it impossible to combat the growing influence of Savonarola. Attempted bribery, covert coercion, even threats – none of these seemed to deter him. By now, Lorenzo's increasing illness was beginning to cloud his judgement. As he gradually lost his grip on life, so he also began to lose his grip on the city. The people flocked to hear Savonarola rail against the wickedness of their rulers. It was the self-proclaimed 'little friar' who now held increasing sway over the people of Florence, rather than their charismatic ruler.

As Lorenzo the Magnificent lay on his deathbed, he decided to make an appeal to Savonarola: he invited him out to his villa at Careggi for a meeting. To Lorenzo's surprise, Savonarola accepted the invitation.

There are several slightly differing eyewitness accounts of this meeting. However, on the salient points they all concur. When Savonarola entered Lorenzo the Magnificent's bedchamber, where his family and friends were gathered about his bed, the 'little friar' appeared totally self-possessed. He was not in the least cowed by the sight of his dying ruler. By this stage, almost in spite of himself, Lorenzo had more than a little sneaking admiration for the uncompromising friar. He opened by asking Savonarola for his blessing. Cautiously, Savonarola agreed that he would bless Lorenzo – but only if he agreed to fulfil three commitments. Lorenzo nodded. Firstly, Savonarola asked Lorenzo if he repented his sins and believed in the one true God. Lorenzo replied that he did. Secondly, Savonarola told Lorenzo that if he wished for his soul to be saved he must renounce the ill-gotten wealth he had accumulated through usury, and restore to the people 'what has wrongly been taken'. To this, Lorenzo replied, 'Father, I will do so, or I will cause my heirs to do it if I cannot.' Lastly, Savonarola demanded that Lorenzo return to the people of Florence their liberty, granting them rule by a truly republican government. To this final demand, Lorenzo did not reply, merely turning his head away to face the wall. Whereupon Savonarola stood in silence for some time, gazing at Lorenzo. At last the 'little friar' appeared to make up his mind. Quickly, he gave Lorenzo his blessing, and then departed.

The following day, Lorenzo the Magnificent died, and was succeeded as ruler of Florence by his firstborn son, Piero.

Girolamo Savonarola was born on 21 September 1452, making him just three years younger than Lorenzo the Magnificent. Unlike almost all the others described in this book, Savonarola was not born in Florence, or even in Tuscany. He hailed from the city-state of Ferrara, across the Apennine mountains some seventy miles to the north. Yet it was in Florence that he would leave his mark, and achieve his life's work. His influence on the republic would be deep and lasting, drawing as it did so deftly on the citizens' legendary faith in their republican liberty, and his ability to kindle the glowing embers of this fading belief. On the other hand, concomitant with this vision of freedom we have Savonarola's restrictive belief in a simple, fundamental Christianity similar to that advocated by Jesus to his disciples. It is important to bear in mind how at all times these two disparate elements – liberty and puritanism – played a crucial role in Savonarola's beliefs. In his mind, social justice and fundamental Christianity would remain inseparable.

The city of Ferrara into which Savonarola was born was no Renaissance republic, but it bore a certain resemblance to Florence. Its absolutist ruler, Duke Borso, was an illegitimate scion of the cultured Este family, and he believed in cultivating his self-image by employing talented local artists. These were set to work adorning the inner walls, halls and chambers of his forbidding moated castle, whose turrets dominated the centre of the city. Savonarola would have had direct knowledge of this flamboyant court through his grandfather Michele, who was employed as court physician and would prove to be a formative influence on young Girolamo.

Michele Savonarola was one of the leading physicians of his age, whose masterwork *The Practice of Medicine from Head to Toe* was said to include all medical knowledge of the period. This enlightened work would have marked Michele out as a pioneer of humanistic thought, had it not been for his increasingly strict, medievalist attitude to life. Indeed, by the time Michele began to educate the five-year-old Savonarola, even his medical works had become permeated with such beliefs. In the words of Savonarola's biographer Roberto Ridolfi, the works that Michele 'wrote in his old age have the quality of being written by a learned anchorite, rather than a doctor of the d'Este court, being as they are so full of pedantry and moralising'. This was the man whose domineering personality would bear down on the intelligent but impressionable young Girolamo Savonarola, filling his eager mind with all the unbending and authoritative principles of an age that in parts of Italy was already fading into history. Savonarola would never forget the teachings of his brilliant but extremist grandfather, who would finally die in 1466 at the age of eighty-one, an exceptional age for the period.

After this early tutoring from his grandfather, Savonarola attended the local public school, where he received an education in the classics, and in a nod towards modern learning he was also taught the poetry of Petrarch. This modern, liberal aspect of his education would continue when he entered the University of Ferrara with the intention of studying medicine and following in the footsteps of his illustrious grandfather. Here Savonarola also received instruction in the new humanism. (When he later attacked these ideas, it would not be from a position of ignorance.)

Savonarola's father, Niccolò, had inherited a small fortune when Michele Savonarola died, and he had entered employment at Duke Borso's court. Here Niccolò was duped by some unscrupulous courtiers who encouraged him to use his inheritance to set up a bank, whereon he quickly lost all his money. (This hardly endeared his son to bankers.) By now Girolamo was having second thoughts about taking up medicine, but his father insisted. The family needed the income provided by a successful physician. Around this time, the young Girolamo began writing poetry. He also fell in love with the girl who lived next door, Laudomia Strozzi, but his proposal of marriage was hurtfully rejected by her on the grounds that he was of inferior social status.*

Indicatively, Savonarola's poetry was not about his disappointment in love. There were more important things in life than the lusts of the flesh. Instead, he wrote poetry with titles such as 'On the Ruin of the World', which dwelt upon apocalyptic scenes, and 'On the Ruin of the Church', which castigated the wickedness of the pope and his court in Rome. A common theme of his poems was social injustice.

Savonarola's increasing preoccupation with religion was encouraged

---

* The Strozzi had been a prosperous Florentine family whose banking fortune had been second only to that of the Medici. In 1433 they had supported the Albizzi when they had driven Cosimo de' Medici into exile. On Cosimo's return the following year, he had engineered a swingeing *catasto* for the Strozzi, which in turn had driven them into exile.

by the fact that his father had lost his inheritance by involving himself in the sin of usury. At the same time, his medical studies and their emphasis on human anatomy inspired in him an increasing distaste for matters of the flesh. All this came to a head in the spring of 1474.

With the arrival of the May holiday, Savonarola decided to get away from Ferrara. He set out on a long walk through the flat green fields and humid air of the Po delta. After walking some fifty miles, he arrived at the small walled city of Faenza, where the streets were thronged with visiting crowds celebrating the holiday. But the sight of all the market stalls, the street hawkers and the puppet booths, with everyone involved in such blatant godless merriment, repelled him, and he sought refuge in the church of Sant'Agostino. Here a friar was delivering the day's sermon, his distant voice echoing through the silent dimness. The text of the friar's sermon was taken from Genesis, where God tells Abraham: 'Get thee out of thy country, and from thy kindred, and from thy father's house...' Savonarola would later recount how he immediately recognized that the voice of God was speaking to him. From that day on, Savonarola determined that he would join the priesthood.

In the event, it would take him a year before he finally plucked up the courage to flee his home, making his way thirty miles south to the large city of Bologna. Here he entered a Dominican friary, taking his vows of poverty, chastity and obedience. Savonarola's intelligence facilitated his rise through the hierarchy, yet at the same time his excessive religiosity irked his superiors, who wished him out of their way. Thus in 1482 Savonarola was assigned to the monastery of San Marco in Florence.

After a long and lonely trek across the mountains, the thirty-year-old Savonarola arrived in Florence. Here he encountered a city of splendours such as he had never seen before. Why, even San Marco was unlike any monastery he had ever visited. As we have seen, its buildings had been refurbished by Cosimo de' Medici during his last years as ruler of Florence, and he had even built himself a sumptuously frescoed private chapel to which he could retire for periods of contemplation. In part to assuage his guilt over the sin of usury, which had enabled him to amass a huge fortune, Cosimo had also generously endowed the monastery itself.

No longer did the Dominican friars live in poverty, or have to rely upon local charity for their subsistence. Each friar had his own furnished cell, and all the monastery food was supplied by Cosimo's grandson, Lorenzo the Magnificent, the present ruler of Florence. The friars dined on an abundance of olives, fish, fruit and eggs; while the senior friars dined in some luxury in their own cells, even on occasion hosting dinner parties for local dignitaries. This was hardly the way of life to which Savonarola was accustomed, nor did he wish to become so.

Savonarola took up his duties, which involved teaching logic to the novices. His intellect, as well as his exemplary asceticism and religious fervour, soon began attracting a devoted following amongst the young novices who attended his classes, and even amongst some of the older friars. There was something charismatic about the 'little friar'. And they too were becoming troubled by the contrasts of everyday life in the city. Side by side with the fine new buildings and gilded reputation of Renaissance Florence was the troubling misery of the poor, who were becoming increasingly affected by the downturn in the wool industry.

Across the street from San Marco was the open space of the gardens which Cosimo de' Medici had set aside for his collection of ancient sculptures. This was now a favourite spot with Lorenzo the Magnificent, who liked to stroll along the shadowy paths amongst the beds of greenery and marble relics. Savonarola's cell happened to overlook these gardens, and according to legend it was from his window that he first caught sight of Lorenzo wandering through his sunlit gardens.

One of Savonarola's duties was to preach the Lenten sermons at the small walled hilltop town of San Gimignano. Savonarola was used to talking earnestly to his circle of novices, but when he used this method to deliver his sermons it was not a success. As he later wrote: 'I had neither the voice, nor the strength, nor the ability to preach, as a result everyone was bored when I delivered my sermons.' And, tellingly: 'I couldn't even have frightened a chicken.'

Savonarola felt humiliated by his inability to preach, and this eventually led to a spiritual crisis, during which he underwent a revelation that 'a scourge of the church was at hand'. He kept this to himself, but the following Lent he decided to make his apocalyptic experience the subject of his sermons at San Gimignano. In the course of delivering these sermons, he became carried away by his vision. He had found his voice – and he had found his subject. Savonarola railed from the pulpit, warning his frightened congregation of the coming of 'the antichrist, war, plague or famine'.

Savonarola said nothing of his new preaching when he returned to Florence. For the next few years he was assigned the task of being an itinerant preacher, wandering from town to town in northern Italy delivering sermons. During this period he gained in self-confidence, and the feeling that he was destined to deliver his apocalyptic message to the world strengthened. In the course of his travels Savonarola happened to attract the attention of Giovanni Pico della Mirandola, a humanist philosopher who was a close friend of Lorenzo the Magnificent. Despite his humanist ideas, Pico della Mirandola found himself deeply impressed by the integrity of Savonarola's preaching.

It so happened that, at this time, Lorenzo the Magnificent was becoming worried about his young son, Giovanni, for whom he had mapped out a career in the Church. Giovanni was intellectually gifted, but there was no denying his laziness and self-indulgence. If he was to fulfil a senior role in the Church with any seriousness, he needed to become conversant with a far stricter theology than was prevalent amongst the artists and thinkers of the circle in the Palazzo Medici. Similarly, Lorenzo the Magnificent was also becoming concerned by the general spiritual malaise which seemed to be prevalent in Florence. He felt that he himself was in part responsible for this, owing to the festivals and bawdy entertainments he was in the habit of putting on. After listening to Pico della Mirandola, Lorenzo the Magnificent decided that perhaps Savonarola's sermons were just what his son and the people of Florence needed at this juncture. Using his influence with the Dominicans, he managed to have Savonarola sent back to Florence, where the 'little friar' took up residence once more at San Marco during the summer of 1490.

Savonarola was by now a highly gifted and practised preacher, capable of swaying any congregation with his ideas. And he was becoming increasingly convinced of where these ideas were leading: the entire Church was in need of reform.

Within a matter of months, Savonarola's preaching in Florence was attracting such large crowds that his sermons were transferred from the church at San Marco to the cathedral. Here he began expanding on his theme of reform. Soon he was denouncing all forms of corrupt authority – especially tyrants who denied the people their rightful freedom. Savonarola also berated the tyrants' supporters: the rich and powerful families who lived lives of luxury while the poor were reduced to misery. These attacks were not personalized; no names were mentioned. As long as Savonarola's attacks remained generalized, they remained in accord with the teachings of Christ.

Initially, the conflict between these teachings and the behaviour of the Church itself was merely implied. Yet as Savonarola became more and more filled with indignation, he became increasingly daring. Soon he was making attacks on the Church itself, and its corrupt clergy. It was time for all to repent before the coming 'divine scourge'.

The effect of Savonarola's teaching on the people of Florence was immediate and drastic. The city had never heard anything like this before. Society became divided, with Savonarola's passionate sermons attracting a growing and ever more fervent following amongst the poor. Meanwhile, the pilloried rich and middle classes took to denouncing his followers, referring to them as *piagnoni* – literally 'snivellers', or 'weepers and wailers'. The situation now took a decisive turn, as Savonarola launched into ever more dire prophecies. At the same time, he also began to experience troubling visions. Filled with the exultation of these visions, he described how he had seen 'the Sword of the Lord suspended above the Earth' and how this would strike down humanity 'swiftly and sure'. Soon he was going even further, predicting that trials and tribulations would smite Rome, and a 'new Cyrus* would come from across the mountains

---

* The sixth-century BC Persian king Cyrus the Great had set free the Israelites from Babylon, allowing them to return to their homeland and rebuild the temple at Jerusalem. Thus, according to Judeo-Christian tradition, Cyrus was seen as the unwitting instrument of God.

bringing death and destruction in his wake'. Only then could there be a renewal of the Church.

The population was seething, and things were plainly getting out of hand. Yet Lorenzo the Magnificent remained seemingly indecisive. And by now he was so stricken with gout that he was reduced to his bed, or had to be carried about on a litter. His friends and advisers insisted that he should banish Savonarola from the city, but Lorenzo was aware that it was he himself who had invited Savonarola to Florence, and he appeared reluctant to go back on his word.

Such was Savonarola's popularity amongst his fellow friars that, in July 1491, he was elected prior of San Marco. The Medici faction was further outraged when Savonarola did not call on Lorenzo the Magnificent, ruler of the city, to give thanks to him, as was the custom with each new prior of San Marco. (This was partly in gratitude for all that Cosimo de' Medici had done for San Marco, but it had also become a local tradition amongst the city's religious institutions over the years of Medici ascendancy.) When the friars of San Marco urged Savonarola to call on Lorenzo, Savonarola demanded of them: 'Who made me prior? God or Lorenzo?' When they replied, 'God,' Savonarola declared: 'Then it is the Lord God who I should thank.'

Lorenzo the Magnificent knew that he must act. But he decided against making any public pronouncement, which would only further divide the city. Instead he dispatched covert messengers to San Marco. First he tried to persuade Savonarola to desist from his inflammatory sermons; then, when this had no effect, he began to issue threats. Although Savonarola still refrained from mentioning anyone by name in his diatribes against corrupt rulers, by now it was evident to all that Lorenzo was the object of his denunciations.

When yet another delegation of Lorenzo the Magnificent's followers arrived at San Marco, Savonarola announced that he had experienced a further vision of deep historic importance. According to Villari, Savonarola:

> began to speak about the city of Florence and the political state of Italy, displaying a depth of knowledge in these matters which

astonished his listeners. It was then that he predicted, in front of the many witnesses who were present in the sacristy of San Marco, that great changes would soon take place in Italy. He then specifically prophesied that Lorenzo the Magnificent, Pope Innocent VIII and King Ferrante of Naples would all soon die.

Word of this prophecy quickly began to spread throughout the city, with the sensational effect which Savonarola had doubtless anticipated.

In fact, Savonarola's prophecies were not quite so sensational as they might at first appear. The monastery of San Marco would have had a significant stream of friars passing through its gates, on their way to and from Rome, as well as to and from other Dominican monasteries throughout Italy. These friars would have carried with them the latest news, or current gossip, from the cities and towns and regions through which they had passed. In Villari's opinion, Savonarola's depth of political knowledge may have astonished his listeners, but it is doubtful that it would have astonished any friars present. As prior of San Marco, Savonarola would have been as well informed as any Medici bank manager concerning the latest political developments in Italy. All of Florence was aware that Lorenzo the Magnificent was seriously ill. Innocent VIII had only been elected as a stopgap pope, with the College of Cardinals persuaded that, given his frail health and his hedonistic lifestyle, he was unlikely to last more than a few years. Indeed, many were surprised that he had already lasted seven years in the Vatican. Meanwhile, it was something of a miracle that King Ferrante of Naples had managed to reach the age of sixty-eight, given his increasing paranoia and other indications of his mental instability. Seen in this light, Savonarola's prophecies appear to be little more than a series of well-informed guesses.

It was at this stage that Lorenzo the Magnificent invited Savonarola to visit him at his villa in Careggi. Indicatively, Savonarola's three questions to Lorenzo concerned his belief in God, renunciation of his worldly goods, and his willingness to grant the people of Florence their true democratic rights. Savonarola's fundamental religious beliefs remained inextricably linked with social justice. After Lorenzo baulked at the third question, it surprised many of those present that Savonarola gave Lorenzo his deathbed blessing. It was clear that Lorenzo had a certain respect for Savonarola's idealism, and it would appear that Savonarola, for his part, also had a grudging respect for his adversary. What had gone through the mind of the ambitious young friar when he had first set eyes on the charismatic figure of Lorenzo the Magnificent wandering through his gardens of ruined statuary? With hindsight, we can see that there was perhaps an unconscious recognition that he too aspired to such power.

Lorenzo died in April 1492. Less than four months later, news arrived that Innocent VIII had died in Rome. Concerning Savonarola's prophecies, only King Ferrante of Naples remained alive. And rumour had it that he too was now ill. The murmurs amongst the people of Florence began to grow. How could Savonarola have possibly known that such things would come to pass, unless he was indeed a true prophet, receiving word directly from God, as he claimed?

Around this time, Savonarola experienced another 'great vision', whose dramatic intensity matched his earlier vision of the sword of the Lord suspended above the earth. In this vision, he claimed to see:

> a black cross which stretched out its arms to cover over the whole of the earth. Upon this cross was inscribed the words '*Crux irae Dei*' [the Cross of the Wrath of God]. The sky was pitch black, lit by flickers of lightning. Thunder roared and a great storm of wind and hailstorms killed a host of people. The sky now cleared and from the centre of Jerusalem there appeared a golden cross which rose into the sky illuminating the entire world. Upon this cross were inscribed the words '*Crux Misericordae Dei*' [the Cross of the Mercy of God], and all nations flocked to adore it.

Given Savonarola's fanatical adherence to the truth, it is highly unlikely that this vision was a pure fabrication. Such a view is unexpectedly supported by modern neuroscience and its investigations concerning the pathology of such 'visions'. During these episodes, localized brain activity indicates that the person undergoing this mental state does actually 'see' what they claim to see. Similarly, when a subject claims to hear 'voices' speaking to them, appropriate brain activity indicates that they are speaking the truth. In neither of these cases does the subject feel that they are in any way responsible for these mental effects, which appear to them to emanate from a powerful outside source.

Regardless of any question concerning the veracity of Savonarola's pronouncements, there can be no doubt that his followers amongst the people of Florence developed a strong superstitious belief in both his visions and his prophecies. And events would only serve to reinforce such a belief. In January 1494, news reached Florence of the death of King Ferrante of Naples. The truth of Savonarola's prophecy had now been fulfilled.

And even more was to follow. Now that Lorenzo the Magnificent was gone, there was no one to maintain the balance of power in the Italian peninsula. The new King of Naples, Alfonso II, allied himself with the new pope, Alexander VI. Ludovico Sforza of Milan saw this as a threat, and invited Charles VIII of France to protect him. Charles VIII had for some time laid claim to the throne of Naples; acting on the pretext of Ludovico's invitation, he set forth with the largest army in Europe and crossed the Alps into Italy to take possession of the Kingdom of Naples, sweeping aside all that lay in his path. Even Ludovico Sforza would eventually lose Milan to the French. Here surely was the 'new Cyrus' who Savonarola had prophesied 'would come from across the mountains bringing death and destruction in his wake'.

Once again, there is no denying the uncanny resemblance to Savonarola's prophecies, which he had made some years earlier, well before any thought of a French invasion. Rational explanation suggests a surprising coincidence here. It was now some forty years since the fall of Constantinople to the Ottoman Turks. Since this time, the Ottomans had advanced inexorably up through the Balkans – reaching within 200 miles of Venice. In 1480, they had even sailed across the Adriatic and briefly occupied the city of Otranto on the southern Italian mainland. Savonarola's prophecy that the new Cyrus would arrive in Italy from 'across the mountains' would thus seem to have been inspired by his fear of an Ottoman conquest, with the conquering army arriving from across the mountains to the east, in the Balkans, rather than the Alps.

After the death of Lorenzo the Magnificent, his oldest son Piero had taken power. Not for nothing would he become known as Piero the Unfortunate. An arrogant and impetuous character, he quickly alienated his father's trusted advisers. When Charles VIII invaded Italy, he soon overran Milan. In preparation for his march south towards Naples, the French king sent word to Piero demanding Florentine support. Piero immediately hired mercenaries to man the fortresses on the Tuscan border, which stood in the path of Charles's large army. But the superior French forces quickly took all but one of the fortresses, slaughtering their defenders.

The hilltop fortress at Sarzanello, which overlooked the road south to Naples, proved more difficult, and the French army were forced to lay siege to this obstacle in their path. Was the French advance halted? Or was this merely a temporary setback, after which they would wreak vengeance on Florence?

By now, the city of Florence was in turmoil. Many were all for surrendering to the demands of Charles VIII. Meanwhile Savonarola continued to preach that the French king and his army were the 'scourge of God'; he called to his congregation: 'O Florence, for your sins, your brutality, your avarice, your lust, many trials and tribulations will be heaped upon you.' The *gonfaloniere*, Piero Capponi, and the *signoria* remained at a loss for what to do.

At this point, Piero de' Medici decided to take matters into his own hands. In emulation of his father's heroic dash to King Ferrante in Naples, Piero decided he would confront Charles VIII. Without consulting the *signoria*, he rode out of the city and headed west for the French camp. He would save Florence single-handed.

But the trouble was, Piero de' Medici had no real plan. When he arrived at the French camp below the walls of Sarzanello, and was taken to see the French king and his court, he found himself overawed. And to make matters worse, the French king and his courtiers treated Piero with disdain. Before Piero could suggest any compromise, Charles VIII began making demands. Sarzanello must surrender at once. The French army must be allowed to occupy the Florentine ports of Livorno and Pisa. Charles VIII was well aware that such a move would leave Florence cut off and at his mercy.

To the astonishment of the French king and his advisers, Piero de' Medici abandoned any pretence at negotiation and immediately agreed to all his demands. Charles VIII conferred with his advisers, and then proceeded to make further demands. To pay for the safety of Florence, the city must grant him 200,000 florins (an outrageous sum). Charles VIII then went on to insist that in order to enforce these measures he and his army must be allowed to pass through Florence. Piero agreed, and even went so far as to offer the French king the use of the Palazzo Medici during his stay. Piero's capitulation could not have been more total or abject.

After a two-week absence, Piero de' Medici arrived back in Florence on 8 November 1494, and news of his capitulation quickly began to spread throughout the city. When Piero and his attendants arrived at the Palazzo della Signoria to relay the news officially to the *gonfaloniere*, the door was slammed in his face. Inside, *gonfaloniere* Capponi ordered *La Vacca* to be rung from the tower, summoning all citizens to a *parlamento* in the piazza. As Piero de' Medici and his men hung about, wondering what to do, the people of Florence began streaming into the piazza from all quarters of the city. They soon began jeering Piero and his attendants, flinging stones and refuse at them. The crowd then started chanting that Piero de' Medici was a traitor. At which point, Piero and his attendants quickly rode off for the safety of the Palazzo Medici.

Piero's younger brother, the nineteen-year-old Cardinal Giovanni, had travelled from Rome as soon as he heard of Piero's mission to Charles VIII. When the humiliated Piero arrived back at the Palazzo Medici, Cardinal Giovanni did his best to rally him, but to no avail. Piero appeared broken – the strain of his mission to Charles VIII, together with his utter rejection by the people of Florence, had all been too much for him. And this time there could be no resort to the time-honoured practice of rallying the Medici supporters and setting in motion the Medici political machine. This now barely existed: there was simply no more money to oil it. According to de Roover:

> The Medici Bank was at this time on the brink of bankruptcy. Most of its branches had been closed, and those still in existence were gasping for breath. Even the Rome branch, for so long the pillar of the Medici Bank, was giving way... the debt of the Medici family to the Rome branch exceeded their equity by 11,243... florins. In addition, Messer Giovanni, the youthful cardinal... owed another 7,500 florins.

With Piero the Unfortunate in a paralysed funk, Cardinal Giovanni decided to make a last valiant effort. Calling together an armed band consisting of the few remaining loyal Medici supporters, he rode through the streets, calling out the famous Medici rallying cry: '*Palle! Palle!*' But this was greeted only by jeers, and answering cries of '*Popolo e Libertà!*' The throng soon became so threatening that Cardinal Giovanni and his men were forced to ride back into the courtyard of the Palazzo Medici, the doors slamming closed behind them.

During the night, Piero the Unfortunate and Cardinal Giovanni frantically gathered together as many valuables as they could carry. Then, under cover of darkness, Piero fled the city, disguised as a poor monk. His brother would soon follow, in a similar disguise. The next day, the *signoria* formally banished Piero the Unfortunate and his family, placing a bounty of 5,000 florins on his head, while the mob broke into the Palazzo Medici and began ransacking its remaining contents. Cosimo de' Medici had predicted 'within fifty years we Medici will have been exiled'. This had come true in just thirty years.

CHAPTER 16

THE BONFIRE OF
THE VANITIES

B Y NOW, A PIVOTAL event had taken place. On 1 November, while
Piero the Unfortunate was away on his mission to Charles VIII,
Savonarola had stepped up into his pulpit and begun delivering a sermon
to the assembled mass of citizens crammed into the cathedral. Only his
voice seemed to hold their attention.

The next day he did the same. And on the third day he delivered yet
another impassioned harangue. According to Ridolfi: 'During the course
of these three days, as he later recalled, he shouted so vehemently from
the pulpit that the vein in his chest almost burst, and he reached such a
point of physical exhaustion that he almost fell seriously ill.'

With Piero de' Medici out of the city and the dwindling Medici
supporters increasingly conflicted, the authorities were reduced to paraly-
sis. Miraculously, only Savonarola's sermons seemed capable of holding
the people to order. According to a dispatch sent by the Mantuan ambassador: 'A Dominican friar has so terrified all the Florentines that they are
wholly given up to his preaching.' In the eyes of the people, the words

of Savonarola – the self-proclaimed voice of God – appeared to be their
only hope.

Reluctantly forced to recognize that power had now effectively passed
into Savonarola's hands, *gonfaloniere* Capponi and the *signoria* summoned
the Council of Seventy, the very body which Lorenzo the Magnificent
had set up to increase Medici power. On 4 November, Capponi suggested
to the assembled members of the council that the only way to save
Florence, or at least stave off the impending threat of Charles VIII, was
to send a delegation to the French king to beg for mercy. This delegation
should consist of four ambassadors, true representatives of the people of
Florence. He himself volunteered to be one of the ambassadors, but in his
opinion the person best suited to lead this delegation was 'a man of holy
life... courageous and intelligent, of high ability and great renown'. He
was, as all realized, referring to Savonarola.

Despite suffering from chronic nervous exhaustion after delivering
his sermons, Savonarola could not bring himself to turn down Capponi's
offer. It would officially confirm him as the leading power in the city.

At this point it is worth questioning the motives of those concerned.
Was Capponi lining up Savonarola as a scapegoat, in case things went
wrong? Was Savonarola simply incapable of repressing his lust for power?
Such mixed motives must be borne in mind throughout the events that
follow.

On 5 November, Savonarola and his fellow ambassadors left the city.
Despite the urgency of the situation, as well as the need to make a digni-
fied impression on the French king and his court, Savonarola insisted
that he would only travel on foot, as befitted a 'little friar'. The others
had no alternative but to follow behind on horseback, decked out in the
city's livery in the customary fashion. Savonarola himself wore his usual
threadbare robes, bearing only his breviary.

Thus the Florentine delegation set out on their way to meet Charles
VIII and his army besieging the fortress at Sarzanello. As they passed
through the countryside, they learned from passing revellers that the
French had left Sarzanello. But where had they gone? No one seemed
to know. The Florentine delegation continued on its way, enquiring at

each village if anyone had heard news concerning the destination of the French army. This was hardly an auspicious start.

On 8 November, the very day of Piero the Unfortunate and Cardinal Giovanni de' Medici's flight from Florence, Charles VIII marched into Pisa, where he was welcomed by the citizenry, who were only too pleased to be freed from Florentine rule. And it was here, some days later, that Savonarola and the Florentine delegation finally arrived to meet the twenty-four-year-old Charles VIII.

Both Charles VIII's personality and his appearance were profoundly marked by the inbreeding of the French royal families. His intellect was limited, his face unsettlingly ugly, and he had short legs with excessively large flat feet. According to the Florentine historian Guicciardini: 'His limbs were so proportioned that he seemed more like a monster than a man.'

Renowned for his naivety, his behaviour was similarly curious. Though beguilingly childish, his habit of muttering to himself in a threatening fashion made many feel uneasy in his presence. Despite this, when seated on his raised throne, surrounded by his counsellors and the trappings of his court, the gnome-like king presented a grand and imposing prospect: Europe's most powerful monarch in all his medieval glory.

The Florentine delegation was duly ushered into the royal marquee. Undaunted, Savonarola at once spoke out, addressing Charles VIII: 'O King! Just as I have been predicting through these last years, thou hast come as the Minister of God, as an emblem of Divine Justice. We welcome thy presence with joyous hearts and smiling faces...'

Charles VIII had already been briefed by his advisers about Savonarola's gift of prophecy – a subject that appealed to the barely literate young king's superstitious nature. He leaned forward, listening intently to Savonarola's words – even when Savonarola abruptly changed his tone and began warning Charles VIII that 'although he was sent by God, Heaven was capable of wreaking a terrible revenge even upon its own instrument' should the French king allow his army to harm Florence.

At the end of the formal audience, Charles VIII allowed the other three Florentine ambassadors to retire, but insisted that Savonarola should remain behind for a private audience. According to the French diplomat Philippe de Commines, who was present, they discussed 'what God had revealed to [Savonarola]'. Despite his appearance, in his shabby robes and sandalled feet, Savonarola seems to have made a deep impression on Charles VIII, as well as perplexing the king's entire court with his fiery faith and unorthodox behaviour.

Savonarola and the other three ambassadors eventually set off back to Florence. On the way, they were greeted with the news that the civil government of the city was on the point of complete breakdown under the leaderless *signoria*. Upon arrival, Savonarola immediately let it be known that he would deliver a sermon in the cathedral later that same day. The people of Florence crammed into the cathedral, with others filling the piazza outside. Savonarola warned the assembled congregation that they should give thanks to God that the Medici had been overthrown. He told them that the French were coming, and would soon be encamped outside the city walls in preparation for entering the city. He assured the sea of frightened faces before him that no harm would come to them, as long as they welcomed the French and did not oppose them with violence.

Less than a week later, Charles VIII led his vast army in through the city gates. As the French soldiers marched along the streets, the citizens of Florence lined their route, cheering them, calling out somewhat nervously, '*Viva Francia! Viva Francia!*' It would take the long column of marching French soldiers no less than two hours to pass through the city gates. In all, they consisted of 10,000 men. According to contemporary reports, a further 10,000 had been left encamped outside Pisa.

All of the 10,000 French soldiers billeted in Florence were assigned to especially marked houses, the front doors daubed with paint. For the next few days the situation remained tense, while the French king carried out negotiations with Capponi and the *signoria* over the 200,000 florins which Piero de' Medici had promised him. Apart from isolated outbreaks of violence, the situation remained under control. An uneasy peace prevailed, but only just. Eventually, Capponi informed Charles VIII that they could only give him 150,000 florins, as that was all the money they had.

On 25 November, Capponi and the *signoria* attended a grand public ceremony in the Piazza della Signoria, where a treaty would be signed before the assembled citizens of Florence. But when the herald began reading out the terms of the treaty, Charles VIII learned that the *signoria* had written down 120,000 florins instead of the promised 150,000. The angry French king leapt to his feet and threatened, 'We will have to sound our trumpets!' This was the signal that would call his men to arms throughout Florence, to begin the sacking of the city. Unabashed, Capponi replied: 'If you sound your trumpets, we will ring our bells.' This was Florence's traditional call to arms, summoning all citizens to defend their city.

For a moment, there was silence. Charles VIII had 10,000 hardened soldiers, but they would be defending themselves against the entire population of the city (estimated to be around 70,000 at the time). And the citizens would have the advantage of knowing all the streets and back alleys. Charles VIII joked, 'O Capponi, Capponi, what a capon [chicken] you are!' Somehow this succeeded in defusing the situation, and the treaty was signed.

But news leaked out that Charles VIII and his soldiers planned to sack the city regardless. When Capponi and the *signoria* reassembled in their council chamber, they summoned Savonarola, and demanded that he confront Charles VIII and persuade him to issue an order restraining his soldiers. According to a contemporary report, Savonarola went straight to the Palazzo Medici, where Charles VIII had taken up residence. Bursting through the soldiers who attempted to restrain him, he entered the king's chamber. Here he found Charles VIII in full armour, preparing to lead his men in the sacking of the city. Savonarola stood before him, raised a brass crucifix, and announced: 'You and all your men will be destroyed by Him unless you cease at once...'

Charles VIII's face fell, and he then greeted Savonarola with childlike respect. But he made no move to take off his armour. Savonarola now began reasoning with him, pointing out that the longer he and his men remained in Florence, the more he lessened the impetus of his campaign against Naples. Eventually, Savonarola declared to Charles VIII: 'Now listen to the voice of God's servant. Continue on your journey without any more delay. Don't try to ruin the city or you'll bring God's anger down on your head.'

To the astonishment of all, the following day the French king and his army marched out of Florence to join up with his soldiers camped outside Pisa, and continued their journey south towards Naples. Savonarola, with a little help from Capponi, had managed to save Florence.

Had the sacking of Florence taken place, it is quite possible that the city would not have recovered. Although the influence of the Renaissance had begun to spread through Italy, would it have persevered if its *fons et origo* had disappeared in flames? Probably. But its character may well have been changed; its full force and influence diminished. As we shall see, Florence still had much to give the Renaissance – especially in art, science and politics. The city's influence in these major fields would prove both quintessentially Florentine and fundamental, inspiring western Europe's transformation into the modern age.

Meanwhile, although Florence had not been destroyed, it seemed as if the very spirit which had given birth to the Renaissance was all but extinguished. Savonarola may have saved Florence physically, but he was also intent upon saving Florence spiritually. And in his very own fashion. For the first time in over a century – since the Ciompi Revolt of 1378–82 – Florence had a government which was freely voted in by the people. Savonarola had brought about a semblance of justice, democracy and republican rule. The citizens at last had their liberty. Yet how were they to express this liberty? Savonarola decided that instead of answering to the Medici, the citizens should now answer to God. Instead of secular injustice, the citizens would have divine justice. They would be equal and free; but equal before God, and only free to embark upon a life of simple piety.*

---

*The establishment of justice in Florence at this particular time begs an important question. Who was the Renaissance for? Who did it benefit? Certainly not the underprivileged. It is arguable that they would benefit from this humanist development in the long run, by the 'trickle-down effect'. However, as the twentieth-century economist John Maynard Keynes observed: 'In the long run we are all dead.' Similarly, the trickle-down effect has proved far from inevitable in any field.

Understandably, the citizens of Florence were hardly unanimous with regard to Savonarola's restrictions on their lifestyle. Two entries by the contemporary Florentine diarist Luca Landucci suggest the problematic nature of what was now taking place in the city. After the new elections, he happily recorded on 1 January 1495 (modern-style dating) that:

> The new Signoria entered into office, and it was a great joy to see the whole Piazza [della Signoria] filled with citizens, quite different from other times, as a new thing, thanking God who had given this impartial government to Florence, and delivered us from subjection. And all this had been done at the instigation of the *Frate* [i.e. Savonarola].

Yet around the same time, Landucci records how, during his sermons, Savonarola 'went on discoursing about State matters, and great fear was felt lest the citizens should not agree. *Chi la volava lesso e chi arrosto* [One wished it boiled, another roasted]: i.e. everyone had a different opinion, one agreed with the *Frate*, and another was against him; and if it had not been for him there would have been bloodshed.'

Savonarola now sought to establish his 'City of God', and over the coming months his fundamental Christianity became more deeply entrenched amongst the citizens of Florence. This entailed some drastic changes. Wives and daughters began taking vows and entering convents, while in public people gave up wearing wigs or brightly coloured clothing – partly of their own accord, but increasingly due to social pressure. Those who valued their position in society made sure that their regular attendance at church was noticed. And soon there were further developments, especially amongst the youth.

By now, many impressionable adolescent boys had become enthusiastic converts to Savonarola's brand of fundamentalism. Consequently, he began organizing them into groups, clad in white for purity, and sending them out into the streets. Altars, complete with crucifixes and candles, were set up at crossroads, where the boys began singing hymns, encouraging passers-by to stop and join them. Stealing a march on the bands of bully boys, who in earlier times had roamed the streets during Carnival demanding money for 'charity', Savonarola's white-clad youths would knock on doors, humbly seeking alms for the poor.

Landucci describes how these bands of 'Savonarola's boys' became increasingly emboldened, their behaviour more and more oppressive: 'Some boys took it upon themselves to confiscate the veil-holder of a girl walking down the Via de' Martegli, and her family created a great uproar about it. This all took place because Savonarola had encouraged the boys to oppose the wearing of unsuitable ornaments by women.'

Savonarola also encouraged similar high-minded behaviour towards gamblers, whom he particularly detested, 'so that whenever anyone said, "Here come Savonarola's boys!", all the gamblers fled, no matter how rough they were'.

Regardless of these puritanical constraints, Savonarola's repression was evidently felt by many to be preferable to the repression from which the more democratic 'City of God' had relieved its citizens. Instead of the subtly pervasive and corrupting repression of Lorenzo the Magnificent and the Medici party machine, the people were seemingly liberated by their new-found holiness. Looking back on these days, Landucci would later declare: 'God be praised that I saw this short period of holiness. I pray that he may give us back that holy and pure life…what a blessed time it was.'

Things came to a head during the early weeks of 1497. Under the previous regime, the days prior to the forty-day fasting of Lent had been given over to the revels of Carnival. Now all remnants of Carnival celebrations were banned, and in their place Savonarola planned a 'bonfire of the vanities'. He ordered the collection throughout the city of any items of luxury. These included all the things that he abominated – from old manuscripts to mirrors and musical instruments; from paintings to the works of ancient philosophers and humanist writers. Even the works of Dante did not escape his damnation. All these were to be piled up in a great heap in the middle of the Piazza della Signoria, to be burned on the day before Lent.

These 'vanities' were collected by the *piagnoni*, who went from door to door, house to house. Filled with self-righteousness, the *piagnoni* now revelled in their nickname, which had previously been intended as an insult. People of all ranks, from the *ciompi* and the *popolo* to members of the *signoria*, were swept up in a wave of collective hysteria. Even Botticelli became a convert, bringing some of his own paintings to place on the pyre. Vasari describes how Botticellli 'was so ardent a partisan that he was thereby induced to abandon his painting, and, having no income to live on, fell into very great distress'.

On Shrove Tuesday, 7 February 1497, the pyre of vanities was ceremoniously set alight in the midst of the piazza. The *gonfaloniere*, the *signoria* and senior members of the administration gazed down from the balcony of the Palazzo della Signoria. As the towering bonfire crackled into life, heraldic trumpets blared from the *palazzo* and *La Vacca* tolled. The large assembled crowd of citizens applauded, and then began joining in the hymns sung by Savonarola's boys.

Throughout Lent, Savonarola delivered a series of ever more fiery sermons from the pulpit of the cathedral. By 4 March, he had worked himself up to such a pitch that he declared: 'Friars have a proverb amongst themselves: "He comes from Rome, do not trust him." O hark unto my words, you wicked Church! At the Court of Rome men are losing their souls all the time, they are lost...' Without mentioning anyone by name, he went on: 'If you meet people who enjoy being in Rome, you know they are cooked. He's cooked, all right. You understand me?' With these words, all knew to whom Savonarola was referring – none other than the pope, and the fact that he would be 'cooked' in Hell.

Savonarola had chosen a formidable enemy. The present occupant of the Vatican was Alexander VI, the infamous Borgia pope. Unlike previous popes, Alexander VI had blatantly recognized his offspring, going so far as to invite some of his grown-up progeny to live with him in the Vatican. These included Cesare Borgia and his sister Lucrezia Borgia, whose notoriety even matched his own. Indeed, the entire family had become notorious for their stolen riches, their decadent 'entertainments', and their involvement in secret assassinations and poisonings.

Alexander VI may have been depraved, but he was also a very powerful and determined man. And he was highly practised in guile and deceit. Although Savonarola had been preaching against the corruption of the Church for some time now, this was the first occasion on which he had condemned the pope himself. This condemnation may have been disguised, but there was no mistaking its meaning. Word of Savonarola's bold move soon reached Rome.

For some time now, Alexander VI had been watching Savonarola's growing power over the people of Florence. As early as July 1495, he had written a papal bull addressed to Savonarola:

> We have heard you proclaim that what you have said concerning future events does not proceed from yourself but comes from God. We therefore desire, as it is the duty of our pastoral office, to discourse with you so that we may gain from you a greater understanding of what is agreeable to God, and put this into practice...

The bull continues in a friendly and disarmingly beguiling tone. Ridolfi characterizes this letter as 'a most peculiar document which might be figuratively compared to the famous poisoned sweets of Borgia'. Savonarola may have been an idealist, but he was no holy fool. He well understood that if ever he ventured to Rome and fell into the clutches of Alexander VI, he would never return to Florence alive.

Savonarola wrote back to Alexander VI, courteously declining his invitation, explaining that he was too exhausted to make the long and arduous journey to Rome. Given Savonarola's insistence upon truth, this was almost certainly the case. His regular passionate sermons, to say nothing of his daily involvement in the politics of Florence, had in fact left him in a state of such exhaustion that he was forced to abandon preaching for a while.

When Savonarola resumed his sermons, Alexander VI decided to try a different tack. By now a growing opposition to Savonarola was beginning to form within Florence. The main opposition group called themselves the *arrabbiati* (enraged ones). They drew supporters from across a wide spectrum of the population, from the *popolo* to the members of the leading families. Indeed, belligerent young aristocrats would play a major role in bullying the *piagnoni*. The *arrabbiati* resented Savonarola's interference in the city's secular government, with some even favouring a return to the old Medici days. Such opposition was reinforced by the declining economic situation. Florence was now cut off from its main export route through the port of Pisa, which had been 'temporarily occupied' by Charles VIII. The situation was then worsened by a prolonged period of unusually heavy rainfall, which resulted in a succession of bad harvests. According to Landucci: 'Throughout this time it never stopped raining, and the rainstorms had gone on for about eleven months, there never once being a whole week with no rain.'

The *arrabbiati* would make two attempts to assassinate Savonarola. After both failed, they wrote imploringly to the pope to intervene. Once again, Alexander VI decided to avoid outright confrontation. In a misguided appeal to Savonarola's vanity, he wrote offering the 'little friar' a cardinal's red hat. Savonarola was stung by the pope's misjudgement of his character, and haughtily replied that he wished only for a hat 'red with blood'. Some have seen this as a reference to martyrdom. Had Savonarola already foreseen this end for himself in his overheated visions? Or was he perhaps coming to the realization that this was the inevitable outcome for him: one that might lead to sainthood and the posthumous fulfilment of his dreams?

Florence began to suffer from an influx of starving peasants, driven from the *contado* by the harvest failures and the flooding. This further increased the divisions amongst the people. Landucci describes how Savonarola now 'divided fathers and children, husbands and wives, brothers and sisters'. The situation hardly improved when in May 1497 an exasperated Alexander VI finally issued a bull excommunicating Savonarola, thus banning him from preaching. But Savonarola decided to ignore his excommunication and continued delivering his sermons. Many were profoundly shocked by the sight of the excommunicated Dominican friar celebrating Mass in the cathedral, and on at least one occasion a riot broke out amongst the congregation, followed by another botched assassination attempt.

During the course of his sermons, Savonarola now began to hint that he would perform a miracle to prove once and for all his divine mission. A Franciscan rival preacher seized upon this opportunity and challenged Savonarola to an ordeal by fire. This involved walking barefoot through a fire consisting of fifty feet of burning coals, where God would decide who would burn to death and who would miraculously emerge unscathed. Savonarola chose to ignore this challenge, but one of his more zealous followers accepted it, insisting that he would take Savanarola's place. The challenge was duly accepted, and a date agreed for the ordeal.

From dawn on 7 April, people began streaming into the Piazza della Signoria, all eager to witness the ordeal by fire and see if a miracle would take place. By noon all entrances to the piazza had been sealed off by the militia to prevent any more people cramming into the open space in front of the Palazzo della Signoria. After a long wait, at 1 p.m. the delegation of 200 Franciscans arrived, accompanying their contestant. Half an hour later, a 250-strong Dominican delegation arrived, bearing candles and singing hymns; they were followed by their contestant, grasping a crucifix. Behind him followed Savonarola, holding aloft a sacramental host, the bread which becomes Christ's body at Holy Communion.

The *signoria* emerged from the *palazzo* to oversee the proceedings. There now followed an extended session of bickering between the two delegations over procedure. This covered a wide range of topics. Typical of these was the Franciscan objection to the Dominican contestant wearing his full-length red cloak, on the grounds that it might be 'bewitched'. Meanwhile the crowd was becoming increasingly restless, impatient for the contest to begin. Disturbances began to break out between the *arrabbiati* and the supporters of Savonarola. The militia stationed at the entrances to the piazza waded into the crowd, attempting to restore order. By now, the presiding *signoria* were at a complete loss as to what to do. In the midst of all this, a sudden violent storm broke out, with thunder and lightning crashing through the heavens, followed by a deluge of rain. Many took this to be an omen of God's displeasure. Despite this, the crowd stood their ground, determined to wait for the miracle – or lack of one – which they had come to witness. Finally the storm ceased as suddenly as it had begun.

But by this stage the *signoria* had come to the conclusion that things had gone too far, and were fearful that the situation could well develop into a wholesale riot. Whereupon they summoned the official heralds from the *palazzo* to announce that the ordeal had been cancelled.

By now it was late afternoon and the light was beginning to fade. The *arrabbiati* began spreading rumours that Savonarola had ordered the Dominican contestant not to take part in the ordeal. Even some of the *piagnoni* began to have their doubts. Why had Savonarola not taken up the challenge himself? The mood of the crowd changed. The Franciscan delegation made their way through the crowd and departed the piazza, but as the Dominicans began to follow suit, the crowd chased after them. After being pursued through the streets, the Dominicans made it back to San Marco and slammed the gates shut behind them.

The next day, the city remained eerily quiet and deserted. Then, in the afternoon, groups of opposing supporters emerged and began scuffling on street corners, some of these conflicts evolving into full-scale fights. By evening, a large crowd had gathered outside San Marco, angrily calling out for Savonarola. Later that night the monastery was stormed by the mob. Eventually, Savonarola was taken captive and marched off to the Bargello, along with two of his most ardent supporters. Over the coming days, he was subjected to the customary torture inflicted upon all indicted inmates. Under torture, Savonarola confessed that all his prophecies and visions had been mere inventions. But afterwards he went back on his confessions. This same process was repeated again... and yet a third time, before he was too weak to deny his confessions.

On 23 May, Savonarola and his two loyal companions were led out into the Piazza della Signoria, where they were condemned as heretics and sentenced to death. All three were then hanged on the scaffold which had been erected in front of the Palazzo della Signoria. Beneath their swinging bodies fires were lit, which consumed them. Finally, the mingled ashes of the fire and the bodies were carried away and scattered in the Arno, so that no holy relics would remain.

Some historians have seen the entire episode of Savonarola's rise to power in Florence as a precursor to the Reformation, which would split the Church into Catholics and Protestants during the following century. Whether or not this is the case, the downfall of Savonarola certainly marked a vital turning point in Florentine history. Freed of any fundamentalist yoke, the city would retain its uncorrupted republican rule for just fifteen years, before the gradual demise of this freedom into troubled rule and ultimate autocracy. Yet it was during this transitional period that Florence would produce three seminal figures whose lives would transform three intrinsic components of the continuing Renaissance – namely, politics, art and science.

CHAPTER 17

MACHIAVELLI

THE VERY ADJECTIVE 'MACHIAVELLIAN' has become a byword for politics of a devious and ruthless nature. Others have seen Machiavelli's ideas, as elaborated in his best-known work, *The Prince,* to be nothing more than the very essence of realpolitik – that is, political life stripped of its civilized (or obfuscating) veneer. *The Prince* contains Machiavelli's ruthless and amoral advice to a prince on how to gain power, and how to retain it. This seemingly simplistic (or realistic) work was the product of a mind well versed in the subtleties and mistakes of politics.

It was in the world of actual politics and diplomacy that Machiavelli gained his wide-ranging expertise, which would be distilled into his longer and more considered work, the oft-neglected *Discourses.* The more nuanced wisdom of this latter work comes through in such remarks as 'The governments of the people are better than those of princes' and 'In a well-ordered republic it should never be necessary to resort to extra-constitutional measures'. Such well-meaning guidance can seldom resist the more immediate amorality of a ruthless tyrant. Yet tyrants are rarely popular, and as history has demonstrated, such optimism frequently prevails in the long run. It is impossible to reconcile the ruthless advice given in *The Prince* with the wealth of political experience contained in the *Discourses*. In his writing, as in his life, Machiavelli remains a paradox.

Machiavelli was an extremely subtle character who was in the habit of undercutting the seriousness of his life, and his works, with a sense of humour. Even in his celebrated official portrait, which depicts him resplendent in his robes of office, his features are enlivened with the ghost of a wry smile. Was Machiavelli being serious in *The Prince*, or was this a work of irony, reflecting only the most pessimistic outlook on life and humanity? This is not an easy question to answer. The light touch of humour (or ironic truth-telling) can even be detected in another of his works, the indubitably serious, eight-volume *Florentine Histories*. Take, for instance, Machiavelli's description of the Battle of Anghiari, regarded by Florence as one of its greatest military victories:

> Nor was there ever an instance of wars being carried on in an enemy's country with less injury to the assailants than at this; for in so great a defeat, and in a battle which continued four hours, only one man died, and he, not from wounds inflicted by hostile weapons, or any honourable means, but, having fallen from his horse, was trampled to death. Combatants then engaged with little danger; being nearly all mounted, covered with armour, and preserved from death whenever they chose to surrender, there was no necessity for risking their lives; while fighting, their armour defended them, and when they could resist no longer, they yielded and were safe.

As many as 8,000 men are said to have taken part in this 'battle'. We have heard how *condottieri* preferred to wage war as a game, rather than in deadly earnest, but Machiavelli's description (or exposé) can hardly be said to have contributed to the greater glory of Florence.

In Machiavelli's work, we can see further evidence of the scientific method beginning to emerge. He relied upon experience (or evidence), and drew empirical judgements from this – regardless of religious, moral or Aristotelian authority. Thus he states in *The Prince*: 'All armed prophets have been victors, and all unarmed prophets have failed.' Amongst the former he includes Moses, Romulus, Cyrus and Muhammad. Amongst the latter he cites Savonarola. While in the *Discourses*, he states, with perhaps unwitting irony: 'Where there is religion one presupposes every kind of goodness, so where there is no religion one presupposes the opposite.' This would very much be Machiavelli's fate: *The Prince* appeals to no religious authority, and its author would thus be vilified for all manner of evil.

The rise and fall of Savonarola would have a formative influence on Machiavelli, who grew up in Florence during this period. We know from Machiavelli's own correspondence that when he was twenty-eight years old he attended two of Savonarola's sermons, on 2 and 3 March 1498. Machiavelli's remarks on these were perceptive, while at the same time reflective of his own character. He observed how Savonarola's sermon 'began with great terrors, with explanations that to those not examining them too closely were quite effective'. He perceived how Savonarola 'follows the mood of the times and shades his lies to suit them'. Yet he also recognized that 'had you heard with what audacity he began to preach... it would have stirred no small amount of admiration'.

Here Machiavelli spoke as an educated man with few illusions. He refused to be taken in by Savonarola, and seemed incapable of accepting either his faith or his integrity. Or did he? Machiavelli was writing no ordinary letter. This was his first important task: writing a report on Savonarola for Ricciardo Becchi, the Florentine ambassador to the Holy See in Rome. Machiavelli would have been aware that, in all likelihood, his words – or at least his assessment – would be passed on to Pope Alexander VI himself. Was Machiavelli perhaps tailoring his words to his likely audience?

By March 1498, Florence was emerging from yet another fierce winter. As Luca Landucci observed: 'At the time the cold was extreme and the Arno was frozen over... there having been frost for more than two months.' The starving peasantry were flooding into Florence, for shelter and relief. Savonarola had been excommunicated by Alexander VI the previous year, and was under an edict expressly forbidding him

from preaching. The endgame between Alexander VI and Savonarola
was rapidly approaching.

Conforming with the pope's wishes, the *signoria* had forbidden
Savonarola from preaching in the cathedral, but Savonarola had circum-
vented this ban by delivering his sermons in his own church at San Marco.
And it was here that Machiavelli attended Savonarola's sermons.

Little wonder that Machiavelli wrote so slightingly of Savonarola.
Only many years later, in *The Prince*, would he compare Savonarola with
the likes of Moses and Muhammad. As we shall see, Machiavelli's 1498
letter was in a way a job application, an opportunity for him to present
himself in the best possible light. A more balanced or perceptive interpretation of Savonarola was not what was required, and he was well aware
of this.

Niccolò Machiavelli was born in Florence on 3 May 1469 in the Oltrarno,
where the Vespucci family were close friends and neighbours. Niccolò was
the oldest son of a notary whose career was blighted by inherited debt,
a circumstance which disbarred one from public office. The Machiavelli
family was descended from ancient aristocracy, but by the late fifteenth
century had fallen into comparatively straitened circumstances. As
Machiavelli would later write: 'I was born poor.'

Despite this, he received a good Latin education: that is, in the
old-style Aristotelian scholarship of rhetoric, logic and grammar, rather
than the more enlightened humanist studies which were now the fashion.
However, his father was a learned man, with a good library of the
ancient classics. Browsing his way through these tomes, young Niccolò
would become enamoured of the first-century BC poet and philosopher
Lucretius, and would remain deeply impressed by his universal scientific
approach and his unflinching vision of humanity.

These were troubled times for Florence, and during his youth and
early manhood Machiavelli would witness a number of historic events.
He would be just nine years old at the time of the Pazzi conspiracy and
its bloody aftermath; in his *Florentine Histories*, he would recall how 'the

streets were filled with the parts of men'. He would later remember the
death of Lorenzo the Magnificent and the expulsion of the Medici, as well
as the bonfire of the vanities and the burning of Savonarola. During this
time the population of the city was around 70,000, small enough for gossip
to circulate freely, which meant that he would have heard fresh accounts of
these events, even if he had not personally witnessed all of them.

Machiavelli's 'job application' letter evidently impressed. Immediately
after Savonarola's downfall, when the administration was purged of *frate-
schi*,* Machiavelli was appointed head of the Second Chancery, a medium-
level executive post in the city administration. Machiavelli evidently had
some influential sponsors, probably through his father's intellectual circle,
which had links with Lorenzo di Pierfrancesco de' Medici, the cousin
whose inheritance had been stolen by Lorenzo the Magnificent. In order
to distance themselves from the main line of the Medici, who had been
driven into exile, this branch of the family remained in Florence and
changed its name from de' Medici to il Popolano (Man of the People).

It was these sponsors who were likely responsible for Machiavelli's
rapid promotion a month later to the Ten of War, the committee
responsible for the Florentine Republic's foreign affairs. Within a year,
Machiavelli was being dispatched on a number of minor – but nonetheless difficult – diplomatic missions, where he acquitted himself with
considerable skill. The clarity and incisiveness of his dispatches back to
Florence reveal that he was a natural at this job, being possessed of an
exceptionally insightful mind. Meanwhile, his private letters back to his
pals in the administration were entertaining and filled with such wit,
usually at his own expense, that he had them 'dying of laughter'. One
particularly scurrilous letter describes a hilarious if somewhat exaggerated
incident in which he was duped in the dark into sleeping with an ugly old
crone. In a wordplay on Machiavelli's name, his friends nicknamed him *il
Macchia*, which had connotations of macho manliness as well as meaning
a 'blot' or 'blemish'; even in these early years he was already something of
a roguish black sheep.

---

* Savonarola sympathizers.

Around this time, Machiavelli's father died and was buried in the family tomb at the church of Santa Croce. This would later involve Machiavelli in a revealing episode. A monk informed him that various bones from other families had fraudulently been buried in the Machiavelli family tomb, suggesting that he have them removed. But Machiavelli replied: 'Well, let them be, for my father was a great lover of conversation, and the more there are to keep him company, the better pleased he will be.' This remark goes to the core of Machiavelli's complex character. Although it appears heartless, without feeling, and to some even unprincipled – on reflection it reveals his affection for his father, as well as his understanding and his disregard for empty pieties.

Having demonstrated his diplomatic skill, Machiavelli was entrusted with his first major mission. He was chosen to be one of a vital two-man delegation to the King of France. This was to prove a mission of considerable complexity and importance, as becomes clear in the light of Florence's parlous situation.

By this stage, Italy had reverted to its habitual turbulent and treacherous state. The difficult Charles VIII had died in 1498, and had been succeeded by his more able cousin, Louis XII. Yet now the situation was transformed by the fact that the French had established a permanent foothold in Italy, having occupied Milan. The astute and devious Pope Alexander VI had seized this opportunity to form an alliance with France, by marrying his son Cesare Borgia into the French royal family. With the pope's blessing, and the assistance of French mercenaries, Cesare launched a campaign to conquer the Romagna, part of the so-called Papal States occupying north-central Italy, across the Apennines from Florence. But it now looked as if Cesare Borgia might have further territorial ambitions, this time west of the Apennines, with a planned invasion of defenceless Florence.

Matters were further complicated by the fact that Florence was at the time engaged in a war to retake the port of Pisa, its gateway to Mediterranean trade. To prosecute this war, Florence had hired a contingent of Italian mercenaries, who were laying siege to Pisa. Yet it soon became clear that the mercenaries were prolonging this siege, unwilling to risk their lives by going so far as to take the city (and thus end their employment). And so Florence found itself engaged in an expensive and farcical war to the west, while at the same time facing a potential threat from the east in the form of the unpredictable Cesare Borgia.

It was now that the *signoria* demonstrated the diplomatic expertise which had for so long enabled the republic to remain independent. They immediately contacted Louis XII in Milan, arranging to hire a contingent of tough Swiss and French mercenaries to replace the wayward Italians they had hired to conduct the war in Pisa. At a stroke, the *signoria* had saved the day. They knew that Borgia could not attack Florence as long as it was using French troops, as he too relied upon such French support. The French soldiers would never attack each other; and besides, by hiring these soldiers Florence had placed itself under the protection of Louis XII.

Yet no sooner was this situation resolved than another difficulty arose. When the French and Swiss mercenaries arrived outside Pisa, they refused to fight until they were paid a large sum. According to their commanders, they had not been paid for some time and were owed a considerable amount in back wages. Unfortunately, their former employer, Louis XII, had by now left Milan and returned to France.

Machiavelli's joint diplomatic mission to France was intended to resolve this seeming impasse. He was also briefed to do this as inexpensively and speedily as possible. At the time, a Florentine diplomat not only needed extraordinary diplomatic skills; he also required similar physical strength. Riding post-haste on horseback through northern Italy and over the Alps was a feat of some endurance. Nevertheless, after setting out on 18 July 1500, Machiavelli and his fellow envoy managed to cover the 500 miles from Florence to the French court at Nevers in central France in less than three weeks. Here they were soon put in their place, and treated as mere small fry. According to Cardinal Georges d'Amboise, Louis XII's senior adviser, the king was involved in more important matters. He was negotiating with Spain, the second-most powerful nation in Europe, over how they could conquer and divide between them the Kingdom of Naples. The problems of Florence would have to wait.

It would be a good thirteen days before the Florentine delegation was granted an audience with Louis XII. Machiavelli refused to be overawed by the situation, and would perceptively remark in his dispatch back to Florence that Louis XII's 'haughtiness masks his indecision'. Such insight was all very well, but – as Machiavelli was well aware – this indecision was costing Florence dearly, and might even cost the city its independence. In Machiavelli's next dispatch, he painted a depressing picture: 'The French are blinded by their own power, and only consider those who are armed or ready to give them money to be worthy of their esteem.'

Negotiations dragged on, and Machiavelli was forced to report in his dispatches: 'The King complains about having to pay the Swiss [mercenaries] 38,000 ducats... which he says you ought to have paid, and he threatened to make Pisa and its surrounding territory an independent state.'

The *signoria* dithered over whether to try to raise this sum from its already hard-pressed citizens. Meanwhile, Machiavelli himself was becoming short on funds, and wrote to the *signoria* accordingly. Yet no money was forthcoming, and he was forced to hang about the court kicking his heels as summer passed into autumn. Back in Florence, the *signoria* watched as Cesare Borgia marched into Rimini, just seventy miles east across the Apennines from Florence. They then learned that Pope Alexander VI and his son were intent upon restoring Medici rule to Florence; Piero the Unfortunate was in exile in Rome, and was said to be gathering an army of his own. In a panic, the *signoria* wrote telling Machiavelli to inform the king that they were willing to pay all the money he wanted. Machiavelli's reply was hardly reassuring: 'Concerning the matters which may arise in Italy, the King holds the Pope in higher esteem than any other Italian power.'

Despite this apparent setback, Machiavelli managed to obtain a copy of a letter dictated by Louis XII warning Borgia not to make any foray into Florentine territory. By now, winter was coming on, and Machiavelli found himself so short of money that he could no longer afford to send his dispatches by fast courier, and was having difficulty keeping his clothes clean enough to appear at the court. He begged the *signoria* to allow him to return, but they insisted he remain in France until he had secured a reliable written treaty, signed and sealed by Louis XII himself, that guaranteed French protection for Florence.

Machiavelli had not been wasting his time at the French court. Whenever he was sent on a mission, he always made sure that alongside his diplomatic papers his saddlebag was stuffed with books. On this occasion he is known to have taken Caesar's *Commentaries*, a highly instructive text. Machiavelli would have been well aware that Caesar's clear, incisive descriptions of his military campaigns in Gaul (France) always masked his ulterior political motives. Yet Machiavelli was not only learning from history. He had succeeded in ingratiating himself with the French court to the extent that he was now on friendly terms with the learned and powerful Cardinal d'Amboise.

Machiavelli was never bashful concerning his own diplomatic and political knowledge, and in conversation with the cardinal he was not above making suggestions concerning French policy. If Louis XII wished to succeed in his aim of dominating Italy, he should pay attention to the lessons of history. As Machiavelli would later generalize in *The Prince*: 'If a king wished to rule a nation whose customs and culture are different from his own, he should cultivate the friendship of those who were naturally sympathetic towards him.' In the present case, as he explained to Cardinal d'Amboise, this meant Florence. And what the king should not do was increase the power of those he could not trust, such as Alexander VI and the Church, 'for by this policy he was making himself weak'. Furthermore, he would do well not to make the same error as Ludovico Sforza of Milan, who had brought about his own ruin by inviting into Italy a powerful foreign nation – the French. At this very moment, Louis XII was in the process of making precisely the same mistake over Naples, where he was inviting into Italy the only foreign power to rival France, namely Spain, so that they could share the Kingdom of Naples.

Machiavelli would recall Cardinal d'Amboise's response: '[He] said to me that the Italians knew nothing of war, but I answered that the French knew nothing of politics...' Machiavelli remarked: 'It is possible to conclude a general rule, which almost always applies: whoever is responsible for allowing another to become powerful only ruins himself.'

Although his conclusions here were in fact made with hindsight, the tenor of his reply to Cardinal d'Amboise suggests that he was already beginning to think along such lines. Machiavelli was acquiring a competence and grasp of politics, both in practice and in theory. And here lay the strength of his analysis: even at this early stage, he always sought to understand the underlying principles of what was taking place. As such, he showed the mind of a philosopher: he wished to underpin the flesh and blood of politics and historical events with the bones of science.

Machiavelli would not return to Florence until January 1501, a good six months after he had set out. He found the city once more reduced to a precarious state. The exchequer was empty, the city had no armed force to call upon, and despite the efforts of Louis XII, the hot-headed Cesare Borgia remained an ever-present threat.

That spring, Machiavelli turned thirty-two years old, and in the summer he entered an arranged marriage. His bride was the teenage Marietta Corsini – the daughter of his boss, the head of the Ten of War. Machiavelli's star was evidently rising. Despite this business-like marriage, Machiavelli seems to have grown fond of his new young bride, and would always miss her when he was sent away on a lengthy mission. Or so it would appear. His hilarious letters back to his friends take on a more outrageous tone.

Just a year later, Machiavelli would become involved in one of his longest and most important missions. Along with Francesco Soderini, Bishop of Volterra, he would be dispatched as an envoy to Cesare Borgia, with instructions to discover Borgia's true intentions towards Florence. This would prove one of the most nerve-racking experiences of Machiavelli's life.

Borgia stage-managed his reception of the Florentine delegation to maximum effect. Immediately on their arrival at Urbino, after a hard two days' riding across the mountains, Machiavelli and Bishop Soderini were hustled into the dark and deserted ducal palace. Here they were confronted by Borgia, dressed all in black, his bearded features eerily illuminated by the light of a single flickering candle.

Borgia proceeded to berate Machiavelli and the bishop, angrily threatening them with all manner of retribution if Florence did not invite him to become its *condottiere*. This would have given Borgia control over the unarmed city. Despite being more than a little scared by Borgia's display, Machiavelli shrewdly assessed that the duke was bluffing. And when Borgia sent him back to Florence for an 'answer', Machiavelli was able to reassure the *signoria* that there was no immediate threat. The *signoria* remained unconvinced, as well they might. So Machiavelli was ordered to return to Borgia to act as Florence's 'diplomatic mission', with instructions to follow him and his court wherever they went, all the while reporting back with regular dispatches to Florence.

The following six months would be one of the most harrowing and formative periods in Machiavelli's entire career. During these months Borgia would exhibit to the full the treachery and vindictiveness which would justly earn him a place in the rogues' gallery of history. Murder, betrayal, an almost unhinged need for vengeance, more murders, along with wanton depravity – all these would feature heavily in Borgia's behaviour. It was vital that the *signoria* knew precisely what Borgia was doing. Yet Machiavelli knew that each of his dispatches was secretly being opened and read by Borgia. Here was a situation requiring diplomatic subtlety, sleight of hand, and covert implication of the highest order. Little wonder that in his later years Machiavelli would write: 'For a long time I have not said what I believed, nor do I ever believe what I say, and if indeed I do happen to tell the truth, I hide it amongst so many lies that it is hard to find.'

However, as the months went by, Machiavelli found himself being curiously drawn to Borgia, almost in spite of himself. Aside from all the horror and depravity, there was no denying the duke's charisma. And, more than that, his success. Little wonder that Machiavelli would later feature Borgia as one of his exemplars in *The Prince*.

In keeping with Machiavelli's quest for generalizations, Borgia would lead him to an understanding that in order to succeed, and go on succeeding, a prince requires '*virtù e fortuna*'. This phrase, or prescriptive maxim, is open to a wide variety of interpretations. *Virtù* covers all ground from 'virtue' to 'virility'. It has connotations of manliness (*vir*, Latin for 'man') as well as strength. This was the power which Borgia exhibited. But Machiavelli recognized that without the accompanying *fortuna*, this power was as nothing. *Fortuna* was luck, or fate, or opportunity (to be seized). As long as Borgia took advantage of this, his opportunism succeeded.

The following year, Machiavelli would be sent to Rome after Cesare Borgia's father, Pope Alexander VI, had taken ill and died. Cesare had been laid low with the same affliction – probably malaria, rather than the widely rumoured joint poisoning. Soon, his father's greatest enemy would be elected Pope Julius II. The *fortuna* that had accompanied Borgia's campaigning in the Romagna, when Machiavelli had been attached to his 'court', had now eluded him. His luck had run out. The figure whom Machiavelli visited on his sickbed was a changed man. No one could rule their fate once *fortuna* had deserted them.

Just nine years later, Machiavelli would suffer a similar reversal of fortune. Cardinal Giovanni de' Medici, now thirty-six years old, would be entrusted with the papal troops by Julius II. Piero the Unfortunate had died back in 1503, and in September 1512 his younger brother would march into Florence, toppling the republican government which Machiavelli had served so loyally, and restoring the Medici to power. By decree, Machiavelli was 'dismissed, deprived and totally removed' from his post. On top of this, he was fined 1,000 florins, effectively rendering him bankrupt. He was also banished from the city, forcing him to live on his smallholding at the hamlet of Sant'Andrea in Percussina, some five miles south of the city walls.

Worse was to come. Barely had Machiavelli and his family removed themselves to Sant'Andrea than an anti-Medici plot was uncovered in Florence. The plotters had drawn up a list of likely sympathizers, and this included Machiavelli's name. As soon as Machiavelli heard of this, he hastened to Florence to explain his innocence. On arrival he was at once arrested and confined to a cell in the Bargello. In line with current practice, he was then subjected to torture. The traditional Florentine method of torture at that time was the *strappado*. This involved the victim's hands being strapped behind his back and attached to a rope. The rope was then hauled up over a pulley, with the victim being suspended in the air. The rope was released, letting the victim fall, until it abruptly halted his descent before his feet touched the ground. This would sharply jerk his wrists further up behind his back with an excruciating jolt. The victim felt as if his shoulders were breaking, or his arms were being wrenched out of their sockets – either of which sometimes happened. Machiavelli would be subjected to six such 'drops', but confessed to nothing. (Three drops had been enough to make Savonarola confess that he was a heretic.) He would later write, concerning these tortures: 'I have borne them so straightforwardly that I am proud of myself for it and consider myself more of a man than I believed I was.' He had almost certainly known nothing of the plot, but he would probably have had his suspicions as to who was involved. Machiavelli knew that, had he confessed to anything – just to avoid further agony – he would have been executed.

One morning, he was woken in his cell before dawn by the sound of some of the condemned conspirators being led to their execution, accompanied by the customary small choir singing hymns. (This was intended to drown out the howls and imprecations of the condemned.) For weeks Machiavelli languished in his cell amidst what he would later describe as the 'stomach-churning suffocating stench… with metal shackles around [my] ankles, listening to the screams of those enduring the drop… woken near dawn by the choir accompanying the condemned being led to their execution.'

In March 1513, news reached Florence that Julius II had died in Rome, and had been succeeded by Cardinal Giovanni de' Medici, who had become Pope Leo X. As part of the celebrations an amnesty was granted to prisoners, and Machiavelli found himself freed. A pale spectre, he made his way out through the city gate amongst the celebrating crowds, and off down the road to Sant'Andrea and exile on his smallholding. At the age of forty-three, it looked as if Machiavelli's life was to all intents and purposes finished.

For the next dozen years or so, Machiavelli would live in exile, tantalizingly close to the city he loved and regarded as his home. Ironically, if he had not been forced into such isolation, we would probably never have heard of him. He would have gone down in history as an official serving in the administration during Florence's brief period of republican rule.

But Machiavelli refused to be daunted by the fact that *fortuna* had deserted him. During his years in exile he would turn to writing, in the desperate hope of producing a work that would win favour with the authorities. He longed to be reinstated; to win back his former eminence.

The years of composing dispatches had made him fully practised in the craft of writing. Yet those years of diplomatic guile and carefully crafted dissimulations, to say nothing of the lies masquerading as truth and the truth masquerading as lies, had left their mark. As he constantly reminded himself, 'I have not said what I believed, nor do I ever believe what I say.' And this deceptive trait would forever permeate his writing, undercutting it with ambiguity.

The first book which Machiavelli wrote would be *The Prince* – a work seemingly devoid of moral scruples, filled with cold-blooded prescriptions for those seeking power and for those wishing to retain power. Machiavelli began writing the short work in the summer of 1513, and in the white heat of inspiration it was completed in a matter of months. In *The Prince*, Machiavelli would not only draw on his own experience, but also on a host of historical examples derived from his extensive reading, undertaken during the hours of tedium waiting for an audience in foreign courts. This surely would win favour with the new Medici regime. Or was its intent even more devious than this?

The contemporary American political theorist Mary G. Dietz has even gone so far as to suggest that Machiavelli was in fact 'offering carefully crafted advice (such as arming the people) designed to undo the ruler if taken seriously and followed'. And the text certainly contains elements which would seem to support this self-defeating point of view. On the other hand, the final chapter of *The Prince* would appear to go beyond irony or duplicitous motives, suggesting another ulterior aim in writing this work. This last chapter is headed 'An Exhortation

St Augustine by Botticelli.

The Birth of Venus by Botticelli.

Primavera (Spring) by Botticelli.

Left: Verrocchio's *Baptism of Christ*. The kneeling angel on the left is believed to have been painted by Leonardo.

Below: Leonardo's *The Adoration of the Magi*.

Girolamo Savonarola.

Machiavelli at the height of his powers, wearing his Florentine robes of office.

The ruthless Cesare Borgia, who would become an exemplary figure in Machiavelli's *The Prince*.

Girolamo Savonarola being burnt at the stake in the Piazza della Signoria.

Woodcut of Florence from the *Nuremberg Chronicle*, 1493.

Michelangelo's *David*.

The Creation of Adam by Michelangelo.

Michelangelo's *Pietà*.

A contemporary portrait of Galileo.

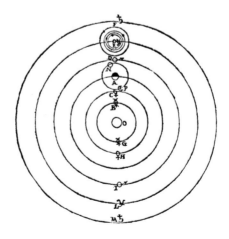

Galileo's diagram of the Copernican (heliocentric) system of the universe, which also shows his own discovery, the four satellites (moons) of Jupiter.

to Liberate Italy from the Barbarians'. The 'barbarians' to which Machiavelli refers are the foreign powers that had invaded Italy, such as the French and the Spanish, whose armies were destroying the country Machiavelli loved.

Assuming this was indeed Machiavelli's motive, then the amorality he preached can be seen not as an end in itself, but as a means for a strong leader to drive out the foreign armies, and protect the freedom and security of their citizens. In this way, Italy would be returned to its former greatness, as in the era of the Roman Empire. Such a united Italy had long been the dream of many Italians, and Machiavelli appears to have subscribed to this too. Yet here again there remains a self-contradictory element. With such methods as Machiavelli advocated for his prince, the freedom, security and greatness of Italy's subjects would seem to be the prince's least concern. *The Prince* was an instruction manual for a dictator, rather than a liberator.

A further indication of the ambiguous motives behind *The Prince* can be found in its dedication. The work was originally dedicated to Giuliano di Lorenzo de' Medici, the third son of Lorenzo the Magnificent. This was the very man who had replaced the republican government Machiavelli had served so faithfully throughout his working life. Unfortunately, by the time Machiavelli had finished *The Prince*, Giuliano had returned to Rome, and his twenty-three-year-old cousin Lorenzo di Piero de' Medici had taken over as ruler of Florence. So Machiavelli changed his dedication accordingly. This was followed by the necessary adjustments to the text: the identity of the great prince who would lead Italy to liberation and greatness now appeared to be of little concern – the main point was that he recognized the author of this exemplary political work, appreciated his political expertise, and reinstated him to his former post in the administration.

But the ruler of Florence, or indeed any member of the Medici family, proved unwilling to reinstate Machiavelli. To all intents and purposes he remained alone, and in disgrace. So for the time being he turned to literature, whose imaginative aspects were ideally suited to his personality and his talents. Amongst several pieces, he wrote a drama entitled *La*

Mandragola (The Mandrake), which is now widely regarded as the first comic masterpiece written in the new Italian language.

Machiavelli obstinately clung to the hope that one day he would be restored to his old position. And for fleeting moments, his hope appeared justified. When the Medici pope, Leo X, was faced with a political crisis (largely of his own making), he secretly dispatched an agent to seek out Machiavelli's advice. In the event, this advice was ignored – to Leo X's detriment.

It is likely that at least one person appreciated Machiavelli's advice and acumen. In 1521, Pope Leo X died; two years later, his illegitimate cousin and confidant, Cardinal Giulio de' Medici, was elected Pope Clement VII. Prior to this, Cardinal Giulio de' Medici had commissioned Machiavelli to write a history of Florence. Under the circumstances, it is hardly surprising that this work was slanted in favour of the Medici. Yet as we have seen in Machiavelli's description of Florence's great victory at the Battle of Anghiari, his history was not without its ironic elements. And it was during these years that Machiavelli would also complete his lengthy and more considered political treatise known as the *Discourses*, which was more republican in its sympathies.

Machiavelli's *Florentine Histories* was well received by Clement VII, and as a result Machiavelli was given a post in the Florentine Medici administration. Yet this post was derisory considering his former position and talents: Machiavelli would be appointed supervisor of the city walls. Later, he would be entrusted with an insignificant diplomatic mission to Lucca. Never again did he attain high office. He would die in 1527 at the age of fifty-eight, an impoverished and disappointed man.

However, Machiavelli's afterlife would exceed even his wildest dreams. Not until 1532 would *The Prince* finally be published, and Machiavelli would certainly have savoured the hypocritical opprobrium which this work provoked amongst rulers throughout Europe. (The same rulers, such as King Henry VIII of England, who read it and followed its advice to the letter.) And through the centuries *The Prince* would continue to be both vilified and appreciated. Napoleon, Lenin, Stalin, Mussolini, Hitler and Saddam Hussein are all known to have had Machiavelli's work on their bedside table.

CHAPTER 18

MICHELANGELO

MACHIAVELLI'S *PRINCE* COULD BE said to have taken Renaissance humanist thought to its logical conclusion. This was the ultimate individualism – but it was only for the ruler. In this way, it is ironically anti-humanist.

Michelangelo would achieve much the same in his art. What can be more human than Michelangelo's statue of David? Here is the ultimate symbol of humanity. He is strong, larger than life, yet naked and thus vulnerable. He is biblical, yet he is utterly a product of his humanistic era. He carries the sling which vanquished the Philistine giant Goliath. (What resonance in that simple fact!) And the Florentine people came to see him as a symbol of their struggle against their enemies – from the Medici to the overwhelming power of Rome.

Like Machiavelli, Michelangelo's formative years would be spent during the period when Savonarola held sway in Florence. Yet if this was the common heritage out of which they grew, which nurtured them both, their reactions to it could not have been more disparate. As personalities, Machiavelli and Michelangelo would prove almost polar opposites.

Michelangelo was earnest, proud, irascible and obsessively hard-working. He also had a profound belief in God, and it is from Michelangelo that we learn something of Savonarola's bewitching powers.

As a young man, Michelangelo was in the habit of honing his sculpture skills in the gardens set up by Cosimo de' Medici close by the monastery of San Marco. In the midst of his labours, he frequently heard Savonarola preaching to his fellow friars beneath the damask rose tree in the monastery garden across the road – an experience he would never forget. Michelangelo's character had been imbued with a deep spirituality from the earliest years of his childhood, and he soon found himself listening intently to what Savonarola was saying. But more than this, Michelangelo found himself so enchanted by the manner in which the 'little friar' spoke that more than sixty years later he would confide to his favourite pupil, Ascanio Condivi, that 'he could still hear [Savonarola's] living voice ringing out in his mind'.

Despite this, Michelangelo would never be tempted by Savonarola's asceticism to the point of abandoning his art. Unlike Botticelli, whose final years were so blighted by his love for Savonarola's teachings, Michelangelo's religious faith was inextricably bound up with his artistic drive. He could no more abandon his overweening pride in his art than he could abandon his belief in the humility of Christ. This spiritual conflict would continue to torment him throughout his life.

Michelangelo Buonarroti was born in 1475 in the village of Caprese, some thirty-five miles south-east of Florence in the Tuscan *contado*. For generations, his family had been minor bankers, but the family bank had failed during his father's time. Michelangelo's father seems to have been rescued from penury by obtaining a post in the local administration of the Florentine Republic, where he held a position equivalent to that of village mayor. The Buonarroti family were proud of their ancient heritage, believing that they were descended from Countess Mathilde of Canossa, the so-called *gran contessa* who ruled Tuscany in the late eleventh century. There is no evidence whatsoever to support this belief, but it is essential to understanding Michelangelo's proud character and self-confidence.

Michelangelo's mother suffered from a prolonged illness during his childhood; as a result, the infant Michelangelo was farmed out to a wet nurse, who eventually became his full-time nanny and surrogate mother. She lived in the village of Settignano in the upper Arno valley, where her husband worked at the local marble quarry. This appears to have had a decisive influence on Michelangelo. According to Vasari, he would boast: 'If there is good in me, it is because I grew up in the countryside. I absorbed with my [nurse's] milk the knack of handling the hammer and chisels with which I make my sculptures.' This too has its mythic element. The infant Michelangelo may have heard the continuous sound of hammer and chisel, but he had been far too young to have handled these implements in the quarry.

Around the age of thirteen, Michelangelo was sent to live with his father in Florence. (His mother had died when he was six.) The family home was in the Santa Croce district, on a respectable street but uncomfortably close to the slums and ramshackle hovels of the impoverished fishermen. His father maintained the social aloofness of his imagined ancestors, and young Michelangelo was brought up in an atmosphere of stifling adherence to the 'old ways'. Like Machiavelli, he too received an old-school education, learning grammar, rhetoric and logic rather than the more modern humanist studies.

Michelangelo soon grew bored with learning by rote and took to drawing to pass the time. He decided that he wanted to be an artist and became interested in the art he saw all around him in Renaissance Florence. In particular, he was fascinated by Ghiberti's bronze doors to the Baptistery, with their ten panels depicting scenes from the Old Testament. Michelangelo would later refer to these as 'the Gates of Paradise', and such was the force of their impression on him that their influence would be unmistakable in his frescoes in the Sistine Chapel, which he would not complete until some twenty years later. Michelangelo also became intrigued by the works of art he saw in the nearby old churches – in particular the solid, gesturing figures he saw in the frescoes by Giotto. Florence in the late fifteenth century was a treasury of Renaissance works, but it is noticeable that Michelangelo was drawn to the masterpieces of early Renaissance art, which still retained unmistakable elements of stylized pre-Renaissance spirituality.

Michelangelo's father disapproved of his son's wish to become an artist, a profession he considered to be beneath the dignity of a family of such standing. There were rows, and according to Michelangelo he was 'often severely beaten'. But obstinacy ran in the family, and the young Michelangelo's stubbornness eventually prevailed. His father packed him off to the studio of Ghirlandaio, the artist who had spurred Botticelli to excel himself.

Michelangelo was thirteen when he entered Ghirlandaio's studio; this was unusually late, as most were apprenticed at the age of ten. But Michelangelo proved to be a quick learner, and some have seen Ghirlandaio's influence in the lifelike quality of the figures that inhabit his paintings. Others have commented on how little Michelangelo was influenced by the great generation of Florentine artists who immediately preceded him – most notably Leonardo and Botticelli. Michelangelo was temperamentally averse to such figures, both in real life and in art. As his biographer Robert S. Liebert enigmatically observes: 'Michelangelo was partly able to leap forward in style by reaching significantly back in time.'

According to Vasari, in 1488 Lorenzo the Magnificent decided to open up his gardens near San Marco and establish this as a school for sculptors. When he began making enquiries for suitable students, Ghirlandaio immediately recommended the fourteen-year-old Michelangelo. The school was run by Donatello's former pupil Bertoldo di Giovanni, a talented sculptor in bronze who 'was so old that he could no longer work'. As a result, Michelangelo was largely left to his own devices, and spent his time painstakingly copying the Ancient Roman statues and fragments dotted about the garden.

In later life, Michelangelo would frequently claim that he was entirely self-taught as an artist, and that his gift came from God alone. Evidence from his work gives the lie to this boast. It appears that the seventy-year-old Bertoldo taught Michelangelo how to model figures in clay and wax. Even early in his career Michelangelo had a remarkable ability to carve marble so that it acquired a soft, waxen appearance.

Vasari recounts a story of what was probably Michelangelo's first real encounter with Lorenzo the Magnificent, an event which would prove a turning point in his life. Michelangelo was in the sculpture garden attempting to sculpt a copy in marble of an antique satyr's head. This was 'very old and wrinkled, with the nose damaged and a laughing mouth'. Michelangelo was so absorbed in his work that he did not notice Lorenzo standing behind him, gazing in awe at the precocious craftsmanship of the young pupil. Michelangelo was attempting to improve upon the battered old satyr's face, hollowing out the mouth to reveal the tongue and two rows of perfect teeth. Suddenly aware of someone behind him, Michelangelo spun round. He blushed as Lorenzo smiled, attempting to put the boy at ease. Lorenzo leaned forward, indicating the mouth of the satyr, pointing out that it was not quite correct. No old satyr would still be possessed of a mouth filled with perfect teeth. Michelangelo waited until Lorenzo passed on, and then chipped off one of the satyr's teeth, digging into the gum to give it further authenticity, as if the tooth had just fallen out. When Lorenzo next passed by, he was amused; but most of all he remained amazed by the exceptional talent he had observed in the young sculptor. Following this incident, Michelangelo was invited to live and work in the Palazzo Medici. He was given a room of his own, and the equivalent of almost five florins a month (more than half the wage which a fully qualified craftsman would need to support himself and his entire family). When Michelangelo moved in to the *palazzo*, Lorenzo gave him a violet cloak, and compensated his father by appointing him to a post in the city's customs administration.

For the next three years or so, Michelangelo would become a member of the Medici household, dining at the table with Lorenzo and his family, along with other distinguished guests. Thus he found himself in the company of such figures as the Platonist philosopher Ficino and the humanist poet Poliziano. He also attended occasional meetings of Lorenzo's informal discussion group, known as the Academy. Unlike many of the artists who had been invited into Lorenzo's circle, Michelangelo had received an education and was thus able to follow the drift of the philosophical arguments. In this way, Platonic philosophy would lend a breadth to the narrow intensity of Michelangelo's religious faith, and the poetry declaimed by Poliziano inspired him to write poetry of his own. But Michelangelo did not show these early efforts to anyone, nor indeed did he join in the Academy's high-minded discussions. To the others, he appeared as a gauche teenager; he was shy and felt tongue-tied in the presence of such brilliant intellectuals.

But this was not the only reason for Michelangelo's diffidence. Several amongst Lorenzo's intellectual circle were homosexual, and made little effort to conceal this within the privacy of the Palazzo Medici. Michelangelo recognized in these others feelings which he too possessed – but was ashamed to express. This often made him appear awkward or brusque in manner. A fine early stanza of his poetry expresses how he saw himself:

> Burning, I remain in the shadow,
> As the setting sun retreats into its glow.
> The others have gone to their life of pleasure,
> I alone lie grieving, with the earth my measure.

There was just one figure in the Medici household with whom he felt an affinity – a talented sculptor called Pietro Torrigiano, who was just three years older than him and slipped into the role of older brother. Yet even here things soon became difficult. As Michelangelo and Torrigiano worked together, it became apparent to Torrigiano that Michelangelo's work far outclassed his own. His jealousy soon led to friction between them. Torrigiano was notorious for losing his temper, and according to the contemporary sculptor Benvenuto Cellini, Torrigiano told him that one day, when he was with Michelangelo: 'I got more angry than usual, and clenching my fist, gave him such a blow on the nose, that I felt bone and cartilage go down like biscuit beneath my knuckles; and this mark of mine he will carry with him to the grave.' Torrigiano's assessment of this injury was correct: all contemporary depictions of Michelangelo emphasize his squashed nose.*

Michelangelo's inner life remained a struggle. He found it difficult to reconcile his strong religious faith with his natural feelings, especially when they were drawn to the naked male form. Even looking back in his later life, he could not resolve the agony of his early years:

> If in my youth I had realized the sustaining splendour of beauty with which I was in love would one day flood back into my heart, there to ignite a flame that would torture me without end, how gladly would I have put out the light of my eyes.

Such self-destructive feelings would only be resolved in the creativity of his art. This is embodied in one of Michelangelo's early works, a frieze called *Battle of the Centaurs*, suggested by lines from a poem by Poliziano. In keeping with Renaissance tradition, this poem is itself adapted from a work by the Ancient Roman poet Ovid, writing in the first century BC. According to classical legend, a group of centaurs became so drunk at the wedding party of the Greek king Pirithous that they attempted to carry off and rape his bride and other women present. With youthful intensity, Michelangelo depicts a riot of tangled, struggling naked bodies. It is possible to detect the influence of Ghiberti's Baptistery doors; but this is no Gates of Paradise. Instead, we see an inferno of writhing bodies sensuously depicted in polished, waxen marble. This may have the mark of a subconscious fantasy emanating from an overheated young mind, but its disorder is realized with a consummate and meticulously composed skill. This tension between order and chaos can be seen as an aesthetic

---

* When Lorenzo the Magnificent was informed of this incident, he became so incensed that Torrigiano fled from Florence. Years later, he would end up in England, where he was instrumental in introducing Renaissance art to this northern land. He would be commissioned by Henry VIII to create a tomb for his father, Henry VII. This includes a terracotta bust of Henry VII which can still be seen in Westminster Abbey. Torrigiano's work would be acclaimed by the twentieth-century art historian John Pope-Hennessy as 'the finest Renaissance tomb north of the Alps'.

embodiment of the agonizing conflict raging in Michelangelo's heart. Indicatively, *Battle of the Centaurs* remained in Michelangelo's possession, and it was never finished.

Lorenzo the Magnificent died in April 1492, just as Michelangelo was nearing the end of this sculpture, and some have suggested that the emotional impact of his mentor's death was the reason why it was not completed. Others claim that this work was intentionally *non finito*, and marks a seminal advance in this sculpting technique. In support of this view, the seemingly unfinished, rough-hewn background and upper level of the frieze certainly serve to emphasize the smooth musculature and skin of the struggling figures.

Condivi relates that, following Lorenzo the Magnificent's death, Michelangelo 'was so grief-stricken… that for many days he could do simply nothing'. He appears to have left the Palazzo Medici and returned home to his father's house. Although Michelangelo is known to have later gone back to the Palazzo Medici, Lorenzo's successor, Piero the Unfortunate, did not commission him to create any serious works. According to Liebert: 'It is symbolic of the ending of the glorious era of Medici patronage that during Piero's brief rule the only recorded commission given to Michelangelo was a snowman!' It would have been little consolation for Michelangelo that his great rival Leonardo was at that very time forced to waste his talent in similar fashion – carving ice sculptures for Ludovico Sforza in Milan.

Florence was now entering troubled times. These were the years following Savonarola's prophecy that a 'new Cyrus would come from across the mountains bringing death and destruction in his wake'. And now this appeared to be coming true: Charles VIII had crossed the Alps with a large French army and was making his way south. In October 1494, Michelangelo began having troubled dreams.* According to Condivi: 'Lorenzo de' Medici had appeared to him in a black robe, all in rags over his nakedness, and commanded him to tell his son [Piero the Unfortunate] that he would shortly be driven from his house, never to return.'

---

* Condivi describes how Michelangelo told him that 'a friend' had experienced these dreams. It is widely accepted that this 'friend' was Michelangelo himself.

The dream implies a close relationship between Michelangelo and Lorenzo the Magnificent. Some have gone so far as to suggest that Lorenzo's near nakedness implies a homosexual attraction on Michelangelo's part. Either way, Michelangelo then described a second instance where 'Lorenzo appeared dressed as he was before... while [Michelangelo] was awake and staring, he struck him with a heavy blow to the cheek because he had not told his son Piero what he had dreamt.' The nineteen-year-old Michelangelo was so frightened by what he had dreamt that he fled the city. The following month, Piero the Unfortunate would also flee Florence, heralding the end of the Medici dominance of the republic.

Two years later, Michelangelo would end up in Rome. And here he would eventually complete his first consummate masterpiece. This is the *Pietà* (Pity), commissioned by the French Cardinal of Saint-Denis for his tombstone. It depicts the body of Christ after his crucifixion, held in the lap of his mother Mary. In striking contrast to the *Battle of the Centaurs*, this is a work of transcendent serenity. Christ's lolling head and lean naked body are draped across Mary's lap, his features tranquil in their deathly repose, his body limp and lifeless. There is little evidence of the passionate agony he has undergone on the cross, or indeed of the traumatic experience undergone by Mary. These are implied. The mark of the nail which penetrated Christ's hand, and the wound in his side which he received while hanging from the cross, are just discernible in the smooth marble of his skin. What we are witnessing is Mary's ineffable pity, the long moment presaging the miracle when Christ will rise again from the dead and save all who believe in him. Mary's youthful features have a simple beauty, almost mystic in their depth of contained emotion.

This very youthfulness in Mary's face would prompt Condivi to question how one so young could have given birth to the thirty-three-year-old Christ in her lap. She should have been a woman in her fifties. Michelangelo replied: 'Do you not know that chaste women stay fresh much more than those who are not chaste? How much more in the case of the Virgin, who had never experienced the least lascivious desire that might change her body?'

Michelangelo may well have believed this, but Vasari suggests an alternative possibility. Michelangelo's deep-felt image of Mary's youthful motherhood could have derived from the fact that both his mother and the nanny who consequently looked after him had died when they were young. Motherhood and innocent adolescence would remain forever identified in his mind.

Michelangelo's personal psychology would frequently play an intrinsic role in his work. Vasari claimed that his 'manner of speech was very veiled and ambiguous, his utterances having in a sense two meanings'. Much the same can be said of his art, especially in its inspiration. His finest works achieve an inextricable blend of secular (often sexual) psychology and a profound spirituality.

Michelangelo would not return to Florence until 1500. By now the Medici were long gone, and Savonarola had been dead two years. Yet the city remained in a volatile state. The economic downturn dragged on, as did the war against Pisa. The cost of paying the mercenaries who were fighting the war was growing ever more unpopular, especially amongst those whose taxes were continually being raised to support them. The populace was disgruntled, with the streets becoming increasingly lawless.

A telling image of the city's state is reflected in the pitiful condition to which Botticelli would be reduced over the coming years. The glory days of his transcendent, colourful paintings for the Medici were long over, and even his renunciation at the feet of Savonarola was a thing of the past. People stopped to watch as he shuffled on crutches through the streets beneath a drab, threadbare cloak – aged, sick and incapable. He would finally die in 1510, after which his reputation would all but vanish. Even Vasari's mention of him is distinctly dismissive, going so far as to muddle him up with another painter, a minor Florentine contemporary with a similar name. Astonishingly, it would be over 300 years before *The Birth of Venus* was put on display in the Uffizi Gallery. Even then it was almost another century before his 'overnight discovery' by the Victorian aesthete Walter Pater on a visit to Florence – whereupon Botticelli finally regained the recognition he deserved.

Back in Florence in the early 1500s, as Botticelli hauled himself through the streets in rags, the government remained rudderless and all but impotent. Even Savonarola's populist reforms were forgotten. This state of affairs was exaggerated by the fact that the *golfaloniere* was changed every two months, and with each new appointment came another fruitless shift of policy. Then, in 1502, a radical change in the city's constitution was introduced: Piero Soderini was elected *gonfaloniere* for life. Within a few years, following Machiavelli's advice, Soderini introduced a new militia, recruited from amongst the youth of the city. From now on, Florence would fight its own wars, and no longer have to rely upon corrupt and untrustworthy *condottieri*.

Soderini was an honest politician, though of limited ability in this sphere. At the time, this proved to be an advantage. The last thing Florence needed was a skilled and ambitious leader, bent upon improving the city's reputation throughout Italy. However, he did have one ambition, which would leave its mark on the city of Florence forever. He was enthused by the achievements of the city's great artists, and was determined that they should be put to good use. Just prior to Soderini's election (and possibly at his instigation), the authorities commissioned Michelangelo to create a statue of David out of a large block of marble which had been left in a warehouse near the cathedral. The neglected marble may have been partially damaged, but it had originated from Carrara in northern Tuscany, whose quarry was renowned for producing the finest white marble in Italy.

The commissioning of a statue of David was intended to restore the civic pride of the city, and Soderini ensured that the twenty-six-year-old Michelangelo was able to work alone and unmolested in the warehouse by the cathedral. He knew that Michelangelo had a phobia about his work being seen before it was finished: the comments of ignorant spectators had been known to drive him into a fury. Despite such ideal conditions, and the freedom of interpretation allowed him by Soderini, Michelangelo found himself confronted with a formidable task. Several other artists had already made attempts on the eighteen-foot block, leaving it in a distressingly mutilated condition. Worse still was the fact that the block was now forty years old. According to Michelangelo's recent biographer William E. Wallace: 'Marble is best carved when it is fresh from the quarries; with age and exposure to the elements it becomes increasingly intractable.'

Michelangelo set to work with a will, and was soon chiselling away obsessively at his overwhelming block of marble. Day and night he hacked, chipped and smoothed the brittle stone. Months passed in solitude, with the curious passers-by only aware of the constant sound of hammer and chisel emanating from behind the large wooden warehouse doors. During the sweltering summer, Michelangelo worked stripped to the waist, the sweat dribbling into his eyes; during the frigid months of winter, when his fingers froze, he worked swathed like a mummy, the steam of his breath obscuring his vision. Soon he began to identify totally with the statue he was carving. We now know that this inclination was evident from the outset, as indicated by a brief poem he wrote on one of his preliminary sketches:

> *Davicte cholla fromba*
> *e io choll'archo*
> *Michelangelo*
> [David with his sling
> and I with my bow
> Michelangelo]

'My bow' refers to the wooden instrument which Michelangelo used to drill smooth holes into the stone. The poem captures Michelangelo's pride, as he likens himself to David setting forth to do battle.

It would take Michelangelo three years to complete his twice-life-sized statue. Intriguingly, according to a contemporary report, the statue was originally intended to stand on the roof of the cathedral beneath Brunelleschi's dome. This may account for some of the exaggeration which gives the statue its power. It was to be viewed from street level; its physicality and expression thus needed to be overemphasized in order to convey these aspects to the spectator far below. Up close, as the statue is seen now, these aspects lend the finished statue its *terribilità*, its awesome yet contained power.

The finished work is profoundly humanistic, a magnificent celebration of what it means to be human. Yet at the same time it is also imbued with an unmistakably idealistic quality: the embodiment of a Platonic ideal. From this time on, Michelangelo's work would become increasingly mannerist, emphasizing the aspect of *terribilità* in both his sculpture and his painting. This would be particularly evident in the frescoes he was to paint on the ceiling of the Sistine Chapel.

In 1505, Michelangelo was summoned to Rome by Pope Julius II, known as the warrior pope, who not only took his papal name from Julius Caesar but personally led his army in campaigns to capture Perugia and Bologna (ordering all the cardinals resident in Rome to accompany him). Julius II was intent upon leaving behind him a legacy unrivalled by any previous Renaissance pope. He decided that his tomb should be designed, built and decorated by the man he deemed to be the finest artist of his time – namely, Michelangelo. This tomb was intended to include forty statues by Michelangelo and his assistants, who were ordered to complete the task in five years. Julius II was a determined character: he was now sixty-two years old, but was bent on seeing for himself his magnificent mausoleum before the time came for him to occupy it.

Over the years, this tomb would inspire another of Michelangelo's transcendent masterpieces. This was his statue of the massively bearded, muscular figure of Moses, seated with the tablets of the Ten Commandments in his lap and his legendary horns protruding from his head. These last stem from Exodus 34:29, which was translated from Hebrew into Latin in the fifth century by St Jerome: 'And when Moses came down from the Mount Sinai, he held the two tablets of the testimony, and he knew not that his face was horned from the conversation of the

Lord.'* The overpowering presence of Michelangelo's statue, which can be seen today in the church of San Pietro in Vincoli in central Rome, is all but impossible to articulate.† It is *terribilità* personified.

Fortunately, there were occasions when Michelangelo was interrupted in the seemingly impossible task of completing Julius II's tomb, and diverted to other projects. The greatest of these 'diversions' was the almost equally Herculean task of painting the ceiling of the Sistine Chapel. According to Condivi, the architect Donato Bramante, who was at work building St Peter's Basilica, had grown jealous of Michelangelo. Bramante felt that he was the one who should have been chosen to build Julius II's tomb. In an effort to displace Michelangelo from the task, and also to discredit him, Bramante persuaded the pope to commission Michelangelo to paint the ceiling of the Sistine Chapel. Bramante suspected that Michelangelo was unpractised in the art of painting, a defect which would be particularly exposed in the use of fresco, which entails a speedy commitment to brushstrokes while the plaster is still damp and 'fresh' (*fresco*).

Michelangelo was initially reluctant to undertake this commission, but Julius II was not a man to brook rejection, and even Michelangelo was cowed into submission. However, just as Michelangelo was about to start on his work, Julius II again became involved in the Italian Wars and led his army into battle, this time against the French. While Julius II was away from Rome, Michelangelo took the opportunity to flee the city, hurriedly making his way back to Florence. Here he once again took up his favourite pursuit of sculpture.

---

* This verse has inspired all manner of interpretation. Some sources claim that in this instance Moses's face was radiant, 'sending forth rays of light like horns'. Others go so far as to suggest that St Jerome simply made a mistake, misinterpreting the Hebrew word קָרַן [*qāran*], which means 'shining' or 'emitting rays'.

† In the early twentieth century, Sigmund Freud would spend many hours in the presence of this mighty work, attempting to psychoanalyse its meaning and effect. The more he attempted to unravel the feelings it generated in him, the more he was reduced to breaking the statue down to simplistic description and imaginative supposition. The effect of Michelangelo's *Moses* is, quite simply, indescribable.

When Julius II eventually learned what had happened, he was furious, and dispatched no less than five consecutive couriers to Florence demanding that Michelangelo return at once. When Michelangelo chose to ignore these, Julius II sent a threatening letter to *gonfaloniere* Piero Soderini, who also ignored the pope's request, 'because he hoped that the Pope's anger would pass'. But Soderini had misjudged Julius II, and when he received a second and then a third letter from the pope, he finally summoned Michelangelo. According to Condivi, Soderini told Michelangelo: 'You've tried and tested the Pope as not even the King of France would dare... We have no wish to be plunged into a war with Julius II over you, and put the entire Republic at risk. So do as you are told, and return to Rome.'

At this, Michelangelo became fearful of the pope's anger. According to several sources, instead of returning to Rome, he made plans to travel to the East. Sometime previously, the Ottoman sultan Bayezid II had heard tell of Michelangelo's architectural prowess, and through the agency of the Franciscan order had conveyed an invitation for him to come to Constantinople and build a bridge across the Golden Horn.* Soderini managed to dissuade Michelangelo from this wild scheme, and he eventually returned to Rome to face Julius II.

Michelangelo now began work in earnest on the Sistine Chapel ceiling. The pope had in mind twelve large figures of the Apostles. However, when it came to his art, Michelangelo could be just as obdurate as Julius II, who was persuaded by his employee to allow him to 'do as I liked'.

Michelangelo's scheme was nothing if not ambitious, and Julius II's project paled in comparison. Instead of twelve figures, Michelangelo proposed to cover the entire ceiling with 300 figures, illustrating many

---

* Unlikely as it seems, this story is in fact true. We know that Sultan Bayezid II had earlier sent a similar invitation to Leonardo da Vinci. Evidence of Leonardo's design for this bridge can be found in his notebook for 1502. With a span of almost 500 feet this would have been by far the largest bridge in the world at the time, but Leonardo abandoned the idea. Almost 500 years later, in 2001, a scaled-down model of this bridge was in fact completed across the E18 highway at Ås, some fifteen miles south of Oslo.

of the major scenes described in the Bible. This work would occupy him for more than four years, and would be an extraordinary physical and creative feat. The Sistine Chapel ceiling is over 130 feet long and over 40 feet wide; it is also 65 feet above the chapel floor. In order to paint this, Michelangelo would require specially constructed scaffolding, which could be moved as his work progressed across the ceiling. Contrary to popular myth, Michelangelo did not lie on his back, but painted standing on his feet, reaching up to the ceiling above his head. According to Vasari, 'the work was carried out in extremely uncomfortable conditions, and having to work with his head tilted upwards'.

The resulting fresco is overwhelming in its vastness and complexity, yet on close examination it bears images of such striking originality that they would become archetypes of western art. The best-known of these is the panel in which Michelangelo depicts God, borne aloft by angels, leaning down with his index finger outstretched towards the extended finger of Adam lying on earth. This is nothing less than the moment prior to the imparting of the spark of life to the first human.

Lesser known, but similarly illuminating, is the image of God reaching up to part the clouds in order to create heaven and earth. This image echoes a drawing which Michelangelo made of himself reaching up as he painted the ceiling; and, like God's act of creation, it was said to have been completed during the course of a single day. As ever, Michelangelo was identifying with his subject.

Yet although he aspired to deity in his art, he was all too aware of his mortal frailty during the course of his work. In a poem, he describes the effect of those long hours spent working alone, high up on his platform: 'I grew a goitre living in the cage [of scaffolding]...'

My beard turns up to heaven; my nape falls in,
Fixed on my spine; my breast-bone twists into a harp,
My face is scarred with drips and drabs
Of paint. My loins grow into my paunch.
My buttocks bear my weight like a saddle,
My unguided feet wander to and fro.

Yet out of this suffering came such sublime images as God dividing the waters of Creation; humanity scrambling in terror as it flees from the Flood; the horror and hideous torment of the damned at the Last Judgement...

Michelangelo claimed that he knew all of Dante's *Divine Comedy* by heart. This was almost certainly an exaggeration, yet what he may not have known in extent he certainly knew in profundity. Indeed, Michelangelo's own poetry contained many echoes of Dante, as well as achieving its own unique, tormented spirituality. In one of his final poems, Michelangelo writes:

> Dear to me is sleep; still more to sleep
> in stone while harm and shame persist;
> not to see, not to feel, is bliss;
> speak softly, do not wake me, do not weep.

Only an exhausted man who had driven himself so hard throughout his long life, spending hours, day after day, hewing and polishing great blocks of marble, could so long for sleep. And 'still more' to sleep in stone: that is, in his work which would live on after him.

According to Vasari, Michelangelo would excel 'not in one art, but in all three'. His sculpture would one day inspire Rodin, his Sistine Chapel informed the postures and colouring of the likes of Raphael and Tintoretto, and his poetry would in turn inspire great poets from Leopardi to Rilke. In the late twentieth century, Michelangelo's poetry would even inspire a practitioner of the one art in which he did not excel – namely music. The Russian composer Shostakovich would incorporate Michelangelo's poems into a late symphony, using Michelangelo's spiritual torment to give voice to his own modernist agony.

Michelangelo's late poem, quoted in its entirety above, was written in reply to his Florentine admirer Giovanni Strozzi, who had suggested that his sculpture of the figure of Night, on the Medici tomb in the church of San Lorenzo in Florence, was so lifelike that it 'would speak if awoken'. Michelangelo's poem disagrees: no, his statue would forever sleep, as he too longed to sleep. This poem was probably written on one of his last visits to Florence, where the Medici had now returned to power; it is also said to reflect his disillusionment with the state of Florence under the restored Medici. Although he loved his native city, ironically he would spend his last years in Rome, before dying in 1564 at the age of eighty-eight.

In his long lifetime, Michelangelo would be employed by six popes. After working for Julius II, whose tomb would not be completed until thirty-two years after his death, he would work for both Medici popes, Leo X and his cousin Clement VII, and then for Paul III, Paul IV and Pius IV, largely overseeing the completion of St Peter's.

During the course of Michelangelo's life he would also witness a transformation in the fortunes of the Medici family. As we have seen, following the death of Savonarola and the republican rule of the *gonfaloniere* Piero Soderini, Cardinal Giovanni de' Medici (later Pope Leo X) would reconquer the city with the help of the army of Julius II. From 1513 until 1537 the city would be ruled, somewhat ineptly, by a succession of relatives and descendants of Piero the Unfortunate. Then, in 1537, Medici rule would revert to the branch of the family descended from Pierfrancesco de' Medici, whose son Lorenzo di Pierfrancesco had proved such a generous patron to Botticelli and other early Renaissance artists. Lorenzo di Pierfrancesco's grand-nephew, named Cosimo de' Medici after his illustrious predecessor who had been proclaimed *pater patriae*, would become ruler of Florence, assuming the title Cosimo I de' Medici, Grand Duke of Tuscany.

By means of a series of strategic marriages, the Medici family were by now recognized as leading European aristocracy. In the early 1530s, Pope Clement VII arranged for his young cousin Caterina de' Medici to marry the heir to the French throne. Caterina's husband would eventually become King Henry II of France, and she would become his queen. When Henry II died in 1559, Catherine de Médicis (as she was now known) effectively became the ruler of France, a position she would hold for the next forty years.

Grand Duke Cosimo I ruled Florence from 1537 until 1569. The days of the Republic of Florence were long since over, both politically and in name. Tuscany was now recognized as a grand duchy – along with the likes of Muscovy [Moscow] and Luxembourg. Grand Duke Cosimo I established himself as an autocratic ruler, putting in place an extensive and efficient administration. This was housed in the large building known as the Uffizi, the present-day city's main art gallery. As its name implies, this was initially intended as the *uffizi* (offices) to house the grand duke's administration.

Grand Duke Cosimo I also became renowned for his patronage, particularly with regard to two Florentine artists who would ironically be best remembered for their achievements in literature. The first of these was Giorgio Vasari, who was commissioned by Cosimo I to design the Uffizi. Yet Vasari would achieve lasting fame for his voluminous literary masterpiece *The Lives of the Most Eminent Painters, Sculptors and Architects*. Though not always reliable, this work contains a host of unknown details and anecdotes concerning a wide range of (mainly Florentine) artists who played both major and minor roles in the Renaissance. Much of the unverified gossip he retails has a convincing air of veracity, and he vividly captures the milieu in which these artists – from Cimabue to Michelangelo – contributed to the formative transformation of European art. Vasari was born in 1511, and would become a friend of his older contemporary Michelangelo, whose worth he fully appreciated and described so perceptively in his *Lives*.

The other artist patronized by Cosimo I was Benvenuto Cellini, whose mannerist works follow on directly from Michelangelo's. But Cellini would be best remembered for his *Autobiography*, which he began in 1558 at the age of fifty-eight. This contains all manner of picaresque detail concerning his often racy life, which included fathering several illegitimate children, sodomy, imprisonment, and eluding his enemies – all of which ensured that he was a frequent traveller. He was also present at a number of historic events, most notably the Sack of Rome in 1527 by the mutinous *Landsknechte*, German mercenaries supposedly in the service of the Holy Roman Emperor Charles V. This took place during the reign of Cellini's friend, the Medici pope Clement VII, with whom he took refuge in the Castel Sant'Angelo, the papal fortress. From high on the battlements he watched as the *Landsknechte* slaughtered, pillaged, raped and burned their way through the Eternal City.

Cellini also visited France during the reign of Francis I, who in his youth had befriended the ageing Leonardo da Vinci a quarter of a century earlier. Indeed, we may well owe the story of Leonardo's death in the arms of the young Francis I to Cellini, as well as the knowledge that after Leonardo's death the *Mona Lisa* ended up in the French king's bathroom. Vasari never saw the *Mona Lisa*, yet in his *Lives* he gives a detailed description of the painting which he could only have heard from an eyewitness – possibly Cellini, whom he met several times in the course of their often troubled relationship.

Though the last word on this enigmatic painting, in which the mysterious shade of dusk somehow serves to illuminate its subject's famous smile, should certainly remain with Leonardo himself. In his *Treatise on Painting*, he wrote: 'In the streets, when night is falling, in bad weather, observe what delicacy and grace appear in the faces of men and women.' This undeniably captures the light of the painting, and even its effect, yet the suggestion in Mona Lisa's smile goes far deeper than any surface effect.

CHAPTER 19

GALILEO

T HIS BRINGS US TO the final member of the trio of Florentines whose contributions to the late period of the Renaissance would transform the western world. After the politics of Machiavelli and the transcendent art of Michelangelo came the first scientist of the modern era – namely, Galileo.

Yet before we come to Galileo himself, it is worth a short detour to describe his father, Vincenzo Galilei, who also made a significant contribution to the Renaissance. Vincenzo was descended from an old Florentine family whose fortune had all but disappeared, leaving him a somewhat embittered and cantankerous character. However, in his youth he had proved a talented mathematician and a highly gifted lutenist. In the latter capacity he was sent to Venice by his patron, Giovanni de' Bardi, in order to further his musical education. At the time, Venice outstripped all Italy in the performance and theory of music. Here Vincenzo studied under Gioseffo Zarlino, by far the greatest musical theorist of the time, who was a firm believer in the classical tradition of counterpoint. This involves the technique of writing, or playing, one melody in conjunction with another, according to a series of strict rules, thus producing a polyphonic (many-sounded) harmony. This had developed into a high art during the medieval era, producing a sophisticated and almost mathematical concision and beauty, as sublime in sound as in the appearance of its formal abstraction on the page of a musical score.

It was this constrictive aspect which irked the creative inclinations of the more free-spirited Vincenzo Galilei. He insisted that music should impart lyrical beauty to the ear more than the mind, and set about trying to compose vocal music which fulfilled such an aim. Thus Vincenzo played a role in freeing music from the past – paving the way for the birth of opera. Once again, the Renaissance template prevailed: setting humanity free from medieval constriction by harking back to an ancient, lyric past.

Although Vincenzo Galilei's combative temperament won him few friends as a musician at the Tuscan court, he nonetheless became a leading member of the humanist circle, who formed the Camerata de' Bardi, the group which met regularly at Count Giovanni de' Bardi's house. Here the Florentine scholar Girolamo Mei introduced the theory that Ancient Greek drama had in fact been sung, rather than simply spoken. Prompted by this idea, in 1582 Galilei produced a setting of the treasonous politician Ugolino's lament from Dante's *Inferno*, which proved a pivotal work. Around 1597, the musician Jacopo Peri and the poet Ottavio Rinuccini collaborated to produce what is now regarded as the first opera, *Dafne*, which tells the story from Ancient Greek mythology of the god Apollo falling in love with the nymph Daphne. The narrative unfolds in dramatic form, with the individual characters singing their separate roles. Once again – this time in a sphere in which Florence had not previously excelled – the city became responsible for yet another aspect of the Renaissance.

Vincenzo's son Galileo Galilei was born in 1564, while the family was living in Pisa; they would return to Florence when Galileo was ten. It soon became evident that this bumptious redhead had his father's temperament, as well as his mathematical abilities. Life at home was far from peaceful. Vincenzo's wife, Giulia, who came from the distinguished Tuscan Ammannati family, considered that she had married beneath her, and to an argumentative ne'er-do-well at that. Apart from nagging her husband, Giulia focused her attention on her bright and difficult young son. Galileo became used to being the centre of attention, and his self-confidence bloomed accordingly, yet beneath his ebullience there always lurked the uncertainty bred of his stormy home life. His conceit would always mask a driving ambition, while his arrogance would be undercut by more needy emotions.

Soon after the family's move to Florence, Galileo was dispatched to a monastery school some fifteen miles south-east of the city, where he was given a traditional education in grammar, rhetoric and logic. When Galileo showed signs of wishing to become a monk, his father withdrew him from the monastery and then sent him to the University of Pisa to study medicine at the age of sixteen. It was anticipated that this profession would provide the family with some much-needed cash. Two years later, while Galileo was on holiday back in Florence, he happened to attend a lecture by the court mathematician Ostilio Ricci. Prior to this, Galileo's mathematical abilities had consisted largely of precocious feats of numerical learning and the like. Ricci's lecture on Euclid introduced him to the real thing: the rigour of Ancient Greek proof, and an entire abstract world built upon a set of self-evident axioms.

At Pisa, Galileo's studies mainly consisted of Galen's medicine and Aristotelian science. Both of these Ancient Greeks had proved giants in their separate fields, yet over the course of one and a half millennia gaping errors had been revealed in their works. For instance, Aristotle claimed that a projectile such as an arrow, or a thrown stone, began by travelling in a straight line but then suddenly ran out of impetus, crashing vertically to the ground. This was patently not the case, as any observer would have noted. However, it was not possible to question such errors for the simple reason that Aristotle was an 'authority', and as such his works were sacrosanct. Galileo's temperament and way of thought led him not only to question such learning, but also to seek an explanation of his own.

There are two stories which have become attached to this period of Galileo's life. Both are probably mythical, yet they are certainly illustrative of his way of thought. The first concerns bodies falling through the air. According to Aristotle, a heavier object always falls to the ground faster than a lighter one. Legend has it that Galileo carried out a public experiment, dropping two objects of different masses from the top of the famous Leaning Tower of Pisa. As he would later write:

> Aristotle says that a hundred-pound ball falling from a height of one hundred cubits* hits the ground before a one-pound ball has travelled one cubit. I say they arrive at the same time. You find, on making the test, that the larger ball beats the smaller ball by two inches. Now, behind these two inches you want to hide Aristotle's ninety-nine cubits, and, speaking only of my tiny error, remain silent about this enormous mistake...

Galileo had made his point. (As we now know, this two-inch discrepancy would be accounted for by air resistance.) And he had made his point by conducting a *cimento*, meaning an 'ordeal' or 'test' – in other words, an experiment. Galileo's emphasis on experiment as a scientific method would later lead his Florentine students to found an *Accademia del Cimento*. In this case, science and experiment are virtually synonymous. This is the heart of Galileo's thinking, and the essence of the Scientific Revolution in which he would play a leading role. As he would go on to say: 'In questions of science, the authority of a thousand is not worth the humble reasoning of a single individual.' The word of a thousand scholastics could be disproved by a single experiment.

But science is more than simply experiment. First we have to recognize the purpose of an experiment, or what to experiment upon. It is in this sphere that science requires imagination. Or, as Galileo put it: 'All truths are easy to understand once they are discovered; the point is to discover them.' Galileo had now moved on from Euclid to the more practical applications of mathematics to be found in Archimedes, who remained famous for his many ingenious devices. These included a polished mirror which concentrated the sun's rays in order to burn the wooden ships of an enemy, and his

---

* Similar to the earlier-mentioned *braccio*, i.e. around two feet. Thus 100 cubits is the approximate height of the Leaning Tower of Pisa.

rotating screw which could be turned to raise water from a lower level to a higher one. Science may be a matter of experiment, but it is also a matter of invention. And this second point is illustrated by the second of the two stories which originate from Galileo's student days in Pisa.

One Sunday morning, while Galileo was sitting in the Pisa cathedral listening to a sermon, his attention was distracted by a lamp suspended on a long wire from the high ceiling. The lamp was swinging like a pendulum, and using the pulse of his wrist Galileo managed to measure the duration of each swing. He discovered that whatever the length of the arc covered by each swing of the lamp, it always took the same amount of time to complete the arc. In a flash of inspiration, Galileo's thought reversed the situation. What if a pendulum could be used for timing a person's pulse? On his return to his student lodgings, Galileo began a series of experiments, comparing pendulums with different lengths of string and differing weights. He finally managed to make a pendulum which could be used for timing a person's pulse. (An extension of this idea would result in the pendulum clock, the first accurate timepiece of its kind – though this would not be developed until almost a century later, by the Dutch scientist Christiaan Huygens.)

Excited by his discovery, Galileo rushed to show it to his teachers at the university medical school. Galileo's professor was so impressed with his young pupil's invention that he immediately stole it. Despite this setback, the *pulsilogium* (as it came to be known) brought Galileo a certain local renown. Examples of this device were soon being used at university medical schools all over Italy, though Galileo received neither full recognition nor any money for his discovery. The concept of patents, with laws to protect inventions and reward their inventors, was still not yet widely recognized.*

---

* In Venice, in 1450, a decree had been issued requiring inventors to register their invention with the authorities, whereupon they received protection for ten years. As we have seen, a similar decree had been issued in Florence some thirty years before this, and had been used by Brunelleschi to patent his ill-fated paddle-barge *Il Badalone*. But this had only protected patents for three years, and had largely fallen into abeyance in Tuscany by Galileo's time.

For this reason, secrecy, spying and plagiarism continued to play a major role in the science of the period. Here true science was forced to conform with the practices of pseudosciences, such as alchemy and astrology. Surprisingly, although Galileo would in time become one of the major astronomers of his age, he would prove all too willing to revert to astrology when the occasion arose – usually when he found himself short of cash. And this was a predicament in which he would frequently find himself, during both his student days and the decades to come. For as well as achieving a measure of renown in Pisa as an inventor, Galileo also achieved notoriety as a roisterer in the taverns and bordellos.

On the few occasions when he did attend classes, Galileo was in the habit of interrupting the lecturer with awkward questions. Why, for instance, did all hailstones, regardless of their size, hit the ground at the same speed, when Aristotle said that heavier bodies fell faster than lighter ones? On this occasion, the lecturer had a ready reply: the lighter hailstones fell from lower in the sky, so that they only *appeared* to fall at the same speed. Such explanations were derided by Galileo, but he was making himself few friends. It soon became evident to all, including his fellow students, that Galileo was too clever for his own good. Consequently, after four years at the University of Pisa, Galileo left with no degree and no money.

His father was less than pleased when he arrived back in Florence devoid of the doctor's certificate which was intended to rescue the family finances. However, this lack of qualifications did nothing to dent Galileo's self-confidence, and he forthwith set about establishing himself as a mathematician, giving a series of public lectures. These were so ill-attended that he soon abandoned the idea. Eventually, Vincenzo managed to pull a few strings at court; thus Galileo was able to deliver the occasional lecture to the prestigious Platonic Academy. This semi-formal humanist institution, which had been established over a century previously under the auspices of Cosimo de' Medici, had been revived a decade earlier by Grand Duke Cosimo I. Ironically, the brief Galileo was given for his lectures had little to do with humanistic science, and was but tenuously linked to mathematics. Galileo was requested to settle a controversy which was raging amongst the older academicians, and pronounce once and for all on the geography and proportions of Hell, as described in Dante's *Inferno*.

By now, Grand Duke Cosimo I had been succeeded by his son Grand Duke Francesco I, who was so interested in science that he even set up his own laboratory in the Palazzo Medici. Unfortunately he proved of little assistance to Galileo, as in 1587 he concocted an elixir to cure himself of fever. According to Galileo's biographer James Reston, this 'was extracted from the ducts of the crocodile and mixed with secretions from the porcupine, the Peruvian goat, and the Indian gazelle'. Grand Duke Francesco's demise was predictably gruesome and painful. It soon became clear to Galileo that he would never be able to realize his dream of becoming a great scientist in Florence.

Astonishingly, in 1589 Galileo managed to secure for himself the post of professor of mathematics at his alma mater, Pisa University. Predictably this did not last long, but it was during this period that Galileo completed his first major work, *De Motu* (On Motion). This set down his revolutionary new ideas on the movement of bodies through air and water. He even had the audacity to attempt an improvement on Archimedes' famous experiment on flotation (the one which involved his celebrated 'Eureka!' moment). In order to achieve this, Galileo invented a scale known as *la bilancetta* (the little balance). This extremely delicate instrument required a great amount of technical expertise to construct and operate, but was capable of detecting very small differences in weight. Such instruments would increasingly be required as scientists began conducting ever more sophisticated experiments.

More importantly, Galileo began applying the rigour of proof to physics, using what he had learned from Euclid. Likewise, he used mathematical measurement to reinforce his ideas. Here, in embryo, we see the beginning of the Scientific Revolution, and the parting of the ways between science and Aristotelian thought. Mathematics was largely scorned by Aristotelian academics, many of whom regarded it as little better than an adjunct to astrology.*

In *De Motu*, Galileo also demonstrated what was to be his other great scientific method: his ability to filch, and improve upon, the ideas of scientific contemporaries. His main justification for this – both in his own eyes, and in the eyes of history – was that he would frequently see to the very essence of an idea, which its discoverer (or inventor) had only grasped in a more superficial aspect. An example of this can be seen in Galileo's ideas concerning falling objects, such as had appeared in his legendary Leaning Tower of Pisa experiment. His original inspiration for this was 'derived' from the Ancient Greek astronomer Hipparchus of Rhodes, who had lived in the second century BC. As part of the Renaissance revival of classical learning, Hipparchus's ideas concerning the simultaneity of falling bodies had begun circulating in Italy, particularly in Florence. Even so, there remained that tiny discrepancy between the actual rate at which the bodies fell, due to air resistance. Galileo insisted that, despite this discrepancy, his ideas were correct: all bodies fall at the same rate. Boldly, he suggested that bodies would fall at *precisely* the same rate if the experiment was conducted in a vacuum. (This would be dramatically vindicated almost four centuries later, when in 1971 David Scott dropped a hammer and a feather on the moon, exclaiming when they hit the surface simultaneously: 'You see, Galileo was right.')

In 1591, Galileo's father died, leaving him as the sole provider for the family, which included his mother and a number of young siblings. Galileo's salary at the university was a derisory sixty florins a year – an indication of the regard in which he was held by his fellow members of staff, most of whom received at least double this sum. Consequently, he began searching for a more lucrative post elsewhere. Fortunately, word of Galileo's unique scientific expertise had begun to spread, even reaching the ear of the new grand duke of Tuscany, Ferdinando I, who

---

* As previously mentioned, just as alchemy developed many of the experimental techniques which would be incorporated into the new science of chemistry, astrology instigated a number of mathematical techniques in its calculations of the passage and conjunction of the planets and zodiac signs as they moved across the heavens.

spoke of him as 'one of Tuscany's finest mathematicians'. Aided by this recommendation, Galileo was appointed professor of mathematics at the prestigious University of Padua in the Venetian Republic. Here he would teach geometry, medicine and astronomy (earning occasional fees for astrological readings on the side in times of need).

It was in Padua that Galileo would do much of his finest work. Here his salary was initially 180 florins, which was barely enough to cover the debts he had left behind with his family in Florence. However, he was soon to increase his income with the invention of a 'geometric and military compass'. This was a masterpiece of simplicity, involving just two hinged brass rulers attached to a lower semicircular brass arc, all of which were engraved with lines of measurement. As its name suggests, the instrument could be used for geometric purposes, such as the construction of a regular polygon. More pertinently, it could also be used to calculate the trajectory of a projectile, such as a cannonball. This directly contradicted the Aristotelian description of the course of a projectile – but most importantly of all, it worked.

For obvious reasons, this instrument was soon in great demand, earning Galileo a good supplementary income. And for equally obvious reasons, in particular its simplicity of construction, the income accruing to its inventor soon dried up as others learned how to reproduce the instrument. However, the ever-ingenious Galileo did manage to recoup some further cash from his invention – by charging his students for instruction in the use of the device for ingenious geometric purposes, such as dividing circumferences into equal parts, and the advanced task of transforming a parallelepiped* into a cube.

Galileo continued to support his family back in Florence as best he could, but this was hardly helped by the irregularities of his income. And this in turn was hardly helped by his irregular lifestyle. He was soon enjoying the intellectual and hedonistic delights of Venice, which was just twenty-five miles away. At the same time, he continued his bohemian life at home – where he set up house with a local woman called Marina Gamba, by whom he would eventually have three children.

---

* A three-dimensional six-sided shape, of which each face is a parallelogram.

It was in Venice that Galileo began developing his theory of tides. He had already learned of the heliocentric ideas proposed by the Polish priest Copernicus half a century previously. These described how the earth and the planets moved in circular orbits around the sun, in contradiction to the Church's teaching that the earth was the centre of the universe. According to Galileo's theory, the tides were caused by the movement of water in the seas, caused by the earth's revolution on its axis as it passed around the sun. This was explicitly attacked by the Tuscan-born Cardinal Bellarmine, who asserted that the Copernican system could only be vindicated by 'a true physical demonstration that the sun does not circle the earth, but that the earth circles the sun'. Galileo claimed that his theory of tides did just that.*

It was a remarkably similar comedy of errors and plagiarisms which would lead Galileo to one of his most significant achievements. In July 1609 he happened to be spending the weekend with his intellectual friends in Venice, when they learned of a rumour that a Dutch spectacle-maker from Middelburg named Hans Lippershey had invented an instrument that could make distant objects appear very close. It was said to consist of two lenses in a tube, and was known as a *perspicillum*.

Without ever having seen one of these miraculous instruments, Galileo immediately grasped how it worked, and set off for Padua to construct one for himself. He quickly understood how to improve its

---

* This was both true and not true. We now know that Galileo's theory of tides was wrong, as these are influenced by the gravitational attraction of the moon. However, the conclusion that Galileo drew from this faulty theorem was correct. This is far from being unique in science: a number of mistaken theories have led to correct conclusions. We have already seen how Columbus's mistaken theory that he was sailing west to China led to the European rediscovery of the Americas. In the seventeenth century the German alchemist Joachim Becher suggested that a mysterious fire-like substance called phlogiston explained a number of well-known chemical reactions. This prompted the discovery of further reactions, even though it was later shown that phlogiston did not in fact exist. Likewise aether, an air-like substance that was believed to surround the earth, enabled nineteenth-century physicists to explain the transmission of electromagnetism, light and gravity – until it too was shown to be non-existent by Einstein's theory of relativity.

magnifying effect by a power of ten. From the outset, Galileo realized the enormous commercial potential of the *perspicillum*. Within two weeks, he was back in Venice attempting to sell his instrument to the Doge and his ruling council. As he explained, this device could be vital to the defence of the city, enabling it to spot enemy ships far on the horizon, hours before any attack.

Fortunately, at this point one of Galileo's Venetian friends enlightened him concerning the devious political ways of the Venetian authorities. Instead of trying to sell his new instrument to the Doge, he should offer it to him for free, 'for the benefit of the Republic'. This proved an auspicious move. The authorities were hugely impressed with Galileo's generosity, and in gratitude granted him a gift of 500 ducats, at the same time ordering the University of Padua to increase his annual salary to 1,000 ducats for life. This news came just in the nick of time. Within a week the first *perspicilla* were reaching Venice and flooding the market, selling for less than a ducat each. Galileo dismissed these as mere toys: their magnification was insignificant, and by now he had improved on his own *perspicillum* to the point where it had a magnification of thirty-two times.

Galileo then launched a pre-emptive strike in order to assert his right to be called the inventor of the *perspicillum*. He gave it a new name, calling it a 'telescope' (from the Ancient Greek *tele*, meaning 'distant'; and *scope*, meaning 'see'). Galileo's response to those who denied his claim to this invention was characteristically robust: 'Any idiot can discover such a thing by accident. I was the one who discovered it by reason, which requires genuine originality.'

Yet Galileo's greatest claim to fame would come when he conceived the idea of raising his telescope to the night heavens and using it for astronomical observation. Here again Galileo was not the first to do this. Some four months prior to Galileo even hearing about the *perspicillum*, the English scientist Thomas Harriot had used one with a six-times magnification to examine the moon, even going so far as to draw a rudimentary map of its surface. However, Galileo's first examination of a half-moon would not only prove far more detailed, but would be aided

by an increased understanding of what he was seeing. And, more significantly, what this meant. Instead of a radiant, partly shaded, semicircular
white disc, he saw a large and mysterious world. Close examination of its
surface revealed unmistakable round craters, mountain ranges and what
looked like seas. This was the end of Aristotelian astronomy, he realized.
The heavenly bodies were not perfect spheres after all; they were worlds
with a geography much like our own.

Over the next few years Galileo conducted a systematic exploration of the solar system, making a series of sensational discoveries. He
observed the sun, and found that it had black spots 'which appeared to
consume themselves'. He observed the 'phases of Venus' – similar to the
phases of the moon as it waxes and wanes. He also made drawings of the
rings of Saturn. And he discovered that Jupiter had satellites: four moons
similar to the one circling Earth. These he named *Medicea Sidera* (the
Medici Stars) in gratitude to the ruler of Florence, who had sponsored
his application to become a professor at Padua. The present ruler, Grand
Duke Cosimo II, was so flattered by the immortalizing of his family that
he appointed Galileo 'first philosopher and mathematician' in Tuscany.
Along with this post came a good salary, as well as palatial accommodation in the Villa di Bellosguardo in the hills overlooking Florence.

Galileo left Padua with his family, though without his mistress
Marina, who preferred to remain behind in the house he had bought
for her. (She would marry within a year of him leaving, using the dowry
Galileo had left her.) Once again Galileo was financially secure, but he
now found himself in far higher regard than had been the case in Venice.
This adulation encouraged him no end. Not only did he continue with
his research, but he decided it was time to make his findings public. He
was convinced that these proved beyond all doubt that he was correct
concerning a heliocentric solar system.

In Rome, Galileo's work once more came to the attention of Cardinal
Bellarmine, who had now risen to a senior post in the Vatican: the equivalent of head of the Roman Inquisition. In 1600, Bellarmine had been
in charge of the prosecution and punishment of Giordano Bruno, the
Dominican friar and individualistic thinker. Bruno had been a curious mix

of a genuinely original scientist and an out-and-out Hermeticist, involving belief in all manner of metaphysical practices, from astrology to alchemy. He was both a medievalist and a Renaissance man. His cosmological thinking was way ahead of its time: he espoused Copernican heliocentric ideas, as well as a belief that the universe was infinite and contained other solar systems. His refusal to recant before Cardinal Bellarmine's court led to him being sentenced to death for heresy. Consequently he was burned at the stake – naked, upside down, and with his mouth gagged so that he could not make public his beliefs.

In 1616, Galileo was summoned to Rome by Cardinal Bellarmine to defend his views. By this stage Bellarmine appears to have developed a certain sympathy with the heliocentric view, though he maintained deep reservations about how this could be made to square with the teachings of the Bible. Surprisingly, Cardinal Bellarmine decided to let Galileo off with a warning. He was informed that he must not 'hold or defend' the Copernican view of the world, though he could still discuss it as a 'mathematical supposition'.

Galileo returned to Florence, privately maintaining: 'The Bible shows the way to go to heaven, not the way the heavens go.' In 1621 Cardinal Bellarmine died, and two years later Urban VIII became pope. Galileo was given papal permission to write a book containing arguments in support of both the Copernican view and the orthodox 'Aristotelian' view.

In 1632 Galileo completed his *Dialogue Concerning the Two Chief World Systems*, which was in many ways a summary of a lifetime's scientific thought. The 'dialogue' in question was between 'the wise Salviati and the hapless Simplicio'. Inevitably it was the aptly named Simplicio who defended the Church's cosmology, subtly making a bungling mockery of this orthodoxy.

Galileo was summoned to Rome to explain himself. In February 1633, he was put on trial. Although Galileo was aware of the seriousness of his situation, he still insisted upon maintaining his innocence. According to the story, sometime in July he was apparently shown the instruments of torture to which he would be subjected if he refused to confess his heresy. Badly frightened, Galileo agreed that he 'abjured, cursed and detested' his theory that the earth moved around the sun. Though it is said that immediately afterwards he muttered under his breath, 'But still it moves.'

He was saved from torture and the possibility of following Bruno to the stake. Instead, he was sentenced to life imprisonment. He was now sixty-nine years old; in view of his advanced age, and the powerful nature of his support from the Medici, he was allowed to return to Florence and remain under house arrest in the Villa di Bellosguardo.

Galileo may have been imprisoned, but his scientific ideas were less susceptible to containment. By now the students who had been attracted from countries across Europe to his lectures in Padua had long since returned home. Many had become professors in their native lands. Galileo's work was published in the Netherlands, and soon copies of this were circulating throughout the major European universities. The Scientific Revolution was beginning, and would prove unstoppable.

It was now half a century since Martin Luther had instigated the Reformation, which would split Europe. The Roman Church no longer held power over the newly Protestant lands, which extended through the German-speaking territories, England, Scandinavia and beyond. Historically, Galileo would be recognized as on a par with the other great thinkers and innovators of his age – such as the French philosopher and mathematician René Descartes; the English physician William Harvey, whose discovery of the circulation of the blood would revolutionize medicine; and the German astronomer Johannes Kepler, who calculated the true spherical orbits of the planets around the sun, modifying with mathematics the idea first proposed by Copernicus. Science was now moving from speculation to measurement. As Galileo famously put it: 'The world is written in the language of mathematics.' This was to prove one of humanity's most decisive insights.

Galileo would eventually die at the age of seventy-seven. By this stage, he was infirm and blind (almost certainly as a result of focusing his telescope on the sun). A year after Galileo's death, Isaac Newton would be born in England. The scientific succession had passed on.

EPILOGUE

WHAT HAD BEGUN IN Florence as a rebirth of classical knowledge, at first affecting architecture and inspiring humanist thought, had been reinforced in a new style of painting. A greater reality had entered humanity's vision of the world. This had quickly spread to all manner of human knowledge and endeavour. Not for nothing would Galileo be compared to Columbus setting foot on a New World.

Out of its first inklings in Florence, the Renaissance had spread its wings, enabling the modern age to take flight across a continent. Western Europe was now open to new ideas, and new methods of utilizing and testing those ideas. It was this openness which was the key: the openness which arose in a small Italian city-state whose citizens believed in its (somewhat corrupt) democracy. Ironically, it may well have been this very corruption which provided the city with sufficient stability.

The world to which these new ideas gave birth remained open to ideas from other cultures. From Arabic mathematics to Chinese printing and gunpowder; from Far East spices to New World vegetables, every aspect of human life, especially in the West, was transformed. Cartography, politics, astronomy, philosophy – indeed all the arts and sciences – would never be the same again.

The new methods introduced into all these fields would spread from Florence throughout Italy, across Europe, and beyond, laying the foundations of the modern world. Galileo's questioning of received wisdom, to say nothing of his bold and imaginative insights – which he then subjected to reason and experiment – were the very culmination of Renaissance thinking. Such thought was progressive. Paradoxically it would lead to both an age of progress and a new sceptical outlook which questioned all 'received' truths.

Such a paradoxical ethos would have a profound effect upon ensuing generations. The seventeenth-century Frenchman René Descartes was both a highly talented creative scientist and a philosopher. His discovery of so-called Cartesian coordinates would lead to an amalgamation of two apparently disparate branches of mathematics. Algebra, which used formulas that included unknown quantities, could now be mapped on a plane in the form of a graph. Algebra and geometry became united. The calculation of unknown quantities and the solution of spatial problems were one and the same.

Yet along with his creativity, Descartes was also a profound sceptic, and it would be this which would lead to him being regarded as the first modern philosopher. In this philosophical capacity, Descartes began to question all knowledge – to doubt all our thoughts and perceptions. How could we know that our perceptions were not simply a dreamlike illusion? Descartes burrowed down, questioning the deepest foundations of our thought and experience. In the end he came to one final, incontrovertible conclusion: *Cogito, ergo sum* (I think, therefore I am). No matter how he might be deceived in every other way, this alone held true. This alone remained beyond question. And upon this incontestable fact the new knowledge would be founded.

Some years later, across the Channel in Britain, the philosopher David Hume would embark upon a similar programme of doubt. His conclusions would lead him to advocate a similar foundation to that of Galileo, with his belief that experience was the bedrock of knowledge and that all such knowledge could only be confirmed by practical experiment.

Art, too, would evolve beyond its Renaissance humanism, to encompass the expressive inner profundity of the Dutch painter Rembrandt and the technical perception of Velázquez. At the same time, many sought freedom of thought by crossing the Atlantic to the New World. The radical minds who settled the distant northern half of the new continent would in their isolation develop an independent way of looking at the world, which encouraged them to break free from the old certainties of Europe and establish a revolutionary independence of their own, based on the reborn Renaissance idea of democracy. This revolutionary idea then spread back to the Old World, further undermining outmoded European certainties and leading to its own revolutions.

At the same time, the mechanical ingenuity of Leonardo and the inventiveness of Galileo would inspire a scientific democracy. Thus the Renaissance would evolve into the Age of Enlightenment, which in turn became the Industrial Revolution. The world as we know it now was coming into being, founded on an earlier, more primitive era of dreams, pride, greed, political realism, techniques, fantasies, bitterness, and so much more. The seeds of ideas which had been sown amongst the warring towers of dark medieval Florence had miraculously blossomed and spread, to become the well-ordered garden – and accompanying dung heap – of our contemporary world.

SOURCES AND FURTHER READING

BECAUSE THIS IS INTENDED as a popular book, rather than an academic work, I have not included a long and exhaustive list of precise citations, which can often stretch out over dozens of pages, thus considerably adding to the cost of the book.

For each chapter, I have listed a number of the books that I have consulted, and also those I recommend for further in-depth reading.

The works from which quotations are cited are mostly indicated in the text. Others are taken from the recommended reading for each chapter. In both cases, checking the exact source of a quotation can often readily be achieved using the index of the work indicated; Project Gutenberg and similar websites are even easier to use for tracing sources, in particular older ones whose copyright has lapsed. Simply type in the quotation, and the search engine will lead you to the precise book and page. In a small number of cases, the translations which appear in this work are my own.

GENERAL READING

Burckhardt, Jacob, *The Civilization of the Renaissance in Italy*, trans. S. G. C. Middlemore, Penguin Books, 1990.

Cronin, Vincent, *The Florentine Renaissance*, Pimlico, 1992.

Gillispie, Charles Coulston, *Dictionary of Scientific Biography*, Scribner's, multiple volumes and ongoing supplements, beginning 1970. (This work is of particular reference throughout many chapters.)

Grendler, Paul F. (ed.), *Encyclopedia of the Renaissance*, six vols, Scribner's, 1999.

Hale, John Rigby, *The Civilization of Europe in the Renaissance*, Athaneum, 1994.

Johnson, Paul, *The Renaissance: A Short History*, Modern Library, 2000.

Miller, David, et al. (eds), *The Blackwell Encyclopaedia of Political Thought*, Wiley-Blackwell, 1998.

Nauert, Charles Garfield, *Historical Dictionary of the Renaissance*, Scarecrow Press, 2004.

Plumb, J. H., *The Italian Renaissance*, Houghton Mifflin, 2001.

Vasari, Giorgio, *The Lives of the Artists*, two vols, ed. and trans. George Bull, Penguin Classics, 2003, 2004. (This work is a frequent source throughout many chapters, especially those concerning the artists.)

I. DANTE AND FLORENCE

Burge, James, *Dante: An Introduction*, Sharpe Books, 2018.

Burge, James, *Dante's Invention*, History Press, 2010.

Dante, *Divine Comedy*, three vols, trans. Dorothy L. Sayers, Penguin, 1962.

Dante, *Vita Nova*, trans. Andrew Frisardi, Northwestern University Presa, 2012.

Villani, Giovanni, *Villani's Chronicle: Being Selections from the First Nine Books of the Croniche Fiorentine*, trans. Rose E. Selfe, ed. Philip H. Wicksteed, Archibald Constable & Co., 1906.

2. WEALTH, FREEDOM AND TALENT

Brucker, Gene A., *Florence, the Golden Age, 1138–1737*, Abbeville Press, 1984.

de Roover, Raymond, *The Rise and Decline of the Medici Bank, 1397–1494*, W. W. Norton, 1966.

Devlin, Keith, *The Man of Numbers: Fibonacci's Arithmetic Revolution*, Bloomsbury, 2012.

Reinhard, Wolfgang (ed.), *Power Elites and State Building*, Clarendon Press, 1996.

Staley, Edgcumbe, *The Guilds of Florence*, FB&C Ltd, 2015. (Especially regarding bankers and money-changers.)

3. A CLEAR EYE AMIDST TROUBLED TIMES

Encyclopedia Britannica, 'Dolce stil nuovo – Italian literature', 2019, https://www.britannica.com/art/dolce-stil-nuovo.

Martines, Lauro, *Power and Imagination: City-states in Renaissance Italy*, Pimlico, 2002.

Vasari, *Lives of the Artists*, 'Giotto'.

4. BOCCACCIO AND PETRARCH

Boccaccio, Giovanni, *The Decameron*, trans. G. H. McWilliam, Penguin Classics, 2003.

Hollway-Calthrop, H. C., *Petrarch: His Life and Times*, Methuen, 1907.

Jansen, Katherine L., Joanna Drell and Frances Andrews (eds), *Medieval Italy: Texts in Translation*, University of Pennsylvania Press, 2009.

Symonds, John Addington, *Giovanni Boccaccio as Man and Author*, Leopold
   Classic Library, 2015.

5. WAR AND PEACE

Caferro, William, *John Hawkwood: An English Mercenary in Fourteenth-Century
   Italy*, Johns Hopkins University Press, 2015.
Mallett, Michael, and William Caferro, *Mercenaries and Their Masters: Warfare in
   Renaissance Italy*, Pen & Sword Military, 2009.
Origo, Iris, *The Merchant of Prato: Daily Life in a Medieval Italian City*, Penguin
   Modern Classics, 2017.
Saunders, Frances Stonor, *Hawkwood: The Diabolical Englishman*, Faber & Faber,
   2004.
Also Antonino Pierozzi, Antonino, Archbishop of Florence, *Chronicles*; the
   anonymous Ferrarese contemporary who wrote the *Chronicon Estense*; Marco
   Battaglia, the chronicler of Rimini; and Donato di Neri, *Chronach Senese*. (To
   trace these chroniclers, see Saunders's masterful bibliography.)

6. THE DOME

Coonin, A. Victor, *Donatello and the Dawn of Renaissance Art*, Reaktion Books,
   2019.
King, Ross, *Brunelleschi's Dome: The Story of the Great Cathedral in Florence*,
   Vintage, 2008.
Manetti, Antonio, *The Life of Brunelleschi*, Pennsylvania State University Press, 1970.

7. THE MATHEMATICAL ARTISTS

Bertelli, Carlo, *Piero della Francesca*, trans. Edward Farrelly, Yale University Press,
   1992.
Borsi, Franco, and Stefano Borsi, *Paolo Uccello*, Thames & Hudson, 1994.
Gombrich, E. H. J., and D. Eribon, *A Lifelong Interest: Conversations on Art and
   Science*, Thames & Hudson, 1993.
Hudson, Hugh, *Paolo Uccello: Artist of the Florentine Renaissance Republic*, VDM
   Verlag, 2008.
van der Waeren, Bartel L., *A History of Algebra*, Springer, 1985.

8. THOSE WHO PAID THE BILLS

Kent, Dale, *Cosimo de' Medici and the Florentine Renaissance: The Patron's Oeuvre*,
   Yale University Press, 2000.
Cavalcanti, Guido, *Complete Poems*, trans. Anthony Mortimer, OneWorld
   Classics, 2010.
Vasari, *Lives of the Artists*. (See particular artists under individual chapters.)

Strathern, Paul, *The Medici: Godfathers of the Renaissance*, Jonathan Cape, 2003.

Ross, Janet, *Lives of the Early Medici: As Told in Their Correspondence*, R. G. Badger, 1911.

9. THE RENAISSANCE SPREADS ITS WINGS

Asimov, Isaac, *Asimov's Biographical Encyclopedia of Science and Technology*, Doubleday, 1964. (See in particular the entries for Alberti and Toscanelli.)

de Roover, *The Rise and Decline of the Medici Bank*.

Fernández-Armesto, Felipe, *Amerigo: The Man Who Gave His Name to America*, Random House, 2008.

Hibbert, Christopher, *Florence: The Biography of a City*, Penguin Books, 1994.

Pohl, Frederick Julius, *Amerigo Vespucci: Pilot Major*, Octagon Books, 1966.

Tavernor, Robert, *On Alberti and the Art of Building*, Yale University Press, 1998.

Vespucci, Amerigo, *The Letters of Amerigo Vespucci and Other Documents Illustrative of his Career*, trans. Clements R. Markham, Gale Ecco, 2012.

10. MEDICI RISING

Frieda, Leonie, *Catherine de Medici: A Biography*, Phoenix, 2005.

Gill, Joseph, *The Council of Florence*, Cambridge University Press, 1959.

Hibbert, Christopher, *The House of Medici: Its Rise and Fall*, William Morrow and Company, 1975.

Kent, Dale, *Cosimo de' Medici and the Florentine Renaissance*, Yale University Press, 2000.

Martines, Lauro, *April Blood: Florence and the Plot Against the Medici*, Oxford University Press, 2003.

Strathern, *The Medici*.

11. A MEDICI ARTIST

Burckhardt, *The Civilization of the Renaissance in Italy*.

Campbell, Lorne, *Renaissance Portraits, European Portrait-Painting in the 14th, 15th, and 16th Centuries*, Yale University Press, 1990.

Legouix, Susan, *Botticelli*, Chaucer Press, 2004.

Lightbown, R. W., *Sandro Botticelli: Life and Work*, Abbeville Press, 1989.

Vasari, *Lives of the Artists*. (He may not have fully appreciated Botticelli's worth, but he is good on his life, friends and milieu.)

12. IL MAGNIFICO

de' Medici, Lorenzo, *The Complete Literary Works*, ed. and trans. Guido A. Guarino, Italica Press, 2016.

Hibbert, *The House of Medici*.

Roscoe, William, *The Life of Lorenzo de' Medici: Called the Magnificent*, ed. Thomas Roscoe, Carey and Hart, 1842. (This is the classic biography.)

Unger, Miles J., *Magnifico: The Brilliant Life and Violent Times of Lorenzo de' Medici*, Simon and Schuster, 2008.

Strathern, *The Medici*.

13. LEONARDO

Bramly, Serge, *Leonardo: The Artist and the Man*, Penguin Books, 1994.

Kemp, Martin, *Leonardo*, Oxford University Press, 2004.

Nicholl, Charles, *Leonardo da Vinci: The Flights of the Mind*, Allen Lane, 2004.

White, Michael, *Leonardo: The First Scientist*, Little, Brown, 2000.

14. SHIFTING GROUND

de Roover, *The Rise and Decline of the Medici Bank*.

Parks, Tim, *Medici Money: Banking, Metaphysics and Art in Fifteenth-Century Florence*, Profile Books, 2004.

15. UNDERCURRENTS

Plumb, J. H. (ed.), *The Penguin Book of the Renaissance*, Penguin Books, 1982.

Villari, Pasquale, *Savonarola*, two vols, trans. Linda Villari, T. F. Unwin, 1888.

16. THE BONFIRE OF THE VANITIES

Landucci, Luca, *A Florentine Diary from 1450 to 1516*, trans. Alice de Rosen Jervis, J. M. Dent & Sons, 1927.

Martines, Lauro, *Power and Imagination*.

Martines, Lauro, *Scourge and Fire: Savonarola and Renaissance Italy*, Jonathan Cape, 2006.

Strathern, Paul, *Death in Florence: The Medici, Savanarola, and the Battle for the Soul of the Renaissance City*, Vintage, 2010.

17. MACHIAVELLI

Capponi, Niccolò, *An Unlikely Prince: The Life and Times of Machiavelli*, Hachette Books, 2010.

Machiavelli, Niccolò, *Discourses* (on Livy), trans. Harvey C. Mansfield and Nathan Tarcov, University of Chicago Press, 2009.

Machiavelli, Niccolò, *Florentine Histories*, trans. Laura F. Banfield and Harvey Mansfield, Princeton University Press, 1988.

Machiavelli, Niccolò, *Machiavelli and His Friends: Their Personal Correspondence*, trans. James B. Atkinson and David Sices, Northern Illinois University Press, 2004.

Machiavelli, Niccolò, *The Prince*, trans. Tim Parks, Penguin Classics, 2014.
Viroli, Maurizio, *Niccolò's Smile: A Biography of Machiavelli*, I. B. Tauris, 2001.

18. MICHELANGELO

Condivi, Ascanio, *The Life of Michelangelo*, trans. Charles Holroyd, Scribner's, 1903.
Harford, John S., *The Life of Michael Angelo Buonarroti; With Translations of Many of His Poems and Letters.* Also, *Memoirs of Savonarola, Raphael, and Vittoria Colonna*, Longman, Brown, Green, Longmans, and Roberts, 1857.
Vasari, *Lives of the Artists*.
von Einem, Herbert, *Michelangelo*, Methuen, 1973.

19. GALILEO

Drake, Stillman, *Galileo at Work: His Scientific Biography*, Dover Publication, 1995.
Galilei, Galileo, *Sidereus Nuncius* (The Starry Messenger), 1610.
Galilei, Galileo, *De Motu Antiquiora* (On Motion), c.1590. (Translations of Galileo's works are freely available on Project Gutenberg.)
Reston, James, *Galileo: A Life*, HarperCollins Publishers, 1994.
White, Michael, *Galileo Antichrist: A Biography*, Weidenfeld & Nicolson, 2007.

ACKNOWLEDGEMENTS

As usual, assistance, guidance and encouragement whilst researching and writing and re-writing this work have come from many sources, of which I can mention but a few. My apologies to those who feel left out. First of all, I must thank my agent extraordinaire, Julian Alexander, of The Soho Agency, who was instrumental in making it all happen. Also, thanks to James Nightingale at Atlantic Books for his help.

Many residents and those familiar with the city of Florence have passed on all manner of advice, insight, tips and so forth – as well as guiding me to many invaluable sources. I have consulted works in many libraries, but most particularly the London Library and the British Library. And, as ever, in the latter, my particular thanks go to the kind and friendly staff of the Humanities 2 Reading Room. My only regret is that during the last phase of writing this book these libraries were closed on account of the Covid-19 lockdowns. This inevitably limited my access to sources and facts which I wanted to double-check.

At the editorial stage, Gemma Wain, working in faraway Toronto during lockdown, proved more than valuable. Her knowledge and perceptive suggestions did much to shape the final stage of this work. My partner Amanda Bush also supplied several suggestions, drawing on her decades of teaching experience both in Britain and abroad, as well as her expert knowledge of natural life. (This work is dedicated to her daughter.)

Despite all the assistance I have received, and the expert sources on which I have drawn, I would like to stress that any errors of fact in this text are entirely my own responsibility.

ILLUSTRATIONS

Section two

St Augustine by Botticelli (*Wikimedia Commons*)

The Birth of Venus by Botticelli (*Wikimedia Commons*)

Primavera by Botticelli (*Wikimedia Commons*)

Baptism of Christ by Verrocchio (*Wikimedia Commons*)

The Adoration of the Magi by Leonardo (*Fine Art Images/Heritage Images/ Getty Images*)

Portrait of Girolamo Savonarola (*Leemage/Corbis via Getty Images*)

Portrait of Machiavelli (*DeAgostini/Getty Images*)

Portrait of Cesare Borgia (*The Picture Art Collection/Alamy Stock Photo*)

Girolamo Savonarola being burnt at the stake in the Piazza della Signoria (*Leemage/Corbis via Getty Images*)

Woodcut of Florence from the *Nuremberg Chronicle*, 1493 (*Wikimedia Commons*)

David by Michelangelo (*Wikimedia Commons*)

The Creation of Adam by Michelangelo (*Wikimedia Commons*)

Pietà by Michelangelo (*pandapaw/Shutterstock.com*)

Portrait of Galileo (*Mondadori Portfolio via Getty Images*)

Galileo's diagram of the Copernican system of the universe (*Photo12/ Universal Images Group via Getty Images*)

INDEX

A NOTE ABOUT
THE AUTHOR

PAUL STRATHERN STUDIED PHILOSOPHY at Trinity College, Dublin, and has lectured in philosophy and mathematics. He is a Somerset Maugham Prize-winning novelist; author of two series of books (*Philosophers in 90 Minutes* and *The Big Idea: Scientists Who Changed the World*); *Mendeleyev's Dream* (shortlisted for the Aventis Science Book Prize); *Dr Strangelove's Game; The Medici; Napoleon in Egypt; The Artist, the Philosopher and the Warrior; Spirit of Venice; Death in Florence* and *The Borgias.*